How to Cure the Classroom Management Blues

A Self-Help Survival Guide for Teachers

Barbara G. Foster

Spalding University

Fostrom Press
New Albany, Indiana

How to Cure the Classroom Management Blues: A Self-Help Survival Guide for Teachers
© Copyright 2012 by Barbara G. Foster

Order online at
www.classroommanagementblues.com

Quantity discounts are available for educational and training purposes. Discounts are also available to schools and other organizations. Contact Fostrom Press at inquiries@fostrompress.com

Library of Congress Cataloging-in-Publication Data

LCCN   2012935220

Foster, Barbara G
    How to cure the classroom management blues: a self-help survival guide for teachers
    / Barbara G. Foster

    1. Classroom management.   2. Behavior management.   3. Effective teaching.

    Includes bibliographical references and index
    ISBN-10: 0976537311
    ISBN-13: 978-09765373-1-1

Fostrom Press

Substantive Editor by Marie Sanders, EdD
Graphics Design by Jennifer Martin, Jen Wren GRAPHICS
Cover Design by Mary Ann Bowman, Creative Media for Learning
Interior Layout and Design by Barbara G. Foster, EdD
Cover Photograph by Photos.com

Brief Contents

How to Cure the Classroom Management Blues

Contents

How to Cure the Classroom Management Blues

STEP TWO   Take Prescriptions

Session 8

⚕ R$_X$ 4—Encourage Trustworthy Behavior

217

Active Ingredients	Principles, Rules, Consequences, Documentation, Procedures

Session 9   **Rₓ 5—Maintain Effective Communication**

| Active Ingredients | Advocacy, Feedback, Dialogue, Collaboration, Professionalism | **281** |

STEP THREE   Prevent a Relapse

Epilogue   Do No Harm   357

Today's assignment:

Learn How to Use This Book

Photos.com

Learn How to Use This Book

The word "blue" has been associated with the idea of melancholia or depression since the Elizabethan era. The American writer Washington Irving is credited with coining the term "the blues," as it is now defined. . . . The blues musical tradition is traced through oral tradition as far back as the 1860s.

Robert M. Baker
A Brief History of the Blues

As a classroom teacher, principal, and teacher educator for more than 35 years, I have seen how excited preservice and beginning teachers are about teaching. When they find themselves spending more time managing student behavior than teaching, many leave the profession after only a few years in the classroom.

 blues [blo͞oz] *pl. n.*

1. state of depression or melancholy, often used with "the"

2. style of music that evolved from southern African American secular songs

The American Heritage Dictionary of the English Language

I have talked with experienced teachers who were overwhelmed with the pressures of the job. Many seem to have lost their passion for teaching. When asked why I am still passionate about teaching in K–12 and post-secondary classrooms after all these years, my resounding answer are **effective classroom management**.

If you are a new or veteran teacher singing "the blues" about students, standardized testing, or an ever-changing curriculum, this self-help survival guide is for you. Grounded in learning theory, instructional design, and research-based practice, the effective classroom management strategies I will share in this book will help you gain control in your classroom and sustain or renew your passion for teaching.

In *How the Brain Learns,* David A. Sousa (2006) says a metaphor helps explain; provides rich imagery, familiarity, and novelty; and makes it easier for learners to gain insights into relationships among ideas for a more in-depth understanding of complex concepts. To help you understand the complexities of teaching and behavior management, I have chosen a medicine metaphor. To learn *How to Cure the Classroom Management Blues,* a teacher dialogues with me, a doctor of education, throughout this book just as a patient talks with a doctor of medicine about an illness.

How to Use This Book

This self-help survival guide takes you step-by-step from a diagnosis of the ***Classroom Management Blues*** through personalized treatment and checkups in 10 chapters, or sessions. In the first four sessions, I will help you make a diagnosis. In each of the next five sessions, you will learn about prescriptions to cure the ***Classroom Management Blues***. In the final session, our topic will be how to prevent a relapse of "the blues" and sustain or renew your passion for teaching.

STEP ONE: ♫ **Make a Diagnosis**

As stress, anxiety, and the blues may lead to depression and burnout, learn to recognize the symptoms and determine how often you experience these warning signs in the classroom. Then, discover historical, educational, and cultural events since the Civil War that changed education for generations and are at the core of what happens in schools today. Next, examine the effects standardized and high-stakes tests have on you and your students. After an analysis of these data, you will make a diagnosis and learn how to personalize treatment.

STEP TWO: 🍎 **Take Prescriptions**

Hippocrates, a Greek physician circa 400 BCE, and the ancient Romans believed apples had the power to cure the sick. In civilizations from the eastern Mediterranean to China, apples symbolize knowledge (Allen & Allen, 2005). Apples still represent good health and education.

> If you cut an apple in half, you will find a Pythagorean pentagram (a five-pointed star). Five is a holistic number and represents the self-actualized person (Lumb, 2002).

Learn about five apples or **prescriptions** with the power to sustain or renew your passion for teaching. The **active ingredients** found in these prescriptions contain practical, research-based strategies to help you prevent or cure the ***Classroom Management Blues***.

Prescriptions for the Classroom Management Blues

🍎 Apply **ACTIVE ENGAGEMENT** to learning activities *every morning and afternoon.*

🍎 Repeat **HIGH EXPECTATIONS** *daily* to inspire ALL students to achieve academic and personal goals.

🍎 Use **APPROPRIATE ASSESSMENTS** *as needed* to foster student learning.

🍎 Encourage **TRUSTWORTHY BEHAVIOR** and support self-discipline *throughout the school day.*

🍎 Maintain **EFFECTIVE COMMUNICATION** *as directed* with students, families, and other educators.

STEP THREE: ☑ **Prevent a Relapse**

In the final session, learn how to personalize treatment and complete regular checkups. Use the checklists provided to monitor and record your progress toward a lasting cure for the ***Classroom Management Blues***.

Special Features

IN PRACTICE—See Classroom Applications

Doctors of education and psychology, education consultants, and other professional educators practice teaching in schools much like medical doctors practice medicine in hospitals; each acquires knowledge and sharpens the skills needed to be successful. **In Practice** inserts show how to apply the concepts and implement the strategies and best practices within your classroom.

PRAXIS JOURNAL—Take Steps toward a Cure

Paulo Freire calls the process of combining action and reflection *praxis*— a set of practices informed by reflection ("TAP," 2000). You are encouraged to write **praxis journal** entries after each session. According to Henriette Anne Klauser (2000), "Writing something down is a commitment." Make the commitment to find a cure for the *Classroom Management Blues*.

A DOSE OF REALITY—Learn from Life Stories

Every human being becomes his or her own person with life stories that reflect many texts and models in a given society (Foster, 1995). In the search for truth and personal understanding, people look to the real and fictional lives of others thought to be admirable and inspiring (Kekes, 1992). **Dose of Reality** inserts contain stories about real teachers, students, and experiences that have had a profound effect on me as an educator. I hope these stories will be inspirational to you.

A DOSE OF HUMOR—Take a Brain Break

Dose of Humor inserts provide mental breaks from the complex concepts and difficult situations you and the teacher in this book experience in the classroom. I learned from David A. Sousa (2006) that humor promotes retention and enhances the learning climate. When we laugh, more oxygen gets into the bloodstream. This fuels the brain and increases the probability that we will remember what we learn and recall it later. The same is true for students.

> Laughter empowers us. When we feel low, depressed or down, laughter helps pull us out of the hole. . . . Laughter is healthy and uplifting. It heals . . . It builds success. It motivates people. It makes us feel good. It can be, as many have said, the best medicine. (Peterson, 2004, pp. 66, 70)

REFLECTIONS—Think, Respond, and Check

Self-assessment drives reflection and the development of subject matter, pedagogical, and pedagogical-content knowledge (Hoffman-Kipp, Artiles, & Lopez-Torres, 2003). Questions and prompts give you the opportunity to think about, respond to, and check your understanding of the information shared in each session.

RESOURCES—Access More Information

Countless books, articles, websites, and other **resources** are available for the topics we will discuss in our sessions together. When you want to learn more, find the **Resources** and **My Bookshelves** *pages* on the *Classroom Management Blues* website at *www.classroommanagementblues.com* for lists of my favorite books and other resources.

SUPPLEMENTS—Download Additional Materials

Supplements for each prescription contain the blackline masters, detailed explanations, and step-by-step directions to put concepts and strategies into practice in your classroom. Select **Supplements** on the *Classroom Management Blues* website at *www.classroommanagementblues.com* to read and download these materials.

DIALOGUE—Be an Active Listener

Jane Vella's academic research asserts that adults learn best through **dialogue**—the most fundamental of human abilities that enhances comprehension and attention. Drawn from the work of such theorists as Paulo Freire, Malcolm Knowles, Kurt Lewin, and Benjamin Bloom, "dialogue education shifts the focus from what the teacher says to what the learner does, from learner passivity to learners as active participants in the dialogue that leads to learning" ("Global Learning Partners," 2006b as cited in "Dialogue Education," 2010, para. 1–2). Listen actively to the dialogue between **A. Teacher** and **Dr. Foster** throughout this book and discover *How to Cure the Classroom Management Blues.*

A. Teacher: *When I began teaching, I could not wait to get to my classroom. Now, it takes all my energy to get to school on time.*

I became a teacher to make a difference in the lives of my students. More and more, I feel like I am failing them!

What can I do to stop feeling this way?

Dr. Foster: *Talk with me about the problems you experience in the classroom, and I will help you learn **How to Cure the Classroom Management Blues** and regain your passion for teaching.*

About the Author

Barbara G. Foster, EdD, earned a Master of Science degree in elementary education and Specialist in Education degree in administration and supervision from Indiana University. After Barbara completed her doctorate in leadership education at Spalding University in Louisville, Kentucky, she joined the faculty and now teaches undergraduate and graduate education courses in classroom management, curriculum and methods, and instructional design.

With more than 25 years of experience in both public and private schools as an effective teacher and principal, Dr. Foster speaks and provides workshops at international, national, and state conferences and district schools on research-based practices related to classroom management and instructional design.

Barbara Foster is available to conduct self-help workshops for teachers on how to actively engage learners, communicate high expectations, use appropriate assessments, implement a trustworthy behavior support system, maintain effective communication, and *Cure the Classroom Management Blues*. She designs workshops to meet the needs of 21st-century teachers and schools. Contact her at drfoster@classroommanagementblues.com about a speaking engagement, workshop, interview, or appearance.

My Support and Inspiration

Dedication

To my husband, Michael, who supported me throughout my professional career and the writing of this book.

To the students in my public, private, and university classrooms, who inspired me to write this book.

Acknowledgments

The author would like to thank and acknowledge the valuable contributions made to this book: Marie M. Sanders for her suggestions and honest review of the content; Peggy DeKay for advice about book layout, components, and graphics; Frank and Joe De Sensi of Educational Directions for their review and suggestion to include chapter reflections; Joseph L. Mills, Jr., of CurrTech Integrations for his support and Assessment Task Level Rubric; DeDe Wohlfarth for information about Prochaska and DiClemente's Stages of Change Model; and Victoria Murden McClure, president of Spalding University, for her inspiring words about standardized testing.

I also owe much to the authors of books I frequently pull from my bookshelf: Stephen R. Covey's *Seven Habits of Highly Effective People* and *The 8th Habit: From Effectiveness to Greatness;* Robert J. Marzano's *The Art and Science of Teaching: A Comprehensive Framework of Effective Instruction;* David A. Sousa's *How the Brain Learns: A Classroom Teacher's Guide* and *How the Brain Influences Behavior: Management Strategies for Every Classroom;* Randy Sprick, Mickey Garrison, and Lisa M. Howard's *Champs: A Proactive & Positive Approach to Classroom Management for Grades K–9*; and Richard J. Stiggins' *Student-Involved Assessment FOR Learning.*

Disclaimers

This book is not a substitute for the medical advice of physicians. Readers should not self-diagnose or treat stress, depression, or any other medical condition using the information contained in this book.

The author and publisher make no claims that the metaphorical prescriptions, active ingredients, and supplements are the only ones with the potential to help teachers with classroom management.

"The word *doctor* has its roots in the Latin words *doctus* and *docere*, which mean 'teacher' and 'to teach'" (Hoegerl, 2005, para.1). Unless otherwise identified, the doctors cited in this book are doctors of education, philosophy, or psychology—not medical doctors.

The author changed the names and identifying details of teachers and students in the *In Practice, Dose of Reality,* and *Dose of Humor* inserts to protect the privacy of individuals.

Although the author and publisher made every effort to ensure that the information in this book and on the **Classroom Management Blues** website was correct at press time—the most accurate information, some websites, and other specific information may have changed.

STEP ONE: **MAKE A DIAGNOSIS**

Today's assignment:

Identify
Warning Signs

Session 1

Photos.com

Identify Warning Signs

The blues lyrics contain some of the most fantastically penetrating autobiographical and revealing statements in the Western musical tradition . . . Blues lyrics are often intensely personal . . . [and] deal with the pain of . . . unhappy situations.

Robert M. Baker
A Brief History of the Blues

To deal with unhappy situations at school, you may tell colleagues, friends, and family members, or you might try to resolve the problems on your own. When you experience pain, you may talk to family members, colleagues, or friends, but you most likely go to a doctor of medicine for a diagnosis and something to help with the pain. This is what you might overhear if **A. Teacher** were to visit a doctor of education's office to get help with problems in the classroom and find out if he or she suffers from the ***Classroom Management Blues.***

> 📄 **di·ag·no·sis** [dī′əg nō′sis] *n.*
>
> The act of identifying the nature and cause of a disease through evaluation of patient history, a physical examination, and laboratory test data
>
> *The American Heritage Stedman's Medical Dictionary*

Dr. Foster: *What brings you here today?*

A. Teacher: *I'm really busy at school and feel stressed. I don't know if it is related, but I am not sleeping at night. I lose my temper at the slightest thing; my family takes the brunt of it. I feel as though I'm on a treadmill. I go to school, get home exhausted, go to bed, and do the same thing the next day ("FAQS," 2005).*

I'm overwhelmed with paperwork, and everyone expects me to do more at school and at home than I already do. I'm normally a very caring person, but I seem to yell at my students more every day ("FAQS," 2005).

Dr. Foster: *Do you have any pain?*

A. Teacher: *Yes. I frequently have a headache, chest pains, and an upset stomach during or after school (Bradshaw, 1991; Carter, 1994).*

What is wrong with me?

Dr. Foster: *From the symptoms you have described, some possible conditions might be burnout or "the blues." To make a proper diagnosis, we need more information. Read "Do You Feel Lucky?" to see that you are not alone.*

Do You Feel Lucky?

In "Avoiding Teacher Burnout," Beth Lewis says we teachers play many roles: "nurse, babysitter, counselor, administrator, parental doormat, paper pusher, and maybe, if we're lucky, educator" (n.d. para. 1). She was surprised after her first year of teaching that the least of her problems were actually in the classroom. Dealing with students was the easy part. "The before school, lunchtime, and afternoon meetings, not to mention the obnoxious amounts of paperwork, [were] enough to drive even the sanest teacher to the sanitarium" (para. 2).

The *reality* is that teaching is one of the professions with the highest degree of career turnover (Lewis, n.d.).

What is the interrelationship among stress, the blues, burnout, depression, and anxiety? The **blues** is a state of melancholy, or sadness. When symptoms become *extreme*, the blues can develop into **depression**, a psychoneurotic or psychotic disorder. **Stress** is a physical or psychological stimulus that may produce physiological reactions or anxiety that may lead to illness.

> Anxiety is an unpleasant emotional state characterized by fearfulness and unwanted and distressing physical symptoms. It is a normal and appropriate response to have stress but it becomes pathological when it is disproportionate to the severity of the stress, continues after the stressor has gone, or occurs in the absence of any external stressor. (Skapinakis, 2003)

Extreme symptoms of stress might cause depression; *long-term* stress could lead to physical or emotional exhaustion, or **burnout**. Someone with burnout expresses anger at those who make demands and explodes easily at inconsequential things.

A. Teacher: *I knew it was normal to have **some** stress and anxiety, but I was not aware that I could become ill or develop burnout if my stress and anxiety becomes extreme or lasts for a long time.*

What are the symptoms?

Dr. Foster: *I will use Bloom's Domains of Educational Activities as a framework to classify the symptoms because they affect the whole person—what he or she thinks, feels, and does in response to stress, depression, and burnout.*

In the 1950s, Benjamin Bloom and a group of educational psychologists determined that learners' mental and physical skill development and emotional growth were the result of educational activities within the cognitive (mental), affective (emotional), and psychomotor (physical) domains (Bloom, 1956). For example, a learner *thinks* about mathematics during a lesson to understand new *knowledge;* but a negative *disposition* (attitude) about math may impede his or her ability (*skill*) to *do* a math assignment. Whether activities are within the cognitive, affective, or psychomotor domain, they are interrelated and may impede or facilitate one's ability to be successful in school and in life.

Table 1.1

Bloom's Domains of Educational Activities		
Domains	**Activities**	**Goals**
Cognitive	Thinking	Knowledge
Affective	Feeling	Disposition
Psychomotor	Doing	Skill

What are some cognitive, affective, and physical symptoms of stress, burnout, and depression? The cognitive or psychological symptoms of stress, depression, and burnout include a lack of interest, ideas, and concentration, as well as the inability to make decisions (Bradshaw, 1991; Carter, 1994; Skapinakis, 2003). Thoughts of suicide and harming someone are signs of depression (Skapinakis, 2003).

The affective or emotional responses of those who suffer from stress, depression, and burnout include feelings of inadequacy, guilt, hopelessness, helplessness, and being overwhelmed (Bradshaw, 1991; Carter, 1994; Skapinakis, 2003). In "Signs of Burnout and How to Help You Avoid It," Henry Neils defines burnout as emotional exhaustion or chronic fatigue (para. 7).

Stress, burnout, and depression share physical symptoms like weight loss or gain, change in appetite, abnormal breathing, and sleeplessness (Bradshaw, 1991; Carter, 1994; Skapinakis, 2003). According to Bradshaw (1991), the symptoms that signal high stress levels and could lead to depression or burnout include increased muscle tension, frequent headaches, a fast heartbeat, cold feet and hands, and frequent colds and bouts with the flu.

How do the behaviors attributable to depression and negative stress compare with the warning signs of the *Classroom Management Blues*? Attributes of negative stress and depression may be a reduction in social activities and less contact with friends. Skapinakis (2003) and Bradshaw (1991) associate the following behaviors with high levels of stress and indicate that they could lead to depression or burnout: difficulties at home and work; infrequent or lack of enjoyment and humor; inattention to dress and grooming; perfectionism and rushing around; and increased risk taking, gambling, and overspending.

A. Teacher: *I have many symptoms. I must be depressed and have burnout.*

Dr. Foster: *You should consult with a medical doctor to find out if you suffer from depression or burnout and receive proper treatment.*

*If you have the **Classroom Management Blues**, I can help.*

Dr. Foster: *To find out if you have the Classroom Management Blues, please answer these questions.*

Table 1.2

Warning Signs of the Classroom Management Blues		
1. I frequently have a headache during or after school.	❑ Yes	❑ No
2. I frequently lose my temper with students.	❑ Yes	❑ No
3. I frequently lack the energy to go to school.	❑ Yes	❑ No
4. I frequently frown or overreact to small things.	❑ Yes	❑ No
5. I frequently experience paper overload.	❑ Yes	❑ No
6. I frequently feel like a failure as a teacher.	❑ Yes	❑ No
7. I frequently feel sad, disappointed, aggravated, or frustrated during the school day.	❑ Yes	❑ No
8. I frequently blame others for what is happening in my classroom.	❑ Yes	❑ No
9. I frequently believe I lack the skills to cope with my teaching responsibilities.	❑ Yes	❑ No
10. I frequently give up on or am too critical of some students.	❑ Yes	❑ No

A. Teacher: *I frequently experience many of these warning signs, so I must have the blues!*

Dr. Foster: *If you answer yes to one or more of the warning signs, you **may** have the **Classroom Management Blues**. We cannot make a diagnosis until we discuss your educational history and standardized test results.*

A. Teacher: *What information about my educational history do you want me to bring to the next session?*

Dr. Foster: *Bring the answers to these questions:*

1. Which historical, educational, and cultural events had the greatest effect on your mother's education? If possible, answer the same question for at least three generations on your mother's side of the family (e.g., grandmother, great-grandmother, great-great-grandmother).

*2. Which historical, educational, and cultural events had the greatest effect on **your** education?*

3. What aspects of teaching were you most and least prepared to handle as a beginning teacher?

A. Teacher: *Why do you want me to focus on my mother's side of the family?*

Dr. Foster: *Links exist between the education levels of both parents and children's health and health-related behaviors, and research shows that increases in the education level of the mother have been associated with improvements in children's academic performance ("Mother's Education Level," 2008).*

A. Teacher: *What if I can't find information about my family history?*

Dr. Foster: *Discover what you can. I will help you fill in the gaps.*

Concluding Remarks

Stress is inherent in teaching, so you must be aware of the warning signs. Factors at school that you cannot control add to stress. In our sessions, you will learn about the factors that you **can** control to reduce your stress level and potential for burnout. In the next session, we will look at the history of education and discover factors that may add to the ***Classroom Management Blues*** and put you and your students and school at risk.

Resources—Access More Information

Find links to online stress tests and more information about teacher burnout and stress management on the ***Classroom Management Blues*** website. Locate the **Resources** page, then **Warning Signs** at *www.classroommanagementblues.com* for a list of books, articles, websites, and other resources.

Praxis Journal—Take Steps toward a Cure

Write responses to these prompts and questions before the next session:

- **Think about what you have learned about the warning signs of stress and burnout.** How does teacher stress and burnout affect teacher effectiveness and student learning?
- **Based on what you have learned in this session, set a goal and develop a plan.** How do you plan to achieve your goal and solve one or more related problems?
- **Implement and evaluate your plan.** How did your actions affect you as a teacher and your students as learners?
- **Reflect on future goals and actions.** What will you do in the future?

Today's assignment:

Discover Educational Histories

Session 2

Photos.com

Discover Educational Histories

*The word "blue" has been associated with the idea of melancholia or depression since the Elizabethan era. . . . Following the Civil War (according to **Rolling Stone**), the blues arose as "a distillate of the African music brought over by slaves."*

Robert M. Baker
A Brief History of the Blues

You may experience one or more warning signs of the ***Classroom Management Blues***, but just as a medical doctor asks patients about their medical history before making a diagnosis, we must examine your educational history to determine whether you are at a low, medium, or high risk for the blues. Family medical histories capture the shared social, cultural, and environmental risk factors that may lead to an illness ("Calculating Genetic Risk," 2010). Similarly, historical, social, educational, and cultural events of past generations point to factors at the core of what is happening in schools today and may put students, teachers, and schools at risk in the years to come.

> **his·to·ry** [his′tə rē] *n.*
>
> 1. a record or account, often chronological in approach, of past events, developments
>
> 2. the discipline of recording and interpreting past events involving human beings
>
> *The Collins English Dictionary*

Dr. Foster: *In this session, we will discuss your educational history to determine whether you are at a low, medium, or high risk for the **Classroom Management Blues**. Though we will explore the historical, educational, and cultural events of past generations on your mother's side of the family, paternal family members of the same generation would have experienced the same events.*

I made an ancestry chart to help you keep the historical, educational, and cultural events of each generation in perspective. You may want to refer to this chart as we talk about the effects of these events on education in the United States. (See Figure 2.1 on page 19.)

 What did you learn about your family's educational history?

A. Teacher: *I was only able to get information as far back as my great-grandmother, who was born in 1925. There is a lot I do not know.*

Dr. Foster: *Before you tell me about your great-grandmother, let me fill you in on the events after the Civil War began in 1861 up to the year she was born. Your great-grandmother's mother, grandmother, and great-grandmother would have used many inventions still evolving today. These include the typewriter, telephone, light bulb, camera, airplane, and automobile.*

A. Teacher: *Tell me about the schools.*

Dr. Foster: *The establishment of schools and standardized tests occurred by the early 1900s. After 1875, high schools were common, and children up to age 16 were required to attend school in most states (Travers & Rebore, 2000).*

A. Teacher: *I was not aware that standardized testing in schools began so long ago. I do remember learning that most people only had a grade school education.*

Dr. Foster: *If your great-great-great-great grandmother could read, she might have read about the Fourteenth Amendment in 1868.*

Which events from 1868 to 1945 changed education for generations? Congress passed the *Fourteenth Amendment* in 1868 that overruled the decision in the *Dred Scott v. Sandford* case of 1857, which denied Constitutional rights to slaves and their descendants. It was not until 1954 that the Supreme Court reversed the "separate but equal" doctrine of the *Fourteenth Amendment*, which imposed segregation as long as states provided similar facilities.

> ### Congress Passes the Fourteenth Amendment
>
> *July 1868*
>
> No state shall make or enforce any law which shall abridge the privileges or immunities of citizens of the United States; nor shall any state deprive any person of life, liberty, or property, without due process of law; nor deny to any person with-in its jurisdiction the equal protection of the laws.
>
> ———————————
>
> Excerpted from the 14th Amendment

A. Teacher: *I can't believe it took so long to gets laws passed to improve the life and liberty of **all** citizens of the United States.*

Dr. Foster: *Although there was progress in the nineteenth century, your great-great grandmother and great-great-great grandmother had to wait until the end of World War I in 1918 before **all** states required children to attend at least elementary school.*

Let's get back to your great-grandmother who was born in 1925—seven years after World War I and two years before the invention of the television.

    What did you learn about your great-grandmother?

A. Teacher: *My grandmother told me her mother, my great-grandmother, did not have a television in the house until after she and my great-grandfather graduated from high school. They were high school sweethearts and never divorced.*

Dr. Foster: *Your great-grandparents were of the* **Builders and Veterans Generation**, *who were born between 1925 and 1945. They lived through the Great Depression and World War II.*

A. Teacher: *In what generation would my grandmother belong? She was born in 1946.*

Dr. Foster: *Your grandmother was one of the 76 million* **baby boomers** *born in the 15 years after World War II. Her generation lived through the civil rights movement and Vietnam War; many received college degrees ("Generational Characteristics," n.d.).*

Your grandparents would most likely remember when the Supreme Court banned segregation in public schools.

How did the events from 1945 to 1980 transform education for the Baby Boom Generation and Generation X? In the landmark case of *Brown v. Board of Education*, Topeka, Kansas, a little girl's parents sued so she could attend an all-white neighborhood school ("*Brown v. Board of Education*," 2008). In 1954, the U.S. Supreme Court reversed the District Court of Kansas decision and declared that the doctrine "separate but equal" was inherently unequal. The decision did not fully desegregate public education in the United States, but it galvanized the civil rights movement and put the *Constitution* on the side of racial equality (McBride, 2006).

A. Teacher: *That must have been a celebratory and turbulent time for teachers and students.*

Dr. Foster: *It was also a time of discovery. The* **Sputnik** *spacecraft mission revolutionized education and the world three years after* **Brown v. Board of Education**.

The Soviet Union launched the Sputnik, a satellite the size of a basketball, into orbit in 1957. This historical event led to new political, military, technological, and scientific developments (Launius, n.d.), and the race was on between the United States and Soviet Union to put a man on the moon.

> ## High Court Bans Segregation in Public Schools
>
> *May 1954*
>
> The court reversed the District Court of Kansas decision. The court concluded that "in the field of public education, the doctrine 'separate but equal' has no place. Separate educational facilities are inherently unequal. Therefore, we hold that the plaintiffs and others similarly situated for whom the actions have been brought are, by reason of the segregation complained of, deprived of the equal protection of the laws guaranteed by the Fourteenth Amendment."
>
> Excerpted from "Brown v. Board of Education: National Historic Site"

After Sputnik, Americans began to worry about schools and competition against the Soviet Union. "Consequently, in 1958 the National Defense Education Act (NDEA) was passed so that the better students would become competent in mathematics, the sciences, and foreign languages" (Travers & Rebore, 2000, p. 55).

A. Teacher: *It has been over 50 years since Sputnik, and people are still worried about the math and science abilities of our students.*

Born in 1965, my mother watched the U.S. moon landing on television in 1969. She remembers Sesame Street, *which began in 1969, the video game "Pong" in 1972, and Nintendo in 1983.*

Dr. Foster: *As a member of* **Generation X** *(1965–1980), she would also have seen the fall of the Berlin Wall and reports of the AIDS epidemic on television. At that time, there were many single parent and blended families ("Generational Characteristics," n.d., p. 1).*

 What did your mother tell you about her school years?

A. Teacher: *She went to Head Start, played sports, received help with reading in elementary and middle school, and attended high school classes with children who had special needs.*

Dr. Foster: *Several federal laws passed in the years between 1965 and 1975 that enhanced the educational opportunities of girls, children of low-income families, and students with mental, physical, or emotional challenges.*

Table 2.1

Federal Education Laws 1965–1975
1965 **Elementary and Secondary Education Act (ESEA) Title I**—Students who were academically behind and from low-income families received supplemental academic assistance to succeed in school.
1972 **Title IX of the Educational Amendment**—Females were to be treated equally with few restrictions in reference to funding, access to curricular offerings (once limited to males), and other opportunities like athletics. Agencies could lose federal funds with evidence of sex discrimination.
1973 **The Rehabilitation Act and Section 504**—These regulations required school districts to provide a "free appropriate public education" to each qualified student with a disability. Schools had to provide "regular or special education and related aids and services to meet the student's individual educational needs as adequately as the needs of the nondisabled students" ("Protecting Students," 2009, para. 1).
1974 **Family Educational Rights and Privacy Act (FERPA)**—Parents and guardians of children under eighteen had the right to inspect, copy, and challenge, if necessary, written comments or other data on official school records.
1975 **All Handicapped Children Act (P.L. 94-142)**—Children and youth with special needs between the ages of three and twenty-one were to receive an appropriate education (an individualized education program) in a least restrictive environment, and parents were to participate in decision making. The act called for mainstreaming children with special needs in appropriate classrooms with children without disabilities,

From Travers & Rebore, 2000 and "Protecting Students," 2009

A. Teacher: *It took many federal laws to give **all** children an equal opportunity for an appropriate education. I can imagine the stress teachers felt with the changes in schools during those years.*

I was born in 1981. My generation and I surf the net and have DVDs, MP3 players, cell phones, iPods, and over 100 TV channels. We live in a world of globalization and the war on terror.

Dr. Foster: *You are a member of **Generation Y Nexters**, who were born between 1981 and 2001. The homeschooling movement began, and computers appeared in classrooms the year you were born. **A Nation at Risk** was in the news when you were two years old.*

Which events from 1981 to 2009 may affect education for future generations? Only 26 years after Sputnik, the National Commission on Educational Excellence reported "a rising tide of mediocrity" in education that put the nation at risk. "The promise that all, regardless of race or class or economic status, are entitled to a fair chance and to the tools for developing their individual powers of mind and spirit to the utmost" was at risk ("Nation at Risk," 1983). The commission received documentation of the following risk indicators (para. 12–13):

- About 13 percent of all 17-year-olds in the United States were functionally illiterate. Functional illiteracy among minority youth may have been as high as 40 percent.

- Many 17-year-olds did not possess the "higher-order" intellectual skills expected of them. Nearly 40 percent could not draw inferences from written material; only one-fifth could write a persuasive essay; and only one-third could solve a mathematics problem that required several steps.

- Between 1975 and 1980, remedial mathematics courses in public four-year colleges increased by 72 percent and in 1983 constituted one-quarter of all mathematics courses.

- Business and military leaders complained that they had to spend millions of dollars on remedial education in basic skills like reading, writing, spelling, and computation.

> ### A Nation at Risk
>
> *April 1983*
>
> Our Nation is at risk. Our once unchallenged preeminence in commerce, industry, science, and technological innovation is being overtaken by competitors throughout the world. This report is concerned with only one of the many causes and dimensions of the problem, but it is the one that undergirds American prosperity, security, and civility. We report to the American people that while we can take justifiable pride in what our schools and colleges have historically accomplished and contributed to the United States and the well-being of its people, the educational foundations of our society are presently being eroded by a rising tide of mediocrity that threatens our very future as a Nation and a people.
>
> ---
>
> Excerpted from *A Nation at Risk*

A. Teacher: *That was really bad news. After this report, I am sure the nation took more interest in schools.*

Dr. Foster: *Federal education programs made changes after this report.*

The repealed Education Consolidation and Improvement Act of 1981 along with other federal programs became the revitalized Elementary and Secondary Education Act in 1988. Chapter 1 (now Title I) was essentially the same, but the funding was "almost 20 percent of the total annual federal educational budget" (Travers & Rebore, 2000, p. 56). Other changes in the 1990s included the Americans with Disabilities Act and the Individuals with Disabilities Education Act (IDEA).

Congress passed the Americans with Disabilities Act in 1990 and guaranteed equal opportunity in employment, public accommodation, and transportation for individuals with a disability. Congress also passed the Education of the Handicapped Act Amendments, which changed the name of P.L. 94-142 to IDEA. This act mandated transition and assistive technology in students' individualized education programs, and required greater support for students with autism, traumatic brain injury, emotional disturbance and attention deficit disorder (Travers & Rebore, 2000).

A. Teacher: *These laws passed when I was in elementary school. Were there some national goals about that same time?*

Dr. Foster: *The six national goals for public schools, announced in 1991, were to raise the graduation rate to at least 90% by the year 2000.*

A. Teacher: *We are well beyond the year 2000 and still strive to achieve these goals. What happened?*

Dr. Foster: *In 1991, the states received federal funds for alternative certification, professional development for teachers, and several other programs, but the assistance was not adequate to reform schools (Travers & Rebore, 2000). Others would argue that the funds were adequate.*

National Goals for Public Schools Announced

April 1991

America 2000: An Education Strategy was introduced along with six National Education Goals agreed upon by the President and governors at a 1989 Education Summit. The Goals state that by the year 2000:

1. All children will be ready to learn when they begin school;
2. The high school graduation rate will be at least 90 percent;
3. Students will demonstrate competency in the core content of mathematics, English, science, history, and reasoning skills;
4. U.S. students will rank first in international competition in mathematics and science;
5. Adults will be literate to succeed in a global community; and
6. Schools will be free of drugs and violence.

From Travers & Rebore (2000). *Foundations of Education: Becoming a Teacher*

In a PBS interview on *Frontline* in 2000, Caroline M. Hoxby said:

Education spending has gone up about 85% in real dollars since 1970. So I think that the spending has been going up because people want to have education that's getting a lot better over time, and having it stay about the same or getting a little bit better is not making people happy. (para. 3)

Title I continued to be under scrutiny in the 1990s. The federal government spent about $7.2 billion a year on Title I programs without any overwhelming evidence that the funding had made a difference in achievement gains, especially in reading and mathematics. After an evaluation in 1995, the focus shifted to "school reforms on children's achievement rather than on analysis of individual progress" toward academic gains (Travers & Rebore, 2000, p. 56).

In the *Education Manifesto: A Nation Still at Risk,* published seven years after America 2000 and fifteen years after *A Nation at Risk,* the National Commission on Excellence in Education asked why educators continue to do what doesn't work even though they know how to teach children to read, what a well-trained teacher does, and how an outstanding principal leads in exemplary schools (i.e., schools that succeed with extremely disadvantaged students). The commission stated, "The educational gaps between advantaged and disadvantaged students are huge, handicapping poor children in their pursuit of higher education, good jobs and a better life" ("Education Manifesto," 1998, para. 23).

The National Commission on Excellence reported some improvements. Charter schools had proliferated, choices had spread, and privately managed public schools had long waiting lists (para. 48).

A Nation Still at Risk

April 1998

This is no time for complacency. The risk posed to tomorrow's well-being by the sea of educational mediocrity that still engulfs us is acute. Large numbers of students remain at risk. Intellectually and morally, America's educational system is failing far too many people. . . .

What truly threatens public education is clinging to an ineffective status quo. What will save it are educators, parents and other citizens who insist on reinvigorating and reinventing it.

What is at stake is parents' confidence that their children's future will be bright thanks to the excellent education that they are getting; taxpayers' confidence that the typical graduate of the typical U.S. High school will be ready for the workplace; and our citizens' confidence that American education is among the best in the world.

Excerpted from *Education Manifesto: A Nation Still at Risk*

Dr. Foster: *When you were a senior in college, Congress passed the **No Child Left Behind Act of 2001** that required even more changes in schools.*

No Child Left Behind Act Is Signed into Law

January 2002

The act, which passed with overwhelming bipartisan support, embodies four key principles—stronger accountability for results; greater flexibility for states, school districts and schools in the use of federal funds; more choices for parents of children from disadvantaged backgrounds; and an emphasis on teaching methods that have been demonstrated to work. The act also places an increased emphasis on reading, especially for young children, enhancing the quality of our nation's teachers, and ensuring that all children in America's schools learn English.

Excerpted from "No Child Left Behind: A Desktop Reference"

A. Teacher: *The year after the **No Child Left Behind Act** became law, I was a first year teacher. Some of the teachers in my school said, "This too shall pass." and "We will continue to teach in spite of **NCLB**."*

It is not that we teachers do not want to change; we are just overwhelmed with all the changes in the laws after the election of each new Congress and president. I am concerned about the implications of new legislation on teaching and student learning. Many of us teachers fear a transfer to another school or losing our jobs.

Most teachers would be more willing to change if they were involved in the change effort, given information beforehand about the disadvantages and advantages of the proposed change, and supported with professional training ("Six Change Approaches," n.d., para. 1–2).

Dr. Foster: *I understand why you and other teachers are concerned about the new legislation. The firing of teachers in underperforming schools has appeared in recent headlines, and so has **Race to the Top**.*

All Teachers Fired at Underperforming School in Rhode Island

February 2010

The blue-and-white banner exclaiming "anticipation" on the front of Central Falls High School seems like a cruel joke for an institution so chronically troubled that its leaders decided to fire every teacher by year's end.

The mass firings were approved by the school district's board of trustees Tuesday night after talks failed between the superintendent and the local teachers' union over implementing changes, including offering more after-school tutoring and a longer school day. The teachers say they want more pay for the additional work.

The shake-up comes as Rhode Island's new education commissioner pushes the state to compete for nearly $13 million in federal funding to reform the worst 5 percent of its schools in Central Falls. To get the money, schools must choose one of four paths set under federal law, including mass firings. Initially the hope was to avoid layoffs by adopting a plan that would have lengthened the school day and required teachers to get additional training and offer more after-school tutoring.

Excerpted from Associated Press
Central Falls, Rhode Island

A U.S. Department of Education program, *Race to the Top*, granted money to states that were "leading the way with ambitious yet achievable plans for implementing coherent, compelling, and comprehensive education reform" ("Race to the Top," 2010, para. 2). The winners were to help trail-blaze effective reforms and provide examples for states and local school districts throughout the country. In March 2010, Delaware and Tennessee won the first *Race to the Top* grants.

A. Teacher: *When states compete for federal funding, they place even more pressure on school districts. This pressure trickles down to the students and teachers.*

I am sure lawmakers want to improve schools, but their mandates often take away from what we try to do—teach.

No matter what the public and lawmakers think about us teachers, I am dedicated to teaching and care about my students.

Dr. Foster: *You possess the traits that Americans who responded to the Annual Phi Delta Kappa /Gallup Poll in 2009 want for their children—caring teachers who are dedicated to the teaching profession. The 43rd annual PDK/Gallup poll did not ask respondents about these traits on in 2011.*

Americans Speak Out

September 2011

The *43rd Annual Phi Delta Kappa/Gallup Poll of the Public's Attitudes Toward the Public Schools* asked Americans what they thought was the biggest problem that the public schools must deal with. For the 12th consecutive year, the public thinks it is a lack of funding.

The survey confirms the public's overall trust and confidence in the women and men who teach in our schools . . . Despite their positive feelings, poll respondents indicate that they are more likely to hear "bad stories" than "good stories" about teachers in the news media.

Excerpted from *2011 PDK/Gallup Poll*

Initiative after initiative, the United States has spent billions of dollars to reform schools. "Despite all this activity, even the most ardent reformers must admit that public schools and student learning have improved only slightly, if at all" (Wolk, 2010, p. 16). Paulo Freire wrote in *Education for Critical Consciousness*, "Education is an act of love and courage. It cannot fear the analysis of reality, or under pain revealing itself . . . [to] avoid creative discussion" ("TAP," 2000, p. 2).

A. Teacher: *I am not afraid to discuss what happens in my classroom. If I **do** have the **Classroom Management Blues**, I want to find the cure and regain my enthusiasm for teaching.*

It will take much courage to overcome all the stressors we have talked about in these first sessions, but we have yet to discuss the characteristics of students in classrooms today. They are considerably more complex than students of past generations.

Dr. Foster: *Some refer to today's students as **Generation Z**, the N-[for Net] **Generation** or D-[for digital] **Generation**. Prensky (2001) calls the students of this generation "Digital Natives. . . . 'native speakers' of the digital language of computers, video games and the Internet" (p. 1). Those of us who were **not** born into the digital world are "Digital Immigrants" (p. 2).*

Some young people who have grown up with digital media may experience learning challenges in the classroom.

How do the digital natives in classrooms today compare with students of past generations? Digital natives, or Generation Z, have grown up with digital media. "Their brains have been conditioned by using computers to play games, send email, exchange instant messages, or videoconference through Skype" (Small & Vorgan, 2008, cited in Sprenger, 2009, p. 34).

In a study of 2,000 students between the ages of 8 and 18, Tapscott found that students spent an average of 6 hours a day connected to some digital communication device, often several simultaneously. "They do homework while listening to iPods, sending instant messages, or watching movies on their computers" (p. 34). The use of digital devices can enhance memory at first, but over time the stress of trying to multitask can lower the effectiveness of the immune system, reduce the ability to solve problems, weaken cognitive function, and cause depression (p. 36).

Hyperconnectedness leads to multitasking. Linda Stone (2007) says the result is *continuous partial attention*. As the brain can only attend to one thing at a time, multitasking is "not only unproductive, it's impossible" (Sprenger, 2009, p. 35). To help students build emotional literacy, teachers can encourage students to reflect, take technology breaks, use interactive whiteboards, and teach peers (Sprenger, 2009, pp. 37–38). (Visit *www.classroommanagement blues.com* for more information about hyperconnectivity. Select the **Resources** page, and then locate **History** and **Hyperconnectivity**.)

Being physically present has become less important to this digital generation while "responding instantly is highly prized" (p. 36). With fewer face-to-face interactions, relationships may suffer and the young can lose the ability to empathize and read faces and gestures (p. 34). According Larrivee (2009), these challenges put students "at risk for what has been termed *broken cords*—the failure to develop healthy human attachments" (p. 4). (Read some of the alarming statistics in "Hit the Alarm Button!")

Hit the Alarm Button!

The U.S. Department of Health and Human Services (2009) reported some alarming statistics about our students:

- There were about 3.3 million referrals related to alleged **abuse and neglect** of about 6 million children.
- Ten percent of young adults aged 12 to 17" were **illicit drug users**.
- Among young people aged 12 or 13, the rate of current **alcohol use** was 3.5 percent; the rate was 13 percent for those aged 14 or 15, and 26.3 percent for 16 or 17 year olds.

The *reality* is that our young people must learn to deal with problems outside the classroom that put them at risk for failure in school and in life.

In 2009, there were 409,840 live births for mothers aged 15–19 years, a **birth rate** of 39.1 per 1,000 women in this age group (down from 434,758 births and a birth rate of 41.5 in 2008). The Hispanic, American Indian/Alaska Native, and non-Hispanic black teen pregnancy rates were more than twice as high as the non-Hispanic white teen birth rate ("Centers for Disease Control," n.d., para. 1).

School-related statistics show that our young people must deal with problems that put them at risk inside and outside the classroom. Here are some of the disturbing statistics:

- In 2008, among students ages 12–18, about 1.2 million were victims of nonfatal **crimes at school** (Bureau of Justice Statistics, 2010, para. 3).

- **Suicide** was the third leading cause of death in 2007 for people ages 15 to 24. In each age group, the following number died by suicide: children ages 10 to 14—0.9 per 100,000 and adolescents ages 15 to 19—6.9 per 100,000 (National Institute of Mental Health, n.d.).

- The National Center for Education Statistics (2010) reported that during the 2007 school year: about 32% of the students were **bullied** at school; 21% were made fun of; 18% were the subject of rumors; 11% were pushed, shoved, tripped, or spit on; 6% were threatened with harm; 5% were excluded from activities on purpose; and 4% reported that someone tried to make them do things they did not want to do and their property was destroyed on purpose.

- About 4% of students had experienced **cyber bullying** on or off school property during the 2007 school year; 2 percent of the students who had experienced cyber-bullying had hurtful information about them posted on the Internet by another student (National Center for Education Services, 2010).

> ### More Students Disciplined Following Girl's Suicide
>
> *March 2010*
>
> More students have been removed from a Massachusetts school in the investigation of the alleged bullying campaign against a 15-year-old girl who committed suicide. . . . Their charges included violation of civil rights with bodily injury resulting, criminal harassment and disturbance of a school assembly . . . criminal harassment and assault by means of a dangerous weapon.
>
> Though initial news reports blamed Phoebe's suicide on cyber bullying . . . the students' actions were "primarily conducted on school grounds during school hours and while school was in session."
>
> The bullying of Phoebe was common knowledge to most of the student body and to certain faculty, staff and administrators.
>
> Excerpted from CNN Justice

A. Teacher: *All these statistics disturb and cause me to have more questions than answers. How can bullied students stay focused on learning? Why do some young people turn to illicit drugs, alcohol use, and violence?*

Dr. Foster: *As teachers, we are concerned with students' cognitive and skill development when they do not learn to cope with academic deficiencies and trauma inside and outside the classroom.*

A. Teacher: *What do you mean by trauma?*

Dr. Foster: *Trauma is an emotional wound or physical injury that creates lasting damage to a person's psychological development (The American Heritage Stedman's Medical Dictionary, 2002).*

A. Teacher: *All this information causes me extreme emotional stress. You asked me to reflect on what I was prepared to handle in my first years as a teacher. I was most ready to teach the content and least prepared to handle student misbehavior, like bullying.*

Dr. Foster: *Because of your educational history and emotional stress level, you are at high risk for the **Classroom Management Blues**. Once we look at some test results, we will be able to make a diagnosis.*

   I hope this ancestry chart helps put the historical, educational, and cultural events in context and allows you a deeper understanding of how they affect you and your students (see Figure 2.1 on the opposite page).

Concluding Remarks

You cannot change your genetic makeup or educational history, but you can use this information to make decisions about the changes you **can** make to improve your life and the lives of your students. You cannot control whether your students succeed in life, but you can help them be successful in your classroom. "Whether we 'leave no child behind' or 'race to the top,' our primary concern, always and without exception, must be the children we pledge to serve" (Rooney, 2010, p. 88).

In our next session, we will look at standardized and high-stakes test results. You will learn about their effect on how and what we teach, as well as how standardized testing affects students, teachers, and other educators.

Resources—Access More Information

Discover more about education law, hyperconnectivity, and generations on the **Classroom Management Blues** website. Select **Resources**, then **History** at *www.classroommanagementblues.com* for a list of books, articles, websites, and other resources.

Praxis Journal—Take Steps toward a Cure

Write responses to these prompts and questions before the next session:

- **Think about what you have learned about educational histories.** How do legislative mandates and generational differences affect teacher effectiveness and student learning?

- **Based on what you have learned in this session, set a goal and develop a plan.** How do you plan to achieve your goal and solve one or more related problems?

- **Implement and evaluate your plan.** How did your actions affect you as a teacher and your students as learners?

- **Reflect on future goals and actions.** What will you do in the future?

Figure 2.1

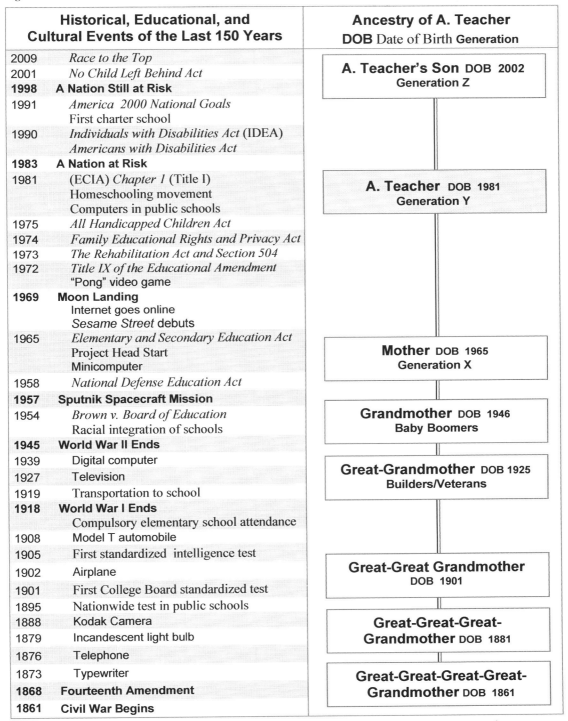

Historical, Educational, and Cultural Events of the Last 150 Years	
2009	*Race to the Top*
2001	*No Child Left Behind Act*
1998	**A Nation Still at Risk**
1991	*America 2000 National Goals*
	First charter school
1990	*Individuals with Disabilities Act* (IDEA)
	Americans with Disabilities Act
1983	**A Nation at Risk**
1981	(ECIA) *Chapter 1* (Title I)
	Homeschooling movement
	Computers in public schools
1975	*All Handicapped Children Act*
1974	*Family Educational Rights and Privacy Act*
1973	*The Rehabilitation Act and Section 504*
1972	*Title IX of the Educational Amendment*
	"Pong" video game
1969	**Moon Landing**
	Internet goes online
	Sesame Street debuts
1965	*Elementary and Secondary Education Act*
	Project Head Start
	Minicomputer
1958	*National Defense Education Act*
1957	**Sputnik Spacecraft Mission**
1954	*Brown v. Board of Education*
	Racial integration of schools
1945	**World War II Ends**
1939	Digital computer
1927	Television
1919	Transportation to school
1918	**World War I Ends**
	Compulsory elementary school attendance
1908	Model T automobile
1905	First standardized intelligence test
1902	Airplane
1901	First College Board standardized test
1895	Nationwide test in public schools
1888	Kodak Camera
1879	Incandescent light bulb
1876	Telephone
1873	Typewriter
1868	**Fourteenth Amendment**
1861	**Civil War Begins**

Ancestry of A. Teacher
DOB Date of Birth **Generation**

A. Teacher's Son DOB 2002
Generation Z

A. Teacher DOB 1981
Generation Y

Mother DOB 1965
Generation X

Grandmother DOB 1946
Baby Boomers

Great-Grandmother DOB 1925
Builders/Veterans

Great-Great Grandmother
DOB 1901

Great-Great-Great-Grandmother DOB 1881

Great-Great-Great-Great-Grandmother DOB 1861

STEP ONE: **MAKE A DIAGNOSIS**

Today's assignment:

Examine
Test Results

Session 3

Photos.com

Session 3

Examine Test Results

There are a number of different ideas as to what the blues really are: a scale structure, a note out of tune or out of key, a chord structure; a philosophy? . . . The blues weren't sung according to the European ideas of even tempered pitch, but with a much freer use of bent pitches and otherwise emotionally inflected vocal sounds . . . These 'bent' pitches are known as 'blue notes.'

Robert M. Baker
A Brief History of the Blues

In our first two sessions, we discussed the symptoms of stress, identified the warning signs of the ***Classroom Management Blues***, and learned about the history of education in America to gauge the collective impact on you as a teacher in today's classroom. Just as medical doctors collect data about the health of a patient from diagnostic tests to determine whether the patient suffers from a medical condition, our next step is to examine how the results of high-stakes tests affect teachers, learners, and schools in the United States and around the world. We will use these data to make a diagnosis and help determine the best treatment for a lasting recovery.

 re·sults [rĭ-zŭltz′] *n.*

1. *expressions, quantities, etc., obtained by calculation*

2. *effects, outcomes, or consequences*

Random House Dictionary

A. Teacher may evidence one or more warning signs and have an educational history similar to teachers of past generations that point to the ***Classroom Management Blues***, but a proper diagnosis requires an analysis of test results. If the results show **A. Teacher** has the blues, he or she will receive personalized treatment. Checkups and further tests will indicate how effective the treatment is to support his or her well-being and recovery.

Dr. Foster: *In this session, we will discuss some of the pros and cons of using standardized tests to evaluate students, teachers, and schools. We will examine National standardized test results along with international rankings and comparisons. With the pressure that comes with high-stakes testing, you will learn about the physical and emotional effects on students and teachers.*

A. Teacher: *Just the mention of standardized tests and high-stakes testing causes me angst and makes me sick to my stomach!*

In elementary school, I was so exhausted during a test that I doodled on the test paper. In middle school, I felt "pressured by the principal during an all-school rally to do well on the test so that the campus would be recognized as a top school . . . [and] treated to a pizza party" (Jain, 2009, para. 3–4).

Now I am a teacher and "my school has also fallen victim to testing mania. The overwhelming pressure has pushed our district to over-emphasize testing. We had our first testing pep rally this year. Although, in the spirit of being a teamplayer, I have wholeheartedly participated in our testing mania overkill, in my heart I know that what we are participating in is . . . not what is best for our students. I reason that I am not the one who has made the situation, I am just dealing with it—I didn't make the game, I'm just playing it" (Stephanie, 2008).

I do not know why politicians put this heavy burden on students, teachers, principals, and school communities.

Dr. Foster: *That is the most critical question for which many teachers, parents, students, and principals have no answer. Let's discuss both sides of the argument, compare U.S. and international test results, and discover ways standardized tests can be used to inform rather than punish teachers, learners, and schools.*

In a letter to the editor of *The New York Times*, Monty Neill, interim executive director of *FairTest,* wrote:

> By judging classrooms primarily on standardized exams, they [officials] encouraged testing gamesmanship. The predictable result, inflated scores without improved educational quality . . . Parents, children and taxpayers would be far better served if politicians understood the well-documented limitations of standardized exams rather than continuing to pursue misguided high-stakes testing policies that undermine real learning. (2010, para. 7)

What are the benefits of standardized tests? Stephen G. Sireci, director of the Center for Educational Assessment at the University of Massachusetts at Amherst, says that standardized tests can provide "independent and unbiased information" about student achievement (Jain, 2009). The research of Eric Hanushek, distinguished professor at Stanford University's Hoover Institution, "has shown that strong academic accountability systems—most often those that utilize standardized testing—are associated with greater school learning and achievement" (para. 26). He maintains that standardized testing promotes fairness and provides a level playing field for what is tested and how the administration of tests pinpoints whether the schools of students from disadvantaged backgrounds receive an enriched curriculum and focus everyone on achievement—ensuring that schools do their jobs (Jain, 2009).

Buck, Ritter, Jensen, and Rose (2010) interviewed 42 teachers in five Arkansas schools in 2009 to find out how testing influenced their classroom instruction. The researchers expected to hear that testing was a negative force as was evidenced in 90% of the literature examined, but most of the teachers had positive things to say about how accountability and data were useful, collaboration and creativity were encouraged, and "standards provided a road map for the year's instruction" (p. 52).

A. Teacher: *I somewhat agree with the teachers interviewed in Arkansas. I bet they were not in low-achieving schools.*

Dr. Foster: *The teachers were not in schools that were under constant accountability pressure, but they worked "each day in typical American schools, with good but not great student performance" (p. 54). The researchers suspected they did not stumble upon the only teachers in the country who saw the benefits of student testing.*

"Some claim that no one benefits [from standardized testing], but if that was true, the tests would have been discontinued long ago" (Johnson, n.d., para. 1).

What is a brief history of standardized testing? The Chinese government gave the first written standardized test to those who wanted to work for the government in the seventh century. In America, Horace Mann tested students' knowledge of spelling, geography, and math in 1845 (Hall, n.d.), and Joseph Rice found that phonics led to better reading results than word methods when he tested 33,000 public school children in 1883 (Brown, 2006).

In 1900, the College Entrance Exam Board developed a series of exams to test a potential college student's knowledge of math, science, literature, and Latin. By the end of 1941, the College Board was using only the SAT multiple-choice exam (Hall, n.d.); it was faster and easier to grade. U.S. colleges use the SAT as a common national measure to predict future success in higher education. High school essays, GPAs, and recommendations are not as reliable (Kemmerling, 2005).

Some believe standardized tests reward teachers to improve instruction, motivate students to work harder in school, and promote the development of mentoring relationships between teachers and students. Others say tests hold school districts accountable and help with "the reallocation of funds to schools who perform well and deserve a reward, and to those schools most in need" (Kemmerling, 2005, para. 7).

A. Teacher: *Standardized tests may have some benefits, but when used to reward and punish schools, students, teachers, and other educators feel the pressure.*

Dr. Foster: *When decisions based on the results of standardized tests may harm or cause students to be at risk, these tests become "high-stakes."*

High-stakes . . . tests are used to validate the system of rewards and punishments. . . . By labeling schools as low performing failures, we expect to humiliate them into improvement. There is no research to prove that this strategy does anything other than to drive good staff away from the very children who need them the most. (Murden McClure, 2010)

How should America's schools use test results? "With greater importance given to a standardized test, the power of that test over students and educators increases" (Jones, 1996, para. 6). Test results determine whether districts receive federal funds, and in many states, school districts tie results to salaries and evaluations to measure teacher and principal effectiveness. For students, test results determine grade advancement, retention and graduation; remediation and special services; and entrance into kindergarten, advanced classes, and college (Herbert, 2007; Strauss, 2006).

A. Teacher: *When schools make important decisions solely on test results, many teachers teach to the test.*

Dr. Foster: *Teaching the content based on the standards tested is not the problem. What is questionable is that 71% of standardized tests nationally are multiple-choice only, even though we know multiple-choice tests have faults (Jones, 1996). Though cheaper and easier to grade, standardized, multiple-choice tests encourage rote memorization. Many times the teaching methods used in classrooms conform to the questioning methods on 'high-stakes' tests (para. 14).*

A. Teacher: *"We've got to stop using assessment as a hammer and begin to use it appropriately, as a diagnostic and learning tool" (Barton, 2007, para. 14).*

Dr. Foster: *I agree with you. Dr. W. James Popham describes classroom assessment **for** learning as "a marvelous, cost-effective way of enhancing student learning." He says, "Solid research evidence confirms that it works, assessment experts endorse it, and teachers adore it" (2007, p. 70).*

We will discuss how to use assessment FOR learning in a future session.

> If state departments of education could step outside the box of the testing mindset, they could play a more constructive role in assessment. The model of School Quality Review (SQR) teams allows state boards of education to become involved in helping to create teaching and learning capacity, rather than just focusing on the limited outcomes of standardized tests. Tests could still be used, but they would not have high stakes attached. (Stoskopf, 2001, para. 45)

A. Teacher: *If education in the United States is so poor, why do so many international students want to come here to pursue an education?*

I think our students are just as smart as students in other countries are. What do you think?

Dr. Foster: *To answer your question, let's look at National Assessment of Education Progress results to assess the condition of education in the United States and the results of the Programme of International Student Assessment to compare and contrast student performance between the United States and other countries.*

What do results from the National Assessment of Education Progress show about the condition of education in the United States? The National Assessment of Educational Progress (NAEP) serves as a common metric for all states and selected urban districts. As the assessment stays the same from year to year, it provides results over time on subject-matter achievement, instructional experiences, and school environment for students in grades 4, 8, and 12 and groups within those populations (e.g., female students, Hispanic students). The subjects include mathematics, reading, science, writing, the arts, civics, economics, geography, and U.S. history (National Assessment, 2010).

In the "Commissioner's Statement: The Condition of Education 2010," Stuart Kerachsky, the deputy commissioner of the National Center for Education Statistics, writes, "Overall progress on national assessments in reading and mathematics has been made among 4th- and 8th-graders since the early 1990s" ("Independent," n.d., para. 1). Significant gaps remain among racial and ethnic groups in both reading and mathematics assessments but narrower among White and Black 4th-graders.

A. Teacher: *A few years ago, I read an article that described the results of 10 urban districts that participated in the NAEP. The author said No Child Left Behind was a failure. Grade 8 Reading showed no progress and only in grade 8 Math was progress faster than the national* rate *("Independent," n.d., para. 2).*

Dr. Foster: *There is little or no agreement about NCLB. In June 2008, Maria Glod wrote in the* **Washington Post***, "Students are performing better on state reading and math tests since enactment of the landmark No Child Left Behind law six years ago" (para. 1).*

 Here are some NEAP results. What do you think?

Table 3.1

NAEP Results—Grade 8 *National Assessment of Educational Progress* Average Scale Score		National	Public	Private	Large City
READING	2009 All Students	264	262	282	252
	2003 All Students	264	263	281	250
MATHEMATICS	2009 All Students	283	282	296	271
	2000 All Students	273	272	286	-
SCIENCE	2009 All Students	149	147	-	132
	1996 All Students	150	148	-	162

Retrieved from NAEP Data Explorer:
http://nces.ed.gov/nationsreportcard/naepdata/report.aspx

A. Teacher: *I see that the national reading and science scores are stable, and math scores are up 10 points over the last six years. I can't say it was because of NCLB, but this was really good news! It should have been more widely reported.*

A. Teacher: *I also noticed that the scores in private schools were higher, and those in large city schools were lower than the national average. I was not surprised!*

Dr. Foster: Look at this table and compare the scores of minority and White students.

Table 3.2

2009 NAEP Results—Grade 8 National Assessment of Educational Progress Average Scale Score–% Students		National	%	Public	%	Private	%	Large City	%
READING	All Students	264	100	262	100	282	100	252	100
	Asian/Pacific	274	5	273	5	268	5	268	8
	White	273	58	271	57	284	74	272	22
	Hispanic	249	20	248	20	273	10	245	41
	Native American	251	1	252	1	-	-	252	1
	Black	246	15	245	16	264	8	243	27
MATHEMATICS	All Students	283	100	282	100	296	100	271	100
	Asian/Pacific	301	5	300	5	310	6	299	8
	White	293	58	292	56	300	74	294	21
	Hispanic	266	20	266	21	278	10	264	42
	Native American	266	1	267	1	-	-	271	1
	Black	261	15	260	16	272	8	256	27
SCIENCE	All Students	149	100	147	100	-	-	132	100
	White	160	61	159	60	-	-	158	23
	Asian/Pacific	156	4	155	4	-	-	147	8
	Hispanic	129	16	127	17	-	-	123	35
	Native American	128	1	134	1	-	-	137	1
	Black	124	17	123	17	-	-	119	33

Retrieved from NAEP Data Explorer: http://nces.ed.gov/nationsreportcard/naepdata/report.aspx

A. Teacher: *I see that Asian/Pacific and White students score much higher than the national average, while Hispanic, Native American, and Black students have similar scores—well below the national average and the scores of Asian/Pacific and White students.*

Dr. Foster: *For Hispanic and Black students in private schools, reading scores are at or above the national average of all students, and math scores are 12 points higher than their counterparts' in the public schools.*

A. Teacher: *What about testing and assessment in charter schools?*

Dr. Foster: *The "charter" for these nonsectarian public schools establishes methods of assessment to measure success. These schools are usually accountable to a state or local school board for academic results to renew the charter ("US Charter Schools," n.d.).*

In "The Myth of Charter Schools," Ravitch (2010) says a film like *Waiting for "Superman"* suggests, "The only hope for the future of our society, especially for poor black and Hispanic children, is escape from public schools, especially to charter schools, which are mostly funded by the government but controlled by private organizations, many of them operating to make a profit" (para. 3). The CREDO study evaluated progress on math tests in 2,500 of the nation's charter schools and found that amazing results are smaller than 17% for charter schools (para. 12).

Although studies show a link between income and test scores, Ravitch asserts that David Guggenheim, the director of *Waiting for "Superman,"* believes "teachers alone can overcome the effects of student poverty." She disagrees and cites studies that show teacher quality accounts for only about 7.5%–10% of student test score gains. "The same body of research shows that about 60 percent of achievement is explained by nonschool factors, such as family income" (para. 15). (Read "Luck of the Draw" for more information about charter schools.)

Luck of the Draw

 Many charter schools do not serve the neediest students (Liam, 2010). Charter schools in New York City have significantly fewer students eligible for free lunch than public schools. Similarly, charter schools enroll less than 4 percent of English language learners. "As for special education students, charter schools are enrolling 9.5 percent, while public schools enroll 16.4 percent" (Horn, 2010, para. 2).

In the final moments of *Waiting for "Superman,"* the children and their parents assemble in auditoriums in New York City, Washington, DC, Los Angeles, and Silicon Valley, waiting nervously to see if they will win the lottery [for admission to a charter school]. As the camera pans the room, you see tears rolling down the cheeks of children and adults alike, all their hopes focused on a listing of numbers or names. Many people react to the scene with their own tears, sad for the children who lose. I had a different reaction. . . . I felt an immense sense of gratitude to the much-maligned American public education system, where no one has to win a lottery to gain admission. (Ravitch, 2010, para. 34)

The *reality* is that students should not have to win a quality education with the **luck of the draw**. All students should be winners and receive a quality education, whether they attend a public, private, or charter school.

A. Teacher: *There seem to be inconsistencies among research findings about which factors account for student test score gains. Do the NAEP scores indicate whether family income or poverty affects test scores?*

Dr. Foster: *Compare the scores of students who were eligible for the school lunch program with the scores of students who were not eligible.*

Table 3.3

NAEP Results—Grade 8 National Assessment of Educational Progress Average Scale Score–% Students		National	%	Public	%	Private	%	Large City	%
READING	2009 All Students	264	100	262	100	282	100	252	100
	2003 All Students	264	100	263	100	281	100	250	100
	2009 Eligible School Lunch	249	39	249	43	264	6	244	65
	2009 Not Eligible	273	54	273	56	282	31	268	33
	2003 Eligible School Lunch	249	31	249	34	267	7	242	56
	2003 Not Eligible	272	54	271	57	281	24	268	34
MATHEMATICS	2009 All Students	283	100	282	100	296	100	271	100
	2000 All Students	273	100	272	100	286	100	-	-
	2009 Eligible School Lunch	266	39	256	43	271	6	262	66
	2009 Not Eligible	294	54	293	56	298	31	289	32
	2000 Eligible School Lunch	253	29	253	31	257	5	-	-
	2000 Not Eligible	283	51	283	54	286	31	-	-
SCIENCE	2009 All Students	149	100	147	100	-	-	132	100
	1996 All Students	150	100	148	100	-	-	162	100
	2009 Eligible School Lunch	130	37	130	39	-	-	122	62
	2009 Not Eligible	159	55	158	58	-	-	150	35
	1996 Eligible School Lunch	133	26	133	29	133	7	-	-
	1996 Not Eligible	156	51	155	51	165	49	-	-

Retrieved from NAEP Data Explorer: http://nces.ed.gov/nationsreportcard/naepdata/report.aspx

A. Teacher: *I noticed that the national percentage of students eligible for the school lunch program increased 8%–10% for reading, mathematics, and science. Despite the increase in poverty as measured by eligibility for the school lunch program, national scores in all three subjects remained about the same or increased. These results were similar for the high-poverty public and large city schools. From these results, I think teachers **do** make a difference in student learning.*

A. Teacher: *After an analysis of these test results, it makes sense that schools use test results for low-stakes decision making about the curriculum, instruction, and services to support students and teachers. Schools should not use scores to punish schools in which nonschool factors, like family income and poverty, have a greater effect on learning and achievement results.*

We spend far more on educational testing in this country than do any of our competitors. In higher achieving states like Connecticut and New Jersey, administrators use test scores to inform decisions about curriculum, teacher training, and whether to augment opportunities for teacher mentoring and professional collaboration. This is called low stakes testing because poor scores lead to greater investment and more supportive services. (Murden McClure, 2010)

Dr. Foster: *Let's see if international test results support your belief that American students are just as smart as students in other countries.*

How effective is education in the United States as compared to other countries? Representative 15-year-olds take the Programme for International Student Assessment (PISA) every three years. In 2009, participants represented 65 countries and the Chinese cities of Shanghai, Hong Kong, and Taipei. Table 3.4 shows the results of the top-scoring countries and the Organization for Economic Cooperation and Development (OECD) average for all the participating countries and cities.

Dr. Foster: *What do you notice about the top-scoring countries in this table?*

Table 3.4

PISA 2009 Results *Programme for International Student Assessment* **% of students in schools . . .**	Shanghai China	Korea	Finland	Hong Kong China	Japan	Germany	United States	Chinese Taipei	OECD average
That give standardized tests 1 to 5 times a year	90.9	96.5	96.3	98.4	63.0	40.0	95.3	63.2	68.8
That make achievement data public	0.6	33.0	2.5	48.4	3.7	10.6	89.3	19.4	36.6
That use achievement data to evaluate teachers' performance	80.2	45.3	10.9	55.0	23.6	23.7	41.0	25.5	44.8
Rank for correct responses	**1**	**2**	**3**	**4**	**7**	**15**	**17**	**19**	

Results for the PISA 2009 Assessment at http://nces.ed.gov/surveys/pisa/

A. Teacher: *One of the first things I noticed was that 89% of the U.S. participants attended schools that made achievement data public—far more than the other countries and cities in the OECD. It was surprising that 80% of the students from Shanghai, China attended schools that used achievement data to evaluate teachers' performance.*

Dr. Foster: *Compare and contrast the 2006 and 2009 reading, mathematics, and science scores for the top-scoring countries and cities in this table.*

Table 3.5

PISA Results *Programme for International Student Assessment* Representative 15-year-olds			Shanghai China	Finland	Hong Kong China	Korea	Japan	United States	Germany	Chinese Taipei	OECD Average
Reading	Rank	2009	1	3	4	2	7	14	16	18	
	Rank	2006		2	3	1	15	*	17	16	
	Mean	2009	556	536	533	539	520	500	497	495	499
	Mean	2006		547	536	556	498	*	495	496	495
Mathematics	Rank	2009	1	5	2	3	8	29	15	4	
	Rank	2006		2	3	3	8	28	16	1	
	Mean	2009	600	541	555	546	529	487	513	543	499
	Mean	2006		548	547	547	523	474	504	549	497
Science	Rank	2009	1	2	3	5	4	20	11	11	
	Rank	2006		1	2	10	5	27	12	4	
	Mean	2009	575	554	549	538	539	502	520	520	501
	Mean	2006		563	542	522	531	489	516	532	498

Results for the PISA 2003, 2006, and 2009 Assessments retrieved from http://bit.ly/qvyGkgPISA and http://nces.ed.gov/surveys/pisa/ (* Error in printing test booklets)

A. Teacher: *The table shows that 15-year-old students from Shanghai far outscored all the other participating countries in reading, math, and science. Except for Finland, the top scores were from cities or countries in the East in which there is less diversity and students share a common language. Are there other possible explanations for these results?*

Dr. Foster: *The academic performance of the Chinese cities, Shanghai and Hong Kong, does not represent the performance of an entire country (Gumbel, 2010). Only 35% of Chinese students enter high school—those with test-taking abilities (Riddile, 2010). Chinese authorities have significantly increased the pay and training of teachers, reduced the emphasis on rote learning, and focused on problem solving (Gumbel, 2010).*

> Nations with high-performing school systems—whether Korea, Singapore, Finland, or Japan—have succeeded not by privatizing their schools or closing those with low scores, but by strengthening the education profession. (Ravitch, 2010, para. 8)

Dr. Foster: *Excluding the achievement results in Chinese cities from the 2009 PISA report, Finland and Korea would have ranked at or near the top. These two countries "have been at the pinnacle of international education" in recent years (Gumbel, 2010, para. 4).*

A. Teacher: *How have Korea and Finland maintained their high rankings over the years?*

Dr. Foster: *In her inaugural address at Spalding University in 2010, President Victoria Murden McClure said, "Korea built a national curriculum that focuses on learning goals, high order thinking, inquiry, innovation, and the integration of technology throughout the curriculum. They teach this challenging curriculum to every student. Today, Korean students rank first in the world in problem solving, second in reading, and third in math."*

In contrast, the attributes of the Finnish education system include high-quality teachers, low rates of immigrants, conservative direct instruction, effective student discipline, fast diagnosis and treatment of learning problems, special schools, and a culture that knows that people only survive with effort ("Research on Causes," 2011). Finland also stopped using mandated standardized tests, reduced the gap between rich and poor, and focused on 21st-century skills like creative problem solving, not test preparation (Jehlen, 2010).

Finland has a national curriculum, which is not restricted to the basic skills of reading and math, but includes the arts, sciences, history, foreign languages, and other subjects that are essential to a good, rounded education. Finland also strengthened its social welfare programs for children and families. (Ravitch, 2010, para. 7)

A. Teacher: *So Finland did something about poverty. I would like to find out what they did to strengthen welfare programs for children and families to improve student learning.*

Dr. Foster: *I urge you to do the research!*

Here are more PISA results that may shed some light on the effect of family income on student achievement.

Table 3.6

PISA Results *Programme for International Student Assessment* Representative 15-year-olds		Shanghai China	Korea	Finland	Hong Kong China	Japan	Germany	Chinese Taipei	United States
2007–2008	% of the population below 50% of median income			5.4		11.8	8.4		17
2009	% with correct responses (Rank)	1	2	3	4	7	15	10	17
	% of disadvantaged low achievers	0.32	1.28	2.23	0.67	3.34	5.09	2.95	4.6
	% single-parent families	10.6	12.8	20.4	12.3	15.0	17.4	13.6	24.3

Results for PISA 2007–2009 Assessments retrieved from http://nces.ed.gov/surveys/pisa/

Riddile (2010) says, "PISA reports average scores. The problem is that the U.S. is not average. While the U.S. is the top country in global competitiveness, we also have the highest percentage of students who live in poverty and regretfully, poverty impacts test scores" (para. 36). When adjusted for poverty, the United States outperforms other countries in areas with a poverty rate of 10% to 25% (especially in areas with less than 10% poverty).

Dr. Foster: *Think about what you have learned about education and student achievement in the United States and other countries. What do you think is most important?*

A. Teacher: *First, as Mel Riddile says, "poverty impacts test scores." We ranked 17 out of the 68 countries and cities that took the PISA. This is great because we educate the highest percentage of children with low-income families.*

Next, schools in the countries and Chinese cities with the highest PISA scores increased teacher pay, focused on teacher education, and included problem solving in the curriculum.

*Finally, the United States, like South Korea, educates **all** children. Chinese students scored the highest, but only a select number of Chinese students (high performers on tests) go to high school.*

Maura Pfeifer says that the focus of China on the test scores is so strong that it consumes all of a students' time. "Chinese parents know their teaching is by memorization and memorization never created a Silicon Valley so they are trying to learn originality and to reach the ultimate dream of an American university education" (as cited in Sawyer, 2010).

According to Yong Zhao, Director of the U.S.-China Center for Research on Educational Excellence at Michigan State University:

Math, science, and literacy are . . . very important basics for all students but they are by no means the only components of a good education—what about morality, passion, creativity, understanding of history, society, and humanities, arts, music, social responsibility, and the ability to work together? That's why test scores have been shown to be poor predictors of future successes of individuals (Goleman, 1995) and nations (Baker, 2007; Tienken, 2008). (Zhao, 2009, para. 11)

A. Teacher: *I agree. There is more to education than math, science, and literacy. The Chinese recognize this. That's why they want their children to attend our universities. American educators must do something right!*

Dr. Foster: *As high scores on tests have been shown to be a poor predictor of future success, let's look at the Nobel prizes for literature, chemistry, peace, economics, medicine, and physics. Although we do not know how the recipients scored on tests when in school, they have been successful—products of the education provided in their respective countries.*

 Look at this table and tell me where the United States ranks in the number of Nobel prizes awarded as compared to the high-ranking countries on the PISA. (see Table 3.7 on the next page).

Table 3.7

		Birth County of U.S. Prize Winners	Total Nobel Prizes 829 Awarded	Chemistry	Literature	Peace	Physics	Medicine	Economics	Prizes awarded from 2000 to 2010	
Rank	**Country**									**Total**	**%**
1	United States	243	326	63	12	22	88	94	47	73	22
3	Germany	15	102	29	10	6	32	23	2	8	8
9	Japan	3	19	8	2	1	7	1		10	53
14	China	5	9	1	1	2	5			4	44
18	Finland		4	1	1	1		1		1	25
21	South Korea	1	1			1				1	100
21	Taiwan	1	1	1						0	0
21	Hong Kong		1				1			1	100

Nobel Laureates 1901–2010 of Select Countries

Nobel Laureates by Country retrieved from http://en.wikipedia.org/wiki/List_of_Nobel_laureates_by_country

A. Teacher: *The United States won more Nobel prizes than any other country—nearly half of the prizes awarded. We should be proud!*

Dr. Foster: *Yes, but we should strive to improve. Japan, China, Finland, and Korea have earned a higher percentage of their prizes in the last ten years.*

We also need to continue to improve in math and science and encourage creative thinking to remain #1 in global competetiveness (Riddile, 2010).

American education is at a crossroads. There are two paths in front of us: one in which we destroy our strengths in order to "catch up" with others in test scores and one in which we build on our strengths so we can keep the lead in innovation and creativity. The current push for more standardization, centralization, high-stakes testing, and test-based accountability is rushing us down the first path while what will truly keep America strong and Americans prosperous should be the latter, the one that cherishes individual talents, cultivates creativity, celebrates diversity, and inspires curiosity. (Zhao, 2009, p. 198)

A. Teacher: *All this talk about high-stakes testing and test results makes my head spin. Do politicians understand how high-stakes testing affects us as a nation?*

Dr. Foster: *Those, who design and mandate high-stakes tests, may be well intentioned, but in many cases, many believe they have caused more harm than good.*

Politicians, educators, and parents must be concerned about the knowledge and skills development of students to foster innovation and creativity, as well as the effects high-stakes testing has on learners' physical and emotional well-being.

What effect does high-stakes testing have on students, teachers, parents, and principals?
The pressure of international competition and high-stakes testing causes stress in schools across the
globe. Politicians who have mandated high-stakes tests for school improvement have ignored that
it leads to punishments, insidious incentives, and needless worry, anxiety, and stress (Nichols
& Berliner, 2007). Some stress is normal, but extreme pressure can produce physiological reactions
that may lead to illness and depression. (For a few examples, read "I'm Going to Be Sick.")

I'm Going to Be Sick

 Pressure is the reality of high-stakes testing. "Pressure
cookers, with just the right amount of heat, can speed up
the meal and increase the efficiency of cooking. Too much
heat, however, always results in pressure cookers exploding"
(Nichols & Berliner, 2007, p. 156). Here are some "sickening"
stories about students, teachers, and principals during
testing week.

- An elementary principal opened the large carton containing tests and
  answer sheets. She found instructions to put on latex gloves, insert the test
  booklets that children had vomited on into the ziplock bag, and return
  those tests along with the others to the Department of Education (Nichols
  & Berliner, 2007).

- In a Texas survey, 47 percent of students often or always developed
  headaches, 40 percent had upset stomachs, 38 percent showed irritability,
  35 percent displayed increased aggression, 34 percent "froze up," and
  29 percent vomited while taking the TAAS test (Hoffman, Assaf, & Paris,
  2001).

- "It's awful. I just cringe every time I walk in the teacher's room because
  these tests are the only topic of conversation in there, and it raises your
  anxiety just to hear how scared everybody is. A few years ago, I really
  loved teaching, but this pressure is just so intense. . . . I'm not sure how
  long I can take it" (Barksdale & Thomas, 2000, p. 390).

- Betty Robinson, principal of the Simonton School, attended a meeting in
  which Gwinnett County School officials discussed school performance—
  based almost entirely on standardized test scores. Simonton had been one
  of four schools included on a list of 436 Georgia schools that were failing
  new standards. Early the next morning, before her students were to take
  yet another important test, Robinson shot herself in the head (Nichols &
  Berliner, 2007).

The *reality* is that "we have to hire extra janitorial staff on high-stakes testing
days to clean up the vomit" (Johnson & Johnson, 2006, p. 224).

Few research studies address school-related stress and its effect on student health. "A 2008 assessment among 10- to 13-year old[s] in Sweden found that 21 percent of boys [and] 30 percent of girls experienced headache[s], and 17 percent of boys and 28 percent of girls experienced abdominal pain at least once per week" (as cited in "Children in China," 2010, para. 16).

A. Teacher: *Is school-related pressure unique to Sweden and the United States?*

Dr. Foster: *No. Chinese students feel the pressure, too. With China's rise in prosperity and their one-child policy, "many parents, who had limited educational opportunities themselves are now investing in their only children" ("Children in China," 2010, para. 13–15). In a study of 2,101 students aged nine to 12 in nine urban and rural schools in a somewhat prosperous eastern province in China, 81% of the students said they worried "a lot" about exams. Parents physically punished 73% of the children for test results, 63% feared their teacher would punish them, and one-third reported headaches or abdominal pains at least once a week (para. 3–6). Read more about students "Facing Pressure" in China.*

Facing Pressure

 Host of *ABC News and World Report* Diane Sawyer visited with Chinese students who average 41 more school days a year than Americans students. "Most of these children are enrolled in extra classes on the weekends. They average 30% more hours of instruction every year than American students" (Sawyer, 2010).

Sawyer spoke with some high school students in an upscale school in Shanghai. Here are two questions she asked about China.

Diane Sawyer: *What's the best thing about China?*

Students: *Pressure.*

Diane Sawyer: *Pressure?*

And what is the worst thing about China?

Students: *Pressure.*

Sawyer goes on to say, "Sometimes one picture says it all. Here are the third grade children stopping twice a day to use ancient acupressure techniques to relax their eyes, then their muscles from all that work. And after all, they face a lot of high pressure exams to determine if they get their shot at the future, college" (Sawyer, 2010).

From "Educating China: See a Chinese Classroom Firsthand" by D. Sawyer (Host), 2010

The ***reality*** is that pressure is dichotomous.
Can students learn to cope with the good and the bad?

Dr. Foster: *This table shows how people in the United States and other countries responded to the question, "How much pressure are parents putting on students?" What do you think about their perceptions?*

Table 3.8

Pew Research Center—Global Attitudes Survey			
Parental pressure on students	Not enough	Right amount	Too much
United States	56%	24%	15%
China	11%	20%	63%
Japan	9%	20%	59%

From Wike, R., & Horowitz, J. M., 2006

A. Teacher: *The Americans who responded to this survey believe parental pressure on students is "not enough." Those who responded in China and Japan say it is too much, and yet students in these and other Asian countries score high on the PISA.*

I hope American politicians do not think more pressure is needed to raise test scores and forget about the "flesh-and-blood students," teachers, and principals in our schools (Rooney, 2010, p. 88). We need parental support, not pressure.

Nichols, Glass, and Berliner created an Accountability Pressure Rating (APR) scale that quantified the pressure felt by students, teachers, administrators, and parents. They found that "as the pressure to pass tests goes up, so do dropout rates" especially for Hispanic students. Their findings "add to a growing body of literature that suggests high-stakes testing, particularly high school exit exams, may disproportionately disadvantage minority youth" (Nichols & Berliner, 2007, pp. 90–91).

In the nine years since Congress reauthorized the Elementary and Secondary Education Act (ESEA) as the No Child Left Behind Act (NCLB), startling growth has occurred in what is often described as the "School-to-Prison Pipeline"—the use of educational policies and practices that have the effect of pushing students, especially students of color and students with disabilities, out of schools and toward the juvenile and criminal justice systems. This phenomenon has proved incredibly damaging to students, families, and communities. It has also proved tremendously costly, not only in terms of lost human potential but also in dollars . . . No Child Left Behind's "get-tough" approach to accountability has led to more students being left behind, thus feeding the dropout crisis and the School-to-Prison Pipeline. ("Advancement," 2010, p. 1)

A. Teacher: *I think schools should eliminate the use of test scores to track and retain students. Low-income and minority students are "more likely to be retained in grade, placed in a lower track, or put in special or remedial education programs" ("How Standardized," n.d., para. 3). Many of these students drop out or find themselves in failing schools.*

A. Teacher: *I know highly qualified teachers who avoid public and large city schools with a high concentration of the neediest students because they do not want to receive punishments or lose their job. Thus, more of the teachers in these schools are new and not ready to teach children different from themselves in relation to economic status, race, and religion (Sanders, 2002).*

Education departments should not use test results to reward and punish schools, teachers, and students. "Numbers have meaning and can give direction. . . . [but] should never become the consuming part of our agenda no matter what the political or social realities" (Rooney, 2010, p. 89).

> High-stakes testing that is designed to punish schools for poor performance acerbates the problem by creating a revolving door that places novice teachers in front of our most challenging students. It is estimated that the negative effect of being taught by a new or poorly qualified teacher is about one-third of a grade level. These negative effects are cumulative; having two or three new teachers in a row cost a child the learning equivalent of a full grade level. (Murden McClure, 2010)

Dr. Foster: *How should American schools address the pressure of high-stakes testing?*

A. Teacher: *I didn't think it would ever happen but Secretary of Education Arne Duncan announced in August 2011 that he is waiving the No Child Left Behind Act's "proficiency requirements for states that have adopted their own testing and accountability programs and are making strides toward better schools" (as cited in Dillon, 2011, para. 2). Secretary Duncan said, "The current law serves as a disincentive to higher standards, rather than as an incentive" (para. 8). From what I have learned in this session about what other countries like Korea and Finland have done to improve education, I am glad states will have the opportunity to design school accountability systems locally that have the potential to improve education in the United States.*

Dr. Foster: *The intent of the No Child Left Behind Act and standardized testing might have been to improve learning, but people do not learn when they feel threatened. "People learn in a supportive environment. That's the nature of human beings. So if you want . . . [children] to learn, you have to give them a lot of support and a lot of encouragement. You can't threaten a child or a school or a school district into learning" (Hirsch, 2001, para. 11).*

> When the brain is thinking negatively or is threatened, it prepares the body to defend itself. As blood flow is reduced to the brain, one is not able to think at higher levels, and the body does not perform appropriately. (Tate, 2007, p. 101)

I can tell you feel overwhelmed with all the pressure from parents, principals, and politicians to improve standardized test scores. Read "Humor Me! I Need a Laugh!" We both need to take a break and have a good laugh!

Humor Me! I Need a Laugh!

Humor reduces stress and mental and physical tension and increases creativity and productivity (Burgess, 2000; Feigelson, 1998; Tate, 2007). After a discussion of a serious topic like high-stakes testing, **humor me! I need a laugh!**

Jones (1996) says, "I'm reminded of a phrase that I heard once from a farmer which is applicable to standardized testing."

"Cows grow faster when you feed them than when you weigh them."

Here are some quotations that might relieve some mental and physical tension (Humor, n.d.).

○ *Due to financial constraints, the light at the end of the tunnel has been turned off.*

○ *Even on clear days, I can't see the point.*

○ *First rule of holes: when you are in one, stop digging.*

○ *If you think small things can't make a difference—*
try going to sleep with a mosquito in the room!

○ *Minds are like parachutes: they only function when open.*

○ *Teachers open the door, but you must enter yourself.*

○ *Nothing improves the memory more than trying to forget.*

○ *Smile, they said, life could be worse. So I did and it was.*

○ *There are too many people trying to change this world who could not change a fuse.*

○ *Most people would sooner die than think, and most people succeed in this.*

○ *There are three kinds of people: those who can count, and those who can't.*

○ *You become what you spend your time being.*

When it comes to high-stakes testing . . .
"Results are what you expect, and consequences are what you get!" (Humor, n.d.)

Concluding Remarks

You might or might not have a voice in whether standardized tests are required in your school, but you can share what you have learned about the effects of high-stakes testing with those who have a voice. Contact national and state legislators as well as members of your local school board.

You might not be able to control how your school district uses test results, but you do control how **you** use test results to inform your teaching. It is also in your power to help students cope with the pressure and anxiety related to the tests you give and those mandated in your school system.

In our next session, you will find out if you suffer from the *Classroom Management Blues*. If so, you will learn how to personalize your own treatment to sustain or renew your passion for teaching. It is within your power to prevent or cure the *Classroom Management Blues*!

> We need to stop blaming teachers and punishing students . . . Let's demand that those who are most invested in education—families and teachers—have a voice in determining the course of educational reform. . . . The education of our children is far too important to reduce it to a high stakes game of testing roulette. (Marker, n.d., para. 16)

Resources—Access More Information

Learn more about national and international data, high-stakes testing, test anxiety, and creativity on the *Classroom Management Blues* website. Locate **Resources**, and then select **Testing** at *www.classroommanagementblues.com* for a list of books, articles, websites, and other resources.

Praxis Journal—Take Steps toward a Cure

Write responses to these prompts and questions before the next session:

- **Think about what you have learned about high-stakes testing.** How do high-stakes testing and school-related pressures affect teacher effectiveness and student learning?

- **Based on what you learned in this session, set a goal and develop a plan.** How do you plan to achieve your goal and solve one or more related problems?

- **Implement and evaluate your plan.** How did your actions affect you as a teacher and your students as learners?

- **Reflect on future goals and actions.** What will you do in the future?

STEP ONE: **MAKE A DIAGNOSIS**

Today's assignment:

Begin
Personalized Treatment

Session 4

Session 4

Begin Personalized Treatment

You don't make progress by standing on the sidelines, whimpering and complaining. You make progress by implementing ideas.

Shirley Chisholm
Teacher and U.S. Congresswoman

In previous sessions, we have discussed the warning signs of the ***Classroom Management Blues***, factors in your educational history, and the effects of high-stakes testing that can put teachers and students at risk. In this session, we will analyze this information and make a diagnosis. You will self-assess the severity of your condition, determine your stage of readiness for change, learn about the prescriptions for the ***Classroom Management Blues,*** and discover how to personalize treatment.

> **treat·ment** [trēt′mənt] *n.*
>
> **Synonyms:** cure, prescription, help, assistance, remedy
>
> *Roget's 21st Century Thesaurus*

A. Teacher: *I expect you will tell me I have the **Classroom Management Blues** and need help to survive in the classroom!*

Dr. Foster: *Before we make a diagnosis and discuss options for treatment, let's review your symptoms, educational history, and the effects standardized test results have had on you as a teacher.*

 Which warning signs did you identify in our first session? (See page 4.)

A. Teacher: *I identified four warning signs that seem to be the most severe.*

- *I feel sad and frustrated during the school day.*
- *I blame parents and students for what is happening in my classroom.*
- *I give up on and am too critical of some students.*
- *I get headaches during or after school.*

Dr. Foster: *How do you feel about your educational history and the aftereffects of high-stakes testing on your teaching effectiveness?*

A. Teacher: *I understand how my educational history and high-stakes testing affects aspects of what I believe and do in the classroom. I feel helpless and hopeless about ever-changing laws; inappropriate use of high-stakes testing that adversely affects student learning; comparisons between international and U.S. students when their attributes are not comparable; and negative comments from politicians and the community about the teaching profession!*

Dr. Foster: *I empathize with how you feel about what you have experienced in the classroom. Schools are under extreme pressure to raise standardized test scores and more effectively educate young people to compete globally. You need to learn how to cope with the pressure of high-stakes testing and the effects on your physical and emotional well-being. The good news is I will share ways you can cope with these pressures and gain more control in your classroom.*

What is the diagnosis? With a diagnosis comes fear and anxiety about the severity, treatment, and possibility of a relapse, but a person can learn to exert control over his or her life and cope with these challenges. Success depends on the stage of physical and mental readiness for treatment.

Dr. Foster: *After much discussion about your symptoms, educational history, and response to high-stakes test results, I am confident you have a case of the **Classroom Management Blues**.*

A. Teacher: *I am not surprised. It distresses me to think I am in this condition. I was so passionate about teaching when I became a teacher.*

What kind of treatment do I need? How fast can I get started?

Dr. Foster: *There is no easy, "one size fits all" method to cure the **Classroom Management Blues**—what works for one teacher may not work for another. You will learn how to personalize, or modify, the recommended treatment with my guidance.*

How quickly you begin and advance through treatment will depend upon what you choose to do and how you feel about the changes you make in your classroom.

In the late 1970s and early 1980s, James Prochaska and Carlo DiClemente developed the *Stages of Change Model* (SCM) at the University of Rhode Island. The idea behind the mind and body stages is that change includes many steps, not one. People move through these stages on their way to successful change at different rates (Kern, 2008).

> Each person must decide for himself or herself when a stage is completed and when it is time to move on to the next stage. Moreover, this decision must come from inside . . . stable, long-term change cannot be externally imposed. (para. 5–6)

Dr. Foster: *I have a chart that shows how to identify, accept, and make long-lasting, positive changes. I think you will find the **Stages of Change Model** helpful as you begin the change process to cure the **Classroom Management Blues**.*

 Look at this chart (see Table 4.1). What is your current stage for change?

Table 4.1

Stages of Change Model	
Precontemplation Not considering change	• I do not believe I have a problem. • I do not need to change.
Contemplation Thinking about change	• I know I have a problem, but I am not yet ready to change. • I weighed the pros and cons of change, but I doubt the long-term benefits will outweigh the short-term costs. • I am open to educational information, but I do not know for sure that the strategies will work perfectly.
Preparation—Determination Getting ready to change	• I am committed to making a change and want information about what I need to do. • I want to know what strategies and resources are available to help me change.
Action—Willpower Practicing the change	• I believe I have the ability to change. • I use different strategies to change. • I am open to help and seek support from others.
Maintenance Maintaining the change	• I am on track and avoid temptations. • I remind myself of how much progress I have made. • I have acquired new skills to avoid a relapse. • I anticipate the situations in which a relapse could happen and prepare coping strategies in advance. • I understand it often takes a while to let go of old behavior patterns and practice new ones until they are second nature. • I recognize that it is normal to regress—to attain one stage and fall back to a preceding stage. • I re-evaluate my progress up and down through these stages.
Relapse Resuming old behaviors	• I am discouraged because I have returned to my old ways. • I am unable to recognize environmental cues and high-risk situations that tempt me.
Transcendence From Kern (2008) Not returning to old ways	• I no longer go back to my old ways. If I do, it seems abnormal. • I am not tempted to return to my old ways.

From Kern, 2008; "Prochaska and DiClemente's Stages," n.d.;
and "Prochaska and DiClemente's Stages of Change Model," n.d.

A. Teacher: *I am not at the precontemplation stage. I know I have a problem.*

Though I am open to educational information, I don't know for sure if the strategies will work perfectly. I don't believe anything works perfectly because situations and people change.

*I **am** frustrated with what happens in my classroom and want to know if strategies and resources are available to help me, so I must be at the preparation and determination stage.*

Dr. Foster: *People often skip the preparation and determination stage. "They try to move directly from contemplation into action and fall flat on their faces because they haven't adequately researched or accepted what it is going to take to make" a major change (Kern, 2008, para. 19).*

*Your commitment is evident as this is our fourth session. You seem to be **mentally** ready to follow through with the recommended treatment.*

 *Are you **physically** ready to begin treatment? Are you in good health?*

A. Teacher: *I do need to get more sleep. When I have less stress in the classroom, I am confident I will sleep and feel better.*

Dr. Foster: *The healthier you are, the easier it will be for you to advance through the Stages of Change. I recommend a checkup with your family doctor as you might choose to make important changes in your physical activity to reduce stress ("Caring for the Whole Patient," 2009, para. 19).*

It is important for you to make informed decisions about treatment and seek support throughout this ongoing process.

A. Teacher: *I understand. Tell me about the treatment.*

What is the recommended treatment for the Classroom Management Blues? The primary components of treatment for the ***Classroom Management Blues*** are **prescriptions** for active engagement, high expectations, appropriate assessments, trustworthy behavior, and effective communication. Each prescription contains many **active ingredients** grounded in learning theory, instructional design, and research-based practice. **Supplements** are available to help teachers put the theories and strategies found in each prescription into practice in the classroom.

Dr. Foster: *In each of the next five sessions, you will learn about one prescription and five of its most **active ingredients**. In addition, you will receive **supplements** to help put into practice the theories and strategies found in each prescription to cure the **Classroom Management Blues**.*

A. Teacher: *It sounds complicated! I had hoped there was an easy solution. I trust you will show me step-by-step what I need to do to be successful!*

Dr. Foster: *Yes. I will be your guide as you learn to cure yourself of the **Classroom Management Blues**.*

"Teacher, Heal Thyself" is the title of Carl Hoegerl's letter to the editor of *The Journal of the American Osteopathic Association*. He encouraged osteopathic medical students, residents, and program directors to take time to learn and to teach, but his advice applies to any teacher.

> According to *The American Heritage Dictionary of the English Language* (2000), the word *doctor* has its roots in the Latin words *doctus* and *docere*, which mean "teacher" and "to teach." Those who become good learners will become good teachers. Learn to become a good teacher, and teach to become a good learner—and start early. Bring the profession to a new level. (Hoegerl, 2005, para.1, 6)

A. Teacher: *I get it! I am ready to learn how to cure my **Classroom Management Blues**.*

Dr. Foster: *Apples symbolize knowledge, good health, and education. I am confident that the prescriptions, or apples, I recommend will help you cure your **Classroom Management Blues**.*

Table 4.2

Prescriptions for the Classroom Management Blues

- Apply **ACTIVE ENGAGEMENT** to learning activities *every morning and afternoon*.
- Repeat **HIGH EXPECTATIONS** *daily* to inspire ALL students to achieve academic and personal goals.
- Use **APPROPRIATE ASSESSMENTS** *as needed* to foster student learning.
- Encourage **TRUSTWORTHY BEHAVIOR** and support self-discipline *throughout the school day*.
- Maintain **EFFECTIVE COMMUNICATION** *as directed* with students, families, and other educators.

Active Engagement	High Expectations	Appropriate Assessments	Trustworthy Behavior	Effective Communication
Active Ingredients	*Active Ingredients*	*Active Ingredients*	*Active Ingredients*	*Active Ingredients*
• Brain Research	• Efficacy	• Expectancy	• Principles	• Advocacy
• Constructivism	• Authenticity	• Attribution	• Rules	• Feedback
• Higher-Order Thinking	• Community	• Practice	• Consequences	• Dialogue
• Learning Styles	• Autonomy	• Evaluation	• Documentation	• Collaboration
• Student Interest	• Resiliency	• Reflection	• Procedures	• Professionalism

A. Teacher: *I am familiar with the prescriptions and many of the active ingredients, but I am not sure how they will work together to help me be more effective in the classroom. Do I need all of them? Do I need one more than I need another?*

Dr. Foster: *You need a blend of all five prescriptions, but the dosage will depend on how you and your students react to the active ingredients I have found to be most effective in caring, high-performing classrooms.*

Dr. Foster: *You can use the strategies in these active ingredients or add other active ingredients to "spice up" the effective strategies you already use in your classroom.*

Let me share the wisdom of Bobby Ann Starnes, an educator from Berea, Kentucky, who says, "Good teaching, like making good gravy, requires tapping into your own experiences to discover what works best for you and your students" (2010, p. 72). Read "It Won't Be Your Mother's Gravy" to learn about tapping into your own experiences.

It Won't Be Your Mother's Gravy

Last Thanksgiving, I tried to make my mother's gravy. As always, I failed miserably. Standing at the stove stirring the mixture, getting it wrong yet again, I had a vivid image of the day I asked my mother to teach me.

Mother never used a recipe, and she laughed lightly when I suggested she write out one for me. My mother understood gravy. She just knew how much of this or that she needed—salt, pepper, milk, butter, in quantities of a pinch, a dash, a handful. She knew how to thicken or thin, how to get it just brown enough. She knew how the ingredients interacted. And by watching carefully, she knew when to add each. She could see a problem before it occurred, and she knew how to head it off. She paid attention, and even when she seemed distracted by the potatoes or the bread or crying children, she kept it all in her head and responded to each situation at just the right moment.

I finally gave up on ever being able to make my mother's gravy. Instead, I decided to make my own. I smiled as I remembered myself anxiously trying to copy her every movement exactly. I can't make hers, I thought, but she taught me a lot about gravy. As a result, I learned to make my gravy. And it is good.

Excerpted from "My Mother's Gravy" by B. A. Starnes, January 2010

Bobby Ann Starnes (2010) says, "Good teachers become good by learning what they can from others, by trying again and again, by watching and listening and noticing, and by coming to understand as much as they can about the ingredients" (p. 73). In ***reality,*** what you put into practice from this book will be your classroom management—not mine!

Dr. Foster: *Our sessions together will serve as a **self-help survival guide** to help you cure the Classroom Management Blues. Like other professional development workshops and conferences, some sessions may last an hour while others may extend over several days. It will be your decision how quickly you move through each session and when you put the ideas and strategies into practice in your classroom. Pace yourself, and let me know when you need a break.*

A. Teacher: *Could I start right away? I want to keep my condition from getting worse.*

Dr. Foster: *I understand you want to start treatment as quickly as possible, but it is important for you to take your time and make informed decisions. This will improve your chances to be successful..*

A. Teacher: *I trust you will provide the information and resources I need to make positive changes in my classroom. How long will I need treatment?*

Dr. Foster: *You can realistically expect to practice new behaviors for three to six months ("Prochaska," n.d.). It will take months and years to maintain or sustain a commitment to the new behaviors (para. 5). During the action/willpower and maintenance stages, you must avoid temptations to return to your old behaviors. This requires preparation for complications. Remember, movement up and down through the Stages of Change is normal (Kern, 2008). (See page 43.)*

A. Teacher: *I want to be healthy when I retire from teaching. It took years to get myself in this condition; it will take time to get better.*

Dr. Foster: *A positive attitude will keep you motivated. Once you begin to gain control of your classroom, the temptation to return to your old practices will lessen.*

A. Teacher: *I am hopeful that I will become blues free.*

Dr. Foster: *If you focus, stay energized, and do not rush the process, you will recover.*

What is the prognosis, or chances of recovery? A person's chances of recovery are dependent upon early diagnosis, prescriptions in the right dosage, the ability to anticipate the situations in which a relapse could happen, and the preparation of coping strategies in advance. Joshua Freedman describes a three-part model, or process, that can help teachers become blues free. He developed the EQ Model as an action plan to use emotional intelligence (EQ) in daily life. "The process works when you spin it, like a propeller moving a ship. As you move through these three pursuits you gain positive momentum" (Freedman, 2010, para. 9).

- **Know yourself** (self-awareness)

  Become more aware of your strengths and challenges, *what* you feel and do, and what you want to change

- **Choose yourself** (self-management)

  Become more intentional about *how* to respond proactively to influence yourself and others

- **Give yourself** (self-direction)

  Become more purposeful about *why* you respond to stay focused and energized as you move in a new direction with full integrity (Freedman, 2010; Freedman, Ghini, & Fiedeldey-Van Dijk, 2005)

> What keeps me from getting discouraged when my failures outnumber my successes is to keep thinking long-term. I often must endure a lot of failures to hit the next big breakthrough. So I just plow through those failures as fast as possible. It's like a conveyor belt—there's a new success on that belt somewhere ahead, and the faster the belt moves, the sooner it will arrive. (Pavlina, 2006, para. 19)

Freedman (2010) described specific, measurable competencies for these three pursuits. The *Six Seconds Emotional Intelligence Assessment*—or SEI—can measure the competencies that include the abilities to

- Accurately identify and interpret both simple and compound feelings
- Acknowledge frequently recurring responses and behaviors
- Evaluate the cost and benefits of choices
- Assess, harness, and transform emotions as a strategic resource
- Gain energy from personal values and commitments
- Take a proactive perspective of hope and possibility
- Recognize and appropriately respond to others' emotions
- Connect daily choices with a sense of purpose (para. 11)

A. Teacher: *I noticed the three pursuits involved self-awareness, self-management, and self-direction. The choices I make about the prescriptions are mine!*

*One of the emotional intelligence abilities is being able to evaluate the benefits of choices. I know the prescriptions you recommend will cure the **Classroom Management Blues**, but every prescription has side effects and risks. What are the risks and side effects?*

Dr. Foster: *With any treatment, you **should** be aware of the risks and side effects.*

*Although the risks or cautions vary from prescription to prescription, the side effects of each prescription for the **Classroom Management Blues** are the same— more trust and respect, increased learning, and improved behavior.*

A. Teacher: *I am ready to **learn** about these prescriptions and implement the strategies you recommend in my classroom. The possible side effects are worth the risks!*

Concluding Remarks

No prescription alone will prevent or cure the **Classroom Management Blues**, but the potential for prevention and a cure increases with the use of all the recommended prescriptions, the development of emotional intelligence, and a commitment to move through the Stages of Change until you no longer go back to your old ways. Learn about the prescriptions and blend the practical, research-based strategies with the effective strategies you currently use in your classroom to sustain or renew your passion for teaching. In the next session, learn how the **Active Engagement Prescription** can help increase student learning and improve student behavior.

> Emotional intelligence is the capacity to blend thinking and feeling to make optimal decisions—which is key to having a successful relationship with yourself and others. . . . At the core, emotional intelligence is something to BE. By being more emotionally intelligent, smarter with feelings, you will more accurately recognize emotions in yourself and others. This data will help you make decisions and craft effective solutions to the "life puzzles" you face each day. (Freedman, 2010, para. 1)

Resources—Access More Information

Learn more about change, the benefits of sleep, and emotional intelligence on the *Classroom Management Blues* website. Select **Resources**, then **Treatment** at *www.classroommanagementblues.com* for a list of books, articles, websites, and other resources.

Praxis Journal—Take Steps toward a Cure

Write responses to these prompts and questions before the next session:

- **Think about what you have learned about how to personalize your own treatment for the *Classroom Management Blues*.** How would a cure for the *Classroom Management Blues* affect teacher effectiveness and student learning in your classroom?

- **Based on what you have learned in this session, set a goal and develop a plan.** How do you plan to achieve your goal and solve one or more related problems?

- **Implement and evaluate your plan.** How did your actions affect you as a teacher and your students as learners?

- **Reflect on future goals and actions.** What will you do in the future?

STEP TWO: **TAKE PRESCRIPTIONS**

GARDNER'S PHARMACY

111 Teaching Turnpike
Any Town, USA

Date Filled: First Day in the Classroom
Discard After: Retirement

 0001

Prescription for **ACTIVE ENGAGEMENT**

Patient's Name: **A. Teacher**

Patient's Address: **101 Learning Lane — Any Town, USA**

Apply **ACTIVE ENGAGEMENT** to learning activities
every morning and afternoon.

Doctor: *Barbara G. Foster*

SIDE EFFECTS: More trust and respect, increased learning,
and improved behavior

CAUTION: May cause excitement

Active Ingredients
- **Brain Research**
- **Constructivism**
- **Higher-Order Thinking**
- **Learning Styles**
- **Student Interest**

Unlimited Refills

Session 5

Photos.com

Session 5

Apply Active Engagement

Those helping to row the boat have neither the time nor the desire to rock it.

Cynthia Desrochers
Creating Lessons

When teachers provide experiences that foster student motivation and active engagement in a well-managed classroom, students learn more, stay on task, and are less likely to misbehave (Desrochers, 2000; Jensen, 1998). "Although it is difficult to prescribe a 'one size fits all' method to motivating students, research suggests that some general patterns do appear to hold true" (Anderman & Midgley, 1997, para. 1). In this session you will learn some of the patterns found in the **Active Engagement Prescription**.

 en·gage [ĕn-gāj′] *v.*

1. to attract and hold the attention of; engross

2. to draw into; involve

The American Heritage Dictionary of the English Language

Dr. Foster: *Look at the* **Active Engagement Prescription** *(on the opposite page). How should teachers use this prescription? What are the active ingredients and side effects? What is the caution?*

A. Teacher: *The prescription is for* **ACTIVE ENGAGEMENT**, *and its* **active ingredients** *are brain research, constructivism, higher-order thinking, learning styles, and student interest. If I apply* **ACTIVE ENGAGEMENT** *to learning activities every morning and afternoon, the* **side effects** *will be more trust and respect, increased learning, and improved behavior in my classroom.*

Though it is a **caution**, *I will like to be more excited about teaching and have my students be more excited about learning.*

I could really use this prescription. Many of my students lack motivation!

Dr. Foster: *Understand that more strategies are associated with this prescription than those I will share with you in this session. You are encouraged to add other strategies to the* **Active Engagement Prescription** *to help motivate your students.*

Dr. Foster: *Let's begin with a discussion of brain research. Thanks to research in neuroscience, we know more about human learning and have the potential to be successful with more students (Sousa, 1998). "Although the research is no magic bullet, what we are discovering about learning has the potential for making the greatest contribution to our practice in recent memory" (para. 1).*

Active Ingredient	 Brain Research

The first active ingredient in the **Active Engagement Prescription** is **brain research**. At Davenport Community Schools (2005), brain-compatible classrooms are clean, well-organized, and enriched environments; have calm (green and blue) and reassuring (brown) colors; and contain lamps, classical music, and plants. Brain-compatible classrooms reflect "what is being studied, not just print resources, but also three-dimensional objects and artifacts" (para. 8). Students make more connections, retain more information, and learn faster with greater meaning in these multisensory, interactive environments (Sousa, 1998).

What can teachers do to increase cognition, learning, and retention? Sousa (2006) cites studies on retention of learning conducted in the 1960s by National Training Laboratories of Bethel, Maine. The researchers found that a learner's ability to retain information is dependent on the **primary** teaching method used by the teacher. Figure 5.1 shows the percentage of new learning that students can recall after 24 hours when taught primarily by one teaching method.

Figure 5.1

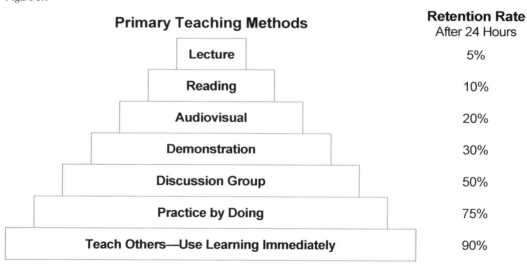

Lecture, with the lowest retention rate of 5%, continues to be "the most prevalent teaching method" in many classrooms (p. 95). To increase retention, students must be more **active** in the learning process. When students participate in discussion groups, the retention rate is about 50%. When students practice by doing, they recall about 75% of the new learning after 24 hours. The highest retention rate of 90% is possible when students **teach others** or use the learning immediately.

A. Teacher: *I know how to provide more opportunities for my students to **practice by doing**, but I don't like using **discussion** or **cooperative learning groups.** My students argue, get off topic, and fail to share the work. My students misbehave and just don't learn very much when they work in small groups. I have more control when we do activities together as a class and I lead the whole class in discussion.*

Dr. Foster: *I understand you want to maintain class control, but when students work in small groups, they use the teaching methods with the highest retention rates (i.e., discussion, practice by doing, and teaching others). It is important that you use small group discussions and cooperative learning in your classroom as often as possible.*

*Visit the **Classroom Management Blues** website for a list of books, articles, websites, and other instructional materials to help you teach the group process and design meaningful cooperative learning activities. Select **Resources** at www.classroommanagementblues.com, then **Engagement** and **Grouping**.*

In my experience, group success and productivity are dependent upon the selection of the group members.

 Let me ask you this. When you want your students to work in groups, how do you select the group members?

A. Teacher: *Most of the time, I group by ability or let the students choose who they want to work with. Sometimes, I have them count off.*

Dr. Foster: *When teachers group students by chance, choice, or ability alone, the probability is high that the groups will not be successful or produce high-quality work.*

If no one in the group is organized or has the ability to understand the content needed to finish an assignment, misbehavior results and the assignment is often not finished.

A. Teacher: *I often have these experiences. Is there a way to establish groups that is more productive?*

Dr. Foster: *Rather than leave the composition of groups to chance, use* 🗁 **Supplement A: Quality Grouping** *to improve the **quality** of the work your students complete and make the diverse **qualities** of your students count. This strategy takes into consideration such qualities as gender, leadership, ethnicity, ability level, communication skills, and the ability to work with others.*

*Select the **Supplements** page, then **A–F** on the **Classroom Management Blues** website at www.classroommanagementblues.com for step-by-step directions and to download the blackline masters for* 🗁 **Supplement A: Quality Grouping**. *For a sneak preview, read "Qualities Count in Groups."*

Qualities Count in Groups

Teachers should carefully think about whether groups would be homogeneous or heterogeneous for gender, social skills, academic ability, ethnicity, leadership skills, disabilities, and ability to work with others (Weinstein & Mignano, 2003). This is not easy to do, so grouping is often by chance.

Adapted from other systems, this *Quality Grouping* strategy allows teachers the flexibility to select the student information and *qualities* needed to help groups be successful on cooperative activities and projects. They record the quality ratings for work habits and organizational skills, content knowledge and skills in one or more subjects, the ability to communicate content to others, as well as interpersonal skills and overall behavior on an index card for each student. Teachers sort index cards using the circled *Total Quality* score to determine group members.

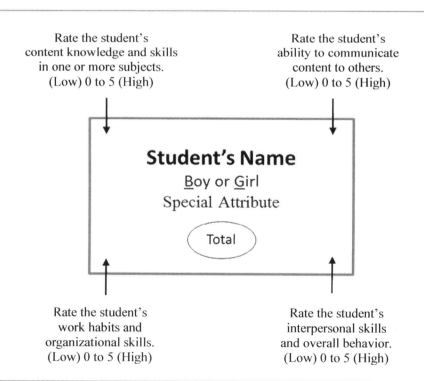

Rate the student's content knowledge and skills in one or more subjects. (Low) 0 to 5 (High)

Rate the student's ability to communicate content to others. (Low) 0 to 5 (High)

Student's Name
Boy or Girl
Special Attribute

Total

Rate the student's work habits and organizational skills. (Low) 0 to 5 (High)

Rate the student's interpersonal skills and overall behavior. (Low) 0 to 5 (High)

Select the **Supplements** page at *www.classroommanagementblues.com*, and then **A–F** to download step-by-step instructions and blackline masters to put **Supplement A: Quality Grouping** into **practice** in your classroom. Try it, and you will see how it works to increase the probability of group success and high-quality group products.

A. Teacher: *I'll try the Quality Grouping strategy, but I question whether my students can **teach each other** to achieve a retention rate of 90%.*

Dr. Foster:  *Think about something you teach. Did you know the skill, subject, or content better before or after you taught it for the first time?*

A. Teacher: *I was more knowledgeable after teaching it for the first time. Is there a strategy that will help my students effectively teach each other?*

Dr. Foster: *Use ▭ **Supplement B: Jigsaw** to structure peer teaching in your classroom. This cooperative learning strategy reduces group conflict, promotes better learning, improves student motivation, and increases enjoyment of the learning experience (Aronson, 2005). Use Jigsaws when you believe the content or skill is at a level that students can comprehend and teach others successfully. Select **Supplements**, then **A–F** and **Supplement B** at www.classroommanagmentblues.com for step-by-step instructions and blackline masters. Read "Putting the Pieces Together" to see a Jigsaw in practice.*

Putting the Pieces Together

A good way to engage students in learning about any concept or topic is to wrap it in a puzzle, or a **Jigsaw**. This collaborative learning strategy, like the **Story Elements Jigsaw** below, can be adapted for learners of all ages and different content areas.

Instruction: I read a story to the class and teach one or more lessons about these story elements: plot, theme, characterization, and setting.

Practice: The students read a different story. I assign each member of the **Home Quad** one of these story *elements*: *Plot, Setting, Theme*, and *Characterization*. On their own, the students write down what they know or have learned about their assigned story element.

Then, students with the same element meet in **Expert Quads** to discuss, clarify, and possibly rehearse what they will teach about the element.

Finally, the experts return to their **Home Quad** and teach their assigned elements. If I want every student to be an expert on each element, I repeat the **Practice** with three other stories.

Evaluation: The students read a different story. Each student completes an assessment independently to demonstrate understanding of *all* the story elements.

Rather than use four story elements, you could assign four different articles, sections of a chapter, subtopics, or vocabulary words. Select the **Supplements** page, then **A–F** at *www.classroommanagementblues.com* to read more examples and download step-by-step directions to put **Supplement B: Jigsaw** into practice in your classroom.

A. Teacher: *I have never thought of my students as teachers. With what students must learn in schools today, how important is it for students to teach each other?*

Dr. Foster: *Every student* **can** *and* **should** *learn to teach because they will teach throughout their lives. No matter the occupation or position held within an organization, everyone teaches or explains something on the job.*

Most people **will** *become parents, some of children with special learning needs. Students who learn to teach others with and without special learning needs will be better able to cope with and help their own children. A parent* **is***, after all, a child's first teacher.*

📁 **Supplement C: LTC** (**L**earner **T**eacher **C**hecker) *will help you model and structure how students can teach each other and instill a sense of pride in helping one another succeed within the classroom community. Use* **LTC** *when one concept or skill is* **best** *taught and learned with one-on-one instruction. Choose* **Supplements***, then* **A–F** *at www.classroommanagementblues.com for detailed directions and blackline masters. Read about how* **LTC** *works in "Learner + Teacher + Checker = Retention."*

Learner + **T**eacher + **C**hecker = Retention

The best way for students to learn a concept or skill is to receive one-on-one instruction. I use **LTC** when so many hands are up that I cannot possibly get to everyone. The example below is like the telephone game you played as a child. Here is one example that shows how to use this strategy.

In Practice

Dr. Foster

Instruction: Student is a **L**earner who does the task.

As **Teacher 1**, I teach **Learner 1** how to *substitute a word in a document with a synonym from the word processor's thesaurus.*

Practice: Learner becomes a **T**eacher who explains the task.

Learner 1 becomes **Teacher 2**, who practices by teaching **Learner 2** how to *use the word processor's thesaurus.*

Evaluation: Teacher becomes a **C**hecker who listens and supports the next teacher.

As the preceding teacher, I now become **Checker 1** and remain with **Teacher 2** to offer support, if needed.

I move on to monitor and assist students with other tasks. **Teacher 2** becomes the **Checker** as **Learner 2** becomes the teacher for the next student. This continues from one student to the next until all the students learn how to *use the word processor's thesaurus.* Finally, the last student teaches me, while the last **Checker** provides support.

Students learn (do), teach (explain), and check (evaluate) the task to get added **practice** and foster **retention**. Select **Supplements** at *www.classroommanagementblues.com*, then **A–F** to download the directions and blackline masters for **Supplement C: LTC**.

| **Active Ingredient** | 🍎 **Constructivism** |

Constructivism is the second active ingredient in the **Active Engagement Prescription**. Like the LTC strategy, "constructivism promotes social and communication skills by creating a classroom environment that emphasizes collaboration and exchange of ideas" ("Concept to Classroom," 2004, para. 6). Davenport Community Schools (2005) believe constructivism is at the heart of brain-friendly classrooms where students learn and retain more when they discuss issues, work together to resolve problems, and help each other contribute to the learning community.

A. Teacher: *If students are **active** participants in the learning process, what is my role in the constructivist classroom? Are my expert knowledge and teaching ability of no value?*

Dr. Foster: *Your role is to **design** instruction and **sequence** real-world problem solving and inquiry-based learning **activities** to guide students as they construct or build knowledge about preexisting concepts rather than reproduce a series of facts ("Concept to Classroom," 2004). Your expert knowledge is essential to help students fill in the gaps and go beyond the content being learned (Patsula, 1999).*

To design and sequence activities to actively engage your students, psychologist Dr. Jerome Bruner describes three stages students must move through to construct understanding and develop intellectually. Here is a diagram that shows Dr. Bruner's stages along with a real-life example (Kennedy & Tipps, 2000).

Figure 5.2

	Enactive	**Iconic**	**Symbolic**
A learner **constructs** understanding by …	Experiencing the world through actions on **objects**	Using **pictures** and **graphic representations**	Thinking in **abstract terms**
A builder **constructs** a house by …	Working with **tools**	Using house **plans**	Thinking about how the house will meet a family's **needs** and weather a storm

Dr. Foster: *Just as a master builder provides a sequence of learning experiences and assesses whether a novice builder can use the tools properly, interpret plans accurately, and envision the needs of the owners and workers, master teachers help learners develop the cognitive, psychomotor, and emotional skills needed to be lifelong learners and teachers. As I stated before, your role is to guide students as they construct and build knowledge. (Read "Teacher as Master Builder" for an example of a constructivist lesson.)*

Teacher as Master Builder

It is important to design and sequence activities to help students construct understanding and develop intellectually. When I taught sixth graders a few years ago, they had difficulty with this symbolic task:

$$4\,Fe + 3\,O_2 \longrightarrow 2\,Fe_2O_3$$

Today, I would use Dr. Jerome Bruner's constructivist stages to design activities and engage my students in tasks like these to learn how to balance chemical reactions.

Enactive—Experience the world through actions on objects

Task 1   Students create molecules using toothpicks and marshmallows (e.g., yellow = carbon, pink = oxygen, green = hydrogen, orange = chlorine) to balance chemical reactions ("SNC2P," n.d.).

Iconic to Symbolic—Use pictures, then letters and numbers

Task 2   For more **practice**, students see pictures that show how the chemical reactions are balanced. The interactive "Chemical Formula" website takes students from pictures to symbols.

Task 3   Students **practice** balancing reactions by playing "Classic Chembalancer." Students insert numbers in front of each molecule until there is the same number of atoms on both sides of the equation and check their responses (Dun, 2005).

Task 4   Students balance at least five equations to demonstrate mastery ("Worksheet," n.d.).

In the example above, students could practice alone or with a partner. Students may succeed alone, but they are more likely to be more successful succeed learning and retaining the ability to balance chemical reactions with the support of a partner.

A. Teacher: *The master builder analogy shows that teachers or someone else guides students to construct new learning.*

Dr. Foster: *"Learning is more than an interaction between the learner and the physical world; it also includes people who provide information and support through language interactions" (Kennedy & Tipps, 2000, p. 96). Dr. Lev Vygotsky, a psychologist and social constructivist, wrote about the interactions that advance student learning within a social environment.*

How do social interactions promote student learning? The **Zone of Proximal Development (ZPD)** is one of the main concepts defined in Lev Vygotsky's book *Mind in Society: The Development of Higher Psychological Processes.* ZPD is "the distance between the actual development level as determined by independent problem solving and the level of potential development as determined through problem solving under adult guidance or in collaboration with more capable persons" (1978, p. 86).

> The ZPD represents the amount of learning possible by a student . . . [when] a teacher and learner (adult/child, tutor/tutee, model/observer, expert/novice, master/apprentice) work together on a task that the learner could not perform independently because of the difficulty level. (Schunk, 2000, p. 244)

Constructivism works best when teachers *provide guidance*, *sequenced activities,* and *collaborative opportunities* that move students from the enactive to the symbolic stage and *help students learn how to think.* When students take ownership in their learning in constructivist classrooms, they learn to question and apply natural curiosity about the world ("Concept to Classroom," 2004).

Active Ingredient	🍎 **Higher-Order Thinking**

The third active ingredient in the **Active Engagement Prescription** is *higher-order thinking*. According to Sousa (2001), Benjamin Bloom's Taxonomy of the Cognitive Domain is consistent with the latest research on brain function. Although Bloom's thinking skills model has been around since the 1950s, Sousa believes it "remains one of the most useful tools for moving students, especially slower learners, to higher levels of thinking" (p. 252).

How does higher-order thinking advance learning in constructivist and brain-friendly classrooms? What Davenport Community Schools (2005) believe about brain-friendly classrooms reflects the characteristics of constructivist teachers. A much greater depth of knowledge results when constructivist teachers ask open-ended questions that require high-order thinking and teach students how to use metacognition—think about their thinking (Brooks & Brooks, 1993).

The divergent thinking processes at the upper levels of Bloom's Taxonomy describe how students process information in constructivist and brain-friendly classrooms. Students **analyze** when they separate, compare, or determine relationships among concepts or ideas; **evaluate** when they make a decision or choose from several options; and **create** (synthesize) when they combine previously learned information, opinions, or concepts into an original response (Bloom, 1956; Dalton & Smith, 1986; Sousa, 2006).

Anderson, Krathwohl, Airasian, Cruikshank, Mayer, Pintrich, Raths, and Witrock *analyzed* and *evaluated* Bloom's original taxonomy and published a new version in 2001 (see Table 5.1). The revised version uses verbs to name each level, as verbs are a better fit to write learning objectives (Sousa, 2006). Synthesis and evaluation were interchanged as "the researchers felt that recent studies in cognitive neuroscience suggest that generating, planning, and producing an original product demands more complex thinking than making judgments based on accepted criteria" (p. 250).

Table 5.1

Levels of Bloom's Taxonomy	
Original 1956	*Revised 2001*
Evaluation	**Create**
Synthesis	**Evaluate**
Analysis	**Analyze**
Application	Apply
Comprehension	Understand
Knowledge	Remember

A. Teacher: *My students show a much greater depth of knowledge when I use the higher-thinking levels; but it takes a lot of time to think up questions for every lesson and assessment.*

Dr. Foster: *Use* 📁 **Supplement D: Higher-Order Thinking (HOT) Question Starters** *in a matter of minutes to add analysis, evaluation, and synthesis questions to lesson plans, activities, projects, and assessments. Select* **Supplements**, *then* **A–F** *at www.classroommanagementblues.com to download a page of* **HOT Question Starters**. *Read how to "Get Started with HOT Question Starters."*

Get Started with HOT Question Starters

In Practice
Dr. Foster

Start with any lesson. I found *Edible Color Wheel* at http://www.princetonol.com/groups/iad/Files/color.htm and looked at the list of **HOT** Question Starters. Below are the **Question Starters** I chose for this lesson.

HOT Questions for the *Edible Color Wheel* Lesson

Analyze	Evaluate	Create
What is the relationship between . . . *primary and secondary colors?*	Based on what you know, how would you explain . . . *tints and shades?*	What way would you design . . . *a chart to remember different color combinations and results?*
What is the difference between . . . *intermediate and tertiary colors?*	How would you decide about . . . *what colors to use in your new bedroom?*	Suppose you could . . . *paint your bedroom and furniture.* What would you do *to show what you know about colors?*

Use **Supplement D: HOT Question Starters** to put higher-order thinking into practice in your classroom. Select **Supplements** at *www.classroommanagementblues.com*, then **A–F** to download a page of question starters. Place it in your plan book for easy reference.

Constructivist teachers ask higher-order thinking questions to help students gain understanding. What's more, students become "expert learners" when they question themselves and their strategies. "This gives them ever-broadening tools to keep learning" ("Concept to Classroom," 2004, para. 3).

Active Ingredient	🍎 Learning Styles

The fourth active ingredient in the **Active Engagement Prescription** is **learning styles**. Mills (2002) says that our natural learning strengths, or styles, are the ways we *perceive* the world, *process* information (think and make decisions), and **attend** to what we value.

Dr. Foster: *Learners use different* **perceptual modalities** *(e.g., visual, auditory, kinesthetic, tactile) to* **perceive** *the world. They affect what learners* **attend** *to and how they* **process** *information.*

 Look at this table. It shows how the general categories of Dennis W. Mills parallel Jerome Bruner's modes of knowledge representation and Bloom's Domains of Educational Activities. Use information from the table and explain some differences among visual, auditory, kinesthetic, and tactile learners.

Table 5.2

Mills 2002	Perceptual Modalities	Information Processing	Personality Patterns
	The way learners **perceive,** respond to, and gather information to make sense of real-life experiences	The way learners **process,** (think about, organize, and retain information); make decisions; and solve real-life problems	The way learners **attend to** real-life experiences and feel about or value academic subjects, jobs, and activities
	Learners are . . .	Learners use . . .	Learners like . . .
	▪ **Visual** ▪ **Auditory** ▪ **Kinesthetic** ▪ **Tactile**	• Pictures and symbols • Sounds • Movement • Touch	• Reading, writing • Music, debates • PE, science • Sculpture, ceramics
Bruner 1964	**Enactive Mode** Experience through objects	**Iconic & Symbolic Mode** Use pictures and think abstractly	
Bloom 1956	**Psychomotor** Domain Doing—physical skills	**Cognitive** Domain Thinking—mental skills	**Affective** Domain Feeling—attitudes

A. Teacher: *Visual learners use pictures and symbols to gather and respond to information whereas auditory learners use sounds and spoken language to think about, organize and retain information; make decisions; and solve real-life problems. When their preferred perceptual modality is kinesthetic, learners attend to academic subjects, jobs, and activities that involve movement (e.g., PE, science). Tactile learners, on the other hand, touch to make sense of the world and might prefer sculpture and ceramics.*

Dr. Foster: *You visually **perceived** the information from the table and **processed** the information by reading and thinking about the words (cognitive domain). You **attended** to the task, which shows that you valued the task (affective domain).*

A. Teacher: *I always thought visual, tactile, kinesthetic, and auditory described learning styles and so did multiple intelligences. Are perceptual modalities, learning styles, and multiple intelligences the same?*

How do perceptual modalities, learning styles, and multiple intelligences compare with one another?
Davenport Community Schools (2005) believe students learn more in constructivist and brain-friendly classrooms when teachers design learning experiences that allow learners to use ALL their perceptual modalities and multiple intelligences. Howard Gardner, a psychologist and professor of neuroscience, is the originator of nine multiple intelligences and "calls for doing away with our 'fast food-food approach to education' to accommodate all children, not just those who find it easy to learn in traditional ways" (Plucker, 2004, para. 5).

Interpersonal, intrapersonal, logical-mathematical, linguistic, spatial-visual, musical-rhythmic, naturalistic, and bodily-kinesthetic are eight of Gardner's **multiple intelligences** (see Table 5.3). The ninth intelligence is existential—"the ability and proclivity to pose (and ponder) questions about life, death, and ultimate realities" ("Educational Resources," n.d., para. 12). Learners have more than one intelligence, or learning style. Though they might prefer one or more **perceptual modalities** (i.e., visual, auditory, kinesthetic, tactile), ALL available modalities are used to perceive, process, and attend to content-specific information and real-life experiences.

Dr. Foster: *In most K–12 classrooms, teachers implement eight of Dr. Gardner's multiple intelligences but **not** the existential intelligence.*

 Study the information about Gardner's multiple intelligences on this chart (on the opposite page) and answer these questions.

1. *Which **auditory** and **visual** representations do **logical-mathematical** learners attend to when they process information and make sense of the world?*

2. ***Logical-mathematical** learners use their **tactile** and **kinesthetic** modalities to discover abstract patterns and relationships, manipulate numbers, and engage in logical activities when making decisions and solving job-related problems in which potential occupations?*

3. *Who are some famous **logic smart** people who embody the **logical-mathematical** learning style?*

A. Teacher: 1. ***Logical-mathematical** learners attend to the representations of numbers, mathematical and scientific patterns and relationships, and logic to process information and make sense of the world.*

2. *The potential careers for **logical-mathematical** learners are engineer, computer programmer, or physician.*

3. *Some famous **logic-smart** people are Albert Einstein, Marie Curie, and Bill Gates.*

Table 5.3

Multiple Intelligences Famous Examples	Learners process information using . . .	Learners attend to . . .
		Potential Occupations
Linguistic *Word Smart* Mark Twain, J. K. Rowling, Toni Morrison	Persuasive, spoken, and written language	Writing, poetry, literature, journalism
		Lawyer, translator
Logical-Mathematical *Logic Smart* Albert Einstein, Marie Curie, Bill Gates	Numbers, logic, and abstract patterns and relationships	Mathematics, science
		Computer programmer, engineer, physician
Spatial-Visual *Picture Smart* Frank Lloyd Wright, Pablo Picasso	Shapes, textures, patterns, and patterns of space	Drawing, designing, building, photographer
		Decorator, cartoonist
Musical-Rhythmic *Music Smart* Wolfgang Mozart, Jennifer Lopez, Ringo Starr	Sounds, tones, rhythms, melodies, and rhymes	Band, listening, poetry
		Musician, singer, lyricist, conductor
Naturalistic *Nature Smart* Charles Darwin, Jane Goodall, Jacques Cousteau	Environmental features and phenomena	Working with living and nonliving things
		Farmer, meteorologist
Interpersonal *People Smart* John Dewey, Oprah Winfrey, Mother Theresa	Personal interactions and feelings of others	Working in groups, teaching
		Salesperson, pastor
Intrapersonal *Self-Smart* Helen Keller, Anne Frank, Aristotle	His or her own feelings, thoughts, and motivations	Working alone, diaries
		Philosopher, writer, psychologist
Bodily-Kinesthetic *Body Smart* Fred Astaire, Michael Jordan, Michelle Kwan	Body awareness, touch, and movements	Sports, dancing, acting, magic, and games
		Surgeon, athlete, dancer

Dr. Foster: *Use* 🗁 **Supplement E: Surveys for Preferred Learning Styles, Conditions, and Activities** *to discover the learning styles, learning conditions, and preferred activities of your students. (Select the* **Supplements** *page, and then* **A–F** *for* **Supplement E** *at www.classroommanagementblues.com to download the surveys.)*

Read "More than One Way to Savor Colors" to learn how students make an edible color wheel. The lesson was adapted to address all perceptual modalities [PM] *and multiple intelligences* [MI].

More than One Way to Savor Colors

See how learners *perceive*, *process*, and *attend to* information about colors in a lesson that has been adapted to address all **Perceptual Modalities**[PM] and **Multiple Intelligences.**[MI]

In Practice

Dr. Foster

Edible Color Wheel by Sandra Hildreth

Adapted from http://www.princetonol.com/groups/iad/Files/color.htm

Step 1: As learners enter the classroom, they hear songs by Greg Percy—"The Red & Yellow Blues" and "Secondary Samba." They see a blank color wheel; vanilla wafer cookies in a bag; and red, yellow, and blue frosting in cups at their tables. **Musical-Rhythmic**[MI] **Spatial-Visual**[MI] **Auditory**[PM]

Step 2: Groups work together to frost 3 cookies using the primary colors and place them on the color wheel. Students discuss how the primary colors make the other colors and answer questions to review secondary colors. **Interpersonal**[MI] **Linguistic**[MI] **Bodily-Kinesthetic**[MI] **Tactile**[PM] **Auditory**[PM]

Step 3: Groups discover how to make the intermediate colors with the primary colors and explain any patterns observed. **Bodily-Kinesthetic**[MI] **Interpersonal**[MI] **Logical-Mathematical**[MI] **Spatial-Visual**[MI] **Auditory**[PM]

Step 4: Once finished, students make a print of the color wheel or take a picture; then eat the cookies. **Bodily-Kinesthetic**[PM] **Spatial-Visual**[MI] **Tactile**[PM]

Step 5: Learners choose to work alone or with a partner to make a list of living and non-living things that exhibit primary, secondary, and intermediate colors. **Intrapersonal**[MI] **Interpersonal**[MI] **Linguistic**[MI] **Naturalistic**[MI] **Spatial-Visual**[MI]

Step 6: For assessment purposes, students imagine redecorating their bedroom. Each learner chooses one of the following: write a description, draw a picture, or make a model including primary, secondary, and intermediate colors, as well as tints and shades. **Intrapersonal**[MI] **Linguistic**[MI] **Spatial-Visual**[MI] **Bodily-Kinesthetic**[MI] **Tactile**[PM]

How would this lesson compare with one in which students receive a color wheel to memorize the location of each color for a test? For active engagement, some of the experiences require the use of specific learning styles; and in others, students could choose. To discover other ways to put learning styles into **practice** in your classroom, select **Resources** at *www.classroommanagementblues.com*, then **Engagement** and **learning styles**.

When teachers design instruction and activities that address learning styles and multiple intelligences, students are motivated to "show their talents and learn in ways that work for them. Then, they can be motivated to learn in new ways that do not come so easily" (Chickering & Gamson, 1987, para. 7). Learning styles link to **student interest**, the last ingredient in the **Active Engagement Prescription**.

Active Ingredient	🍎 Student Interest

Students value, attend to, and have positive feelings about educational activities in which they have an interest (Mills, 2002). The "Objects of Interest" identified by researchers in Table 5.4 include real objects, topics or ideas, and activities. These general components could be physical, cognitive, or affective.

> Because students see little novelty and relevancy in what they are learning, they have a difficult time focusing for extended periods and are easily distracted. For many students, school is seen as a dull, non-engaging environment that is much less interesting than what is happening outside of school. (Sousa, 1998)

Dr. Foster: *Look at this table. It defines the General Components of Objects of Interest and offers examples that show how to connect **multiple intelligences** to **student interests**.*

Use information from the table to describe the Objects of Interest of students who are naturalistic.

Table 5.4

General Components of Objects of Interest (Ainley, 1998; Krapp, 2002; Krapp et. al, 1992)	Real Objects Environmental and Physical (Bloom)	Topics or Ideas Psychological and Cognitive (Bloom)	Activities Personal and Affective (Bloom)
	Concrete objects toward which an interest is directed or needed for engaging in an interest	Active and aroused interest in topics representing a certain domain of knowledge	Disposition toward typical procedures or value-related activities that are connected to specific areas of interest
• **Naturalist** Examples	Rocks	Geology	Make a volcano

A. Teacher: *According to the table, naturalistic students would most likely want to study geology, handle rocks, and make a volcano.*

What can I use to identify my students' interests and learning styles?

Dr. Foster: *Use 🗁 **Supplement E: Surveys for Preferred Learning Styles, Conditions, and Activities** to discover the learning styles, learning conditions, and preferred activities of your students. Then, make connections to topics that emotionally interest them. Select the **Supplements** page, then **A–F** for **Supplement E** at www.classroommanagementblues.com to download the surveys for students of all ages.*

*With knowledge about your students' interests, you can modify and differentiate instruction to **actively engage** learners. To see how you can use the information from these surveys to motivate students, read "Something about Motivating Mary."*

Something about Motivating Mary

Like many students, Mary does not attempt assignments. See how I used what I knew about her learning styles, learning conditions, and preferred learning activities to motivate Mary to learn the meanings of vocabulary words.

Mary circled and checked the following descriptors on the **Supplement E: Surveys for Preferred Learning Styles, Conditions, and Activities**. (To download the surveys, select the **Supplements** page at *www.classroommanagementblues.com*.)

(10.) I am good at understanding people; leading, organizing, or communicating with people; and/or helping others get along. **Interpersonal**

(16.) I am good at imagining things, reading maps and charts, and/or working with colors and pictures. **Spatial-visual**

(38.) I learn best when I can create artwork to go along with what I am learning. **Condition**

Mary indicated with checks that she liked to do the following **activities**.

✓ Collage   ✓ Mobile   ✓ Videotape

Mary refuses to write the definitions of vocabulary words. From Mary's preferred learning styles, learning conditions, and activities, I would give her these options:

◆ Make a **collage** with pictures that depict each word's meaning—include words along with the pictures. **Spatial-visual** and **Artwork**

◆ Make a **mobile** with words, definitions, and pictures. **Spatial-visual** and **Artwork**

◆ Work with a group of students to **video** scenarios that represent the meanings of the words. **Spatial-visual** and **Interpersonal**

Some would argue that it would not be fair to the other students to give Mary a modified assignment; I would ask or respond as follows:

◆ *If Mary is not doing assigned tasks, what is Mary doing?* If Mary tends to disturb other students, then getting her to do an assignment would benefit everyone.

◆ *Is writing definitions the only way students can learn word meanings?* All students could receive the same choices so Mary saves face with her peers.

Use **Supplement E: Surveys for Preferred Learning Styles, Conditions, and Activities** to actively engage your students in assignments. To download the surveys, choose **Supplements** at *www.classroommanagementblues.com*, then **A-F** for **Supplement E**.

Why does student interest foster student learning in constructivist and brain-friendly classrooms? Davenport Community Schools (2005) and Cynthia Desrochers (2000) agree that students learn more in constructivist and brain-friendly classrooms when teachers provide **relevant content and projects** that are developmentally appropriate and meaningful or connected to the world beyond school and of **interest** to learners. They say that teachers should create an enriched environment to elicit curiosity and use emotional hooks to bring in the **interests** and experiences of the learners. Flowerday and Bryant (n.d.) also urge teachers to give students **choices** or some level of control as this increases positive emotions, teaches decision making, and fosters student learning.

A. Teacher: *I know I should give students choices and make content interesting and relevant; however, state and national mandates for accountability and testing do not give me choices in what I teach or my students a choice in what they want to learn (Casey, 2000).*

I want to provide for student interest; I just don't know how I can do this with the curriculum I am required to teach. Do you have something that will help?

Dr. Foster: *You can use **WebQuests**. These inquiry-oriented activities connect relevant content to the world beyond school; elicit curiosity and use emotional hooks; bring in student interests; and give students choices and real-world problems to solve.*

*Many WebQuests are **interdisciplinary**; most include **group activities** enhanced by giving learners **roles to play** (e.g., scientist, detective, reporter) and **real world** scenarios to work within (e.g., you've been asked by the Secretary General of the UN to brief him on what's happening in sub-Saharan Africa this week). While WebQuests require finding information online, students might look at web pages saved to a flash drive or find similar print information in the classroom or library.*

*The official **WebQuest** website, found at http://webquest.org, has links to over 2,500 top WebQuests for almost every content area (kindergarten to adult). Best of all, WebQuests require little or no modifications: you can implement them in your classroom right away for any content area.*

*Though you could develop your own WebQuests, you might want to search online. This is what I found when I typed the **content + WebQuest** at www.google.com.*

- Macbeth + WebQuest   69,000 hits
- Fossils + WebQuest   41,600 hits
- Gettysburg + WebQuest   40,200 hits
- Shapes + WebQuest   166,000 hits

Be sure the content is developmentally appropriate and make modifications to meet the needs of your students. Read "In Search of Answers about WebQuests" to learn about the common components of WebQuests along with a WebQuest that asks students to investigate whether King Tutankhamen's death was murder.

In Search of Answers about WebQuests

What are the common components of WebQuests? The components are shown next to the **King Tutankhamen: Was It Murder?** WebQuest. Note: The underlined phrases are links to other web pages with background information, help for writing a persuasive essay, an assessment, and a rubric to evaluate the essay.

In Practice
Dr. Foster

Common WebQuest Components	King Tutankhamen: Was It Murder? Adapted from http://www.pekin.net/pekin108/wash/webquest/
Introduction Sets the stage and provides background information	The Egyptian government has hired you and your renowned team to determine if King Tut was murdered. Your team will have only 3 days to finish your work.
Task Is doable and interesting	You must learn about the circumstances surrounding the death of King Tut and write a persuasive essay stating and defending your position—**Was it murder?**
Process Gives clear step-by-step directions	▪ Meet with your team of 4 or 5 and choose your roles: medical examiner, reporter, archaeologist, historian, or history professor. ▪ Print out the <u>questions</u> and record your responses as you visit your assigned site. ▪ Work with team members to synthesize the information.
Information Sources Identifies specific websites and resources in the classroom or library	▪ **Medical examiner** visit <u>Mysteries of Egypt: Tutankhamen</u> ▪ **Reporter** visit <u>The Mysterious Death of King Tut</u> ▪ **Archaeologist** visit <u>The Life of King Tutankhamen</u> ▪ **Historian** (optional) visit <u>Tutankhamen's Life</u> ▪ **History professor** visit <u>Who Killed Tut?</u>
Guidance Offers help with tasks	For help with **Writing a Persuasive Essay**, <u>click here</u>.
Evaluation Provides individual and group assessment tasks with rubrics	▪ Read <u>this page</u> to gain some chronological history of the pharaohs of the New Kingdom. You'll need the fun facts you find to answer the questions in the assessment! ▪ Each team member will complete <u>this assessment</u> to check your knowledge. Be sure to click on the button when you have finished the assessment. ▪ Your teacher will use <u>this rubric</u> to evaluate your essay. Print it, evaluate your essay, and make revisions.
Conclusion Brings closure, reviews what has been learned, and encourages further learning	**Well that solves the mystery!** We all know that is not true, but you have done some research, learned to determine what a reliable source is, and learned about ancient Egypt along the way. Maybe someday we will know if Tut was murdered.

Would this WebQuest elicit curiosity, teach decision making, and increase interest?

A. Teacher: *I think my students would be motivated to do this and other WebQuests!*

WebQuests would be especially useful when I need to provide advanced content and challenging activities for my high-achieving students. It takes a lot of time to individualize instruction and plan special activities for these students.

Attending to students' learning styles and interests can have a positive effect on student learning, but how can I address the many learning styles and interests of every student with the limited amount of time I have to plan lessons?

Dr. Foster: 🗁 **Supplement F: Forms for Student Motivation and Class Activity Planning** *can help you motivate individual students, determine the number of students with each learning style in a class, and plan lessons, activities, projects, and assessments that meet the multiple learning styles of an entire class. For example, the form shows that engaging students in a demonstration, WebQuest, or video would meet **ALL** of Dr. Gardner's multiple intelligences.* Select the **Supplements** *page, then* **A–F** *at www.classroommanagementblues.com to download these forms.*

Use Adjectives to Describe a Class

Over the years, my very insightful students have found it difficult to understand the function of adjectives in complex sentences. Here is how I would use **Supplement F** to create a lesson for one of my classes.

According to the **Student Motivation Forms**, 92% of the students in my class are bodily-kinesthetic, 80% interpersonal, and 75% naturalist.

I would have the class participate in one or more of the following *activities* shown on the **Class Activity Planning Form** that meet all three of these styles. The students would also have the choice to work alone or with a partner.

* *Scavenger Hunt*—Give students a list of objects located outside the school. Have the students list at least three adjectives that describe each object found.

* *Collage*—Have students apply pictures and words (adjectives) to describe the pictures.

* *Mobile*—Let students hang pictures or noun cards with adjectives on the back.

To extend these activities, students could write sentences, riddles, poems, or stories using the nouns and adjectives on the list, collage, or mobile. Use the **Class Activity Planning Form**, part of **Supplement F**, to plan lessons, activities, projects, and assessments. Select the **Supplements** page at *www.classroommanagementblues.com* to download this form.

A. Teacher: *I'm not very creative, so a list of activities on the* **Class Activity Planning Form** *will make it easier for me to address the learning styles of all my students.*

A. Teacher: *I believe the* **Active Engagement Prescription** *and its* **supplements** *can help me actively engage my students in meaningful learning.*

Dr. Foster: *I will use a sandwich analogy to summarize* **Active Engagement.** *Learners must be able to think, organize, and remember information, think, and solve problems; these goals represent Dr. Bloom's* **Cognitive Domain** **sandwiched** *between the* **Psychomotor** *and* **Affective** *Domains in this chart (see Figure 5.3). Teachers focus on helping students develop their mental skills (the* **meat** *of the* **Active Engagement** *sandwich); but the ways students perceive the environment and how they feel about what they are learning (the two slices of* **bread**) *must also be considered in preparing learning activities that foster student learning. The quality (flavor) and effectiveness of the* **Active Engagement Prescription** *are dependent upon the presence and concentration of one or more of its* **active ingredients.**

Figure 5.3

Bloom's Domains of Educational Activities	Rx 1 Active Engagement Ingredients				
	Constructivism	**Learning Styles**	**Student Interest**	**Brain Research**	**High-Order Thinking**
Psychomotor *Physical Skills* Learners use their body and senses to respond to the physical environment.	**Enactive** Hands-on Manipulatives	**Perceptual Modalities**	**Real Objects** Environmental Physical	**Practice** by doing	
Cognitive *Mental Skills* Learners gather and remember information, think, and solve problems.	**Iconic and Symbolic** Pictures & Letters/Numbers	**Information Processing**	**Topics or Ideas** Psycholgical Cognitive	**Practice** by discussing in groups and teaching others	**Thinking** Analyze Evaluate Create
Affective *Feelings Attitudes* Learners value, attend to, and have feelings about different activities.		**Personality Patterns**	**Activities** Emotional Personal		

Ham and Bread

Kristina Gipe-Martinez, an LBD resource teacher in Louisville, Kentucky, dialogues with a third grader during a writing conference about a "How To" portfolio piece. While she focuses on *information processing* (cognitive skills), note how the student *perceives* the task and expresses his *feelings*.

Ms. Kristina:	*Okay, tell me how you make a ham sandwich.*
Third Grader:	*I use ham and bread.*
Ms. Kristina:	*How much ham and bread?*
Third Grader:	*Two pieces of ham and two pieces of bread.*
Ms. Kristina:	*What kind of ham (baked or honey) and bread (white or wheat)?*
Third Grader:	*Honey ham and white bread.*
Ms. Kristina:	*Do you put anything else on your sandwich?*
Third Grader:	*No, just ham and bread.*
Ms. Kristina:	*Is there anything else you would like to add to your sandwich? What about some cheese or something else?*
Third Grader:	*No. I just like ham and bread.*
Ms. Kristina:	*Let's keep in mind that other people are going to be reading this, and we want it to be really interesting. So, let's think of some other ingredients for your ham sandwich.*
Third Grader:	*Then it won't be my ham sandwich!*
Ms. Kristina:	*I understand that you only like ham and bread, but we want to have a few more ingredients to make your "How To" piece more interesting. Let's add some cheese and mayonnaise.*
Third Grader:	*Then it will be your sandwich, not mine!*
Ms. Kristina:	*I understand it won't be your exact sandwich. Now it's time to get the reader's attention with an exciting first sentence about your great sandwich!*
Third Grader:	*It's not great! It's not my sandwich!*
Ms. Kristina:	*Let's pretend you love it, and it is your favorite sandwich!*
Third Grader:	*But, I don't love it! It's gross with cheese and mayonnaise!*
Ms. Kristina:	*You're right! "How to Make a Gross Ham and Bread Sandwich" would be more interesting!*

It is funny how wrapped up a student can be in his or her feelings about a task. When teachers attend to the "bread" of an assignment, as well as the "meat," or content, students have the opportunity to learn in a way more palatable and meaningful.

A. Teacher: *I see how important it is to actively engage my students, but how do I effectively use so many active ingredients and supplements?*

Dr. Foster: *Begin with small doses. If you are consistent and increase the usage of each active ingredient and supplement, you will get the desired effects.*

Implement the supplements in the order shown on this checklist to enhance the effectiveness of the **Active Engagement Prescription**.

R$_x$ 1 Implementation Checklist

Select the *Supplements* page at *www.classroommanagementblues.com*
to obtain detailed explanations, step-by-step instructions,
and blackline masters for *Supplements A–F*.

- ☞ **Supplement D—HOT Question Starters**
  Print the page of questions, and begin adding higher-order
  thinking questions to learning activities and assessments.

- ☞ **Supplement E—Survey for Preferred Learning Styles, Conditions, and Activities** Have students respond to the survey.

- ☞ **Supplement F—Student Motivation and Class Activity Planning Forms**
  Use the **Class Activity Planning Form** to plan learning activities and
  the **Student Motivation Form**, as needed, to motivate individual students.

- ☞ **Supplement C—LTC: Learner, Teacher, Checker**
  Start out with simple and linear tasks, then try branching tasks.

- ☞ **Supplement A—Quality Grouping**
  Complete the index cards for the students in a class. Assign short tasks, and adjust
  groupings before moving to complex tasks requiring more than one class period.

- ☞ **Supplement B—Jigsaw Tasks**
  Use the Quality Groups established with Supplement A. Begin with Jigsaws
  students can complete in one class period. Provide information for students
  to learn and teach before requiring students to do their own research.

Concluding Remarks

Blend other information you find about student motivation with the supplements and active ingredients, in this prescription to actively engage students. Before you go, look at the **Active Engagement Prescription** (on the opposite page), and note the caution. Apply the prescription as directed *every* morning and afternoon when you plan lessons, assessments, learning activities, and projects. The **Active Engagement Prescription** alone will not prevent or cure the ***Classroom Management Blues***. In the next session, learn how to use the **High Expectations Prescription**, along with **Active Engagement**, to inspire your students to be efficacious, autonomous, and resilient within the learning community.

GARDNER'S PHARMACY
111 Teaching Turnpike
Any Town, USA

Date Filled: First Day in the Classroom
Discard After: Retirement

 0001   Prescription for **ACTIVE ENGAGEMENT**

Patient's Name: A. Teacher

Patient's Address: 101 Learning Lane — Any Town, USA

Apply **ACTIVE ENGAGEMENT** to learning activities *every morning and afternoon.*

Doctor: *Barbara G. Foster*

SIDE EFFECTS: More trust and respect, increased learning, and improved behavior

CAUTION: May cause excitement

Active Ingredients
• **Brain Research**
• **Constructivism**
• **Higher-Order Thinking**
• **Learning Styles**
• **Student Interest**

Unlimited Refills

Resources—Access More Information

Learn more about brain research, grouping, constructivism, Jigsaws, higher-order thinking, peer teaching, questioning, learning styles, multiple intelligences, and student interest on the ***Classroom Management Blues*** website. Select **Resources**, then **Engagement** at *www.classroommanagementblues.com* for a list of books, articles, websites, and other resources.

Praxis Journal—Take Steps toward a Cure

Write responses to these prompts and questions before the next session:

• **Review the *Active Engagement Prescription* and think about what you have learned.** How does active engagement affect teacher effectiveness and student learning?

• **Based on what you have learned in this session, set a goal and develop a plan.** How do you plan to achieve your goal and solve one or more related problems?

• **Implement and evaluate your plan.** How did your actions affect you as a teacher and your students as learners?

• **Reflect on future goals and actions.** What will you do in the future?

STEP TWO: **TAKE PRESCRIPTIONS**

BANDURA'S PHARMACY
222 Expectations Expressway
Any Town, USA

Date Filled: First Day in the Classroom
Discard After: Retirement

 0002

Prescription for **HIGH EXPECTATIONS**

Patient's Name: A. Teacher

Patient's Address: 102 Attitude Avenue — Any Town, USA

Repeat **HIGH EXPECTATIONS** *daily* to inspire ALL students to achieve academic and personal goals.

Doctor: *Barbara G. Foster*

Active Ingredients
- **Efficacy**
- **Authenticity**
- **Community**
- **Autonomy**
- **Resiliency**

SIDE EFFECTS: More trust and respect, increased learning, and improved behavior

CAUTION: May be contagious

Unlimited Refills

Session 6

Photos.com

Repeat High Expectations

Treat a person as he is, and he will remain as he is.
Treat him as he could be, and he will become what he should be.

Jimmy Johnson (1943–)
The first American football coach to win both
an NCAA Division 1A National Championship and a Super Bowl

To have a well-managed classrooms, teachers must create and maintain an environment where students receive respect and inspiration to learn and behave appropriately. "Although students may appear to accept or even relish lax teachers with low standards, they ultimately come away with more respect for teachers who believe in them enough to [respectfully] demand more, both academically and behaviorally" (Lumsden, 1997, para. 17). Use the strategies found in the **High Expectations Prescription** to inspire your students to strive to achieve their academic and personal goals in the classroom and beyond.

 in·spire [in spīr′] *v.*

1. to exert a beneficial effect upon (a person)

2. to arouse (with a particular emotion)

Collins English Dictionary

Dr. Foster: *Look at the* **High Expectations Prescription** *(on the opposite page). What is the recommended use of this prescription? What are the active ingredients and side effects? What caution is given?*

A. Teacher: *The* **active ingredients** *found in the* **High Expectations Prescription** *are efficacy, authenticity, community, autonomy, and resiliency. If I repeat* **High Expectations** *daily to inspire ALL my students to achieve academic and personal goals, the* **side effects** *will be more trust and respect, increased learning, and improved behavior. I am not concerned about the* **caution***; I hope it is contagious.*

When I became a teacher, I believed all students could learn and be successful in my classroom. It has been difficult to hold on to that belief when so many of my students say "I can't." and "I don't care."

I am eager to learn how the active ingredients can help me be an inspiring teacher who holds to the belief that EVERY student can achieve in my classroom.

Dr. Foster: *Let me remind you that more strategies are associated with the **High Expectations Prescription** than the ones we will discuss in this session. Repeat these and other "inspirational" strategies to maintain high standards and expectations. I believe you will succeed!*

 Before we begin, name some well-known teachers and coaches.

A. Teacher: *It was easy to think of coaches' names—Bear Bryant, Vince Lombardi, Knute Rockne, Pat Riley, and Woody Hayes.*

*I should know more teachers, but I do not. The only famous teachers I can recall are the teacher in the movie **Dangerous Minds**, the principal in the movie **Lean on Me**, and Anne Sullivan, who was Helen Keller's teacher.*

Dr. Foster: *What do the teachers and coaches you listed have in common?*

A. Teacher: *They inspired students or players to perform at high levels in tough situations.*

Dr. Foster: *In this session, you will learn how to maintain high expectations for ALL students, even when other teachers give up on them; it is easier to say than to do. To inspire you to repeat high expectations daily and hold fast to your belief that ALL students can achieve their academic and personal goals, I will share quotations from well-known coaches and teachers throughout our session.*

*You will also learn to repeat **High Expectations** and coach, or inspire your students. Though coaches mainly attend to physical skills and teachers focus on cognition, there is no guarantee of success in a game or classroom. When learners lack physical or cognitive skills or their talents remain underdeveloped, attitudes (affective states) come into play to inspire achievement. Students base their level of motivation, attitudes, and actions more on what they believe about themselves (efficacy) than on what is objectively true (Bandura, 1997).*

Active Ingredient	 Efficacy

The first active ingredient in the **High Expectations Prescription** is **efficacy**, the power, or ability to produce a desired effect or change. Perceived self-efficacy, rooted in the **social cognitive theory** of Albert Bandura, is the belief, expectation, and hope that people have the strengths and capabilities to achieve goals and make positive changes (Bandura, 1994; Benard, n.d.).

What influences self-efficacy? Social cognition focuses on how people perceive and interpret information within a social or cultural context. Bandura identifies information sources people generate themselves (intrapersonal) and from others (interpersonal) to make judgments about their strengths and capabilities.

> *A teacher who is attempting to teach without inspiring the pupil with a desire to learn is hammering on cold iron.*
>
> **Horace Mann**
> (1796–1859)
>
> American
> education reformer

Information sources that influence self-efficacy include one's past performance, physiological or emotional stress reactions, vicarious experiences, and verbal or social persuasion (Huitt, 2002; Sewell & St. George, 2000; Siegle, 2000a). Through cognitive appraisal, the information becomes instructive when deemed relevant to judge personal capabilities (Bandura, 1985).

A. Teacher: *From what I learned in our last session, I see a relationship between self-efficacy and Bloom's psychomotor, cognitive, and affective Domains of Educational Activities. Students **think** about how their capabilities relate to personal **feelings**, how they respond to people they value, and what they attend to in the **physical** environment.*

Dr. Foster: *A connection does exist. You have applied the* **Active Engagement Prescription**.

Let's explore how **efficacy** *manifests itself in students from different information sources related to the interpersonal and intrapersonal learning styles. Then I will give you strategies to promote high **self-efficacy** in your students.*

How does intrapersonal information, or self-knowledge, influence self-efficacy? Students use the **intrapersonal** learning style when they process information about their strengths and capabilities. This self-knowledge comes from past performance and physiological or emotional stress responses in the classroom (Huitt, 2002; Sewell & St. George, 2000).

Successful past performance is the most effective way to create a strong sense of efficacy; this is consistent with the old adage *success breeds success*. "In contrast, failure, especially if it occurs early in the learning experience, undermines one's sense of efficacy" (Sewell & St. George, 2000, para. 4). (See how past performance affects the self-efficacy of two students in "A Tale of Two Subjects.")

> *I hear, I know.*
> *I see, I remember.*
> ***I do, I understand.***
>
> **Confucius**
> (551 BCE–479 BCE)
> _____
> His emphasis was on *study,*
> the Chinese character that
> opens the book.

A Tale of Two Subjects

Once upon a time, there was a young child. While learning to read, she received frowns [☹ s] on papers and was placed in the lowest **reading** group. A few years later, a teacher asked, "Why don't you like to read?"

Mathematics classes were required for graduation. With F's on report cards in every math class, a young adult decided to drop out of high school.

The *reality* is that the way teachers group, assess, and grade has a profound effect on what students choose to do throughout their school years and beyond.

A. Teacher: *As a teacher, I have the power to influence the intrapersonal information or self-knowledge of my students to make sure they are successful in my classroom. I also need to recognize signs of high self-efficacy—I need to celebrate and affirm my students when they makes statements like "I can do this" or " I'll have a go at that" (Sewell & St. George, 2000, para. 3).*

Dr. Foster: *Those strategies will have a positive effect on your students' self-efficacy, learning, and behavior. You will learn more strategies when we discuss the* **Appropriate Assessments Prescription** *in our next session.*

While **past performance** *is the most effective source of intrapersonal information that informs high and low self-efficacy, you might not be aware of the* **physiological and emotional reactions** *(e.g., sweating, trembling, getting butterflies). These are signs of vulnerability to poor performance and might be determining factors of success inside and outside the classroom. Read "I Know how They Feel" to learn how I have experienced physiological and emotional responses in school.)*

I Know how They Feel

The *reality* is many students become physically ill when they enter a school or classroom. Students who experience stress when they do not understand concepts and assignments despite repeated explanations might become ill. **I know how they feel**.

   I vividly recall experiencing extreme stress in a classroom on two occasions. My heart started to pound, and I began to perspire. I was sick to my stomach.

At the age of 16, I took a French class for two weeks at the University of Montpelier in France. The teacher only spoke French; I could not understand her no matter how many times she repeated instructions and questions.

   Back in my room after the first class, my head was spinning. I could not eat anything and wondered whether I would ever be able to understand. My chaperone would not let me quit. I eventually understood the teacher, but I do not know how I successfully finished the course.

In the early 1980s, I took an elective college course called "Computers for Teachers" that required that I learn the FORTRAN computer language. Though the instructor spoke English, I could not understand what he said. After the first hour, I had to leave the class because I felt sick. I returned to class determined to succeed. I got an "A," but it was the most difficult elective course I have ever taken.

I know how it feels to have physiological and emotional responses in difficult learning situations. What is the *reality* for students who have similar symptoms day after day and year after year? Do they misbehave? Do they drop out of school?

A. Teacher: *I've had classes that were difficult, but I have never had any intense physical or emotional reactions in school. It's hard for me to understand how it feels; but I see how these responses and past performance could influence whether a student perseveres or gives up.*

Dr. Foster: *Now we will look at how **interpersonal** information influences self-efficacy.*

> When experience contradicts firmly held judgments of self-efficacy, people may not change their beliefs about themselves if the conditions of performance are such as to lead them to discount the import of their experience. (Bandura, 1994, p. 401)

How does interpersonal information influence self-efficacy? Students use the **interpersonal** learning style when they process information about their strengths and abilities from social models. This information comes from verbal or social persuasion and observing others who are similar in skill level or held in high regard (Bandura, 1985; Huitt, 2002; Sewell & St. George, 2000).

During the formative years from preschool to high school, social persuasion and verbal feedback from teachers, parents, and peers play an important role in the development of self-efficacy. Students process what they hear and give weight or value to the person when they make efficacious judgments (Bandura, 1985).

> *I hear, I know.*
> *I see, I remember.*
> *I do, I understand.*
> ## Confucius
> (551 BCE–479 BCE)
> ---
> Famous thinker, teacher, and social philosopher of China

Dr. Foster: *Take the words "You're really smart!" The influence these words have on a student's self-efficacy depends on the weight and value given to the person who utters these words. Read "Keep It Simple Stupid" and discover the effect the words "You're really smart!" had on one of my fourth graders.*

Keep It Simple Stupid!

Richie believed he was stupid, so Stupit was the name he wrote at the top of his papers. I repeatedly told Richie that he was smart, but he placed little or no value on what a teacher said—he repeated second grade so he did not like teachers.

One day, Richie was able to do something on a computer program that Shaheed, the "smartest kid" in class, had not been able to figure out. When Shaheed saw what Richie had done, he shouted at the top of his lungs, "RICHIE, YOU'RE REALLY SMART!" Richie beamed and began to write his "real" name on papers.

The *reality* is that understanding whose feedback is valuable to a student is **not** simple.

A. Teacher: *I know older students put more weight or value on what peers say. When I tell my 12-year-old son, "You are smart," he says, "You just say that because you're my mother." He values what his friends say more than what I say.*

Dr. Foster: *Sometimes parents or teachers tell children they are **not** smart—children tend to "adopt this perception of themselves" (Lumsden, 1997, para. 5). Do not underestimate the power parents and teachers have on a student's self-efficacy, especially in the early years. In a "Tale of Two Students," I share how my husband and I reacted differently to comments made by teachers about our abilities in school.*

A Tale of Two Students

The ***reality*** is "teachers' expectations for students, whether high or low, can become a self-fulfilling prophecy. That is, students tend to give to teachers as much or as little as teachers expect of them" (Lumsden, 1997, para. 5).

Michael's first grade teacher said, "You're not very smart. You need to repeat first grade." He adored his teacher and believed that a teacher would know whether he was smart or not.

So Michael **acted** like he wasn't very smart throughout elementary and middle school and became a behavior problem. He did just enough to pass.

When he told his teachers that he **could** do electronics in high school, they did not give him the opportunity to take an electronics class because of his past performance. He continued to misbehave in class and did just enough to graduate.

My sixth grade teacher read aloud the names of students that he thought would make the honor roll in middle school. I **knew** he would call my name, but he did not. I could not believe it!

I proved him wrong and made the honor roll. Though I had only done just enough in preceding years to get by, I still **believed** I was capable of making A's.

The ***reality*** is that some parents and teachers persuade children at an early age to believe they lack capabilities. According to Bandura (1994), these children will "avoid challenging activities that cultivate potentialities and give up quickly in the face of difficulties" (para. 9).

Dr. Foster: *Why do you think one student demonstrates high self-efficacy in the face of a teacher's low expectations while another student accepts the negative perceptions of his or her teacher?*

A. Teacher: *I think young children rely more on what a teacher says about their abilities than older students do!*

Dr. Foster: *Successes do build a student's personal efficacy, and "failures undermine it, especially if failures occur **before** a sense of efficacy is firmly established" (Bandura, 1994, para. 4).*

Students also process information about their own abilities when they observe people they admire or perceive to have similar strengths and abilities (Bandura, 1985; Huitt, 2002; Sewell & St. George, 2000). The more similar the models' successes and failures are the more persuasive (Bandura, 1994).

> *I hear, I know.*
> **I see, I remember.**
> *I do, I understand.*
> **Confucius**
> (551 BCE–479 BCE)
> ___
> Started his own school at age 22

A. Teacher: *So when a student sees another student perceived to have similar strengths and abilities succeed in a challenging situation, the student is more likely to believe he or she can succeed. A student is more likely to give up when he or she observes others perceived to be similarly competent fail despite persistent effort.*

Dr. Foster: *Peer influence is more likely when students have little prior experience or are uncertain about their own capabilities (Bandura, 1994).*

A. Teacher: *As young children lack experience and are uncertain about their abilities, the models they attend to are important in the development of high self-efficacy.*

How can I tell if a student has high and low self-efficacy?

What are the recognizable differences between students with high and low self-efficacy? Research over the past 30 years has shown a positive relationship between self-efficacy and persistence, motivation, and academic achievement (Siegle, 2003). Bernard Weiner explains how students perceive and attribute their achievement levels, successes, and failures (see Table 6.1). Albert Bandura offers research-based ways to identify whether a student has high self-efficacy (see Table 6.2).

Table 6.1

Attribution Theory	
High Achievers . . .	**Low Achievers . . .**
• Succeed and say **"I Can"**	• Fail and say **"I Can't"**
• Attribute failure to a faulty or inappropriate strategy they use	• Attribute failure to low ability, bad luck, and factors beyond their control (not their fault)
• Attribute success to high ability and effort of which they are confident	• Attribute success to good luck and factors beyond their control
• Have self-confidence and a sense of responsibility	• Lack confidence and a sense of responsibility

Adapted from "Attribution Theory—Weiner"

Table 6.2

Social Cognitive Theory	
Students with High Self-Efficacy . . .	**Students with Low Self-Efficacy . . .**
• Choose to participate and expend more effort in their learning	• Choose to not work on tasks and to give up easily
• Seek more challenging learning experiences	• Avoid challenging tasks
• Persist longer and cope when faced with difficulty or adversity	• Have a narrow view of how to solve problems, which causes depression and stress
• Use different learning strategies and attribute success to ability	• Use few or no learning strategies
• Possess self-regulatory cognitive and metacognitive strategies	• Depend more on teachers and others
• Set personal goals	• Express little hope for the future
• Are motivated to learn	• Are passive
• Recover from failure more quickly	• Are resigned to failure

Adapted from "Developing Efficacy Beliefs in the Classroom" A. Sewell & A. St. George, 2000

Gender also influences self-efficacy. "Boys tend to attribute their successes to skills, whereas girls often attribute their successes to effort. The reverse is true when viewing poor performance. Girls often attribute their poor performance to low ability, while boys blame theirs on low effort" (Siegle, 2000a, para. 4).

> *Each time you fail, start all over again, and you will grow stronger until you have accomplished a purpose—not the one you began with perhaps, but one you'll be glad to remember.*
>
> **Anne Sullivan** (1866–1936)
>
> Best known as the teacher of Helen Keller

Dr. Foster: *It is easy to undermine perceived efficacy, and more difficult to produce enduring increases in high self-efficacy by persuasion (Bandura, 1985).*

A. Teacher: *I can now recognize the attributes of students with high efficacy and realize that I, too, must have high efficacy—believe in my ability to help my students develop high efficacy. I need to persist in the pursuit of this goal and be motivated to learn several strategies to help my students succeed in the classroom.*

*I want to say **"I Can"** move ALL my students to become high achievers with high self-efficacy, but if what I say has little influence or undermines self-efficacy, I'm not sure what I can do.*

A. Teacher: . *Can you offer any strategies to help me develop high self-efficacy in my students?*

Which strategies foster positive self-efficacy? According to Albert Bandura, learners are more likely to attempt and be successful at tasks in which they perceive themselves to be competent. Teachers must provide specific feedback, implement instructional strategies, and design activities that celebrate high self-efficacy and take account of students' past performance and social influences within the classroom.

> Successful efficacy builders do more than convey positive appraisals. In addition to raising people's beliefs in their capabilities, they structure situations for them in ways that bring success and avoid placing people in situations prematurely where they are likely to fail often. They measure success in terms of self-improvement rather than by triumphs over others. (Bandura, 1994, para. 10)

As past experience is the strongest source of self-efficacy, teachers should implement **goal strategies** to help draw students' attention to their progress toward the lesson objectives (Siegle, 2000b). Here are some of these goal strategies:

- Review accomplishments at the beginning and end of a lesson.

- Post an agenda of the current lesson's objectives before instruction.

- Help students reflect upon accomplishments in the lesson opening or closing.

> *Set a goal and don't quit until you attain it. When you do attain it, set another goal, and don't quit until you reach it. Never quit.*
>
> **Paul William "Bear" Bryant**
> (1913–1983)
> _____
> Most successful college football coach in NCAA Division I

A. Teacher: *I share objectives with my students, but I need to post the objectives on an agenda, review accomplishments before, during, or after lessons, and help my students reflect upon their achievements.*

Dr. Foster: *It is also important to provide **specific feedback** throughout a lesson about students' skill development toward goals and objectives. There are many websites with strategies to help students set goals, document growth, be a peer model, and practice lack-of-effort explanations for poor performance. (Visit Dr. Del Siegle's website at http://www.gifted.uconn.edu/siegle/SelfEfficacy/section3.html for more strategies.)*

In "Help Students Set Goals," Del Siegle (2000b) recommends that teachers provide a form (e.g., My Accomplishment Plan) to help students set personal goals each week (e.g., write three small, specific, attainable goals); reflect on their accomplishments at the end of the week with a spotlight on improvement; and guide students to maintain or develop new goals for the next week. Teachers should also model this process for students. (Dr. Siegle offers more self-efficacy strategies in "I Think I Can—I Think I Can.")

I Think You Can—I Think You Can

According to research over the past 25 years, there are intervention strategies teachers **can** implement easily to help students believe they **can** learn new material and tackle new challenges (Siegle, 2000c). Here are some of these strategies:

- Avoid the appearance of unsolicited help.

    Circulate around the room and randomly stop at desks of several different students before and after a needy student.

- Help students practice lack-of-effort explanations for poor performance.

    Say, "You know how to use a ruler, but you need carefully read the numbers."

- Compliment students on the specific skills they develop.

    Say, "You used insight when you solved this problem" instead of "Good work."

- Promote recognition of progress during a lesson.

    Say, "Look how much we have already learned about . . ."

- Help students set goals.

    Set attainable goals within the student's reach with reasonable effort.

- Help students document their growth.

    Avoid class charts that display individual progress.

- Use peer models.

    Confirm that the student can perform the task correctly before he or she models in front of the class.

- Help students serve as their own model.

    Help students visualize a new task before beginning.

Find more strategies that **I Think You Can** use in your classroom to foster self-efficacy at www.gifted.uconn.edu/siegle/SelfEfficacy/section0.html.

Though peer models in the classroom directly influence student self-efficacy, live and symbolic models in the media viewed repeatedly have a distinct influence over models seldom observed. Students who are not fully secure in their roles have low self-esteem and are prone to emulate these role models, whether positive or negative (Gredler, 1992). In "Take It Step by Step," read about Michael Jordan—a goal setter. When he played professional basketball, young athletes admired and emulated him.

Take It Step by Step

Michael Jordan wrote *I Can't Accept Not Trying: Michael Jordan on the Pursuit of Excellence*—a book about goal setting. He wrote, "I approach everything step by step . . . I had always set short-term goals. As I look back, each one of the steps or successes led to the next one."

When I got cut from the varsity team as a sophomore in high school, I learned something. I knew I never wanted to feel that bad again. . . . So I set a goal of becoming a starter on the varsity. That's what I focused on all summer. When I worked on my game, that's what I thought about. When it happened, I set another goal, a reasonable, manageable goal that I could realistically achieve if I worked hard enough. . . . I guess I approached it with the end in mind. I knew exactly where I wanted to go, and I focused on getting there. As I reached those goals, they built on one another.

All those steps are like pieces of a puzzle. They all come together to form a picture. . . . Not everyone is going to be the greatest. . . . But you can still be considered a success. . . . Step by step, I can't see any other way of accomplishing anything.

Excerpted from *I Can't Accept Not Trying: Michael Jordan on the Pursuit of Excellence* by M. Jordan, 1994

The ***reality*** is that no one is an instant success.

A. Teacher: *In our last session, I remember our discussion about how students are more likely to learn from and attend to what they value. I can see why people would seek role models like Michael Jordan who possess competencies to which they aspire. Students also identify with those models perceived to be similarly competent.*

Dr. Foster: *Role models do transmit knowledge and can teach effective skills and strategies (Bandura, 1994), so share stories from your own life and people who have succeeded despite academic and physical challenges. The **Family Village** website (www.familyvillage.wisc.edu/general/famous.html) provides links to famous people with disabilities (e.g., ADHD, epilepsy, cerebral palsy, autism) who have achieved success. One such example is Dr. Patricia Polacco, a writer and illustrator of children's books. Read about her in "From Caterpillar to Butterfly."*

> *We would accomplish many more things if we did not think of them as impossible.*
> **Vince Lombardi**
> (1913–1970)
>
> One of the most successful coaches in the history of football

From Caterpillar to Butterfly

The life stories of famous people who have succeeded despite academic and physical disabilities can *transmit knowledge* and *teach effective skills and strategies.* Learn how to foster efficacy and integrate the life stories of role models into different subjects.

The Butterfly by Patricia Polacco

Read the book. The amazing life story of the author's Aunt Monique growing up in France during World War II shows the horrors of war in a way that readers can identify with. A fist crushing a butterfly makes a powerful statement that the reader can understand without pictures of blood and violence. Children and young adults have an incredible capacity for compassion and understanding the very dark parts in our history as human beings. "We need to keep telling these stories . . . hopefully we won't repeat our mistakes." This story pays homage to those who have stood up against oppression . . . those who have shown courage . . . and those who know the joy of true friendship.

Share the author's story. Patricia Polacco is a writer and illustrator of children's books, but she did not start writing children's books until she was 41. Patricia majored in fine art and received her PhD in art history. What is so amazing about these accomplishments? Diagnosed with dyslexia, dysnumeria, and dysgraphia, Dr. Polacco did not learn to read well until she was 14 years old. A teacher, Mr. Falker, gave her the additional help she needed to overcome her reading problems!

Adapted from "Center for Disability," 1998 and "Butterfly," 2006

Help students make connections between the book and other subjects.

- **Science**   Metamorphosis from caterpillar to butterfly
- **History**   Oppression, courage, and friendship during WWII
- **Writing**   Symbolism of crushing the butterfly and violence

Help students make personal connections to the author and book.

- **Life Skills**   Overcome academic, physical, and societal adversities

Use children's books at all grade levels to begin lessons on any subject. Access websites (e.g., http://www.familyvillage.wisc.edu/general/famous.html) about famous people with disabilities to help the students in your classroom see that they too can **practice** the life skills needed to change from a "caterpillarto a butterfly."

Dr. Foster: *Students might idolize sports figures, movies stars, pop singers, and other role models in the media, but peer models directly influence how students perceive their capabilities and what they do in the classroom.*

A. Teacher: *I recall "Quality Grouping" as a strategy to foster self-efficacy. It gives students the opportunity to work in cooperative groups with peer models having complementary talents.*

Dr. Foster: *Your thinking is right on target! Competitive practices and ability grouping further diminish one's self-efficacy (Bandura, 1989), so Quality Grouping* **can** *set the stage for students to learn effective skills and strategies from their peers without the fear of failure.*

> Because peers serve as a major influence in the development and validation of self-efficacy, disrupted or impoverished peer relationships can adversely affect the growth of personal efficacy. A low sense of social efficacy can, in turn, create internal obstacles to favorable peer relationships. Thus, children who regard themselves as socially inefficacious withdraw socially, perceive low acceptance by their peers and have a low sense of self-worth. (Bandura, 1994, para. 54)

To counter the effects of low self-efficacy from intrapersonal and interpersonal sources, teachers can integrate **role models** who succeed despite academic and physical challenges, implement **goal strategies** within lessons, give students **specific feedback** about their academic skills development, ask **peer models** to demonstrate effective learning strategies, and use **Quality Grouping** to promote positive influences. Actions speak louder than words when it comes to fostering students' perceived self-efficacy and high expectations of themselves as learners and peer teachers.

Active Ingredient	🍎 Authenticity

"Students experience higher self-efficacy when they are told they are capable by someone they believe is trustworthy" (Siegle, 2000a, para. 9). Thus, **authenticity**, the second active ingredient in the **High Expectations Prescription**, fosters student success in the classroom.

"Either consciously or unconsciously, teachers often behave differently toward students based on the beliefs and assumptions they have about them" (Bamburg, 1994, para. 8). Research has shown that teachers' true feelings color their expectations for students and tend to be self-fulfilling; the old adage "We reap what we sow" applies. Therefore, the challenge for teachers is to communicate high expectations and then "walk the talk."

> As fallible humans, it's natural to make judgments, both positive and negative. A child's socioeconomic status, language ability, past performance, appearance, weight, and numerous other factors can subtly influence our perceptions of that child. What many people don't realize, however, is that the early assumptions we make can often become self-fulfilling prophecies. A student labeled as "gifted" might succeed, while a student branded as a "troublemaker" or as a "low achiever" might fall behind. (Gazin, 2004, para. 2)

A. Teacher: *I want to have high expectations for all my students, even the difficult ones.*

Dr. Foster: *Then you need to learn about the student characteristics that can potentially lower your expectations and the learning strategies that might counter unconscious biases.*

Which student characteristics lower teacher expectations?
Researchers have found that "some teachers do interact with students for whom they hold low expectations in such a way as to limit their development" (Cotton, 2001, para. 40). Until teachers become aware of these factors, they might withhold opportunities, remain unchanged in their expectations, and treat students for whom they have low expectations in ways that inhibit classroom success (Cotton, 2001; Green, 2010). Many factors can lead teachers to hold lower expectations for some students (see Table 6.3).

> *Invest in the human soul. Who knows, it might be a diamond in the rough.*
>
> **Mary McLeod Bethume**
> (1875–1955)
>
> Educator and founder of Bethune-Cookman College

Table 6.3

Factors that May Influence Teacher Expectations	
Socioeconomic Backgrounds	Some teachers expect less from students from lower socioeconomic backgrounds and more from middle-class students or students who exhibit middle-class-like behaviors regardless of their social-class backgrounds.
Kind of School	Some teachers believe students from either inner-city schools or rural schools are less capable.
Appearance	Some teachers perceive students whose work areas or assignments are messy, who have poor grooming habits, who are overweight, or who wear less expensive or out-of-style clothing have lower ability.
Oral and Written Language	Some teachers believe grammar, vocabulary, and nonstandard English-speaking patterns reflect academic ability.
Gender	Some teachers ask girls (especially in science, math, and technical areas) fewer questions than they ask boys. They may assume boys have less drive and will obtain lower results than girls will.
Seating Position	Some teachers treat students who sit at the sides or back of the classroom as if they have lower learning motivation and/or ability.
Placement	Some teachers view classes in which students have already been labeled (e.g., gifted, at risk) or tracked by ability with more or less learning potential.
Temperament	Some teachers reject, request special education placement, or recommend medication for students who they perceive as distractible and too active.
Halo Effect	Some teachers make unfounded assumptions about a student's overall ability or behavior from one student characteristic.
Race/Ethnicity	Some teachers have higher expectations for White students than students from other ethnic groups. The gender, class, and temperament of children of color influence teachers' expectations more than White children do. Educators place more students of color in special education programs and on lower academic tracks than White students.

From Cotton, 2001; "Expectations," 2001; Shaunessy & McHatton, 2009; and Shepherd, 2010

A. Teacher: *I believe I have the same high expectations for all my students, and with this information, I will be more aware of my interactions.*

Many of these factors could influence how students interact with each other.

Dr. Foster: *This was my experience. Read "Mirror, Mirror."*

Mirror, Mirror

Children have very little, or no control over the clothing they wear or where they live. If students are unaccepted by their peers, they run the risk of the same rejection from teachers (Geisler, 2001).

I lived on a farm and rode a bus from a rural community to a middle school in a nearby town. The city kids made fun of us country kids. I did not see the poor, dumb, country bumpkin they saw when I looked in the mirror. No matter what I said or did, they never saw me as I saw myself.

 The *reality* is that a person's social and economic background or clothing does not *reflect* his or her ability and character, but the perceptions others have of them are **real.** Many students are unable to cope with others' perceptions.

A. Teacher: *Teachers, parents, and peers influence how students treat one another. I need to make sure I lead by example. What can I do?*

How can teachers counter unconscious biases and confirm their belief that all students can learn? "Merely HOLDING certain expectations for students has no magical power to affect their performance or attitudes. Instead, it is the translation of these expectations into BEHAVIOR that influences outcomes" (Cotton, 2001, para. 40). First, teachers can avoid the effects of negative expectations and *disregard unreliable sources of information* about students' behavior and learning potential (Jones & Jones, 2001).

A. Teacher: *At the beginning of the school year, teachers bombard me with information about the students I will be teaching. Their comments usually center on the "bad" kids; it is difficult to remain objective.*

Dr. Foster: *I, too, have heard horrible stories about what teachers say about students in teachers' lounges and school hallways, sometimes with parents, staff, and other students present.*

A. Teacher: *I know I shouldn't listen to the negative comments. What kind of information **is** appropriate?*

Dr. Foster: *You should look at test scores and cumulative folders, and talk with teachers you respect at the beginning of the year to gather information about your students. Closely monitor their progress and your expectations of individuals throughout the year (Downey, Steffy, Poston, & English, 2009). Intelligence is fluid rather than static and unchanging (Lumsden, 1997).*

"The negative effects of differential teacher treatment of low-expectation students may be direct (less exposure to learning material) or indirect (treating students in ways that erode their learning motivation and sense of self-efficacy)" (Cotton, 2001, para. 43). Vernon Jones, Louise Jones, and Kathleen Cotton agree that teachers can reduce these negative effects if they implement the following instructional strategies:

> In their attempt to be fair and to protect their pupils' self-esteem, teachers often excuse disadvantaged children from the effort that learning requires. This practice obscures the connection between effort and accomplishment and shields children from the consequences. The practice also sets the stage for later failure. (U.S. Department of Education, 1992, para. 15)

- Give **each** student the same opportunities to learn new and interesting material, research and create their own learning materials, and practice reading and speaking.

- Stretch **each** student's mind and encourage him or her to achieve as much as possible on required tasks and try harder ones for extra credit.

- Develop for **each** student a wide range of challenging tasks with no particular right answer.

- Provide **each** student with different learning materials that show a wide range of ethnic diversity.

- Ask stimulating, interesting, and higher cognitive questions of **each** student.

- Help **each** student improve his or her response and give prompts or rephrase questions rather than give answers or call on someone else.

- Diagnose learning difficulties for **each** student who does not understand and break down tasks or reteach in a different way, rather than repeat the same instructions or give up on the student.

- Use a system to assure **each** student has equal opportunities to participate.

- Give **each** student generous wait time.

Dr. Foster: *You can create a safe learning community if you consistently disregard unreliable sources about students' behavior and learning potential; use effective instructional strategies that give each student opportunities to participate; and send authentic messages about what you expect.*

> *Don't try to fix the students, fix ourselves first. The good teacher makes the poor student good and the good student superior. When our students fail, we, as teachers, too, have failed.*
>
> **Marva Collins** (1936–)
>
> Educator famous for applying classical education successfully with impoverished students

Active Ingredient	🍎 Community

The third active ingredient in the **High Expectations Prescription** is **community**. Effective teachers evidence an unwavering expectation to create and maintain a learning community in their classrooms. Marvin Marshall (2000) says a learning community is a place where both students and teachers learn.

> Schools that encourage critical thinking and inquiry . . . are especially effective at communicating the expectation that students are truly capable of complex problem-solving and decision-making. (High Expectations, n.d., para. 5)

Dr. Foster: *On the first day and throughout the school year, I communicated my expectations. "Our classroom WILL be a place where I teach, and you learn. NOTHING will interfere with these goals."*

A. Teacher: *That sounds good in theory, but how do I make it a reality?*

Dr. Foster: *To create and maintain a learning community in your classroom, it will require that you learn the ABCs.*

Figure 6.1

The **ABC**s of a Learning Community

Appreciation   (Cognitive Domain)

Everyone knows he or she is valued and respected.

Belonging   (Affective Domain)

Everyone feels he or she fits in.

Contribution   (Psychomotor Domain)

Everyone takes responsibility and has a say.

What can authentic teachers do to create a learning community where every student feels *appreciated*? To maintain a learning community, teachers must build trust and show every student he or she is "valued, respected, challenged, and expected to succeed" (Gazin, 2004, para. 8). Teachers can communicate appreciation for students and show they are *valued* members of the learning community if they ask stimulating questions; give one-on-one time in a way that seems right at the moment; and say "I missed you" when they return from any absence, time out, or visit to the office for misbehavior.

To build trust and respect, teachers must develop positive relationships with students. One of the most effective trust-building strategies is to show an interest in students' activities outside the classroom (Albert, 1996). When teachers attend athletic events and other performances, they show that they appreciate and value what students do in school and beyond the classroom.

A. Teacher: *Do you mean I should attend the after-school special events and performances of all my students? I hardly have time to attend those of my own children.*

Dr. Foster: *Reserve this strategy for your most difficult students. Even one event can make a difference as you build trust and promote cooperation!*

A. Teacher: *Is there anything I can do* **in** *my classroom to show I'm interested in what they do outside the classroom?*

Dr. Foster: *Use the* 📁 **Supplement G: About Me Survey** *and weave survey information in lessons and conversations with students. This will motivate students, and they will see that you are interested in them as people. Ask before you share personal information from the survey with other students. (Select* **Supplements**, *then* **G–J** *at www.classroommanagementblues.com to download the survey.)*

What About Me?

On the **About Me Survey**, I ask students "*What* jobs, careers, or occupations do you want to learn more about? Leon, a challenging student, answered **movie director**. So I researched the skills needed to be an effective movie director. Then, it was ACTION!

During the school year, he directed the following movies: "*You Do What?*" a film that showed how to safely use equipment in the science lab and "*Say What?*" a film for young children in which the class improved their writing of dialogue while teaching effective responses to put-downs.

Practice integrating information from **Supplement G: About Me Survey** into lessons, assignments, and other projects to show that you value and respect your students' interests. Select the **Supplements** page at *www.class roommanagementblues.com*, then **G–J** for **Supplement G** to download the survey.

To build trust and respect, teachers must model **appreciation** in what they say and do, listen to give attention, and use enthusiastic and affirmation statements about behavior and abilities (Albert, 1996). Teachers should expect students to demonstrate these same affirming techniques. (Read "Give EACH Student Their Just Desserts" for more examples.)

Give EACH Student Their Just Desserts

In *Inspiring Active Learning: A Handbook for Teachers,* Dr. Merrill Harmin (1994) identified **community** as one of five qualities evidenced in inspirational classrooms. He offers strategies that inspire and encourage students within the learning community. "I Appreciate" Messages and Honest Delights are two of these strategies (pp. 63–64, 72–73).

"I Appreciate" Messages

Description Statements that communicate something honestly appreciated about students

Purpose To remind students that at least one adult appreciates them

Examples
- I appreciate it when you respect the differences in others.
- I appreciate it when you find something positive about people.
- I appreciate it when you listen so well to others.
- I appreciate it when you do more than your share of work without me asking you to do it.

Honest Delights

Description Statements expressing spontaneous delight with a student

Purpose To allow a teacher to be spontaneously expressive and demonstrate the reality that people have the ability to delight others

Examples
- Gloria, your answer was very creative.
- You were truthful, and that was not easy, Pat. I am proud of you.
- Good risk taking, Lee.
- I was delighted to see that you stuck with your friend, LaShawn.

"Honest Delights are warmer and more infused with emotional energy than "I Appreciate" Messages, but they are not exaggerated or artificial . . . Each teacher will find different delights in students. Almost any delight is fine, as long as it is *honestly* delightful to the teacher and not embarrassing to the student or his peers" (Harmin, 1994, pp. 72–73). **Practice** giving **EACH** student his or her "just desserts."

A. Teacher: *What else can I do to build trust and show students I appreciate them?*

Dr. Foster: *Before I give you other strategies, let me ask a few questions. They might seem a little strange, but you will soon see how they connect to our discussion of student appreciation within a learning community.*

How do you feel when you have to take schoolwork home at night—like papers to grade and lessons to prepare?

A. Teacher: *Sometimes I don't mind, but I envy those who don't have to take work home. Right now, I'm not able to pursue any personal interests or spend the time I'd like with my family.*

Dr. Foster: *About how much time do you spend nightly on schoolwork?*

A. Teacher: *Right now, a couple of hours after my kids go to bed. I knew when I became a teacher that I would have to do work at home. I sure would like to know how to cut it back to less than an hour.*

Dr. Foster: *In our next session, we will discuss how you can reduce your workload.*

How much time do your own children spend on homework? How much time do you expect your students to spend?

A. Teacher: *My daughter doesn't spend as much time as she should, while my son spends hours on homework. I give my students about an hour every night. Some spend more time if they don't get their work done in class. The principal and parents expect me to give students homework!*

> Everyone has the right to rest and leisure, including reasonable limitation of working hours and periodic holidays with pay. (Universal Declaration of Human Rights, 2011, Article 24)

Dr. Foster: *Research shows that students **are** more successful in school if they **do** homework, but many are not motivated to do it or resent the time it takes away from things they like to do after school.*

As "all work and no play" is unhealthy for students and teachers alike, educators must rethink their expectations for homework. Teachers can show they value homework and participation in extracurricular activities if they provide meaningful homework activities and reduce the time students must spend on homework.

> *There are two educations. One should teach us how to make a living and the other how to live.*
>
> **John Adams**
> (1797–1801)
>
> Second President of the United States, who taught for one year in Worcester, Massachusetts

A. Teacher: *I have always complained about the schoolwork I take home at night. Now I understand why my students feel the same way.*

A. Teacher: *I'd like to learn how to improve my homework practices.*

Dr. Foster: *Apply the* **Active Engagement Prescription** *and use the* 📁 **Supplement H: Homework Contract** *to design worthwhile homework assignments that students will be motivated to do. Read "It's About Time!" to learn about my homework policies and the homework contract that you can download and modify from* **Classroom Management Blues** *website.*

It's About Time!

Some students spend little or no **time** on homework because it is too easy; they are able to participate in sports and other activities. Many students spend several **hours** on homework because it is too difficult or there is no one who can help.

   It's all **about time!** Many students have the **time** to do homework in school while others spend extra **hours** at home because they have the work they did not finish at school as well as the homework.

Here is what I tell students and parents so they know what is expected and see that I value homework and leisure **time**.

🕐 Students need little or no guidance from parents, as the **homework is review**—does not contain new content or skills.

🕐 If a teacher values the "home" in homework, **students do not do homework at school** unless special circumstances make it appropriate.

🕐 If a teacher values the "school" in schoolwork, **students do not do schoolwork at home** unless special circumstances make it appropriate.

🕐 **Students do homework for a specific amount of time.** Students must adhere to time limits, remain on task, and finish as much as they can in the time allotted.

🕐 If **teachers give homework assignments a week ahead**, students will learn to be responsible and manage the time needed for homework and extracurricular activities.

Put these policies into **practice** and you will hear parents and students say, **It's about time** a teacher *not* only cares about whether homework is turned in, but establishes procedures that show he or she *appreciates* the need for students to have time for reading, family, and extracurricular activities. **Supplement H** provides a **Homework Contract** and more detailed information about homework design and policies. (Select **Supplements** at *www.classroommanagementblues.com,* then **G–J** to locate **Supplement H**.)

Dr. Foster: *Teachers foster* appreciation *and positive student-teacher relationships in classrooms when they use affirming techniques, attend extracurricular activities, integrate students' interests in lessons, and improve homework practices. Now we will address how teachers can promote positive peer relationships within the learning community.*

How can authentic teachers create a learning community where every student feels he or she *belongs*? Research shows higher academic performance is associated with a sense of belonging (Trumbull & Pacheco, 2005). Teachers can help students be themselves and feel accepted if they respect diversity and use team-building strategies in the learning community.

> A group of prospective teachers . . . made the following remarks, "That was a good school. The students liked to be there and you could tell that the teachers were good, genuine people." . . . a place that offers a sense of security and belonging. (Hansen & Childs, 1998, para. 6)

A. Teacher: *I think some of the strategies we've already discussed would give students the opportunity to become team players and respect the diverse qualities of their peers. These include Quality Grouping, participation in icebreakers, and the integration of students' interests and learning styles in lessons.*

Dr. Foster: *You have correctly identified a few of the many effective strategies needed to build a learning community in which all students are accepted and feel they belong.*

Two other strategies are to inspire team identity and establish zero tolerance for put-downs (e.g., name-calling, teasing, insulting). Both require that teachers trust the class to help create a non-threatening, safe climate in which all students can achieve high standards for learning and work to break bad habits and build new, better ones (Crawford, 1998).

The limbic system is where intense emotions are registered—happiness, sadness, anger, jealousy, fear, excitement. The cerebrum is where the highest order of thinking takes place—problem-solving, learning, memorization, thought-processing. The cerebrum is where learning takes place and where we want our students to be when we teach them. However, if the body feels threatened, the brain downshifts until the stem gains control so that the organs continue to function, first and foremost. Obviously, brain down-shifting impedes effective problem solving. . . . The best learning environments are safe—where students are protected from ridicule, embarrassment, and harm so that the highest level of thinking occurs. (Payne, 2010, para. 2–3, 5).

To create and maintain a nonthreatening, safe learning climate, teachers and students must establish and remain committed to mutual respect and zero tolerance for put-downs. This means teachers and students must work as a team to respond proactively to put-downs when they happen.

> *Individual commitment to a group effort— that is what makes a team work.*
>
> **Vince Lombardi** (1913–1970)
>
> One of the most successful football coaches

A. Teacher: *I feel the pressure from parents and administrators to handle put-downs and other bullying behaviors. I address what I hear and observe, but how am I supposed to deal with the bullying behaviors I do not see?*

Dr. Foster: *It is easier to deal with overt put-downs and bullying behaviors. It's not surprising that many bullies use covert tactics that are difficult to detect. Teachers need to empower students to take an active role to create a climate of tolerance and respond proactively to put-downs and bullying when an adult is not present.*

A. Teacher: *It's overwhelming. How can I do this?*

Dr. Foster: *What do you think of the action plan in this diagram?*

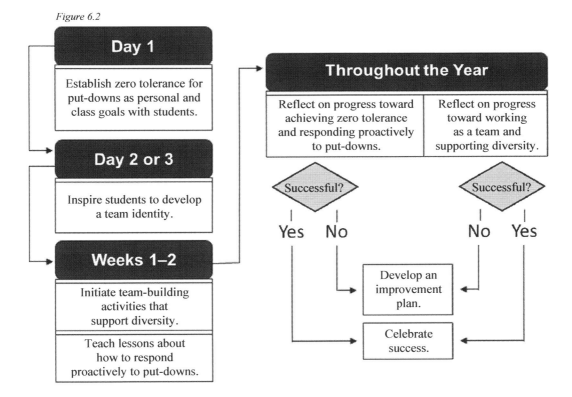

Figure 6.2

A. Teacher: *The plan makes sense, but I will need more information and resources.*

Dr. Foster: *Select **Resources** at www.classroommanagementblues.com, then **Expectations** and **Team Building** for lesson plans and other resources to build teams, support diversity, and address put-downs in the classroom. I also recommend **The Bully Free Classroom** by Dr. Alan L. Beane. This book has tips and strategies to create a positive classroom climate and help the victim and as well as the bully. Read "From Day One!" for some examples from **The Bully Free Classroom**.*

From Day One!

As your teacher, I want to make sure bullying does not happen in our classroom, and if it does, we will have to find a way to stop it. Together we will create a positive learning community—one in which you can feel safe, accepted, and valued (Beane, 1999).

This modified statement is from a parent letter found in the book *The Bully Free Classroom* by Dr. Allan L. Beane. The following excerpts are but a few of the 100 practical prevention and intervention tips and strategies you can begin to use **from day one** to foster a bully-free classroom (pp. 26, 43, 54, 59, 128).

In Practice
Dr. Bean

Create a Positive Classroom

Day 1 **Establish zero tolerance for put-downs as personal and class goals with students.**

Work together to solve a problem . . . when you face a common "enemy" as a group you grow closer to each other in the process. This builds unity, acceptance, and satisfaction as everyone joins forces for a good cause.

Throughout the Year **Reflect on progress to achieve zero tolerance.**

This week in school, another student:

Called me names	Never	Once	More Than Once
Treated me with kindness and respect	Never	Once	More Than Once
Was mean to me because I'm different	Never	Once	More Than Once

Help Victims

Weeks 1–2 **Teach lessons about how to respond proactively to put-downs.**

Cool down. Don't try to resolve a conflict when you or the other person is angry.
When someone bullies you, join other people who are nearby. Bullies generally don't pick on people in groups.

Help Bullies

Throughout the Year **Reflect on progress to achieve zero tolerance.**

It is as important to change bullies' thinking, as it is to change their behavior. Bullies often deny that they have done anything wrong and refuse to take responsibility for their behavior. Challenge their thinking without preaching.
Ask a bully to consider this question and respond verbally or in writing:
Who is right when you think you are not bullying him/her, but he/she thinks you are?

Look for strategies to create a positive classroom and put them into **practice from day one**. Visit *www.classroommanagementblues.com* and locate the **Resources** page about bullying.

A. Teacher: *I am confident I can move my students toward creating a respectful learning community with what I now know about how to establish zero tolerance for put-downs. But I'm not sure what it means to inspire a team identity.*

Dr. Foster: *Excellent resources are available to help create a learning community through team building; educators often overlook team identity.*

Let me ask you this question: "Who are you?"

A. Teacher: *My name is Any Teacher. I'm a parent, teacher, softball player, and gardener.*

Dr. Foster: *After you told me your name, you identified yourself as a member of a family and groups that share a common purpose or interest. We are what we do; and as social beings, we need to belong.*

Belonging to a class, family, team, or group is one of six human needs identified by psychologist Abraham Maslow (1943) that a person must meet before he or she can reach self-actualization. He posited that a teacher could not meet needs at one level before addressing needs at the preceding levels—that a student has little or no change to meet cognitive needs if he or she has self-esteem, belonging, safety, and physiological deficiencies (see Figure 6.3). It is sad but true that social maladjustment and most emotional illnesses relate to the failure to gratify the basic need to belong (Mendler, 2001). Many of our youth choose to belong to a gang despite their physiological and safety needs. (Read about someone who is "Dying to Belong.")

Figure 6.3

Maslow's Hierarchy of Needs

Self-Actualization
Aesthetic
Cognitive
Self-Esteem
Belonging
Safety
Physiological

Dying to Belong

Hi i would like to know something I been in a gang since I was 9 year old. . . . I'm now 20 year old. Everyone I love is dead but a few and everyone that tried to get out was killed so I have something to ask, if I feel that getting out of gang will kill me and staying in will also killing me what do I DO can anyone help? *(*Anonymous, n.d.).

"Already a mighty and revolutionary power with the potential to transform our culture lies dormant within the spiritual depths of each individual within their hopes and dreams, their existential desires and talents, and their intrinsic 'crying out' to belong with others in true human community and this spiritual energy is waiting patiently for the trumpets to call" (Campbell, 2004, para. 8).

The ***reality*** is that some of our youth are willing to die to belong.

A. Teacher: *I have a better understanding about why students look for a group to meet their primary need of belonging regardless of the dangers. I've also noticed that when students are not accepted, they seem to become friends.*

Dr. Foster: *Many students who commit school violence are loners or have been victims or bully-victims (a bully who is or has been a victim). They do not care who they hurt because they believe no one cares about them.*

Students are less likely to identify with inappropriate groups when they have a sense of belonging and feel respected in the classroom. This brings us back to ways to inspire a team identity.

What distinguishes one gang or athletic team from another?

A. Teacher: *Well, they both have unique names, colors, items of clothing, and a location, like a neighborhood or university. They also have symbols or mascots that represent the qualities the members want their team to embody.*

Dr. Foster: *Teams create ways to make themselves known to others.*

In *More than 50 Ways to Build Team Consensus,* Williams (1996) says that when teachers foster a sense of identity, they create an affirming and nurturing bond among team members and increase team effectiveness. Ideas to inspire team spirit and identity include:

★ Post a **team member list** that communicates that everyone belongs;

★ Design and display a **team symbol or flag** that proclaims the team's greatness;

★ Write in a few words a **team motto or cheer** to motivate or keep the team focused;

★ Come up with a **team name** that communicates the team's unique strengths;

★ Create a **team song** to communicate the team's feelings and commitment; and

★ Repeat **team rituals or rites** that remind the team of victories or breakthroughs.

Dr. Foster: *You may purchase commercial programs to build community in your classroom. Tribes TLC® is one example of a community building process for all ages that is a step-by-step sequence of strategies in which quality time is spent to build inclusion within groups. For more information about Tribes TLC® and other programs, search online or select* **Resources***, then* **Expectations** *and* **Trust Building** *at www.classroom managementblues.com.*

The Tribes TLC® process is a way . . . [for] students [to] achieve because they:

- feel included and appreciated by peers and teachers
- are respected for their different abilities, interests, cultures, gender, and dreams
- are actively involved in their own learning
- have positive expectations from others that they will succeed (Gibbs, 2006, para. 2).

A. Teacher: *Won't the kinds of activities you have described take away from the work a team or class needs to do?*

Dr. Foster: *In reality, team identity strategies keep everyone motivated to perform at high levels. As a final point about teams, motivation to keep up their best effort does not always come from the coach or within the team; it comes from the fan base and cheerleaders.*

Members of the class are the fans who **celebrate teamwork** with a mutually agreed upon rite or ritual (gesture, phrase, or object) for individual commitment, individual accountability, shared responsibility, clear goals, team achievement, and diversity (see Figure 6.4). To celebrate cooperative groups' achievements, experts recommend that one group member accept the role of cheerleader, encourager, or supporter to inspire less vocal members to contribute, praise ideas, complete tasks, and urge members when difficulties arise.

Figure 6.4

An example of a gesture teachers and students can use to **celebrate** academic and behavioral team successes is "Kiss Your Brain." The teacher and students take the dominant hand and place it on the lips and then on the top of the head. (Read "Celebrate Good Times, Come On!" on page 239 for other ways to celebrate teamwork.)

There are two ways of exerting one's strength: one is pushing down, and the other is pulling up.

Booker T. Washington
(1856–1915)

Born into slavery he became an important black educator and leader.

As coach, a teacher inspires team identity, supports zero tolerance for put-downs, and teaches students how to interact proactively with peers to create a safe, learning community where everyone works together to achieve common goals. When a teacher maintains a sense of belonging in a nonthreatening learning environment, everyone is free to learn and even laugh together. (Read "Team Building Is NO Joke!" for a good laugh.)

Team Building Is NO Joke!

In "Team Building Humor Strengthens a Team Identity or Spirit," Dr. P. McGhee asserts that put-down jokes destroy a team's moral fiber. Students need to understand the difference between "laughing with" and "laughing at" individuals and groups.

Yogi Berra, a former catcher and manager for the New York Yankees in Major League Baseball, is perhaps the single greatest team player in the history of team sports. He is also famous for **Yogiiisms**—his tendency toward malapropism and fracturing the English language in interesting ways (Wikipedia).

- ○ *I never said half the things I really said.*
- ○ *We made too many wrong mistakes.*
- ○ *Our similarities are different.*
- ○ *You can observe a lot by just watching.*
- ○ *When you get to a fork in the road, take it.*
- ○ *If you don't know where you're going, you'll wind up somewhere else.*

Begin every day with an inspiring team-building joke or quotation about "friendship, peace, peacemaking, self-esteem, assertiveness, tolerance, understanding, acceptance, kindness, respect, and other topics for creating a positive classroom" and inspire a team spirit and identity (Beane, 1999, p. 49).

What can authentic teachers do to give every student the opportunity to *contribute* in the learning community? Albert (1996) recommends that teachers hold class meetings, ask for suggestions from students when making decisions, and encourage peer tutoring. These strategies promote **appreciation** and **belonging** as well as show that teachers trust students to **contribute** in the learning community.

Dr. Foster: *Teaching others was a topic of conversation in our last session. Refer to that information if you need a review. (See pages 53–57.) You will learn more about peer teaching in our session on appropriate assessments.*

*We will discuss openness to students' suggestions and explore opportunities for students to make contributions and decisions about appropriate classroom issues. Although we will talk about class meetings for only a few minutes in this session, there are resources available online to help you implement class meetings at all grade levels. (Select **Resources** at www.classroommanagementblues.com, and then locate **Expectations** and **Problem Solving**.)*

A. Teacher: *I do not feel I can trust **all** my students to make contributions and decisions in my classroom, but I will keep an open mind.*

Teachers demonstrate they trust their students when they give them responsibilities and hold class meetings. These meetings facilitate cohesiveness, respectful interaction, problem solving, and decision making (Marshall, 2000). To be effective, teachers must suggest topics, formulate questions, set an agenda, create the physical environment, serve as facilitator, support conflict resolution, and close and evaluate the meeting.

> *Few things can help an individual more than to place responsibility on him, and to let him know that you trust him.*
>
> **Booker T. Washington**
> (1856–1915)
>
> Enrolled at what is now
> Hampton University at age 16

A. Teacher: *I am sure I sound like a broken record. With everything I have to do, when am I supposed to have class meetings?*

Dr. Foster: *Be creative and weave class meetings into the fabric of what you already do. Read "Meetings' of the Minds" for some ideas.*

"Meetings" of the Minds

Meeting of the Minds is a term in contract law that describes the intentions and common understanding of the parties to form an enforceable contract. In classroom meetings, the learning community meets to set academic and behavioral expectations and to reflect on and make decisions about achieving these shared expectations.

Six Kinds of Class Meetings from "Twenty Kinds of Class Meetings"

1. **Circle Whip** Go around the circle; everyone can either complete the "sentence-starter" or choose to pass. 🎤 A decision I think we should make is . . .

2. **Reflections on Learning** 🎤 What did you learn from . . .

3. **Student Presentation** One or two students present a piece of their work; other class members ask questions and offer appreciative comments.

4. **Problem Solving—Conflict Resolution** Complaints and recommendations: Anyone can complain about a problem but must offer a recommendation to correct it.

5. **Academic Issues** 🎤 Why do you have to study this? 🎤 On the next test . . .?

6. **Classroom Improvement Meeting** 🎤 What changes would make our classroom better? Possibilities: Change the physical arrangement, suggest new learning games

"Meetings" of the Minds give students the opportunity
to contribute to the learning community.

Students become empowered and feel appreciated when teachers ask about and listen to their opinions about relevant topics that interest or concern them. Teachers who implement students' ideas within the learning community demonstrate that their contributions are welcome.

When teachers ask for suggestions and routinely assign classroom jobs, trust builds between teachers and students. To safeguard this trust, checklists **assure** that *every* student has comparable opportunities to contribute. (Read "Depend on Me!" to learn more.)

Depend on Me!

To make sure I give *every* student an equal chance to contribute in my classroom without losing valuable instructional time, I use a checklist. Here are some examples.

In Practice

Dr. Foster

- **Page Recorder**   When I ask students to turn to a particular page in a book, the daily **Page Recorder** writes the page number in a designated location on the board. This helps everyone get on the same page without the need to repeat the page number.

- **Music Director**   The **Music Director** selects and plays instrumental music during work sessions. One student suggested we play music when preparing to leave the classroom to make the transition less hectic. Students do make great suggestions!

- **Share a Story**   Every student has a personal **story to share**, especially younger students. To not hurt feelings and lose instructional time, a checklist makes sure everyone is given the opportunity to share a story, but not always during the same lesson.

- **Read Aloud**   Many students like to **read aloud**, but unless they read loud enough for everyone in the room to hear, it is ineffective. So I am selective about what is read aloud by me and what is read aloud by students. I make sure that I read the most important content in texts. I rarely have every student read aloud in one lesson, so a checklist helps me assure that everyone has the opportunity when reading aloud is appropriate.

Put checklists into **practice** in your classroom to show that when you say **Depend on Me**—your students can depend on you to give everyone a chance to contribute. Select **Supplements**, then **K–P** at http://*www.classroommanagementblues.com* to find **Supplement O** for more information about how to use a **Practice Record Sheet** to record contributions.

English Period 1	Page Recorder	Music Director	Share a story	Read aloud
A. Student		✓		✓

A. Teacher: *The appreciation, belonging, and contribution strategies you have described to create and maintain a learning community might have worked with some of the classes I have had in the past, but not the students in my classroom today.*

Dr. Foster: *Continue to repeat high expectations and use the recommended strategies. "Don't give up. An overall sense of community will not develop overnight, and you may notice lapses in behavior—name-calling, or even fighting. Do not dwell on the negative . . . remember to recognize and praise the students' progress as a group" (Rose, 1999, para. 8).*

Let's take a break. Then we will talk about autonomy—a person's ability to make decisions about and take responsibility for their own learning and behavior.

Active Ingredient	 Autonomy

Not only do students need to take more collective responsibility within the learning *community*, there is an expectation that they maximize their full potential and make choices about and take responsibility for their own learning and behavior (Benson, 2003; Wisniewska, 1998). The freedom for one person to make choices always compromises the obligations to others; so it is "the integration of these two values, community and choice, which defines democracy" (Kohn, 1993, para. 55). **Autonomy**, the ability to make choices and self-regulate, is the fourth active ingredient in the **High Expectations Prescription**.

A. Teacher: *I am still not totally convinced that students can make individual or collective decisions in the classroom, but I will try some of the strategies you recommend.*

*I **really** have doubts about whether my students can learn on their own!*

Dr. Foster: *It does not always mean that students have to learn on their own, but some might learn better alone. People possess and can develop autonomous abilities, attitudes, and capabilities to various degrees, and yet most teachers teach in ways that promote dependence (Benson, 2003; Wisniewska, 1998).*

Like the other active ingredients in the **High Expectations Prescription**, **autonomy** is complex. There is, however, wide agreement that autonomous individuals have self-regulatory mechanisms that maximize the potential to make accurate, consistent proactive, positive, and reflective judgments about their own learning, behavior, and sense of identity.

> Neo-Vygotskian psychology . . . sees learning as a matter of supported performance and emphasizes the interdependence of the cognitive and social-interactive dimensions of the learning process. . . . The teacher's role is to create and maintain a learning environment in which learners can **be autonomous** in order to **become more autonomous**. (Little, 2003, para. 5)

Dr. Foster: *This chart might help clarify the terms. Though the attributes are across from the needs and abilities for which they have a close association, each mechanism, attitude, and ability relates to the other abilities. For example, self-talk and reflective learning are just as important to the ability to cope with new situations as they are to each of the other abilities.*

Table 6.4

The Attributes of Autonomy			
Abilities **Autonomous learners . . .**	Self-Regulatory Mechanisms	Attitudes & Capabilities	Maslow's Needs
• Display self-enhancing biases and the belief that they can achieve goals and solve problems	Self-Concept	Positive Identity	Self-Esteem
• Rely more on their own past successes than the verbal comments of others	Self-Efficacy		
• Set goals and develop action plans or plan personal learning activities • Make decisions and choices	Self-Direction	Proactive Behavior	Cognition
• Act independently and exert control over their environment • Seek support, but can function well without it • Interact with others and give support	Self-Control		
• Monitor learning activities • Evaluate progress and make changes • Learn how to learn from successes and failures	Self-Assessment	Reflective Learning	Self-Actualization
• Cope with new and unforeseen situations • Overcome temporary motivational setbacks	Self-Talk	Multiple Intelligence: Intrapersonal	

From Benard, 1993; Landau & Gathercoal, 2000; Little, 2003; McCarthy, 1998; and Pajares, 2002

A. Teacher: *Again, I see connections between the self-regulatory mechanisms of autonomy and concepts we have already talked about like efficacy and authenticity. I think the strategies for each of these could help my students behave proactively, reflect on their learning, and develop a positive identity.*

Dr. Foster: *The active ingredients in one prescription may be present in others, so the strategies for one **are** applicable for others. For example, the **goal strategies** recommended for efficacy are appropriate for self-direction, one of the self-regulatory mechanisms of autonomy. (See Table 6.5.)*

Table 6.5

The Attributes of Autonomy			
Self-Regulatory Mechanisms	Abilities **Autonomous learners . . .**	Active Ingredients	Prescriptions
Self-Concept	• Display self-enhancing biases and the belief that they can achieve goals and solve problems	Authenticity	High Expectations **Session 6**
Self-Efficacy	• Rely more on their own past successes than the verbal comments of others	Efficacy	
Self-Direction	• Set goals and develop action plans or plan personal learning activities • Make decisions and choices	**Autonomy**	
Self-Control	• Act independently and exert control over their environment		
	• Seek support, but can function well without it • Interact with others and give support	Community	
Self-Talk	• Cope with new and unforeseen situations • Overcome temporary motivational setbacks	Resiliency	
Self-Assessment	• Monitor learning activities • Evaluate progress and make changes • Learn how to learn from successes and failures	Reflection	Appropriate Assessments **Session 7**

Dr. Foster: *The 🗁 **Supplement J: High Expectations Strategy Game** will help you locate strategies that correspond to each active ingredient and self-regulatory mechanism. (Select **Supplements** at www.classroommanagementblues.com, then **G–J** for **Supplement J**.)*

*We have discussed authenticity, efficacy, and community in this session; a discussion of resiliency will follow. Though applicable to autonomy, reflection (self-assessment) is an active ingredient of the **Appropriate Assessments Prescription** that we will talk about in our next session. Right now, our focus will be on how to **empower** students to make choices and act on their own.*

A. Teacher: *I still do not believe all my students can make the right choices in the classroom. Won't they get out of control?*

Dr. Foster: *When conditions are established for empowerment, "control is not lost; it is simply transformed into self-control" (Covey, 2004, p. 256).*

> *The greatest sign of success for a teacher . . . is to be able to say, "The children are now working as if I did not exist."*
>
> **Maria Montessori**
> (1870–1952)
>
> Italian educator, scientist, physician, humanitarian, philosopher, and the first early childhood educator nominated for the Nobel Peace Prize

When a teacher is concerned about how to maintain control and leaves the classroom for a few minutes or is absent, the class is likely to erupt in chaos. "It is in classrooms (and families) where participation is valued above adult control that students have the chance to learn self-control—and are more likely to keep working when the teacher or parent isn't around" (Kohn, 1993, para. 77).

A. Teacher: *I know I don't like to be told what to teach and how to manage my classroom. I was not aware that I have treated my students in the same way that I find offensive (Kohn, 1993).*

How can teachers empower students within the classroom? The answer is to provide opportunities for students to make choices. Researchers in recent years have found that opportunities for self-direction and choice are associated with higher quality teaching that results in more engagement, better performance, and lower dropout rates (Ryan & Deci, 2000b).

John Dewey (1938), the father of progressive schools, and Stephen Covey (2004), the author of *The 8th Habit: From Effectiveness to Greatness*, stress that leaders in education and business cannot leave people to their "own unguided fancies" or abandon them in the name of empowerment. They both agree that a leader in the workplace or classroom must shift from controller to enabler. By removing barriers with agreed-upon guidelines for decision making that do not violate personal rights, leaders become a source of help and support.

> Empowerment . . . is the natural result . . . of trustworthiness, which enables people to identify and unleash their human potential. In other words, empowering enthrones self-control, self-management, and self-organizing. . . . It taps into passion, energy and drive. (Covey, 2004, p. 253)

I have heard teachers give it up after a single attempt, saying, "Children cannot behave responsibly," then remove all further opportunity for students to practice and grow in their responsible behavior. I have also heard teachers say, "Children cannot think for themselves," and proceed thereafter to do children's thinking for them. But these same teachers would never say, "These children cannot read by themselves," and thereafter remove any opportunity for them to learn to read. (Wassermann, 1989, p. 204)

A. Teacher: *I know how to teach reading, but not decision making.*

Dr. Foster: *If you have started to use the constructivist strategies and activities recommended in our last session, then you have already started your students on the road to autonomy. "The entire constructivism tradition is predicated on the idea of student autonomy" (Kohn, 1993, para. 44). Students in constructivist classrooms take ownership in what they learn, learn to question, and apply their natural curiosity to the world (Concept to Classroom, 2004). You can also promote responsible decision making in your classroom when you ask questions.*

What kinds of decisions can students make in the classroom? According to Alfie Kohn (1993), teachers give students opportunities to make academic decisions when they ask ***what, how, why***, and ***how well***. When possible, students might choose *what* topics to study, texts to read, tasks to complete, or questions to answer. They can make decisions about *how* they learn (e.g., work alone, in small groups, as a class) and the criteria to assess *how well* they do assignments. Finally, there may be no better use of classroom time than to discuss with students *why* they are learning content and how the content connects with their real-world concerns and interests. Teachers should give all students opportunities to make decisions in the classroom no matter the age. (Read "Does Age Matter?" for examples of how students can make decisions in K–12 and post-secondary classrooms.)

Does Age Matter?

Dr. Alfie Kohn (1993) says, "The irrefutable fact is that students always have a choice about whether they will learn. We may be able to force them to finish an assignment, but we can't compel them to learn effectively or to care about what they are doing" (para. 32). He cites the following examples.

- When **preschoolers** selected the materials they used to make a collage, their work was more creative than the work of children who used the same materials but did not get to choose them.

- When **second-graders** spent a year in a math classroom without textbooks and rewards in favor of an emphasis on "intellectual autonomy" . . . they developed sophisticated reasoning skills and did not fall behind on basic conceptual tasks.

- When **high school seniors** in Minneapolis worked on chemistry problems with the opportunity to decide for themselves how to find solutions, they consistently produced better write-ups of experiments.

- When **college students** in New York State had the chance to make decisions about the puzzles they wanted to work on and how to allot their time to each of them, they were a lot more interested in working on similar puzzles later in the course than were students who were told what puzzles to do.

There is no question: **choice matters, no matter the age** of the learner. Give students opportunities to make academic decisions and learn firsthand the positive effect on academic performance.

A. Teacher: *Am I supposed to let my students take control of my classroom?*

Dr. Foster: *More student learning happens in classrooms where there is balance between teacher control and student autonomy (Tripod Project, 2002–2003).*

Winning by Losing Control

In *Motivating Others: Nurturing Inner Motivational Resources, Dr.* Johnmarshall Reeve defines "autonomy support" as "the amount of freedom a teacher gives a student so the student can connect his or her behavior to personal goals, interests, and values" (Downing, 2006, para. 5).

Dr. Reeve recommends that teachers use these five behaviors to support students' autonomy:

- Acknowledge students' points of view.
- Encourage students' choices and initiatives.
- Communicate the reason for any behavioral limits or constraints placed on students.
- Acknowledge that negative emotion is a valid response to teacher control.
- Rely on a noncontrolling communication style and offer positive feedback.

The more you **practice** behaviors that support students' autonomy, the more work they do. The more you **lose** control by promoting teamwork, leadership, and decision making the more your students will **win** by developing skills needed for life beyond school (Tripod Project, 2002–2003).

Dr. Foster: *How do you think students respond when teachers give them opportunities to make decisions in the classroom?*

A. Teacher: *I'm sure they love it!*

Dr. Foster: *Not always. Sometimes students resist (Kohn, 1993).*

A. Teacher: *Giving up power in my classroom is frightening and will be difficult. If my students resist, what will I do? (See Table 6.6.)*

People of mediocre ability sometimes achieve outstanding success because they don't know when to quit. Most . . . succeed because they are determined to persevere and get it done. The tougher the job, the greater the reward.

George Allen (1918–1990)

Considered one of the hardest working football coaches in the NFL

Table 6.6

Countering Resistance		
Refusing	Students may protest, and say, "That's your job to decide."	Use as a teachable moment. Engage students in a conversation about their experiences with being controlled and about when they have found learning to be most exciting.
Testing	Students may offer outrageous suggestions or responses to see if the teacher is serious about the invitation to participate.	Meet outlandish ideas with a sense of humor and still take them seriously. If a student says to throw all the books away when asked how to improve school, he or she might be saying something about his or her experience with the curriculum.
Parroting	Students may repeat what adults have said or guess what an adult probably wants to hear. (Thus, a student asked to suggest a rule might say, "We should keep our hands and feet to ourselves.")	It can be hard even to recognize this as a form of resistance—or something undesirable. Getting our ideas to come out of their mouths is not a sign of successful participation and student autonomy. It is an invitation to ask students about their experiences with saying what they know would please a teacher. How different that feels from taking the risk to suggest something that someone might not like.

Adapted from "Choices for Children: Why and How to Let Students Decide" by A. Kohn, 1993

A. Teacher: *I still have a lot to learn about student autonomy and academic decision making.*

Dr. Foster: *Select **Resources** at www.classroommanagementblues.com, then **Expectations** and **Autonomy** for other readings and resources about decision making. In Session 8, we will discuss student autonomy and decision making as they relate to behavior management.*

The significance of autonomy in contrast to control for the maintenance of intrinsic motivation has been observed in studies of classroom learning. . . . Studies have shown that autonomy-supportive (in contrast to controlling) teachers catalyze in their students greater intrinsic motivation, curiosity, and the want for. . . . Students who are too controlled not only lose initiative but learn less well, especially when learning is complex or requires conceptual, creative processing. (Ryan & Deci, 2000a, p. 59)

Active Ingredient	🍎 Resiliency

The fifth active ingredient in the **High Expectations Prescription** is **resiliency**. Bonnie Benard (1993) defines resiliency as the ability to bounce back successfully despite exposure to severe risks like poverty, neglect, abuse, physical handicaps, war, mental illnesses, alcoholism, or criminality of parents.

A. Teacher: *I've read stories about people who succeed despite tragic childhood experiences. How are they able to bounce back?*

Dr. Foster: *According to the Bonnie Benard (1993), resilient children usually possess four attributes: social competence, autonomy, problem-solving skills, and a sense of purpose and future aspirations. The last two strategies that we will discuss in this session are problem solving and self-talk. Resilient children need these strategies to overcome motivational setbacks and cope with new and unforeseen situations.*

 Look at this table to see how the strategies for the active ingredients of the **High Expectations Prescription** *relate to resiliency.*

Table 6.7

Active Ingredients Self-Regulatory Mechanisms	High Expectations	
	Autonomous learners . . .	**Resilient learners . . .**
Authenticity Self-Concept	• Display self-enhancing biases and the belief that they can achieve goals and solve problems	• Have a positive sense of one's own identity
Efficacy Self-Efficacy	• Rely more on their own past successes than the verbal comments of others	• Have a sense of a bright future—hopefulness
Autonomy Self-Direction Self-Control	• Set goals and develop action plans or plan personal learning activities • Make decisions and choices • Act independently and exert control over one's environment	• Have a sense of purpose—educational aspirations • Think abstractly and reflectively • Detach from a dysfunctional family, school, or community environment
Community Self-Control	• Seek support, but can function well without it • Interact with others and give support	• Have social competence—proactive • Elicit positive responses from others—responsiveness, caring, flexibility, empathy, communication skills, and a sense of humor • Establish positive relationships with both adults and peers that help bond them to their family, school, and community • Seek help from others—resourcefulness
Resiliency Self-Talk	• Cope with new and unforeseen situations • Overcome temporary motivational setbacks	• Have the ability to bounce back from adversity • Negotiate the demands of their environment—persistence • Attempt alternate solutions for both cognitive and social problems

From Benard, 1993; Landau & Gathercoal, 2000; Little, 2003; McCarthy, 1998; and Pajares, 2002

A. Teacher: *I'm glad you told me about the strategies for the other active ingredients before you introduced resiliency. I would not have believed that I could help my students develop the ability to bounce back from adversity.*

What can authentic teachers do to create a learning environment that supports resiliency and promotes high expectations? "To prevent children from acquiring or retaining erroneous personal scripts that could have an adverse influence on vital decisions, including the ones they make currently or later in life" (Janis, 1980, p. 181), teachers must help children use positive self-talk and acquire the skills needed to solve problems. Priestley, McGuire, Flegg, Hemsley, and Welham state that to prepare children for the next century, the aims of education should be to help them solve their immediate problems, improve their ability to cope with future problems, and develop new and increasingly better ways to do both (1978, p. 4).

> [By] solving the simple problems encountered in the first stages of life, young children open up new possibilities and challenges for themselves that they can pursue at later stages. . . . the mainspring of cognitive development lies in the pursuit of these challenges. (Gredler, 1992, p. 235)

For children to manage the interactions and problems of everyday life successfully, they need effective problem-solving skills. The "Ten Steps for Lifelong Learning and Problem Solving" represent a synthesis of eleven problem–solving models that date from 1910 to 1991 (Foster, 1995, pp. 43, 72).

Table 6.8

Ten Steps for Lifelong Learning and Problem Solving			
Frame	**Step 1** *Focus*	State the vision, goal, or problem.
	Step 2 *Research*	Gather information.
Process Information	**Step 3** *Interpret*	Analyze information and clarify the vision, goal, or problem.
	Step 4 *Predict*	Consider outcomes, resources, and obstacles.
	Step 5 *Brainstorm*	Generate objectives, hypotheses, or possible solutions.
Decide	**Step 6** *Choose*	Make decisions about timelines and evaluations.
Plan	**Step 7** *Design*	Develop action plans and monitoring and assessment systems.
Implement	**Step 8** *Act*	Put plans in action and fine-tune.
Learn from Experience	**Step 9** *Evaluate*	Value and verify assessment results.
	Step 10 *Transfer*	Reflect on future goals and problems.

From Bellanca & Fogarty, 1986; Covey, 1991; Dewey, 1973; Elias & Tobias, 1990; Gagné, 1985; Polya, 2004; Priestley, McGuire, Flegg, Hemsley, & Welham, 1978; Russo & Schoemaker, 1989; Silva, 1990; "The steps," 1987; and Whetten & Cameron, 1991—see references on page 384

A. Teacher: *I admit that when you first mentioned problem solving, I wasn't sure my students could do it. Now I believe they can because I already teach many of the skills in the "Ten Steps for Lifelong Learning and Problem Solving," like the ability to interpret, predict, and brainstorm.*

Dr. Foster: *Your evidenced understanding by the quantity and quality of the connections you have made about problem solving. Help your students make connections between what they learn in the classroom to problems they face beyond school. This will foster understanding and resiliency.*

Problem-based learning is a total approach to education that challenges students to learn through engagement in a real life problem. It is both a curriculum and a process. It consists of carefully selected and designed problems that demand from the learner acquisition of critical knowledge, problem-solving proficiency, self-directed learning strategies, and team participation skills. It also replicates the commonly used systematic approach to resolving problems or meeting challenges that are encountered in life and career. (Rattanavich, 2008, p. 2)

A. Teacher: *Do you have other suggestions to help me develop well-designed problems and implement problem-based learning?*

Problems are challenges, dilemmas, and triggers—students design and create something; find a better, more ethical, or cheaper way to do something, or seek to understand a puzzling phenomenon or concept (Barnett, 2005). Many resources are available to help students with problem solving. (Select **Resources** at *www.classroommanagementblues.com*, then **Expectations** and **Problem Solving**.)

Dr. Foster: *Along with problem solving, positive self-talk can help students become resilient and cope with new and unforeseen situations, as well as overcome temporary motivational setbacks.*

Self-talk has been shown, in research by medical and communication professionals, to have psychophysiological underpinnings. Thought patterns generated by self-talk affect health-states. . . . People can begin to harness the power in their minds by taking an active role in deciding what to think, enhancing the positive messages they send themselves. It also involves being realistic, identifying the causes for any negativity, realizing it is a signal to act. By doing so, people can face challenges—health related or otherwise—with the knowledge they can succeed. (Weikle, 1993, para. 16)

A. Teacher: *Some laugh at or call people crazy when they talk to themselves.*

Dr. Foster: *"It is not crazy to talk to yourself in your mind. It is normal. Everybody does it, every day, most of the time. The problem is that most people do not realize the hypnotic power of the messages that pass repeatedly through their minds" (Craven & Farrow, 1997, para. 2).*

Those who understand personal development and success regard self-talk as intelligent. More important, silent, positive self-talk is not nearly as effective as when we talk aloud to ourselves (Wayne, 2005, p. 16).

A. Teacher: *You've convinced me that self-talk is a positive mental and oral activity that would help my students be successful in school and beyond.*

Should I recommend that my students talk aloud when alone if they are worried about what others may think?

Dr. Foster: *You have just demonstrated your ability to solve problems. When you model problem solving and positive self-talk in the classroom, you foster resiliency in your students.*

A. Teacher: *I think self-talk is like the intrapersonal multiple intelligence?*

> *You cannot hope to build a better world without improving the individuals. To this end, each of us must work for our own improvement.*
> **Marie Curie** (1867–1934)
> Thinkquest
>
> Marie Curie enjoyed science and mathematics and graduated at the top of her class. She became the first female professor at the Sorbonne.

Dr. Foster: *Yes. Intrapersonal communication does include activities like self-evaluation, the evaluation of others, planning for the future, emotional catharsis, internal problem solving, and internal conflict resolution (Pearson & Nelson, 1985).*

Intrapersonal communication affects self-efficacy, so self-efficacy also affects resiliency. It gives a person hope and a sense of a bright future. (See page 77.) Let's look at other ways to use self-talk to foster self-efficacy and resiliency.

How does self-talk help students cope with adversity? The language that the mind uses to communicate with the body is imagery. Images are more than visual; they can be sounds, tastes, smells, or a combination of sensations. Over 10,000 thoughts or images flash through an average person's mind each day—at least half are negative ("Guided Imagery," 2007, para. 9). To counter these negative images or thoughts, students need to learn to use appropriate affirmations.

An affirmation is a positive statement of an accomplished goal. With repeated affirmations, the subconscious mind finds ways to make the affirmation come true. Through affirmations—good or bad—we shape our lives according to the image that the words in the affirmation create (Sasson, 2007, para. 4–5).

A. Teacher: *Now I understand why you say I need to "repeat" the* **High Expectations Prescription**. *If I routinely communicate my belief in my students' ability to achieve at high levels, their subconscious minds will find a way to achieve at high levels.*

Dr. Foster: *Exactly. "Tapping into the higher reaches of human genius and motivation—what we call voice—requires a new mind-set, a new tool-set" (Covey, 2004, p. 4). Affirmations give "voice" to a person's inner self—whether in spoken word, thoughts, or writing,.*

Good affirmations are short, memorable declarations stated in present tense. They are positive, hopeful, emotional, passionate, visual, visionary, and disciplined (Boe, 2005; Covey, 2004; Sasson, 2007). In "Wise Men Say . . ." Harmin (1994) offers some examples.

Wise Men Say . . .

*When the mind is thinking
it is talking to itself.*

Plato (428/427 BC–348/347 BC)

*The more man meditates upon good thoughts,
the better will be his world
and the world at large.*

Confucius (551 BC–479 BC)

**In Practice
Dr. Harmin**

Dr. Merrill Harmin, a professor of education, offers strategies that inspire and encourage students within the learning community. The following "I" *Affirm* messages are adaptations of his "I *Appreciate*" messages for teachers (1994, pp. 63–64).

"I" *Affirm* Messages

Description	Statements that communicate something honestly appreciated about oneself
Examples	▪ I go one more step when I am ready to give up. ▪ I reach down for my ability to persist when I need it. ▪ I ask for help when I need it. ▪ I ignore distractions. ▪ I take initiative. ▪ I remind myself not to be negative.

"Imagery has been considered a healing tool in virtually all the world's cultures. . . . Navajo Indians, for example, practice an elaborate form of imagery that encourages a person to 'see' himself as healthy" (Guided Imagery, 2007, para. 13). **Wise men say . . .** *affirm* students when they speak or write *good* affirmations about their ability to achieve their goals and aspirations.

"The mind regards often-repeated thoughts and phrases as commands, and starts looking for ways to manifest them in our lives. The mind does not make distinctions between negative and positive self-talk, and treats them both in the same way" (Sasson, 2007, para. 3). Two ways to become resilient to negative thoughts are the "placebo effect" and truth telling.

The placebo effect is the ability of the mind to cure an illness even when the procedure or medicine is worthless (De Witt, 2005; Lord, 1999). Just as the power of a patient's beliefs alone produce improvement, self-efficacy, affirmations and high expectations have the potential to help the subconscious minds of students achieve academic and personal goals. In "The Truth about Affirmations," De Witt (2005) asserts that negative thinking "always stems from a wound in the soul" for which affirmations, like bandages, merely cover up the wound. To heal, one must get at the truth or core of the wound (para. 13).

> **A. Teacher:**   *So, whether proven or not, what someone believes to be true is true.*
>
> **Dr. Foster:**   *"The truth is that the act of simply believing in ourselves can be enough to give us the necessary confidence to do the impossible, achieve greatness, and pick ourselves up when we fall" (Betterini, 2007, para. 1). Whether positive or negative, affirmations and self-talk move us to change.*
>
> *The first step is to recognize the need for change in ourselves and then change who we are, how we feel, and what we do. I did not blame my students when I came home exhausted, frustrated with their behavior, and feeling I did not do what I wanted during the school day. I reflected on what **I did** that influenced their behavior. Did I only see the negative that day?*
>
> *I would vow to change my attitude and behavior the next day, give myself a pep talk before class, and write on my plans in big, bold, colorful letters an important phrase (e.g., Be positive) to help focus on my goal. When I followed through, my students were better, and I was able to bounce back from the stresses of the job.*
>
> **A. Teacher:**   *The truth is that when I become frustrated, I blame everyone but myself. Now I will reflect on my thoughts and behavior.*
>
> **Dr. Foster:**   *"Your belief system, like your computer, doesn't judge or even question what you input; it merely accepts your thoughts as the truth" (Boe, 2005, para. 2).*

> Watch your thoughts, for they become words. Choose your words, for they become actions. Understand your actions, for they become habits. Study your habits, for they will become your character. Develop your character, for it becomes your destiny. (Anonymous. In Boe, 2005, para. 15)

Problem solving is the "outer game" that requires cognitive strategies; learners use affective strategies when we engage in the "inner game" of self-talk. Rebecca Oxford (1990) identified three kinds of affective strategies that teachers can use to regulate learner attitudes, motivation, and emotions for winning the "inner game" of life (p. 163):

- Use progressive relaxation and deep breathing exercises, classical music, and appropriate laughter to **reduce anxiety**.
- Make positive statements, take risks wisely, and administer self-rewards for **self-encouragement**.
- Listen to the body, complete a checklist, write a learning diary, and discuss feelings with peers to **monitor emotions**.

To Tell the Truth or Consequences

"There is always an inner game being played in your mind no matter what outer game you are playing. How aware you are of this game can make the difference between success and failure in the outer game" (Gallwey, "What is," para. 1). The question is, "Do teachers have game?"

According to French philosopher Paul Valéry, a game is enjoyable if entry is a conscious choice. "A game may be seen as a powerful expression of creative freedom and triumph over the burdensome determinism of things or social status, all within perfectly circumscribed limits" (Wikipedia). Read about a true **Game of Life** that played out in Erin Gruwell's classroom and inspired the book *The Freedom Writers Diary: How a Teacher and 150 Teens Used Writing to Change Themselves and the World Around Them* (1999).

"The First Entry" in Ms. Gruwell's Classroom: *Questioning the Game*

Where was the game played?	**Inside: Room 203:** Wilson High School in Long Beach, California **Outside:** School community and in a violent intercity neighborhood
Who were the opposing teams?	**Inside Room 203:** Ms. Gruwell, a 23-year-old English teacher, and nearly 150 kids who had been ignored or written off as "sure-to-drop-out" **Outside:** Distinguished scholars, teachers, administrators, gangs, families
Who were the coaches?	**Inside Room 203:** Erin Gruwell, whose namesake was Hank Aaron, a legendary baseball player who challenged the status quo **Outside:** Erin's father
What equipment did they use?	**Ms. Gruwell provided:** New books designated for advanced placement classes **School provided:** Hand-me-down textbooks riddled with graffiti
What were the rules?	**Honor code of mutual respect between teacher and students in Room 203:** • No right or wrong answers • All entries typed in the same font and written anonymously, with numbers rather than names to designate the authors • No sensationalizing of reality **Teachers and Department Head:** "You're making us look bad. . . . Things are based on seniority around here."
What was the goal?	**In Room 203:** Diary entries, tolerance, encouraging each other, college **In the school:** Test scores
Who won?	**In Room 203:** Ms. Gruwell and her students **Outside:** The school and community at large

The **reality** is that teachers have the potential to inspire learners to become resilient and win against inner interference. **To tell the truth**, teachers must stand up to outer interference, **or** the **consequences** for learners will be diminished performance in the **Game of Life** beyond the classroom.

A. Teacher: *It's difficult for me to remain hopeful about the future and resilient to the obstacles life puts in my path. Until the ability to solve problems and self-talk fully develops, how is a child or adolescent supposed to be resilient and cope?*

Dr. Foster: *Two of the important protective factors needed within the family, school, and community are at least one adult who cares deeply about the well-being of a child and high, articulated expectations and the purposeful support to meet those expectations (Krovetz, 1999). When these are not present in the family or community, the last hope for students is a supportive teacher.*

A. Teacher: *Oh, my! How is it possible for some children to grow to be caring adults if they don't find caring adults, high expectations, and support within the family, community, **or** the school?*

Dr. Foster: *This might also explain why some children grow up and value their coaches more than their teachers. If not found in the classroom, students may find these protective factors in athletic programs.*

A. Teacher: *Every student deserves to have a teacher who cares, sets high expectations, and provides the support to meet high expectations. You have inspired me to be a teacher who cares enough to repeat high expectations and use the coaching strategies I've learned to help my students meet those expectations.*

However, it concerns me that one year or one class may not be enough for some students. Is there anything I can do to help them remember that I will always care and believe in them when they are no longer in my classroom?

Dr. Foster: 🗁 **Supplement I: Inspirational Frames** *will help the students who need your inspiration to frame their future and remember that you care. Inspirational Frames are words set in an inexpensive frame or on a business card that students can carry with them. They contain a personalized message for each student. The inspirational quotations of famous coaches and teachers shared in this session may also be used on tests, bulletin boards, or challenging assignments for inspiration. (Select* **Supplements***, and then* **G–J** *at www.classroom managementblues.com for* **Supplement I***.)*

One of the greatest things you have in life is that no one has the authority to tell you what you want to be. You're the one who'll decide what you want to be. Respect yourself and respect the integrity of others as well. The greatest thing you have is your self-image, a positive opinion of yourself. You must never let anyone take it from you.

Jaime Escalante
(1930–)

Professor and teacher of mathematics who gained distinction for his work teaching poor minority students calculus from 1974–1991

Cinderella Has a Ball

Q   Why was Cinderella thrown off the basketball team?
A   She ran away from the ball.[a]

Q   Why is Cinderella bad at football?
A   Because she has a pumpkin as a coach.[b]

As a teacher, I always resented that the community placed a higher value on sports and coaches than on academics and teachers. Then I read this news report and watched this basketball game during March Madness in 2006.

George Mason University: A True Cinderella Story

George Mason University's miracle run has brought them to the Final Four. The lowest seed ever to make the Final Four (number 11, tied with the 1986 LSU Tigers), GMU's run has been anything but easy. After upsetting Michigan State, one of the most talented teams, they pulled another upset against Coach of the Year Roy Williams' North Carolina. They next won the battle of the "Mid-Majors" by defeating Wichita State, and advanced to the Final Four off a thrilling overtime upset against top-seeded Connecticut.[c]

I was intrigued at the mention of Cinderella. What did Cinderella have to do with basketball? Why would the lowest seed even show up to play the #1 seed at the big dance if they expected to lose? Could it be that everyone "wants the fairy tale," like Julia Roberts in the movie "Pretty Woman" (1990)?[d] Is that why we root for the underdog?

During this time, I began to research high expectations for this book. The connections between coaching, teaching, and repeating high expectations took root.

It's funny how the term "Cinderella" became popularized as a sports term by Bill Murray in the 1980 comedic hit movie *Caddyshack* in which he pretended to be the announcer in his own golf fantasy. He announced, "Cinderella story. Outta nowhere. A former greens keeper, now about to become the Masters champion." [e]

Complete this **Mad Lib** by substituting different words from the numbered word lists and read aloud to discover how surreal it must feel to be Cinderella and "have" the fairy tale.

At [1] _____ the [2] _____ inspired [3] _____ to overcome [4] _____ and [5] _____.

the ball	fairy godmother	Cinderella	evil step-sisters	find love
the game	coach	the team	obscurity	win the game
school	teacher	the class	low expectations	make an "A"

Adapted from:
[a] **Jokes4all.net** at http://jokes4all.net/jokes/cinderella/jokes.html
[b] **Top20fun.com** at http://www.top20fun.com/funny_jokes/78.html
[c] **The Miscellany News** at http://misc.vassar.edu/archives/2006/03/upset_madness_p.html
[d] **List of 400 Nominees** at http://www.afi.com/Docs/tvevents/pdf/quotes400.pdf
[e] **Wikipedia** at http://en.wikipedia.org/wiki/Cinderella_%28sports%29

Dr. Foster: *A coach uses a clipboard to show players the game plan; this clipboard illustrates the components and active ingredients of the* **High Expectations Prescription** *(see Figure 6.5 below). To become a self-actualized person, each student needs to belong, have a positive self-esteem, and develop cognitive skills. To meet these needs and encourage self-regulatory mechanisms, a teacher must repeat* **high expectations** *and use the verbal and nonverbal strategies of authenticity, community, resiliency, autonomy, and efficacy to inspire students to exceed expectations for learning and behavior.*

As all coaches know, sometimes saying the right thing at the right time can move people to surpass their own expectations, to reach deep down and make those extra efforts. Inspiration has to do with bringing out the *spirit*, the vital force, within us. Once that inner power, or self-motivation, is ignited, people push themselves to do their best. (Harmin, 1994, p. x)

R$_x$ 2 High Expectations

Figure 6.5

Maslow's Hierarchy of Needs	Self-Regulatory Mechanisms*	Active Ingredients affect, shape, influence, change, and inspire	
Self-Actualization	Self-Talk	Resiliency	Problem-Solving skills, a sense of purpose, social competence, and autonomy
Cognition	Self-Direction	Autonomy	Self-regulatory mechanisms*
Self-Esteem	Self-Efficacy	Efficacy	Cognitive appraisal of interpersonal and intrapersonal information sources
	Self-Concept	Authenticity	Trustworthiness and genuineness
Belonging	Self-Control	Community	Appreciation, belonging, and contribution

A. Teacher: *I want to be a coach so that everyone wins in my classroom, but where do I begin? What is the game plan, coach?*

Dr. Foster: *Coaching "is the art of creating an environment, through conversation and a way of being, that facilitates the process" by which you can move toward the desired outcomes (Gallwey, 1999, para.1). As your coach, it is time to put you in the game. I will provide support and inspiration as you move toward your goal to be a coach and win the **High Expectations Strategy Game** in your classroom.*

*The ▭ **Supplement J: High Expectations Strategy Game** contains the directions and resources you need to play the game. The goal is to **score** points when you fully exercise each practice and inspire students to become more successful in the classroom and beyond. The more you **practice** or play the game, the more successful you will be as a high-expectations coach. (Select the **Supplements** page at www.classroommanagementblues.com, then **G–J** for **Supplement J**.)*

*My game plan is to empower you to be a problem solver and develop your own **game plan**. It starts with this formula or winning strategy inspired by W. Timothy Gallwey:* Performance (**P**) = potential (**p**) – interference (**i**)

*You **are** the coach in your classroom! You know the performance "**P**" you want to achieve and have an **awareness** of the obstacles "**i**" that stand in the way. With the active ingredients of the **High Expectations Prescription** and its supplements, you have the potential "**p**" to succeed! **Trust** in your ability. To win (achieve student outcomes), repeat the teacher strategies (best practices). (See Table 6.9.)*

Table 6.9

Score High Expectations		
Teacher Strategies	**Most Active Ingredients**	**Student Outcomes**
Set Goals	**Efficacy**	Be a goal setter.
Model		Be a role model.
Monitor	**Authenticity**	Be equitable.
Communicate		Be respectful.
Build Trust	**Community**	Be trustworthy.
Inspire Teamwork		Be a team player.
Empower	**Autonomy**	Be a decision maker.
Self-Regulate		Be disciplined.
Self-Talk	**Resiliency**	Be affirming.
Problem Solve		Be a problem solver.

A. Teacher: *Wow! I would like to have a class of disciplined problem solvers, but all these **outcomes** will be difficult for my students to achieve.*

Dr. Foster: *That's why the student outcomes are considered **high** expectations. They **are** challenging. Unless you provide sufficient opportunities and support, your students might not attempt to achieve them.*

A. Teacher: *I remember from the last session that Vygotsky's **Zone of Proximal Development** is the amount of learning possible when a teacher provides appropriate instructional conditions and works with learners on difficult tasks they could not do on their own.*

Dr. Foster: *Carefully read the information about the supplements before you use them to enhance the effectiveness of the **High Expectations Prescription**. As you discover more information, be aware that other supplements and prescriptions with different active ingredients will blend with this prescription to inspire **EACH** student to meet and exceed expectations for learning and behavior.*

A. Teacher: *You have given me strategies that I believe will help my students achieve high expectations, but I'm still somewhat unclear about how to get started.*

Dr. Foster: *Though you may begin to implement the supplements in any order, refer to this **Implementation Checklist** for my recommendations.*

R$_x$ 2 Implementation Checklist

Select the *Supplements* page at
www.classroommanagementblues.com
to obtain detailed explanations,
step-by-step instructions, and
blackline masters for *Supplements G–J*.

📁 **Supplement G—About Me Survey**
Weave survey information in lessons to motivate students.

📁 **Supplement H—Homework Contract**
Use at the beginning of the year, or at the beginning
of a grading period.

📁 **Supplement I—Inspiration Frames**
Provide personalized messages to students who need
continued support and inspiration to achieve goals
in school and in life.

📁 **Supplement J—High Expectations Strategy Game**
Increase usage of the teacher strategies and best practices.

Concluding Remarks

The **High Expectations Prescription** alone will not prevent or cure the ***Classroom Management Blues***, but the potential increases when you repeat the strategies for the **High Expectations** and **Active Engagement Prescriptions**. In the next session, learn how use the **Appropriate Assessments Prescription** to help inspire students to be more successful in the classroom and reduce assessment's *interference* on teaching and student learning.

Dr. Foster: *Look at the* **High Expectations Prescription** *and note the caution.*

Repeat the prescription as directed, beginning with small doses to inspire performance. With consistency, you will achieve the desired effects of more trust and respect, increased learning, and improved behavior.

BANDURA'S PHARMACY
222 Expectations Expressway   Date Filled: **First Day in the Classroom**
Any Town, USA   Discard After: **Retirement**

 0002   Prescription for **HIGH EXPECTATIONS**

Patient's Name: **A. Teacher**

Patient's Address: **102 Attitude Avenue — Any Town, USA**

Repeat **HIGH EXPECTATIONS** daily to inspire ALL students to achieve academic and personal goals.

Doctor: *Barbara G. Foster*

Active Ingredients
- **Efficacy**
- **Authenticity**
- **Community**
- **Autonomy**
- **Resiliency**

SIDE EFFECTS: More trust and respect, increased learning, and improved behavior

CAUTION: May be contagious   **Unlimited Refills**

Resources—Access More Information

Learn more about self-talk, communicating trust, empowerment, fostering self-discipline, goal setting, monitoring bias, problem solving, team building, trust building, and self-efficacy on the ***Classroom Management Blues*** website. Choose **Resources**, then **Expectations** at *www.classroommanagementblues.com* for a list of books, articles, websites, and other resources.

Praxis Journal—Take Steps toward a Cure

Write responses to these prompts and questions before the next session:

- **Review the *High Expectations Prescription* and reflect on what you have learned.** How do high expectations affect student learning?
- **Based on what you have learned in this session, set a goal and develop a plan.** How do you plan to achieve your goal and solve one or more related problems?
- **Implement and evaluate your plan.** How did your actions affect you as a teacher and your students as learners?
- **Reflect on future goals and actions.** What will you do in the future?

STEP TWO: **TAKE PRESCRIPTIONS**

POPHAM'S PHARMACY

333 Success Street
Any Town, USA

Date Filled: First Day in the Classroom
Discard After: Retirement

 0003

Prescription for **APPROPRIATE ASSESSMENTS**

Patient's Name: **A. Teacher**

Patient's Address: **103 Practice Parkway — Any Town, USA**

Use **APPROPRIATE ASSESSMENTS** *as needed*
to foster student learning.

Doctor: *Barbara G. Foster*

Active Ingredients
- **Expectancy**
- **Attribution**
- **Practice**
- **Evaluation**
- **Reflection**

SIDE EFFECTS: More trust and respect, increased learning,
and improved behavior

CAUTION: May reduce test anxiety   **Unlimited Refills**

Session 7

Photos.com

Session 7

Use Appropriate Assessments

Everything that can be counted does not necessarily count;
everything that counts cannot necessarily be counted.

Albert Einstein (1879–1955)

When teachers use appropriate assessments to create and maintain a non-threatening learning environment, students have less test anxiety and are more inclined to stay on task and believe they can succeed at high levels. This becomes a self-fulfilling prophesy. As Alexandre Dumas says, "Nothing succeeds like success." With the **Appropriate Assessments Prescription**, you too can motivate your students to reach their academic potential.

> **test** [tĕst] *n.*
>
> A procedure or basis for critical evaluation; a means of determining the presence, quality, or truth of something
>
> *The American Heritage Dictionary of the English Language*

A. Teacher: *I have applied **Active Engagement** and repeated **High Expectations**, but I still have students who do not do their work. I am ready to learn how assessments can motivate my students to stay on task and do their assignments.*

Dr. Foster: *Look at the **Appropriate Assessments Prescription** (on the opposite page). What can you tell me about this prescription?*

A. Teacher: *The active ingredients are expectancy, attribution, practice, evaluation, and reflection. If I use the prescription as needed, I will foster student learning and may reduce test anxiety. I hope this is possible!*

Dr. Foster: *It is possible! Let me share a story about a young boy. Tell me if you think he succeeded in school and in life.*

This boy did not learn to talk until he was three. People initially considered him mentally retarded. He struggled with dysgraphia, dyslexia, and word-finding problems. His teachers said he was slow, lazy, and questioned their authority.

A. Teacher: *I do not think he succeeded in school, but he might have been a successful adult. Who is he?*

Dr. Foster: *His name is synonymous with genius—Albert Einstein.*

You're No Einstein

As far as the laws of mathematics refer to reality,
they are not certain, and as far as they are certain,
they do not refer to reality.

Albert Einstein

Albert Einstein was a poor student, but "excelled in math and science, even though he skipped classes and had to cram for exams." He taught himself geometry at the age of 12, and as a teenager, he developed a "profound mistrust for authority." He questioned his teachers, the established mathematical rules of geometry, and the scientific laws of physics. At 15, he dropped out of school.

Education is what remains after
one has forgotten what one has learned in school.

Albert Einstein

He wrote his first 'science paper' at age 16. That same year, he took an entrance exam for the Swiss Federal Institute of Technology—but failed the language and history sections. Einstein was advised to enroll in a secondary school that encouraged his free thinking. After graduation, he qualified to enter the Federal Institute in Zurich.

I think and think for months and years. Ninety-nine times,
the conclusion is false. The hundredth time I am right.

Albert Einstein

Einstein "enthusiastically enrolled in a math and physics program but found lectures and tests intolerable." With the help of a friend, he "passed the final examination and graduated, but the ordeal was so loathsome that Einstein lost interest in science for an entire year." At the age of 26, he got his PhD and published four ground-breaking articles in physics.

It is a miracle that curiosity survives formal education.

Albert Einstein

As a child, *even Einstein was no Einstein.* Schools valued tests and lectures over stirring curiosity or encouraging creative and critical thinking. The *reality* is that not much has changed in schools over the 100 years since Einstein was in school. The *reality* is that *potential* Einsteins have a chance to succeed in schools and beyond if educators learn to use grades and tests appropriately.

Adapted from Brainyquote, Photo, and American Museum of Natural History—see page 384

A. Teacher: *You mentioned the formula* **Performance** (P) = **potential** (p) - **interference** (i) *in our last session (Gallwey, 1999). Albert Einstein had potential, but lectures and tests interfered with his performance in school.*

Dr. Foster: *You understand the* **importance** *of the formula* P = p - i *to enhance students' performance.*

A. Teacher: *Are there other formulas for success?*

Dr. Foster: *You will learn about other formulas as we discuss the active ingredients of the* **Appropriate Assessments Prescription***. Each has the potential to enhance* **performance** *and reduce the interference created by grades and inappropriate assessments.*

A. Teacher: *I hope I will be able to understand the formulas.*

Dr. Foster: *You have demonstrated that you have the potential to understand. It is my responsibility to make the formulas and active ingredients (expectancy, attribution, practice, evaluation, and reflection) comprehensible.*

Throughout this session, there will be quotations from Albert Einstein and other scientists to inspire you to use assessments appropriately.

> *Most of the fundamental ideas of science are essentially simple, and may, as a rule, be expressed in a language comprehensible to everyone.*
> **Albert Einstein**

Before we discuss the **Appropriate Assessments Prescription***, let us make sure we use the same definitions for and understand the relationships among important assessment terms.*

Figure 7.1

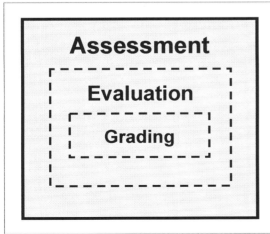

Assessment includes the entire process of grading and evaluation (Pangaro & McGaghie, 2005). Teachers assess how students perform through direct observation and data collection **all the time**.

Evaluation is a **judgment** of the quality and worth of assessment results (Butler, 2001).

Grading means letters, labels, or numbers for the **performance level** achieved (A, B, C; Honors, Pass, Fail; 96%, 86%, 76%) (Pangaro & McGaghie, 2005).

Dr. Foster: *Diagnostic, formative, and summative assessments are three kinds of assessments that should be used to enhance student learning.*

Table 7.1

Kinds of Assessments
Before and during learning experiences, **diagnostic assessments** "provide information to assist teacher planning and guide differentiated instruction" (McTighe & O'Connor, 2005, para. 3). These *pre-assessments* are ungraded and can "check students' prior knowledge and skill levels, identify student misconceptions, profile student interests, and reveal learning-style preferences" (para. 3).
During learning experiences, **formative assessments** help teachers *form* an understanding of what students know and can do. Such an assessment "can be done by teachers as frequently as time will allow, but . . . should also be done formally at specified times, for instance, halfway through an experience" (Pangaro & McGaghie, 2005, p. 143).
After learning experiences, **summative assessments** *sum* up a student's level of performance. This assessment "often includes a *grade* as well as narrative description of performance and recommendations for improvement" (p. 143).

A. Teacher: *These terms are clearer, but I still have questions about grading.*

Dr. Foster: *In this session, you will learn about grading. The challenge "is to craft and use evaluation and grading methods that truly are tools for student improvement not weapons that intimidate" (p. 142) or interfere with student performance in school.*

Each active ingredient in the **Appropriate Assessments Prescription** has the **potential** to help teachers reduce the **interference** created by inappropriate assessment and grading practices. These practices influence whether a student expects to succeed at a task.

Active Ingredient	 Expectancy

The first active ingredient in the **Appropriate Assessments Prescription** is expectancy—*one* factor in Victor Vroom's theory that relates to motivation. Expectancy is the perceived level of confidence at which a student expects to be successful at a task (Sprick, Garrison, & Howard, 1998; Vroom, 2009, para. 3).

A. Teacher: *Expectancy sounds like self-efficacy.*

Dr. Foster: *Yes. "People act on their beliefs about what they can do . . . [and] the likely outcomes of performance. The motivating influence of outcome expectancies is thus partly governed by self-beliefs of efficacy" (Bandura, 1994, para. 19).*

Dr. Foster: *Think about it this way. Self-efficacy is the general belief about one's ability to achieve goals. Expectancy is the belief about one's ability to be successful on a specific task.*

A. Teacher: *So a student might believe he or she can be successful in math class, but not expect to be successful on a long division assignment.*

Dr. Foster: *Right. Even if students expect to be successful on a task, they still might not be motivated to do it. Another factor in Dr. Vroom's expectancy theory that influences motivation is valence, or value.*

*"Valence refers to the emotional orientations people hold with respect to outcomes [rewards]" (Vroom, para. 3). Dr. Julian B. Rotter calls this desirability of an outcome "reinforcement value." He asserts that **Behavior Potential** (BP), **Expectancy** (E), and **Reinforcement Value** (RV) combine in a predictive formula for behavior (Mearns, 2009).*

$$BP = f(E \ \& \ RV)$$

A. Teacher: *Another formula! Let me see if I can explain this one.*

"Behavior potential is a function of expectancy and reinforcement value. . . . In other words, the likelihood of a person exhibiting a particular behavior is a function of the probability that that behavior will lead to a given outcome and the desirability of that outcome. If expectancy and reinforcement value are both high, then behavior potential will be high. If either expectancy or reinforcement value is low, then behavior potential will be low" (Mearns, 2009, para. 17).

Dr. Foster: *Well done. If you want students to reach their potential, you must first get them to do something. Then keep them on task.*

> Isaac Newton used three laws to explain the way objects move. . . . The First Law states that an object that is not being pushed or pulled by some force will stay still, or will keep moving in a straight line at a steady speed. (Bellis, 2012, para. 5)

A. Teacher: *So we motivate students if we show them something desirable, explain how they can get it, and then support them to get there ("Expectancy," n.d., para. 5).*

This sounds good in theory, but I am not sure how to do it.

Dr. Foster: *I will provide the support you need! Read "Zero In on Motivation" for some examples that show how expectancy and value can motivate students to achieve academic and personal goals and expectations.*

Zero In on Motivation

Why is it that *nothing* seems to motivate some students? In *CHAMPs: A Proactive and Positive Approach to Classroom Management for Grades K–9*, Sprick, Garrison, and Howard (1998) help teachers **zero in on** how expectancy and value factor into motivation. They explain that "a person's level of motivation on any given task is a function of both how much the person wants the rewards that accompany success *and* how much he or she expects to be successful" (p. 199). The value factor may include rewards like grades, money, stickers, awards, pride, and enjoyment.

In Practice

Dr. Sprick & Associates

> ## Expectancy multiplied by value equals motivation

"The key implication of the theory is that if the rate for either one of the factors— **expectancy or value**—is zero, no matter what the rate of the other factor is, the motivation will be zero" (p. 200). The examples below show the percentage of motivation for different expectancy and value ratings on a scale from 0 to 10.

Expectancy to succeed on a test	10	X	**Value** of a grade of A	10	=	**100% Motivation**
Expectancy to succeed on a test	0	X	**Value** of a grade of A	10	=	**0% Motivation**
Expectancy to succeed on an assignment	8	X	**Value** of a sticker	0	=	**0% Motivation**
Expectancy to succeed on an assignment	3	X	**Value** of a sticker	4	=	**12% Motivation**
Expectancy to pass math classes	0	X	**Value** of graduating	10	=	**0% Motivation**
Expectancy to pass math classes	7	X	**Value** of graduating	9	=	**63% Motivation**

Sprick, Garrison, and Howard (1998) recommend that when a student is unmotivated, the teacher should **zero in on** whether the "lack of motivation stems from a lack of value, a lack of expectancy, or a lack of both" (p. 200). Teachers may modify the task, reward, or both to motivate students.

Dr. Foster: *Teachers choose learning experiences aligned with the standards-based content goals and objectives established in the curriculum and determine the assessment criteria, grades, and rewards associated with what students need to know and do. This decision-making may or may not consider how these decisions affect a student's motivation to start, persevere, and succeed.*

A. Teacher: *I always thought a good grade would motivate students. Now I need to know how to make decisions that increase the expectancy of my students to get a good grade. This would place the responsibility for learning and earning a grade in the students' locus of control.*

In *A Different Kind of Classroom: Teaching with Dimensions of Learning,* Robert Marzano (1992) describes three factors that influence student motivation to learn and the expectancy for success on assessments. These factors are task clarity, relevance, and potential for success.

How can task clarity and relevance increase students' expectancy for success? Students are more likely to be motivated to learn if they understand what they are expected to learn, know how they will be evaluated, and think the learning goals and assessments are relevant, or meaningful. Teachers can increase expectancy for success if they use rubrics and make connections to prior learning and the real world.

A. Teacher: *From what I learned in the preceding session, I can connect my lessons and assessments to the real world when I use WebQuests and inquiry-based learning. I can also use rubrics and make connections to prior learning, but I need to learn how to use these strategies effectively.*

Dr. Foster: *We can always learn to be more effective. I will offer some tips, but remember, many other helpful strategies and resources are available.*

At the beginning of this session, we talked about **diagnostic assessments**. *Two examples are student interest and learning-style preference surveys (see pages 64, 92).*

A. Teacher: *I remember how an awareness of learning styles and student interests would make the activities I plan relevant and increase expectancy for success.*

Dr. Foster: *"For students to truly learn material and content, it must be meaningful to them emotionally" ("Brain research," 2009, para. 16).*

Diagnostic assessments *or pre-assessments can also check students' skill levels and prior knowledge. These assessments are "as important to teaching as a physical exam is to prescribing an appropriate medical regimen" (McTighe & O'Conner, 2005, para. 8)*

A. Teacher: *I admit I do not use pretests as much as I should, but I do check prior knowledge in other ways. I could use some ideas to be more effective.*

It is important for teachers to know whether students understand the main concepts or have mastered some of the skills before beginning a unit of study. Some students might lack prerequisite skills or have misconceptions about essential concepts.

> Armed with this diagnostic information, A teacher gains greater insight into *what to teach*, by knowing what skill gaps to address or by skipping material mastered earlier; into *how to teach*, by using grouping options and initiating activities based on preferred learning styles and interests; and into *how to connect* the content to students' interests and talents. (McTighe & O'Conner, 2005, para. 8)

Dr. Foster: *Before we talk about strategies, I want to clarify the context in which you assess and integrate prior knowledge.*

 What is your understanding about how and when teachers should assess and integrate prior learning?

A. Teacher: *I know from my experiences as a student in K–12 schools and teacher preparation classes that teachers should assess skill levels and prior knowledge through pretests before they plan instruction and learning activities. It is also my understanding that teachers should review learning from previous lessons at the beginning of each lesson by asking questions.*

Isn't that right?

Dr. Foster: *It is not a question of right and wrong; it is a question of what is appropriate and effective. Teachers should assess skill levels and prior knowledge of each student before they plan instruction and learning activities, but diagnostic assessments are also appropriate throughout a lesson.*

It is appropriate for teachers to review learning from previous lessons, but asking questions of a few students only provides assessment information about the few students answering.

Research findings into how the brain processes information offer new insights into how to ready learners' minds to accept and retain new information (Janac, Kipperman, & Linder, 1997; Sousa, 2006). The focus should be on how to get students to accept and retain accurate information.

> Avoid asking [questions] at the beginning of the lesson. . . . If it is a new topic, the assumption is that most students do not know it. However, there are always some students ready to take a guess—no matter how unrelated. Because this is the time of greatest retention, almost anything that is said, including incorrect information, is likely to be remembered. Give the information and examples yourself to ensure that they are correct. (Sousa, 2006, p. 122)

A. Teacher: *I know little about how the brain processes information and want to know more.*

Dr. Foster: *Because of the advances in neuroscience, we know more. In **How the Brain Learns**, David A. Sousa provides a good explanation of this process. Read about this process in "Does It Make Sense?"*

Does It Make Sense?

In *How the Brain Learns* (2006), Dr. David A. Sousa offers insights into how working memory *makes sense* of what information is stored in short-term or working memory for immediate use and long-term memory for future use. "We tend to remember the best and worst things that happen to us" (pp. 48–49).

What is the likelihood that information in working memory is stored in long-term memory?
Experiences with survival value are **stored quickly**.
Strong emotional experiences have a **high** likelihood of permanent storage.
Past experiences that make sense *and* have meaning have a **very high** likelihood of being stored.
Past experiences that *either* make sense **or** have meaning have **some** likelihood to be stored.
Past experiences that *neither* make sense **nor** have meaning have an **extremely low** likelihood of being stored.

In a "Practitioner's Corner," Dr. Sousa details how closure can enhance sense and meaning. "**Closure** describes the covert process whereby the learner's *working memory* summarizes for itself its perception of what has been learned. It is during closure that a student often finishes the rehearsal process and attaches sense and meaning to the new learning, thereby increasing the probability that it will be retained in *long-term storage*" (p. 69).

Closure may occur at different times in a lesson, and it increases retention of learning because the students do most of the work.

- At the beginning of a lesson: "Think of the two causes of the Civil War we talked about yesterday and be prepared to discuss them."
- During the lesson when the teacher moves from one sublearning to the next (*procedural closure*): "Think of the first two causes of the Civil War and share them with your partner before we learn the third cause."
- At the end (*terminal closure*): "I'm going to give you about two minutes to think of the three causes of the Civil War that we learned today. Be ready to discuss them briefly" (p. 69).

Review is different from closure as the teacher does most of the work. The teacher tells the students the three causes of the Civil War learned in the lesson.

Does it make sense that *closure is better than review*? When students use quiet time to reprocess what students have learned during a lesson, the new learning becomes permanent (pp. 278, 285).

A. Teacher: *It makes sense that one teaching strategy might be appropriate in one situation and not in others.*

Dr. Foster: *With this understanding, you are ready for assessment strategies that can help your students activate prior learning and increase their expectancy for success. (Select **Resources** at www.classroommanagementblues.com, then **Assessments** and **Prior Knowledge** for books, articles, and other resources.)*

    📁 **Supplement K: Unit and Lesson Design** *will help you transfer what you have learned about relevance, prior knowledge, review, and closure to the design of effective units and lessons. (Select the **Supplements** page at www.classroommanagementblues.com, and then locate **K–P** for **Supplement K**.)*

Transfer also "helps students make connections between what they already know and the new learning" (Sousa, 2006, p. 150). Here are examples from different books, articles, and websites that may be appropriate to activate students' prior knowledge and facilitate new learning (positive transfer).

- **Nongraded true-false diagnostic quiz**—Use to discover potential misconceptions for the targeted learning. "In the future, the growing availability of portable, electronic student-response systems will enable educators to obtain this information instantaneously" (McTighe & O'Conner, 2005, para. 19).

- **K-W-L technique**—Post a chart and ask students what they already know (K) and, through discussion, establish what they want (W) to learn. After the activity, discuss and summarize what they have learned (L). "Knowledge-activation routines like this help develop students' metacognitive abilities while providing relevant knowledge connections for specific units of study" (Shepard, 2005, para. 14). Students may use a graphic organizer with this technique.

- **Analogy or storytelling**—"If the present lesson has some similarity to something the learner knows, describe the similarity before presenting new information. . . . Tell a story about a relevant experience that will link to the current subject. Make sure to draw specific parallels during and after the story" (Janac, Kipperman & Linder, 1997, para. 6).

- **Walk around survey**—Give students a topic to study and ask them to move around the room, converse with other students, and record responses. "During these conversations, students will share what they know of the topic and discover what others have learned" (Lipton & Wellman, 1998, para. 2).

- **Interviews**—"In a think-pair-share format, students interview their partners to determine their knowledge levels" (Sousa, 2006, p. 150).

A. Teacher: *From what I have learned, when teachers introduce a **new concept**, walk around survey and interviews are inappropriate.*

Dr. Foster: *Your thinking is on target. If students learn inaccurate information about a new concept, the learning may become permanent. It is important that the information is accurate.*

Dr. Foster: *To **review**, you have learned how relevance influences expectancy for success. Now we will address task clarity. Students are more likely to be motivated to learn if they understand the task and evaluative criteria for the task.*

To help you make sense of task clarity I will use Dr. Richard Stiggins' target metaphor to describe achievement targets. He says, "Achievement targets define academic success—what we want students to know and be able to do. Visualize a target with its concentric circles and a bull's eye in the middle. The center circle defines the highest level of performance students can achieve. . . . Each consecutive outside ring on the target defines a level of performance further from the highest level" (2005, pp. 33–34).

A. Teacher: *It does make it easier to understand when I visualize a target. I can see how this would help students.*

How do achievement targets compare with objectives and outcomes?

Dr. Foster: *The terms may be confusing. Maybe this will help.*

Definitions for goals, achievement targets, standards, objectives, and outcomes vary from educator to educator. However, each term expresses one or more of the following cognitive, psychomotor, and/or affective **expectations**:

- what learners need to *know* and *understand*;

- *patterns of reasoning, performance skills, and dispositions* learners need to develop; and/or

- *products* learners need to create (Stiggins, 2005, p. 43).

Placed on a target (see Figure 7.2), the terms would be aligned along a continuum from general (vague) goals on the outside ring to specific (clear) achievement targets in the center and from complex goals that are difficult to assess to achievement targets that are easier to assess. Though not visible, the bull's eye in this target represents concentric circles or levels of performance identified by Richard Stiggins for achievement targets and assessment tasks.

Figure 7.2

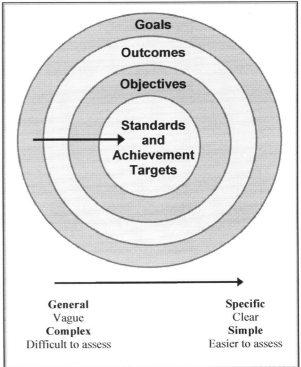

General	Specific
Vague	Clear
Complex	**Simple**
Difficult to assess	Easier to assess

Dr. Foster: *Here is an example from the Kentucky Department of Education for Grade 3 mathematics (see Figure 7.3). The terms may differ for your state or district— notice the movement from general to specific.*

 Think about how many lessons it would take for students to be successful at each level of performance.

Figure 7.3

Kentucky Department of Education: 3rd Grade—Mathematics

Learning Goals

Students are able to use basic communication and mathematics skills for purposes and situations they will encounter throughout their lives.

Students shall develop their abilities to apply core concepts and principles from mathematics to what they encounter throughout their lives.

Academic Expectation

Students use mathematical ideas and procedures to communicate, reason, and solve problems.

Program of Studies: Enduring Understanding (Outcome)

Students will understand that the collection, organization, interpretation, and display of data can answer questions.

Program of Studies: Skills and Concepts (Outcomes)

Students will display, read, and compare data on student-invented graphs.

Students will display, read, and compare data on a pictograph and bar graph.

Common Core State Standard—Represent and Interpret Data (Objectives) (Measurement and Data—Grade 3)

Students will draw a scaled picture graph and a scaled bar graph to represent a data set with several categories.

Students will solve one- and two-step "how many more" and "how many less" problems and use information presented in scaled bar graphs.

Knowledge Targets	Reasoning Targets	Product Targets
I can explain the scale of a graph with a scale greater than one. I can identify the scale of a graph with a scale greater than one.	I can analyze a graph with a scale greater than one. I can choose a proper scale for a bar graph or picture graph. I can interpret a bar/picture graph to solve one- or two-step problems that ask "how many more" and "how many less."	I can create a scaled picture graph to show data. I can create a scaled bar graph to show data.

From Kentucky Department of Education, *Program of Studies with Common Core Standards—* http://bit.ly/programstudiescommoncore and *3rd Grade–Mathematics: Kentucky Core Academic Standards with Targets*—http://bit.ly/KCASGR3MathTargets

A. Teacher: *Although it would take years for students to achieve a goal, the achievement targets would take one or two lessons and would be easier to measure. With this understanding, I am confident I can make sense of the curriculum in my district.*

*With some practice, I could identify clear achievement targets for what I want them to know and understand and the skills and dispositions my students need to develop. As far as the products, I already use the products listed on the **Activity Planning Form** you provided in **Supplement F**. (Select **Supplements** at www.classroom managementblues.com, then **A–F** to find **Supplement F**.)*

I know about synthesis, and analytical and evaluative reasoning, and I want to learn more about achievement targets for other patterns of reasoning.

> Specify clear expectations in your classroom. Do so in writing and publish them for all to see. Eliminate the mystery surrounding the meaning of success in your classroom by letting your students see your vision. If they can see it, they can hit it. But if they cannot see it, their challenge turns into pin the tail on the donkey —blindfolded. (Stiggins, 2005, p. 61)

Dr. Foster: *Books, articles, and websites by Dr. Stiggins and others will help you meet your achievement target. (Select the **Resources** page at www.classroommanage mentblues.com, and then **Assessments**.)*

 The last element of task clarity that promotes expectancy for success is the use of rubrics. Do you have any concerns?

A. Teacher: *Rubrics consume a lot of time.*

Dr. Foster: *Rubrics take time, but so does reteaching what students do not learn and retain. Again, many resources are available to help reduce the time it takes to develop rubrics, but you need to be sure that the rubrics you develop or choose are appropriate for the task or performance.*

Teachers must **match** the kind of assessment with the achievement target it intends to measure (Stiggins, 2005). Even if a rubric is appropriate to assess or evaluate the achievement target, it could have a negative effect on the learning process.

Teachers should not "assume that any collection of evaluative criteria automatically becomes a first-rate rubric" (Popham, 2008, p. 80). According to Stiggins (2005), good rubrics provide "important content (what counts) with sharp clarity (everyone understands) in terms that are practical (easy to use) and that are fair (valid and can be reliably judged)" (p. 157).

> [An] eleven-year-old had a science assignment to complete as homework. Her parent, attempting to help, offered several suggestions for enhancing the project. The child's response to each suggestion was: "No, that's not on the rubric. Here's the rubric. . . . This is **all** we're supposed to do." (Chapman & Inman, 2009, p. 198)

Dr. Foster: *Here are blocks of information on which you can build your* knowledge (see Table 7.2).

Table 7.2

Rubrics are appropriate for formative and summative assessments. They:

- Require clarification of criteria and correct language to express performance expectations
- Give explicit expectations and informative feedback to students
- Generate identical artifacts and restrict problem solving, decision making, and creativity
- Motivate students to reach the specified standards, although some may feel they need to finish the assignment strictly to the rubric rather than taking the initiative to explore their learning
- Give students more control of their learning and the opportunity to succeed at some level, although some students may feel overwhelmed if the criteria are too complex

When all students do the same task and the criteria are similar, consider a *holistic* rubric —a **general rubric** for quick judgments. The feedback for this type of rubric may not be specific enough.	When students do not do the same task, consider a **task-specific rubric**—an analytical rubric. Although it is more reliable than a general one, a task-specific rubric is both time consuming and difficult to construct for unique tasks.

To get a quick, total impression of the task using one level of performance across multiple criteria, consider a **holistic rubric**. It is:
 	
- More difficult as the number of criteria increases
- Not very useful to plan instruction
- Possibly lacking in specific criteria
 	
Judgments may be:
 	
- Satisfactory
  Unsatisfactory
  Not attempted
- Check-plus
  Check
  No check
	To assess complex skills, reasoning, or products with many criteria, consider an **analytical rubric**. Its criteria (essential features) are broken down into levels of performance (descriptors) and assessed separately. This type:
	
	- Provides meaningful and specific feedback along several dimensions to guide instruction and share strengths and weaknesses
	- Provides more consistent scoring across students and grades, but is less consistent among different assessors
	- Helps students better understand quality work, but is more difficult to construct
	- Is time consuming, but better for weighting grades

From "Advantages of Rubrics," 2009; "Basics of Rubrics," 2007; Chapman & Inman, 2009; Leavell, n.d.; and Mueller, 2008

A. Teacher: *Am I supposed to use a rubric for every task and achievement target?*

Dr. Foster: *This RUBRIC will help answer your question.*

Table 7.3

Tiered Instruction and Assessment Task Level RUBRIC					
Qualities	**Level I**	**Level II**	**Level III**	**Level IV**	**Level V**
STANDARDS— TARGETS ASSESSED	One	One	Two or more	Three or more may be interdisciplinary	
DEGREE OF PROBLEM SOLVING AND SOLUTION PATHWAYS	None required		Routine; Requires direct application of strategies; One or more solution pathways	Non-routine; Requires synthesis of multiple strategies; More than one solution pathways	Non-routine; Requires solution of multiple problems with many possible pathways
DEGREE OF COMPLEXITY	Simple calculation or definition	Multiple calculations or processes	Connects concept and process	Connects multiple concepts and processes	
CONTEXT	No context	Minimal superficial	Academic context	Thematic academic context	Thematic real-world context
NATURE OF RESPONSE	Selected response; Brief constructed response		Constructed response	Constructed response	
COMMUNICATION	None		Explanation; "Show your work"	Requires explanation, justification, and representation	
EVALUATIVE CRITERIA	Answer key (Right or wrong)	Answer key— partial credit	Answer key with a narrow range of responses	One or more rubrics	Multiple rubrics

From Analytic Matrix (2010) and Mathematics RUBRIC (2008) on the *CurrTech Integrations*
at http://www.currtechintegrations.com/tieredinstruction_rubric.php

According to Joseph L. Mills, Jr. (2008), assessment tasks range from **Level I** at a minimum level of cognitive demand to **Level V**, which engage students in complex thinking and involve reasoning and problem solving. He recommends that teachers determine the assessment level of a task, then increase or reduce one or more qualities to differentiate instruction; an assessment at **Level II** could be "bumped up" to **Level III** by adding a question for students to explain something.

An assessment at the lowest level of Bloom's Taxonomy (Knowledge) would be at **Level I**. **Level III, IV,** and **V** assessments require the upper levels of Bloom's Taxonomy. Each level is important, but teachers should strive to move students from lower levels at the beginning of a unit of study to the higher levels of thinking and assessment by the end the unit. (Read "Level with Me" to learn more about how to level tasks.)

Level with Me

Joseph L. Mills, Jr., a mathematics assessment consultant, developed the *Tiered Instruction and Assessment Task Level RUBRIC* to help teachers engage students and improve performance. Instruction should match performance levels. See how to **level tasks** for this **Grade 3** standard—collect, organize, and display real-life data and construct tables, bar graphs with several intervals, and pictographs with symbols.

In Practice
Joseph Mills Jr.

Level Tasks (Achievement Targets)	
I	- Given data and a fully labeled graph, I will plot the data.
II	- I will construct an appropriate scale and plot the data given.
III	- Given a table with data, I will create a bar graph with the appropriate scale and labels. - I will provide a written explanation of my graph, scale, and labels.
IV	- I will collect and record my own data. - I will create a bar graph with the appropriate scale and labels. - I will interpret the data and make an appropriate projection (written response).
V	The principal at Jarrettsville Elementary School asked students to make games for a May Day celebration: - I will collect, organize, and display data that shows student interest in a game. - I will prove the game is challenging by collecting, organizing, and displaying supportive data and writing conclusions in a letter to my teacher. - During the celebration, I will collect data to see if the game is challenging and compare the data with previous data. Then I will display results and conclusions.

Look at this Level IV example and test your ability to level tasks . . .

- As you spin the spinner 30 times and record your data.
- Use the data you have collected to construct a bar graph.
- Write two conclusions about the spinner from the bar graph you have constructed.

Level with me. Based on the ©*Tiered Instruction and Assessment Task Level RUBRIC (see Table 7.3)*, why is the example above at Level IV? Most of the qualities are at Level IV. **Benchmarks:** *Three or more* (collect, organize, and display real-life data and construct a bar graph) **Problem Solving:** *Multiple strategies* (interpret, predict). **Complexity:** *Multiple concepts and processes* **Solutions:** *Multiple solutions.* **Communication:** Written response **Evaluative Criteria:** *One or more rubrics*

For Level I, II, and III examples, visit the *CurrTech Integrations* website at http://www.currtech integrations.com/tieredinstruction_grade3.php.

Dr. Foster: *For terminal closure, what have you learned about task clarity?*

A. Teacher: *I have learned that to increase my students' expectancy for success, evaluative criteria for the task must be clear. There are many ways to achieve this purpose and set the stage for new learning, but two are to provide opportunities for students to recall prior knowledge and to use rubrics to articulate assessment criteria.*

Why did we spend so much time and energy on expectancy?

Dr. Foster: *The formula for **motivation** is expectancy times value, and the self-beliefs of efficacy govern the motivating influence of outcome expectancies (see pages 130–133). Whether a student expects to succeed becomes a self-fulfilling prophesy.*

A. Teacher: *I understand. Everything I do to increase expectancy for success increases the motivation of my students to succeed.*

What other factors influence students' expectancy and potential for success? Teachers can effectively create the conditions that draw learners' attention to a topic, but "ultimately students decide whether they feel capable of learning and whether they will do the work" (Chappuis, 2005, para. 1). Task clarity and relevance influence these decisions, and many students factor in grades.

Dr. Foster: *Look at how two teachers calculate a final grade.*

Teacher 1:	**Final Grade**	100%	Tests

Teacher 2:	**Final Grade**	75%	Tests
		10%	Homework
		15%	In-class tasks

 What are your perceptions? What might a student think?

A. Teacher: *Both teachers value tests over homework and in-class tasks.*

*From what Dr. Sprick and his colleagues explained about **expectancy x value**, a student with test anxiety would most likely believe there is no way he or she could pass either class. His or her **expectancy** would be zero.*

*A student with test anxiety might rate the **expectancy** to pass tests at zero. Thus, the student would show little or no motivation to do the tests, homework, or class work because the only thing that really counts is the ability to take tests. (See page 132.)*

Dr. Foster: *You are on target! I will show you how to calculate a final grade when we talk about the active ingredient evaluation. (See Evaluation on page 172.)*

Tests Are NO Joke!

Many teachers complain that the tests required by the state and district do not give a complete picture of what students know. Yet, many of these same teachers use tests as almost the sole criterion for grades in their classrooms.

The value placed on tests by teachers and school districts is no laughing matter!

In "Student Motivation: Factors in Student Motivation," Steven C. Howey (2009) cited Garcia, McKeachie, Pintrich, and Smith (1991), who made this statement about test anxiety:

> Test anxiety has been found to be negatively related to expectancies as +well as to academic performance. Test anxiety is thought to have two components: a worry, or cognitive component, and an emotionality component. The worry component refers to students' negative thoughts that disrupt performance, whereas the emotionality component refers to affective and physiological arousal aspects of anxiety. Cognitive concern and preoccupation with performance have been found to be the greatest sources of performance decrement. (para. 6)

According to Janet Elder, too much stress (e.g., perceived threat) has effects on the brain. "Chronic stress affects thinking, the ability to sort out what's important from what's not, memory formation; it impairs creativity. . . . Too much threat can induce helplessness, leaving students unable to detect patterns, solve complex problems, understand connections, or detect larger levels of organization. . . . Too much threat is paralyzing" (n.d., Item 13).

> Threats, and even harsh comments and sarcasm, trigger chemical imbalances. Serotonin levels fall, and the result is often impulsive, aggressive, or even violent behavior. Students who feel constantly threatened (such as those, for example, who come from an abusive home or live in a dangerous neighborhood) are constantly on alert, scanning constantly for "predators" (or prey). This makes it very difficult to get their attention in the classroom. (Elder, n.d., Item 13)

A. Teacher: *When I was a student, grades worried me. I experienced stress. My focus was to get the "A" I wanted. I did not feel threatened, but I can see how some students would have these feelings.*

Now, I have to give tests and grades as part of my job. I try to keep my personal feelings about grading out of the equation.

Dr. Foster: *You might not take it personally, but students and parents do! See how Richard Stiggins and his daughter felt about the grade she received on her writing assignment in "Don't Take It Personally!"*

Don't Take It Personally!

Dr. Richard J. Stiggins is "the founder and president of the Assessment Training Institute, Inc., Portland, Oregon, a service agency devoted to supporting teachers as they face the day-to-day challenges of classroom assessment" (2005, p. vii). In his book, *Student-Involved Assessment FOR Learning*, he tells this story about his daughter, Kristen Ann, when "she was just beginning to learn to write" (pp. 12–13).

Kristen arrived home one afternoon full of gloom when she was in third grade. She said she knew we were going to be angry with her. She presented us with a sheet of paper—third-grade size with wide lines. On it, she had written a story. Her assignment was to write about someone or something she cared about deeply. She wrote of Kelly, a tiny kitten who had come to be part of our family, but who [we] had to return to the farm after two weeks because of allergies. Kelly's departure had been like the loss of a family member.

On the sheet of paper was an emergent writer's version of this story—not sophisticated, but poignant. Krissy's recounting of events was accurate, and her story captured her very strong sadness and disappointment at losing her new little friend. She did a pretty darn good job of writing, for a beginner.

At the bottom of the page, below the story, was a big red circled "F"! We asked her why, and she told us that the teacher said she had better learn to do it right or she would fail. Questioning further, we found that her teacher had said that students were to fill the page with writing. Krissy had used only three-quarters of the page, so she hadn't followed directions and so she deserved an F.

When she had finished telling us this story, Kristen Ann put the sheet of paper down on the kitchen table and, with a very discouraged look, said in an intimidated voice, "I'll never be a good writer anyway," and left the room. My recollection of this moment remains vivid after 20 years.

She had *succeeded* at hitting the achievement target. She produced some pretty good writing. But her confidence in herself as a writer was deeply shaken because her teacher failed to disentangle her expectation that students comply with directions with her expectations that they demonstrate the ability to write well. . . . Without question, it's quite easy to see if the page is full. But is that the point?

Excerpted from *Student-Involved Assessment FOR Learning* (4th ed.) by R. J. Stiggins, 2005

Some of us teachers **don't take it personally**. "It's a grade that goes in a grade book or a score we average with other scores . . . But for students, it's always far more personal than that." Dr. Stiggins makes this request: "Never lose sight of this very personal dimension of your classroom assessment processes" (p. 13).

The *reality* is that students and parents take grades personally!

Dr. Foster: *Some students give up when stressed about grades; others cheat.*

A. Teacher: *The students who cheat are the ones who get D's and F's.*

Dr. Foster: *Not always. Students with A's may cheat to make grades to stay on an athletic team or to get into and stay in a good university. The pressure may be their own, but parents and coaches may also apply pressure to get the "reward." Read "Cheating Makes the Grade" to learn what students think about cheating.*

Cheating Makes the Grade

According to the *Academic Cheating Fact Sheet* from the Educational Testing Service (1999), "cheating among high school students has risen dramatically during the past 50 years" ("Cheating," Fact 2). While it used to be "the struggling student who was more likely to cheat just to get by," a 1998 poll of Who's Who Among American High School Students reported that 80% cheated to get to the top of their class (Facts 3, 22).

Research has shown that **elementary-age** children believe that cheating "is wrong, but could be acceptable depending on the task" (Fact 18). In a survey of **middle school** students, "2/3 of the respondents reported cheating on exams, while 9/10 reported copying another's homework" (Fact 21).

On National Public Radio's *Talk of the Nation*, a panel of experts and call-in guests discussed cheating in American schools. A student caller said, "I was in honors classes in **high school** because I wanted to get into the best schools, and all of us in those classes cheated; we needed the grades to get into good schools. We were good, moral students; we weren't like unethical people or anything, we just needed to get into good universities, and we had to cheat" ("A Further," n.d., para. 3).

The primary reasons **college** students cheat are "Campus norm; No honor code; Penalties not severe; Faculty support of academic integrity is low; Little chance of being caught" and a heavy workload ("Cheating," 1999, Facts 24–25). "Cheating is seen by many students as a means to a profitable end" (Fact 27).

How do students and parents feel about cheating? The Josephson Institute reported high levels of dishonesty among 29,760 public and private high school students on a 2008 survey. "A whopping 93 percent said they were satisfied with their personal ethics and character and 77 percent said when it comes to doing what is right, I am better than most people I know" ("Ethics of Youth," 2009, para. 3). "Two-thirds of parents say that cheating isn't really so bad: 'All students do it'" ("A Further," n.d., para. 2).

The *reality* is that **cheating is making the grade** for many students. "Even those students who say it is wrong, cheat; if the goal is to get a good grade, they will cheat" ("Cheating," 1999, Fact 20). "Grades, rather than education" will remain "the major focus of many students" at all education levels (Fact 6), as long as grades, not learning, remain the primary focus of educators.

A. Teacher: *So should we abolish grades?*

Dr. Foster: *"Although this might be desirable, especially for younger students, it simply is not going to happen . . . almost everywhere that schools or school systems have tried to remove grades from report cards, they have been faced with community reaction so strongly negative that educators have been forced to return to traditional grades" (O'Connor, 2009, p. 20).*

A. Teacher: *Is there another option?*

Dr. Foster: *Yes. Rather than try to eliminate grades, it would be more productive to make grades more reflective of student learning (O'Connor, p. 20). You will learn how when we discuss the **active ingredient practice**. To motivate students to engage in the learning process with a greater potential for success, teachers must focus less on assessment OF learning (tests and grades) and more on practice, or formative assessments—assessment FOR learning.*

With respect to grades and tests to motivate students, "We all grew up in classrooms in which our teachers believed that the way to maximize learning was to maximize anxiety, and assessment has always been the great intimidator" (Stiggins, 2002, para. 17).

> Psychological research proves that students, and people in general, are more likely to lose interest in what they're doing if they are promised carrots or threatened with sticks. Using grades as a "threat" (stick) or "reward" (carrot) for completion of work is extrinsic, or external, motivation. This type of motivation often results in decreased student focus on the learning objective. (Barnwell, 2008, para. 2)

A. Teacher: *We teachers do need to provide more intrinsic motivation.*

*I **know** how task clarity and relevance increase expectancy and that students' emotions about grades and tests may influence their potential to learn and achieve academic success. I **need to learn** how to promote intrinsic motivation.*

Dr. Foster: *You can learn to promote intrinsic motivation in your classroom with what you know about expectancy and what you will learn about attribution, the next active ingredient.*

> *All true learning is experience.*
> *Everything else is information.*
> **Albert Einstein**

Active Ingredient	 Attribution

Attribution is the second active ingredient in the **Appropriate Assessments Prescription**. Fritz Heider says that an attribution is an explanation for how people interpret events and perceive the causes of behavior. "Behavior is attributed to a disposition (e.g., personality traits, motives, attitudes), or . . . to situations (e.g., external pressures, social norms, peer pressure, accidents of the environment, acts of God, random chance, etc.)" (Heider, 2009, para. 12).

Kurt Lewin influenced Heider's "initial analysis of causal structure" (Gredler, 1992, p. 315). Lewin "contradicted most popular theories in that [his formula] gave importance to a person's momentary situation in understanding his or her behavior, rather than relying entirely on the past" ("Lewin's Equation," 2009, para. 1). Lewin's well-known formula in social psychology is $B = f(P,E)$. Behavior is a function of the person and the environment.

One of the most amazing features of human beings is that we believe we can explain anything. Research by psychologists has revealed that most people are biased in their judgment of who or what is responsible for an event or an action. ("Attribution Theory—Heider," 2009, para. 2)

A. Teacher: *I understand this one, but it has to be more complex than it appears.*

Dr. Foster: *People are complex and so are the environmental factors that can influence what people believe and why they do what they do.*

Bernard Weiner focuses his attribution theory on achievement. In an address he gave in 2009, he explains the development of his attribution-based theory of motivation and places his ideas within a compatible framework (p. 20).

Heider and Rotter did not cite one another, although both were concerned with the perceived causes of success and failure and their locus or location. Rotter acknowledged one internal and one external cause, respectively, skill (ability) and luck (chance), while Heider intuited three causes (ability, effort, and task difficulty). I combined these two lists and proposed four main perceived causes of achievement outcomes—ability, effort, task difficulty, and luck (see Weiner et al., 1971). Two of these are internal to the person (ability and effort) and two are external (task difficulty and luck). (p. 9)

If I have seen farther than others, it is because I was standing on the shoulders of giants.

Isaac Newton
(1643–1727)

Known for developing a theory of gravity and three famous laws of motion

Weiner classifies attributions along three causal dimensions: locus of control, stability, and controllability. The locus of control dimension can be internal or external. "The stability dimension captures whether causes change over time or not. For instance, ability can be a stable, internal cause, and effort classified as unstable and internal. Controllability contrasts causes one can control, such as skill/efficacy, from causes one cannot control, such as aptitude, mood, others' actions, and luck" ("Attribution Theory—Weiner," n.d., para. 2).

Dr. Foster: *"When students have a history of failure in school, it is particularly difficult for them to sustain the motivation to keep trying. Students who believe that their poor performance is caused by factors out of their control are unlikely to see any reason to hope for an improvement" (Anderman & Midgley, 1997, para. 1).*

A. Teacher: *Attribution sounds like expectancy.*

Dr. Foster: *They are similar. **Expectancy** has to do with what a student believes will happen before a task or assessment. After the task or assessment, an **attribution** is the reason for achievement or lack of achievement. According to Dr. Bernard Weiner, attribution influences "expectations about future outcomes" (Gredler, 1992, p. 314).*

> [Attributional] factors serve as conveyors of efficacy information that influence performance largely through their intervening effects on self-percepts of efficacy. (Bandura, 1985, p. 402)

A. Teacher: *Okay. Expectancy is what students believe will happen in a specific situation; attribution is the rationale for that belief.*

*If a student **expects** to fail a test, he or she might **attribute** the failure to having failed other tests in the past. If the student were to pass, the reason given might be, "I got lucky."*

Dr. Foster: *You have a basic understanding of attribution. Before we move on, let's make sure you understand the main causes of achievement outcomes.*

What are the internal and external causes attributable to achievement outcomes? From Lewin's formula (**B**ehavior is a **f**unction of the **P**erson and the **E**nvironment) and Weiner's attribution research, achievement is the **behavior** of interest to teachers. *Ability* and *effort* are the **person's** internal causes while *task difficulty* and *luck* represent external or **environmental** causes.

Dr. Foster: *We will begin with a discussion of the internal causes—ability and effort. Bernard Weiner considers ability stable and effort unstable.*

A. Teacher: *That does not make sense. I agree that ability is more stable than effort, but I think ability can change over time.*

Dr. Foster: *Weiner argues that **ability** and **effort** lead to different expectations for future outcomes. If students attribute a poor grade to lack of ability, they expect it will happen again. As effort is subject to change, students who expend little effort may not expect a poor grade in the future (Gredler, 1992).*

A. Teacher: *I see. As a teacher, I believe that students' effort **and** ability can change. Students may not believe their ability can change.*

On reflection, my beliefs have something to do with my perception of a student's ability. If a student gets an "F" on an assessment, I might say, "This is the best the student can do. No amount of effort will ever change this outcome." In this case, ability and effort are stable.

Dr. Foster: *How do you think your beliefs influence students?*

A. Teacher: *That is complicated. I believe my beliefs could be positive or negative.*

"People can gauge their degree of confidence by the emotional state they experience as they contemplate an action. Strong emotional reactions to a task provide cues about the anticipated success or failure of the outcome" (Pajares, 2002, para. 31). Teachers need to look for these cues.

"Failures that are overcome by determined effort can instill robust percepts of self-efficacy. . . . It is through experience one can eventually master even the most difficult obstacles" (Bandura, 1985, p. 399). See how a teacher and a student perceive effort differently in "You Need to Try Harder!"

> The implications . . . revolve around the importance of understanding what students believe about the reasons for their academic performance. Teachers can unknowingly communicate a range of attitudes about whether ability is fixed or modifiable and their expectations for individual students through their instructional practices. (Anderman & Midgley, 1997; Graham, 1990)

You Need to Try Harder!

"Many teachers factor effort into their grading. . . . They see effort as being related to achievement: Those who try harder learn more" (Stiggins, 2005, p. 285). If teachers say **you need to try harder**, what do they mean? **Effort** is exertion of physical or mental power, an earnest or strenuous attempt, and something done by exertion or hard work. The meaning attributed to effort varies greatly for teachers and students.

In Practice
Dr. Foster

A beginning reader gets an "F" on a reading paper. The teacher tells the student, "You need to try harder." The student gets an "F" on the next reading paper. The teacher asks, "Did you try harder?" The student replies, "Yes, let me show you." As the student writes another answer on the paper, she puts excessive pressure on the pencil point and breaks it.

What does "try harder" mean to this student?

To motivate students to "try harder," there must be a clear definition of "effort." To me, effort means to be **on task.** The ability to stay on task is difficult (hard work); it requires exertion of physical and mental power.

I cannot measure the amount of effort internal to a person, but I can see if a student is on task. When students listen to different speakers during class discussion, I would expect students to look at the speaker or write information in a notebook. I can *observe* these **on task** behaviors.

"After we define effort, we must assess it well. . . . The assessment must arise from a clear target, rely on a proper method of assessment, sample effort in a systematically representative manner, and control for all relevant sources of bias that can distort our assessment and mislead us" (Stiggins, 2005, p. 287). Learn how to grade effort in **Supplement P: Grade Book Magic (Secrets Revealed)**. (Select **Supplements**, then **K–P** at *www.classroommanagementblues.com* for **Supplement P**.)

A. Teacher: *I need to improve my ability to look for the emotional cues my students give about the tasks I assign. I need to provide experiences and assessments at the appropriate level of difficulty. With a better understanding of how students may attribute their success to ability and effort, I expect it will be easier to understand how students attribute task difficulty and luck to their success or failure.*

> Given clear requirements for success, students are better able to gauge the appropriateness of their own preparation and thus gain control over their own academic well-being. Students who feel in control of their own chances for success are more likely to care and to strive for excellence. (Stiggins, 2005, p. 40)

Dr. Foster: *Let's see. Task difficulty is external, stable, and controllable (by the teacher) while luck is external, unstable, and uncontrollable (Weiner, 2009, p. 13).*

 Can you think of a situation in which a student might think luck is internal and stable?

A. Teacher: *It's challenging, but I think I can do it. "A learner may believe he is a 'lucky person'—and for him luck would be an internal and stable characteristic over which he exercises little control. In other words, for this person 'luck' is really... an 'ability' or personality characteristic" (Vockell, 2001a, para. 5).*

Dr. Foster: *To what do you attribute your ability to answer that challenging question?*

A. Teacher: *It was not a lucky guess. I attribute my success to my ability to reason. I am proud that I didn't have to put forth much effort. Task difficulty is more complicated than I originally thought.*

> Causal attributions determine affective reactions to success and failure. For example, one is not likely to experience pride in success, or feelings of competence, when receiving an 'A' from a teacher who gives only that grade, or when defeating a tennis player who always loses. . . . On the other hand, an 'A' from a teacher who gives few high grades or a victory over a highly rated tennis player following a great deal of practice generates great positive affect. (Weiner, 1980, p. 362)

Dr. Foster: *You should be proud. "The harder the task, the more likely that success is ascribed to the self (rather than to the ease of the task) and thus the greater the pride in accomplishment" (Weiner, 2009, p. 11)*

A. Teacher: *There have been times when I have told my students that something is easy. It may be easy for me, but my students might perceive it as difficult. I need to provide challenging tasks, but I do not want them to be so difficult that my students give up.*

Dr. Foster: *Read about how John Watson and I were motivated to do something others thought we could not do in "Challenge Me!"*

Challenge Me!

"Many humans are motivated by the thought of doing something they or others think they cannot do. They don't want to do what they already know they can do" (Geisler, 2001).

In sixth grade, I listened as my teacher read the names of students from his grade book that would make the honor roll in middle school. I just knew he would call my name; he did not.

He did not think I had the ability to make high grades. This experience challenged me to prove him wrong. I did make the honor roll in middle and high school, as well as the dean's list in college!

Years later, I realized that my sixth grade teacher based his perceptions on what he observed. He did not realize that I needed a challenge.

John Watson said, "When I studied Taekwondo, most of the best students were slim, flexible, and young. I was thickset and definitely not flexible! I was also over forty!"

The instructor asked him with some curiosity why he had decided to do something that did not really suit his physical makeup.

John replied, "There was no point in doing something I was already good at or likely to be good at. I wanted a challenge." This answer seemed to make sense to him. (Watson, 2005, para. 2–3)

The *reality* is that challenges are motivating.

A. Teacher: *I think that I should find out from my students how they feel about tasks and assessments through dialogue and observation.*

Is there anything else I can do to help my students persist at difficult tasks and establish a sincere belief that they are competent?

How can teachers counter negative attributions? As relationships exist among efficacy, expectancy, and attribution, the strategies for efficacy and expectancy can have a positive effect on attribution. When teachers plan and implement learning tasks and assessments, they should include methods that address ability, effort, and task difficulty and avoid social comparisons, assess student dispositions, and eliminate excessive competition. (See self-efficacy on pages 76–87.)

Social comparisons tend to lower students' view of their ability when the comparisons are unfavorable. Examples of social comparisons include public displays of only A or mostly correct papers, charts of students' projects and achievements, high and low scores, and ability groups (Ames, 1992; Gredler, 1992). Teachers should discontinue these practices and acknowledge individual progress, improvement, and retention in private, rather than in public.

A. Teacher: *In my school experience and teacher preparation classes, I learned that teachers are supposed to display student work and charts of student progress.*

It never bothered me to have my grades announced or made public, but I made good grades. For students who do not achieve at high levels, I can understand how this would reinforce negative attributions about their ability.

I could make better use of my time if I did not display student work and charts of student progress.

Dr. Foster: *Again, your responses demonstrate your reasoning ability.*

As you stated earlier, find out how your students feel about learning tasks and assessments through dialogue and observation. Use diagnostic and formative assessments for this purpose.

In *Student-Involved Assessment FOR Learning,* Richard J. Stiggins (2005) devotes one chapter to the assessment of dispositions and says, "When we assess dispositions, we tap the feeling dimensions of students . . . the inner motivations or wants that influence their thoughts and their actions" (Stiggins, 2005, p. 200). He cautions teachers to follow three ground rules (pp. 205–206).

Table 7.4

Ground Rules and Cautions for Assessing Dispositions
Ground Rule 1: Remember, this is personal. • Always remain keenly aware of the sensitive nature of student feelings and strive to promote appropriate dispositions through your assessment of them. **Ground Rule 2: Stay in bounds.** • Do not venture into personal territory for which you lack training. You can do great harm if you fail to respond appropriately, even with the most positive intentions. • Stick with those feelings as they relate to school-related objects: dispositions toward particular subjects or classroom activities, academic interests . . . [and] personal dispositions as learners. **Ground Rule 3: If you ask, do something with the results.** • Do not ask how students feel about things just to appear to care. . . . Act on these assessment results [appropriately].

A. Teacher: *I feel competent to follow ground rules one and three appropriately, but the most difficult one for me would be Ground Rule 2: Stay in bounds. What do I do if I encounter deeply troubled students?*

Dr. Foster: *"Listen to your instincts. . . . These are not occasions for you to become an amateur psychologist" (Stiggins, 2005, p. 205).*

Dr. Foster: *Dr. Stiggins and I agree that you should be caring and cautious. The most caring and responsible teachers are those who know when it is time to contact school personnel trained to handle deeply troubled students" (2005, p. 205).*

Feelings, Wo-o-o Feelings

If you ask students how they feel—keep in mind that some **feelings** can be volatile and vary in intensity while others may be more enduring. In order for students to respond honestly to an inquiry, there must be a level of trust. The examples below show how to assess student dispositions (Stiggins, 2005, pp. 213–219).

In Practice
Dr. Stiggins

Create focused and value-neutral questions for **questionnaires**. For example:

Provide a math problem-solving challenge, then ask:
How confident are you that you can solve this kind of math problem appropriately?

a. Very confident   **b.** Quite confident   **c.** Somewhat confident   **d.** Not confident at all

Use **selected response questionnaires** to find out . . .

- If students agree or disagree with specific statements
- How important students regard specific things
- How students would judge the quality of something
- How frequently students feel certain things

For example:

If I do well on a test, it is usually because

a. My teacher taught me well. b. I was lucky. c. I studied hard.

Other types of selected response questions use scales or pictures.

For example:

Use the scale to describe motivation in learning Science.
Put an X on the line that best reflects your feelings.

Very Motivated __ __ __ __ __ Completely Unmotivated

Tell students, *"Color the face that shows how you feel about math."*

Offer **open-ended questions** to which students are free to write responses. For example:

As you think about the readings we did this month, which three did you find most worthwhile? For each choice, specify why you found it worthwhile.

Each assessment method used to find out the **feelings** of students "carries with it specific advantages, limitations, **keys to success**, and pitfalls to avoid" (p. 213). Read more about assessing dispositions in *Student-Involved Assessment FOR Learning*

Not only should teachers avoid social comparisons and carefully assess student dispositions, they should establish a classroom environment in which students learn how to take intelligent risks and attempt challenging, complex work (Black & William, 2006). The elimination of excessive competition is required to achieve this aim.

A. Teacher: *I have concerns about challenging work, competition, and risk taking.*

I know that WebQuests and problem-based learning provide meaningful and challenging learning experiences. Is there anything else I can do that will take less time and still achieve the same purpose.

Dr. Foster: *The easiest way that I have found is to add one or more challenging questions for extra credit on daily assignments, homework, and assessments by using* 📁 **Supplement D: HOT Question Starters**. *(Select the* **Supplements** *page at www.classroommanagementblues.com, then* **A–F** *to locate* **Supplement D**.*)*

Add extra points when you assess these tasks rather than calculate the extra points in the final grade at the end of the term. To encourage students to attempt challenges, give at least one point when they attempt a response. (See page 188.)

A. Teacher: *What can I do to promote intelligent risk taking?*

Dr. Foster: *"The most intelligent risks are those where the potential downside is limited, but the potential upside is virtually unlimited" (Pavlina, 2006, para. 6). These are risks to urge students to take.*

> *A person who never made a mistake never tried anything new.*
> **Albert Einstein**

A. Teacher: *I tell my students, "It is OK to make mistakes."*

Wow! I just realized that I always count the mistakes and grade everything they do. This counters what I say I value.

Dr. Foster: *Your response demonstrates an understanding of why teachers should stop grading for mastery when students learn something new or attempt a challenging task. It is more appropriate to give evaluative grades after students have had time to show mastery of the content or skill.*

The last strategy we will discuss to counter negative attributions is to eliminate excessive competition.

You can increase students' intrinsic motivation and help students learn to manage their emotions when you incorporate win-win competitions (Elder, n.d.).

> Competition will encourage students to persist only to the extent that they believe additional effort will enable them to succeed within the competitive atmosphere. In many instances, success in competition is completely beyond the learner's control—no matter how hard a learner works, another more competent and equally energetic competitor is likely to win. (Vockell, 2001a, Item 6)

A. Teacher: *Isn't "Think: Win/Win" Habit 4 in Dr. Stephen Covey's book,* **The 7 Habits of Highly Effective People**?

Dr. Foster: *Yes. According to Dr. Covey (1995), "Competition has its significant benefits . . . [and individuals] are frequently motivated to perform to their highest potential. But competition can drain creative energy . . . and destroy trust" (para. 7–8).*

A. Teacher: *How do I know when to use competition?*

Dr. Foster: *When individuals are independent of each other, competition within rules and boundaries can be healthy and effective. When individuals "are interdependent with each other, competition can be deadly. The essential principle to create effective interdependence is synergistic cooperation: Think win-win" (1995, para. 9).*

"A win-win situation, also called a win-win game or non-zero-sum game in games theory, is a situation by which cooperation, compromise, or group participation leads to all participants benefiting" (Ellis-Christensen, 2009, para. 1). A zero-sum game or win-lose situation is one in which at least one-person wins while another loses (see Figure 7.4).

Figure 7.4

Non-zero-sum	Win +1	Win +1	Sum +2
Zero-sum	Win +1	Lose -1	Sum 0

Any situation where parties agree to act in both their own interest and in the interest of the group can be a win-win situation. . . . Any participant in a situation or game takes into account the way that his/her own decisions and choices affect all other participants. When this happens, and when all participants develop a strategy which benefits the 'whole,' a win-win situation develops. It should be stated that not everyone in every possible permutation of this scenario wins the same thing or the equivalent amount. (Ellis-Christensen, 2009, para. 7)

A. Teacher: *Do you have any examples of noncompetitive games?*

Dr. Foster: 🗁 **Supplement L: Win-Win Classroom Competitions** *includes classroom competitions like board races and team trials in which each student wins something. For example, everyone would get one or more points on the next test. (Select* **Supplements** *at www.classroommanagementblues.com, then* **K–P** *to locate* **Supplement L** *for more information about classroom competitions.)*

   Before we move on to the active ingredient **practice***, tell me what you have learned about the active ingredient* **attribution***.*

A. Teacher: *First, attribution is the reason a student perceives to be the cause of his or her success or failure. The cause could be ability, effort, task difficulty, or luck.*

   I learned that teachers and students do not agree on the definition of effort. When the definition of effort is **on task***, everyone knows the expectations for on-task behavior.*

A. Teacher: *Finally, students want challenging work and have a greater sense of pride when they succeed on a difficult task.*

Dr. Foster:  *How will you counter negative attributions?*

> The basic principle of attribution theory as it applies to motivation is that a person's own perceptions or attributions for success or failure determine the amount of effort the person will expend on that activity in the future. (Vockell, 2001a, para. 5)

A. Teacher: *I will assess student dispositions carefully, avoid social comparisons, and use win-win competitions.*

Could we take a break? I need some time to process this information.

Dr. Foster: *When you are ready, we will discuss practice and formative assessment.*

Active Ingredient	🍎 Practice

The third active ingredient in the **Appropriate Assessments Prescription** is **practice**. To motivate students to engage in the learning process with a greater potential for success, teachers must focus less on evaluation OF learning (tests and grades) and more on assessment FOR learning (formative assessment). Ample time for **practice** should precede grades and tests for mastery.

When teachers use practice appropriately, they can create a positive learning community and address test anxiety, expectancy of failure, and the fear of making mistakes. "The brain performs better in a positive emotional state. Students must feel physically and emotionally safe before their brains are ready to learn" (Prince, 2005, p. 1). When teachers value **practice**, they can reduce the time needed to grade papers and increase the potential for *every* student to be successful.

> Adopt a brain-friendly, and hence learner-friendly curriculum, one that incorporates practice, practice, practice in a variety of ways, formats, and contexts. Providing multiple contexts for learning the same thing creates the most neural pathways. (Elder, n.d., p. 1)

A. Teacher: *It is hard for me to believe there is something I can do to make my job easier and still increase the potential for all my students to succeed. I am ready to learn.*

Dr. Foster:  *Let me ask. Why are some students not successful in the classroom?*

A. Teacher: *They do not do their schoolwork or homework.*

Dr. Foster: *If you share my* **Pep** *formula with your students and use the related strategies, you will be able to get your students to* **P***ractice (do schoolwork and homework). When you provide* **e***mpowerment and encouragement, you can help your students stay on task and connect their practice with success on* **p***erformances and projects.*

> $$P \bullet e = p$$
> **P**ractice times
> **e**mpowerment
> equals **p**erformance

A. Teacher: *I understand encouragement, projects, and performance. I believe empowerment has to do with what I have already learned about the* **High Expectations Prescription** *and the active ingredients attribution and expectancy.*

I thought I knew what practice was; now I'm not sure.

Dr. Foster: *From the diagnostic information you provided in your self-assessment, I know you are confident about your knowledge of each component of the* **Pep** *formula except for empowerment and practice. As empowerment does connect with what you have already learned about high expectations, expectancy, and attribution, we will center our discussion on practice.*

I will use the **K-W-L technique** *to activate your prior knowledge and facilitate new learning about practice. I will ask what you already* **K***now, establish what you* **W***ant to learn, and have you summarize what you* **L***earn.*

What do you already **K***now about practice?*

A. Teacher: *I* **K***now that when athletes practice, they do several things to prepare for what they will apply in the game. Learners should practice in preparation for tests what they will do on tests.*

Dr. Foster: *What do you* **W***ant to learn?*

A. Teacher: *Once I understand what practice is, I* **W***ant to learn what behaviors I should expect during practice, how I should document the expected behaviors, and how I should factor practice in the calculation of a final grade.*

Dr. Foster: *We have a plan. Let's get started.*

What is the role of practice within the learning process? Practice "begins with the rehearsal of the new skill in working memory, the motor cortex, and the cerebellum. Later, the skill memory is recalled and additional practice follows" (Sousa, 2006, p. 97). With repeated practice, the brain assigns extra neurons to the task. When practice stops, the brain assigns other tasks to the neurons no longer being used (p. 97) and retention declines.

A. Teacher: *I didn't realize how important practice was for retention.*

I thought practice (seatwork) was to keep students busy so I could assist individual students, work with small groups, or do other tasks.

Dr. Foster: *From what you have learned about practice, what effect do you think practice might have on students' performance on high-stakes tests?*

A. Teacher: *It is no wonder many students do not do well on high-stakes tests even when they have had opportunities to learn the content. Some students do not do the practice; some may have practiced but did not practice enough; and finally, some students may not have continued the practice over time to retain the learning.*

Dr. Foster: *You have learned a valuable lesson about how to use practice effectively. Read "Use Practice Effectively, or Else!" to make the learning permanent.*

Use Practice Effectively, or Else!

Dr. David A. Sousa, in *How the Brain Learns,* refers to practice as learners repeating a skill over time. He states, "Practice does not make perfect, it makes *permanent.* . . . Assure that students practice the new learning correctly from the beginning" (2006, pp. 97–98).

Students should do early practice (*guided practice*) in the presence of the teacher. When the practice is correct, the teacher can then assign *independent practice* in which the students can rehearse the skill on their own to enhance retention (p. 98). Teachers must **use practice effectively, or else** risk students learning a skill incorrectly. To unlearn and relearn the skill is very difficult (p. 99) and time-consuming.

Dr. Sousa cites Hunter (2004) who suggests, "If we expect students to retain the information in active storage and to remember how to use it accurately, it should continue to be practiced over increasingly longer time intervals" (2006, p. 125). Thus, students should revisit content and skills throughout the year in the form of homework, as well as closure activities in lessons to connect to prior knowledge.

The *reality* is that what one repeats over time becomes permanent!

A. Teacher: *I spend most of my time planning for what I teach; I need to spend more time planning for what my students practice. If I use practice effectively, it will help with paper overload, and I will have more time to plan practice.*

Dr. Foster: *To help with planning, look at the definitions, keys to understanding, and cautions for guided, independent, massed, and distributed practice in these tables.*

Table 7.5

Guided and Independent Practice
From the work of Madeline C. Hunter

Guided Practice—Students demonstrate a grasp of new learning when they work through an activity or exercise under the guidance of a teacher or another support system. (It is most important for low achievers.) Teachers monitor students as they work to determine the mastery level and provide individual remediation or feedback to help students analyze and improve their practice.

Independent Practice—Students practice the learning after they can perform without support.

Key to understanding—Guided practice and independent practice represent different points on a continuum with no absolute dividing point to discriminate between the two activities.

Caution—Do not give independent practice before guided practice; students might unknowingly learn the skill or information incorrectly.

From "Direct Instruction," n.d.; "Glossary," n.d.; "Lesson Design," n.d.; Schroeder, n.d.; and Sousa, 2006

Table 7.6

Massed and Distributed Practice

Massed Practice—Students try different examples and apply new learning in a short period of time (e.g., cram for an exam).	**Caution**—Chunks of information move quickly into working memory, and people can forget these chunks quickly after an exam.
Distributed Practice—Students review critical information and skills throughout the year and over several grade levels. Spiral review is an example. (Select the **Supplements** page, then **G–J** at *www.classroommanagementblues.com* to locate **Supplement H: Homework Contract**.)	**Key to understanding**—This kind of practice sustains meaning and consolidates the learning in long-term storage in a form that will promote accurate recall and applications in the future.

Adapted from *How the Brain Learns* by D. A. Sousa, 2006, pp. 99–100

A. Teacher: *I have used guided and independent practice appropriately, but not massed and distributed practice. How can I make sure students practice the new learning correctly when they work with a partner, in a small group, or independently?*

Dr. Foster: *Learn how to provide guidance and support in "Supporting Roles."*

Supporting Roles

During guided practice, the teacher plays the leading role by providing guidance to assure students practice the new learning correctly from the beginning (Sousa, 2006). Peers, teacher's editions, and answer sheets play **supporting roles**.

When I worked with small groups or individual students during practice (seatwork), students needed other support systems. On these occasions when I was **not** able to circulate to monitor students as they worked, I provided the **teacher's edition** or an **answer sheet** for the students to check a few answers before they did the whole assignment. Students could also check their work with one or more nearby **peers**.

Students took responsibility for their own learning and did not have to wait one or more days until I had graded their work to see if they had done the work correctly. This reduced the number of papers I had to grade and gave the students immediate feedback.

Give students opportunities to take ownership in their learning, teach each other, and get immediate feedback. These **research-supported** best practices play **supporting roles** and help students retain what they learn.

A. Teacher: *Is there anything else I can do when I circulate to monitor students during guided practice and there are too many hands up for me to help? What do you suggest?*

Dr. Foster: 🗁 **Supplement C: LTC** *(Learner Teacher Checker) is a strategy we have talked about in another session. (See page 56 and select* **Supplements***, then* **A–F** *at www.classroommanagementblues.com to locate* **Supplement C***.)*

A. Teacher: *Thanks for the reminder. I see how this strategy would be effective during practice, but I am still concerned about peer support.*

Dr. Foster: *When you use formative assessment in your classroom, you must give up some control (Black & Wiliam, 1998). You will learn how to manage student behavior and implement peer support in our next session.*

Social interactions advance learning. Think back to the work of Dr. Lev Vygotsky (see page 59). In ZPD [Zone of Proximal Development], "a teacher and learner (adult/child, tutor/tutee, model/observer, expert/novice, master/apprentice) work together on a task that the learner could not perform independently because of the difficulty level" (Schunk, 2000, p. 244).

Peer teaching enables students to learn and retain new learning. In "Theoretical Background of Peer Teaching," Diệp (2009) cited some of the benefits found in the peer teaching literature (para. 10–11, 13):

> The brain is innately social and collaborative. Although the processing takes place in our students independent brains, their learning is enhanced when the environment provides them with the opportunity to discuss their thinking out loud to bounce their ideas off their peers and to produce collaborative work. (Wolfe & Brandt, 1998, para. 4)

- According to Dweck (1993), learners can be responsible to review, organize, and consolidate existing knowledge and material; understand its basic structure; fill in the gaps; find additional meanings; and reformulate knowledge into new conceptual frameworks.

- Farivar and Webb (1994) found that learners who are assisted move away from dependence on teachers and those who give help have the chance to experience and learn that "teaching is the best teacher."

- Researchers Gross and McMullen (1983) concluded that learners seek academic assistance from a similar-age peer, which is often less threatening to the learner's self-esteem than when they seek help from an authority figure.

Practice on easy tasks can help children build automaticity of skills, but they also need to be challenged by tasks to be motivated and learn new skills. Tasks should be set at a level of difficulty where most children in the classroom can master the assignment with some effort. They should not be too easy and especially not so difficult that most children fail at the task (Pintrich & Schunk, 1996).

Dr. Foster: *Take a moment and process what you have learned.*

A. Teacher: *I have Learned about different kinds of practice and support systems that need to be in place for students to be successful during practice.*

In my sessions with you, it has helped to discuss and think aloud about what I am learning. The same would be true for my students.

Dr. Foster: *Through our social interactions, I have enabled you as the learner to gain new knowledge through dialogue and questions.*

 *Here is my next question. Is **practice** formative or summative?*

A. Teacher: *I Know that tests and projects are summative and come after a unit of study. Practice is formative because I form an understanding about what my students know when I assess the activities and exercises they do before a summative assessment.*

Dr. Foster: *I was confident that you would know the answer. Here is what researchers say about the use of formative assessment to raise standards in the classroom.*

> *New learning is like wet cement; it is easily damaged. An error at the beginning of learning can be easily 'set' so that it is harder to eradicate than had it been apprehended immediately.*
>
> **Madeline Cheek Hunter**
> (1916–1994)
>
> ---
>
> Known for developing a model of teaching and learning

In "Inside the Black Box: Raising Standards Through Classroom Assessment," Black and Wiliam contend, "Innovations that include strengthening the practice of formative assessment produce significant and often substantial learning gains" (1998, para. 14). They provide the following suggestions to implement formative assessment effectively across school subjects for preschool to post-secondary students (para. 6, 19–20):

- Formative assessment is at the heart of effective teaching. Pay close attention to the contextualization and timing of formative assessments.

- Avoid too many recall/rote tests and activities as they promote superficial learning.

- Focus more on personal improvement and less on competition.

- Give useful advice and emphasize learning over grading.

- Stress quality in relation to learning rather than quantity.

A. Teacher: *The first three points are a review of what I have learned. Now I am ready to learn how to grade and stress quality over quantity more effectively.*

Dr. Foster: *Let's start with quality over quantity.*

 Think about when you expect students to finish work and when you do not expect work to be complete. Now read "Sometimes, Less Is More!"

Sometimes, Less Is More!

 Like many teachers, I would often say, "You have to complete your work." One day I realized that it did not make sense to expect students to do as much as they could on tests, but expect them to complete everything when learning something new. It also became clear that many students just filled in answers to finish assignments because I emphasized completion over learning.

I remember when I had to diagram sentences in one of my English classes in high school. Let's say I was required to do 30 sentences during a class period. Should the teacher have given me a punishment to take the work home to complete (in addition to the regular homework assignment) when I stayed on task and completed 15 sentences correctly in the class period? If yes, the result would be **less** motivation to take my time and **more** resentment about the class work I had to take home as homework!

Or would it be better if I worked quickly and made mistakes but got the task completed? If yes, the result would be **less** learning and **more** practice learning the task incorrectly!

Some teachers would say, "In the real world you have to finish tasks or lose your job." I agree but would say, "On the job, you would already know, or have mastered, what you are expected to do!"

If teachers agree that students learn at different rates, would it not follow that students complete work at different rates? As teachers, we should be **more** concerned about whether students are on task and learning is evidenced, and **less** concerned about completion! Black and Wiliam (1998) would equate this to more focus on quality rather than quantity.

Dr. Robyn R. Jackson (2009) cited a friend who said, "If less is more, imagine how much more *more* would be!" She said it was a joke, "but many of us subscribe to this philosophy. . . . We want to make our students more competitive, so we give them as much information as possible" (p. 155).

The *reality* is that **sometimes, less is more** and more is less!

A. Teacher: *I have discovered why some of the strategies I use in my classroom have not been effective for all my students.*

Dr. Foster: *Let's continue our dialogue about formative assessment.*

Summarize what you know about tests and quizzes.

A. Teacher: *A test **is not** practice because it is summative. Students take a test after a unit of study to show the mastery level of content and skills. A quiz **is** practice, so it is formative. Teachers give quizzes to form an understanding of what students have learned at different points throughout a unit of study.*

A. Teacher: *I have learned that almost everything students do until the end of a unit of study is formative, so students do practice most of the time.*

Because effective practice is the key to a learner's ability to apply and retain information and skills over time, I need to spend more time to make sure the practice and the formative assessments of the practice are appropriate.

Dr. Foster: *"The more learning, the more connections you make. The greater the number of connections in the brain, the greater the meaning derived from learning" (Hopper, 2009, slide 13). The connections you have made demonstrate your understanding!*

*I have not forgotten that you wanted to know the **behaviors** you should expect during practice. Rather than tell you, I will guide your discovery of the answer.*

What would you tell students before a test?

A. Teacher: *Here are some of my behavioral expectations:*

1. *Do not ask me or anyone else for assistance with answers during the test. If you need help with the directions or do not know a word, raise your hand. I will assist you.*

2. *You have ____ minutes. Do as much as you can.*

3. *Stay on task. If you finish early, work on one or more of the challenge questions.*

Dr. Foster: *Think about the expectations you just listed and what you have **Learned** about practice. What would you tell the students before beginning a practice session?*

A. Teacher: *Expectations for practice would be the same as for tests, except for the first one. Here is how I would revise #1 for practice:*

Begin the practice activity or exercise on your own. Do one or two, then check your answers with a peer, answer sheet, or teacher's edition before you continue.

Dr. Foster: *Think about how your behavioral expectations for practice compare with these research findings.*

Which behaviors should teachers expect students to demonstrate during practice activities? Research has shown that students learn best in a nonthreatening environment where teachers value learning, effort, and peer teaching over competition and grades. So when students practice something new or attempt challenging tasks, they should be empowered and encouraged to *evidence learning, teach others, stay on task, and go beyond what is required.*

A. Teacher: *I hit the target. Let me show you how my behavioral expectations during practice compare with the research-based expectations you shared with me.*

Here is a table that evidences my learning (see Table 7.7 on the next page).

Table 7.7

What I said I would tell students before a practice session	Research-based behavioral expectations
Be on task.	Stay on task.
Check your answers with a peer.	Peer teach.
Do as much as you can.	Evidence learning.
If you finish early, work on one or more challenging questions or tasks.	Attempt challenging tasks and go beyond expectations.

Dr. Foster: *To what do you* attribute *your success?*

A. Teacher: *I was successful because I was able to make connections between what I already knew and what I wanted to learn. I expected to be successful because I trusted that you would ask the questions that would help me make these connections.*

Although I was able to name the behaviors, I still have a few questions and concerns about effective encouragement for these behaviors. I wonder if students will copy from teacher's editions, answer sheets, and other students.

Dr. Foster: *When I dialogue with students about expectations, they learn how I monitor and document learning evidence. We discuss the need to monitor even closer when their* **performance** *is inconsistent with the learning evidenced during* **practice** and on summative assessments.

I do not accuse students of cheating; I just monitor them more closely as promised. There may be a reason other than cheating for inconsistencies in performance (e.g., anxiety, lack of sleep).

A. Teacher: *I know I need to repeat high expectations and trust my students. This will take time and practice.*

Could you explain what to do when students finish early or rush through their work?

> *It's not that I'm so smart, it's just that I stay with problems longer.*
> **Albert Einstein**

Dr. Foster: *Because practice leads to learning new information or skills, a student who finishes early must evidence that he or she has learned the information or skills. If this is the case, the student would work on a more challenging task or something he or she has not mastered or retained.* **Everyone** *works throughout the practice session.*

I value students who evidence learning and support others, not those who finish first. I am sure you remember the fable "The Tortoise and the Hare." It applies here. Discuss the implications or moral of the fable with your students when you explain your behavioral expectations for practice. Read a modified version of the fable in "Who Gets the Last Laugh!"

Who Gets the Last Laugh!

Harry bragged to the other students about how fast he could get his work done. "I have never yet been beaten when I put forth my full speed. I challenge anyone here to race with me."

Another student named Torrence said quietly, "I accept the challenge."

"That is a good joke," said Harry. "I can win even with my eyes closed."

"Keep boasting until you're beaten," answered Torrence. "Shall we race?"

So the assignment was given and the teacher started the race.

Harry started with a burst of speed, but soon stopped to show his contempt for Torrence and put his head down on his desk to have a nap.

Torrence plodded on and on.

The students cheered loudly as Torrence neared the finish. Harry woke up, but could not catch up in time to win the race.

Slow and steady wins the race.

From the fable "The Tortoise and the Hare" at http://www.ivyjoy.com/fables/tortoise.html

Students run races in *some* classrooms every day!

Students who finish the assignments fast get **A**'s, "bragging" rights, and time to play games, work on the computer, or start on their homework.

Students who plod along and do not complete assignments get **F**'s, few privileges, no time to play games or work on the computer, and have to take homework **and** unfinished schoolwork home.

This is **NO** laughing matter. As long as teachers reward speed and completion over perseverance and learning, some students may give up or never start the task.

A. Teacher: *I understand that ALL students work throughout a practice session, and those who finish early should attempt challenging tasks or go beyond expectations (see Table 7.7). I can provide challenging tasks like inquiry-based learning activities (see page 57) and WebQuests (see page 67), but I need some clarification about how to get students to go beyond expectations. Is this something students can do on their own?*

Dr. Foster: *Yes, but you must show your students that you value thinking outside the box and guide them to become critical and creative thinkers.*

Sir Ken Robinson is the author of *Out of Our Minds: Learning to Be Creative* (2009), and a leading expert on innovation and human resources. He defines creativity as "a process, not a single event, and genuine creative process that involves critical thinking as well as imaginative insights and fresh ideas" (2009, p. 23). Robinson offers several ways teachers can facilitate creativity (2009, p. 26; 2006, para. 73, 78). Teachers can:

- Promote skills of divergent thinking through the use of analogies, metaphors, and visual thinking;

- Help students connect with a particular medium or set of materials or processes that excites them;

- Encourage students to experiment, to innovate, not giving them the tools they need to find out what the answer might be or to explore new avenues;

- Give credit for originality, encourage it, and give students some way to reflect on whether the new ideas are more effective than existing ideas;

- Stimulate students' minds with puzzles and questions which will intrigue them;

- Give students problems, rather than just solutions; and

- Ask open questions that students can explore, rather than ones to which they have to find answers already given.

"Collaboration, diversity, the exchange of ideas, and building on other people's achievements are at the heart of the creative process. An education that focuses only on the individual in isolation is bound to frustrate some of those possibilities" (2009, pp. 25–26). Robinson asserts that good teachers know how to form groups, how to get groups to work, and how long to have students collaborate (2006, para. 81). Select the **Supplements** page at *www.classroommanagementblues.com*; then select **A–F** and follow the link to **Supplement A: Quality Grouping** to learn more about grouping.

> *It is the supreme art of the teacher to awaken joy in creative expression and knowledge.*
> **Albert Einstein**

A. **Teacher:** *I understand the value of collaboration and cooperative groups. You offered some good ideas to facilitate creativity, but to be effective, won't I need to invest a lot of time to modify activities and locate resources?*

Dr. Foster: *Select **Resources** at www.classroommanagementblues.com, then **Assessments** and **Critical and Creative Thinking**.*

Dr. Sternberg and Dr. Young propose some creative resources students can learn to become creative thinkers and make decisions about and confront challenging tasks that will be worth the time invested. Read "Invest in Creativity!" to learn how they will pay off!

Invest in Creativity!

Robert J. Sternberg and Todd Lubart proposed an "investment theory of creativity" (Sternberg & Lubart, 1991). According to this theory, creative people persist in the face of resistance, move on to the next new, or unpopular idea, and pursue "ideas that are unknown or out of favor but have growth potential" (Sternberg, 2006, p. 6).

Sternberg "identifies six creative resources that students can be taught to use in order to be creative thinkers" (Young, 2009, p. 5). For Dr. Robert J. Sternberg's creative resources, Dr Linda P. Young describes what teachers can do to **invest in creativity** and guide students to use creative resources to make decisions about and confront problems, projects, and challenging tasks. Here is one example for each resource.

Creative Resources—*Students can . . .   if teachers . . .*

Intellectual Abilities—*Students can* see a problem in new ways and redefine the problem *if teachers* provide the option to redefine problems and avoid a blueprint or step-by-step plan for projects and problem solving.

Knowledge—*Students can* grow in the knowledge of the content field needed to move forward *if teachers* provide the knowledge base and mastery needed to think creatively and problem solve successfully.

Thinking Styles—*Students can* think along new lines, not just generate novel ideas, *if teachers* develop new ways to view problems and the world and help students realize that creative thinking is not just the presentation of something "new" but also an examination of existing structures in a new way.

Personality—*Students can* work to overcome obstacles *if teachers* teach and model perseverance and share information of creative individuals who overcame obstacles through hard work and perseverance.

Motivation—*Students can* ignite a passion for projects or assignments *if teachers* guide students to enjoy the intellectual challenge of the project, set personal goals, and find a real-world connection.

Environment—*Students can* seek an environment and resources that reward creativity *if teachers* create a classroom environment supportive of creativity, reward creative ideas, and allow mistakes in the process.

Young (2009) says that teachers need to understand and have knowledge of creativity and creative processes; successfully teach students to think creatively; assess student growth in creativity and creative thinking; and tie creative thinking to real world applications and experiences. If you want to **invest in creativity**, select the **Resources** page at *www.classroommanagementblues.com*, then locate **Assessments** and **Creativity**.

A. Teacher: *I understand the behaviors I should expect during practice. How do I get started?*

Dr. Foster: *On the first day of school or the first day you are ready to implement* **Pep** *(* **P***erformance =* **e***ncouragement •* **p***ractice), tell a story about someone who had to practice to be a team player and perform at high levels. I talk about Michael Jordan, but it could be a person more familiar to students.*

What Does It Take To Succeed?

On the first day of school, I *dialogue* with my students rather than *tell* them what they need to do to be successful in class. Through this dialogue, the students learn what it takes to succeed and what I expect of them.

In Practice
Dr. Foster

Dr. Foster: *Class. Who is Michael Jordan?*

Student 1: *He is one of the best basketball players of all time.*

Dr. Foster: *Because he was such a good basketball player, he **did not** have to practice. Right?*

Student 2: *No! He **did** have to practice.*

Dr. Foster: *Why?*

Student 3: *He had to practice to stay the best.*

Dr. Foster: *Everyone! **What does it take to succeed** in our class?*

Class: ***Practice!***

When students say they have already done something, I remind them of Michael Jordan. "To stay good at something, what does it take? Practice!"

Dr. Foster: *He was so good he could practice at home. He did not have to practice with the team.*

Student 2: *No! He **did** have to practice with the team.*

Dr. Foster: *Why?*

Student 4: *Because he didn't play the game alone. He had to be able to play with the team.*

Dr. Foster: *Everyone! **What does it take to succeed** in our class?*

Class: ***Be a team player!***

Throughout the year, I remind the students of Michael Jordan. "When we practice, what does it take to succeed?" "Be a team player!"

Through dialogue, my students find out what I value and what it takes to succeed in our classroom (practice and teamwork). To build trust, I have to "walk the talk."

Dr. Foster: *It takes more than talk to communicate expectations. To build trust, you must walk the talk. Read "Do You Walk the Talk?" to see what I mean.*

Do You Walk the Talk?

"Actions speak louder than words."

"If you're going to talk the talk, you've got to walk the walk."

No matter how you say it—if you say something is true, show it through your actions. When it comes to effective practice, be authentic, genuine, and trustworthy. (Fill in the blanks to learn how to walk the talk.)

If you say ___ , do you ___ (walk the talk)?

It's OK to make mistakes.	**Use formative-grading criteria that show learning evidence during guided and independent practice is valued.** • Do **not** evaluate the level of mastery during practice. Focus on the learning, not the mistakes.
Take your time.	**Give students who finish quickly a challenging task about the unit of study or have them assist others to be successful.** • Do **not** reward early completers with fun things to do while others continue to work. "When we practice, we all practice."
Be on task.	**Explain and demonstrate what "on task" means, as it varies from one activity to another.** • Do **not** assume students know. The on-task behaviors for a whole class discussion differ from cooperative learning.
Do your best.	**Show you value on-task behavior and perseverance.** • Do **not** make students "complete" assignments or take unfinished assignments home as homework when they have evidenced learning in class. Think quality, not quantity.
Be a team player.	**Expect students to support each other appropriately during guided practice.** • Do **not** try to keep students from appropriate talk during guided practice—discussion advances learning.
I trust you.	**Give students opportunities to show they are trustworthy.** • Do **not** let students practice work incorrectly. Allow students to grade their own practice with a teacher's edition or answer sheet as well as talk with peers to clarify directions, check answers, and discuss solutions.

The *reality* is that to urge and build trust in the classroom,
teachers must be trustworthy and do what they say!

A. Teacher: *I want to be a teacher who walks the talk! You have given me some practical ways to accomplish this goal.*

Dr. Foster: *Before we conclude our dialogue about* **practice** *and move on to* **evaluation**, *I have one last question to ask.*

Think back to the **Active Engagement Prescription** *and our discussion of the primary teaching methods and the rate of retention after 24 hours. (See page 52.)*

Which of these methods had the highest and lowest retention rates?

Figure 7.5

Teaching Methods	Demonstration Teach others	Discussion group Reading	Audiovisual Practice by doing	Lecture

A. Teacher: *Your question is* **distributed practice** *(see page 160).*

I recall that **lecture** *(5%) was the lowest and* **teach others** *(90%) was the highest. I do not remember all the other percentages, but I do remember that* **discussion group**, **practice by doing**, *and* **teach others** *were the highest.*

Wow! I have come full circle. When my students discuss their work and teach others during practice, they are actively engaged and more likely to retain new learning.

Dr. Foster: *Not only did you pass the test, you went beyond expectations because you made connections to other information and discovered that the active ingredients of one prescription work with those of another.*

A. Teacher: *I have learned a lot, but I need more* **practice** *and help to design effective lessons and practice activities.*

Dr. Foster: *Use* 🗁 **Supplement K: Unit and Lesson Design** *and find other resources to support and improve your practice. (Select the* **Supplements** *page, then* **K–P** *at www.classroommanagementblues.com and follow the link to* **Supplement K**.*)*

I promised to help you with paper overload. Here is the best strategy I have found.

Use 🗁 **Supplement M: Practice Book** *to reduce paper overload and work smarter as a teacher. (Select the* **Supplements** *page at www.classroommanage mentblues.com, then* **K–P** *for* **Supplement K**.*)*

Here is a short explanation of how it works.

A practice book is a spiral notebook in which students do *practice* activities and exercises from texts, worksheets, projection screens, SmartBoard, and the classroom white board, as well as interact with and reflect about learning content. Students can even write responses in the practice book for duplicated materials, so teachers can use the same materials again in other classes or from year to year—saving trees, the money to repurchase, and the time it takes to duplicate the same materials over again.

Dr. Foster: *Practice books never leave the classroom, so the students can keep track of their work, as well as evidence learning over time for other assessment purposes.*

Everything done in the practice book is something that teachers monitor during class time, so they do not have to take the work home or stay after school to grade. (Select **Supplements**, *then* **K–P** *for* **Supplement M: Practice Book** *at www.classroommanagementblues.com for more detailed information.*

This leads us to the other topic you Wanted to Learn about—evaluation, the fourth active ingredient of the **Appropriate Assessments Prescription**.

A. Teacher: *I am ready to learn how to assess and document behavioral expectations during practice and factor practice in the calculation of a final grade!*

Active Ingredient	🍎 Evaluation

Susan Butler (2001) defines **evaluation**, the fourth active ingredient in the **Appropriate Assessments Prescription**, as a judgment about the quality or worth of assessment results. When teachers evaluate or judge the performance level on assessments, they use criteria to assign a grade or numerical value. Butler uses a snapshot and photo album analogy to describe the relationship between assessment and *evaluation*.

> 📄 **e·val·u·ate** [ĭ-văl′yoō-āt′] **v.**
>
> 1. to judge or determine the worth or quality of
> 2. *Mathematics* to ascertain the numerical value of
>
> *Random House Dictionary*

Each classroom assessment is a snapshot of what students know and are able to do. . . . Snapshots can be collected into the photo album of evaluation. However, the evaluative process goes beyond just collecting information; evaluation is concerned with making judgments based upon the collection. (para. 4–5)

A. Teacher: *I am extremely uncomfortable when I have to make judgments about my students' performance and assign report card grades. When a student or parent questions a grade, I lack the confidence to explain because grades do not always reflect student learning. Many of my students coast and get good grades without having learned anything new while others learn more but do not get the best grades (Bartel, 2005).*

> *Whoever undertakes to set himself up as judge of Truth and Knowledge is shipwrecked by the laughter of the gods.*
> **Albert Einstein**

Maybe if I had a better understanding of the evaluation process I would be more confident and effective when I grade my students' performances and projects.

Dr. Foster: *I have confidence in your ability to achieve this goal.*

 Look at this Learning Time Line (see Figure 7.6). Describe what you see.

Figure 7.6

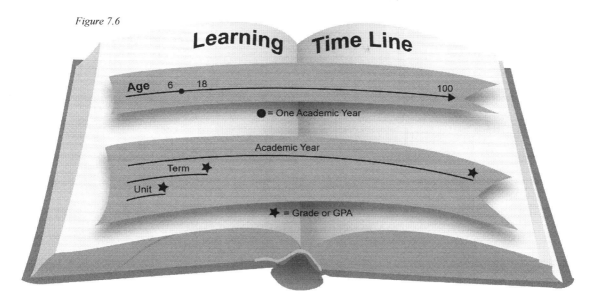

A. Teacher: *The time line arrow represents **lifelong learning**. The academic years between the ages of 6 and 18 make up only a small portion of a person's life; however, these elementary and secondary school years provide the foundation for lifelong learning.*

*I see the end of the unit, term, and academic year as the place in time when a teacher examines and judges multiple assessments and calculates a final grade or GPA. According to Butler's analogy, the multiple assessments in the photo album of evaluation to calculate a **final grade** or GPA are the snapshots of what a student knows and is able to do throughout the grading period.*

*The final grade and GPA are summative as they are the **sum** of a student's level of performance at one point in time. The multiple assessments could be either formative or summative.*

This time line was helpful, but I need a clearer picture of how to evaluate student work and calculate final grades and GPAs.

Dr. Foster: *Mark Conley, the author of **Connecting Standards and Assessment through Literacy**, offers some advice that can help you understand the full scope of how to evaluate student achievement. He says, "Good assessment **should** showcase a student's growth and achievement—both the journey and the destination— to provide a more comprehensive picture of what a student has achieved and what it took to get there" (2005, p. 14).*

 *Now, interpret the **Learning Time Line** based on Dr. Conley's description of good assessment.*

A. Teacher: *It takes a lot of time for me to think through these exercises. Why don't you just tell me the information?*

Dr. Foster: *You know the answer to that question.*

A. Teacher: *Yes. Learning takes time; I want to rush the learning process. If I take an active role in the learning, I am more likely to retain the information over time. You help me learn; I need to do more of this for my students.*

In the diagram (see Figure 7.6), the time-line arrow represents the journey—lifelong learning. The academic years between the ages of 6 and 18 represent legs of the journey. The end of the unit, term, and academic year are destinations—places in time along the journey.

Snapshots in a photo album help tell the story of the journey to each destination. So to get an overall picture of what my students have achieved, I need to look at each snapshot or classroom assessment when I assess students' growth and achievement.

I think audio and video make the achievement picture even clearer.

Dr. Foster: *Again, you have gone beyond expectations.*

As technology continues to advance, it will become easier and easier to use audio and video to evidence learning.

You are ready to apply what you have learned to the development of clear and fair grading practices.

*In its simplest form, the formula I use to calculate a final **g**rade/GPA is the **sum** of **f**ormative and **s**ummative assessment grades.*

$$f + s = g$$

Assessment numbers and labels take on meaning only as each individual teacher makes them mean something. Confusion emerges when the numbers and labels tend to mean too many things or when it is impossible for students and parents to tell whether they mean anything at all. . . . Not everyone needs to assess in identical ways. However, there can be considerable benefits in clarity and fairness for everyone if educators can reach some agreement with regard to the meanings and messages underlying our assessment practices. (Conley, 2005, p. 151)

A. Teacher: *This is consistent with Dr. Conley's description of good assessment; it would provide an overall picture (final **g**rade) for what a student has achieved (**s**ummative assessments) and what it took to get there (**f**ormative assessments).*

Do summative and formative assessments count equally in the formula to calculate a final grade? How should I grade formative assessments?

A. Teacher: *I have many questions and recall from our discussion of practice that it is appropriate to grade summative assessments, **not** formative assessments. Please clarify.*

Dr. Foster: *First, I will clarify how to grade formative assessments. Then, I will show you how to **weight** formative and summative assessments when a final grade is calculated.*

Which criteria are appropriate for grading formative and summative assessments? Teachers use different criteria to evaluate students' performances on formative and summative assessments and assign grades or numerical values. It is appropriate for teachers to grade summative **performance** assessments after a unit of study for knowledge and skill mastery. The criteria for grading **practice**, or formative assessments when students learn new information, include evidence of learning, on-task behavior, and appropriate support of others during practice.

> There are no hard-and-fast rules about the best ways to grade. In fact, as Erickson and Strommer (1991) point out, how you grade depends a great deal on your values, assumptions, and educational philosophy. (Davis, 2002, para. 1)

A. Teacher: *Now it makes sense! I have asked about how to calculate a final grade; but before I could understand how to grade, I needed to have knowledge about practice and assessments—otherwise I would just use the formula.*

*I think formative assessments should count more than summative assessments when I calculate final grades or GPAs because students spend more time **learning** (journey) than on **achievement** tests and projects at the end of the unit of study (destination).*

Dr. Foster: *You know you have performed well!*

A. Teacher: *Show me how you grade practice and formative assessments.*

Dr. Foster: *Fair enough. Here is the holistic rubric I use when I grade practice, which includes learning activities like class participation and cooperative learning.*

Table 7.8

		Formative Assessment—Grading Criteria Expectations for Practice
A+	> 4	Evidences learning, is consistently on task, supports others, and goes beyond expectations
→ **A**	**4**	**Evidences learning, is *consistently* on task, and supports others**
B	3	Evidences learning, is *mostly* on task, and supports others
C	2	Evidences learning, is *somewhat* on task, and supports others
D	1	Evidences learning
F	0	Makes no attempt to evidence learning, be on task, or support others

A. Teacher: *I see you give points for what you value—**learning**, **on-task** behavior (effort), and appropriate **support of others** (peer teaching). I think the expectancy would be high for all students to hit the target. The rubric urges students to attempt the task and evidence learning for a passing grade.*

Why do you use the word "support" rather than "assist?"

> When students are individually evaluated regarding their personal effort in the classroom rather than their status in comparison to other students, they are likely to be task centered rather than grade centered in their view of evaluation (Guthrie, 2001; Rosenholtz & Simpson, 1984).

Dr. Foster: *Pretend you are in a stadium to watch your favorite player. Only those on the field or court may assist him or her, but you can provide support by your presence and cheers of encouragement.*

Before a practice session begins, establish the expectations for support. Students may be guides, assistants, cheerleaders, observers, or active listeners.

*You will get detailed information about how to handle student behavior during practice when we discuss the **Trustworthy Behavior Prescription**.*

 *Look at the Grading Scale for Mastery (see Figure 7.7). The rubric contains criteria that represent the percentage of knowledge or skills mastered or retained after a term or unit of study. Teachers use the rubric to assign grades for the summative assessments or **performances**. Grading scales for mastery vary from school to school.*

Figure 7.7

Grading Scale for Mastery

Grade	Percent	4.0 Scale
A	90–100	3.5–4.0
B	80–89	2.5–3.4
C	70–79	1.5–2.4
D	60–69	0.5–1.4
F	0–59	0–0.4

A. Teacher: *So you say that I should use the **Formative Assessment—Grading Criteria for Practice** (formative assessments) and my school's **Grading Scale for Mastery** when I grade **performance** (summative assessments).*

What should I use for practice tests and quizzes?

Dr. Foster: *Look at this Venn diagram. What do you think?*

Figure 7.8

Practice Formative Assessments | **Practice Tests** Quizzes | **Performance** Summative Assessments

A. Teacher: *Practice tests and quizzes share attributes of both practice and performance. Use the grading scale for performance **and** criteria for practice to evaluate evidence of learning. Students who make an attempt receive a passing grade. For the Grading Scale for Mastery, the lowest percentage for a passing grade would be 60 for a student who makes an attempt and evidences some learning.*

Dr. Foster: *You've got it. By removing the fear of failure, students would most likely attempt and do their best on the practice test or quiz! Read about Ms. Julie Johnson— "She's Got It," too.*

She's Got It!

According to Pangaro and McGaghie (2005), "evaluations are seen by learners as hurdles grounded in threat. . . . Evaluation is a process to which most . . . learners grudgingly submit. It is rarely a process they seek and enjoy" (p. 134). In *The First Days of School,* Harry and Rosemary Wong (1998) included a letter that shows how a kindergarten teacher in Biwabik, Minnesota, uses **tests appropriately** (p. 241). Ms. Julie Johnson's students want to show her they've got it!

In Practice
Julie Johnson

They Beg Me to Test Them

I decide exactly what it is I want students to know or be able to do. And then I show them how to do it. We practice together. They practice on their own. And then I test them the same way we practice. As we begin each new unit, the first thing I do is tell my students what they will be learning and how they will show me that they have learned it—in other words, how they will be tested. This way we all know exactly what we are learning and how we will know when and if we have learned it. There are no secrets as to what is expected of them. When I do this, they all succeed. In my class, test is not a bad word. It is something my students look forward to. It is their chance to show me what they have learned. They can't wait for their turn to be tested because after all the instruction and practice, the test is the easiest part—at least that's what my students tell me. They beg me to test them. They even stand in line waiting for their turn to show me what they have learned.

Julie Johnson

Use the same strategies for practice **tests** and quizzes and you will hear your students say, **"We've got it! Please, test us!"**

A. Teacher: *I understand the criteria to grade practice, summative assessments, and practice tests and quizzes. What concerns me is the extra time it will take to keep a grade book and use all the practice grades to calculate a final grade.*

How can teachers efficiently document formative assessment results? Teachers should use formative assessments to modify instruction and reteach before incorrect practice becomes permanent. Waiting until after a test to find out whether students have evidenced learning is too late, teachers need an effective record-keeping system. Carol Ann Tomlinson, coauthor of *Leadership for Differentiating Schools and Classrooms*, recommends that teachers carry a clipboard "around the room to spot-check student work in progress for particular proficiencies" and to store and retrieve informative data easily about students as individuals and learners (2007, p. 13).

> During my early teaching years . . . I simply knew I was supposed to give tests and grades. . . . With no understanding of the role of assessment in a dynamic and success-oriented classroom, I initially ignored assessment when I could and did it when I had to. (Tomlinson, 2007, para. 3)

Dr. Foster: *Like Dr. Carol Ann Tomlinson, I used a record-keeping page on a clipboard to **check off** progress as I monitored student work during practice and to **record** a daily practice grade for each subject or class period.*

    📂 **Supplement N: Practice Record Sheet** *is the record-keeping page I used to document evidence of student learning during practice and other activities like participation in class discussions. I will provide some information now, but you will find a more detailed explanation about how to use this record sheet on my website. (Select **Supplements** at www.classroommanagementblues.com, then **K–P** and locate **Supplement N**.)*

A. Teacher: *I know athletic coaches use clipboards, but I never thought about using one in my classroom.*

Dr. Foster: *Whether you use a clipboard, iPad or other tablet-like device, recording formative data is as simple as a check, plus, and minus can inform your teaching.*

*When I monitored students as they worked, I chose to spot check a couple of answers. If I observed that a student answered correctly without guidance from me or another student, I recorded a (**+**). When I guided the student to respond correctly, I recorded a (✓). The most telling sign was the (**−**); I used this sign to show that a student struggled to respond even with guidance.*

A. Teacher: *These data would be helpful, but I am a little confused.*

How do I know when to use the Formative Assessment—Grading Criteria numbers to record practice grades and when to use the check, plus, minus system?

Dr. Foster: *Let me show you. Read "Check It Out! (on the next page) to check it out in more detail.*

Check It Out!

In my classroom, I documented the results of formative assessments daily during practice for each subject or class period on a Practice Record Sheet. I used these data to modify instruction and reteach individual students or small groups before the end of the unit of study. **Check it out!**

Progress Criteria . . . to assess particular proficiencies
- **+**   Evidences learning *without* guidance from teacher
- **✓**   Evidences learning *with* guidance from teacher
- **−**   Little or no evidence of learning with guidance from teacher

Formative Assessment—Grading Criteria . . . to record a daily practice score
- **> 4**   Evidences learning, is consistently on task, supports others, and goes beyond expectations
- **4**   Evidences learning, is consistently on task, and supports others
- **3**   Evidences learning, is mostly on task, and supports others
- **2**   Evidences learning, is somewhat on task, and supports others
- **1**   Evidences learning
- **0**   Makes no attempt to evidence learning, be on task, or support others

Practice Record Sheet

Example English Practice Week 2	Day 1 9/14	Day 2 9/15	Day 3 9/16	Homework 9/16	Day 4 CL 9/17	Day 5 D 9/18	Learning Journal	WEEK 2	Identify Nouns Text p 12 9/15	Identify Verbs Text p 13 9/6	Identify Nouns Worksheet 8 9/17	Quiz Nouns 9/21
Able, Annie	3	3	3	4.2	3	4	4	**3.5**	✓	−	✓	75
Bright, Bobby	4	4	3	4	3	4.2	4	**3.7**	+	+	✓	93
Capable, Chris	4	4	3	0	3	3	4	**3**	−	−	✓	60

CL = Cooperative Learning   D = Discussion

Annie Able was *mostly* on task, supported others appropriately, and evidenced learning. I need to work one-on-one in a small group with Annie to reteach verb identification.

Chris Capable was consistently on task during practice, but I need to closely monitor and spend time one-on-one and in small groups to assist with identifying nouns and verbs.

Teachers who "check out" how students are doing during practice can reteach before incorrect practice becomes permanent. To learn more about how to monitor and document practice, locate **Supplement N: Practice Record Sheet** at *www.classroommanagement blues.com*. **Check it out!** (Select the **Supplements** page, then **K-P** for **Supplement N**.)

A. Teacher: *I am ready to use a clipboard and document formative assessments. It sounds like a lot of work, but I think I will enjoy teaching more when I see evidence that my students have learned throughout the unit of study rather than be disappointed after the final exam, or another summative assessment, to find they did not learn as much as I had expected. I can also use the formative results to reteach and modify my instruction. You are right; I usually do not reteach after the summative assessment because I feel pressured to move on and cover more of the curriculum.*

Dr. Foster: 📂 **Supplement V: Clipboard Management** *explains how to set up the clipboard. (Select* **Supplements** *at www.classroommanagementblues.com, then* **Q–V** *for* **Supplement V**.*)*

An added benefit of **evaluation** *and the other active ingredients of the* **Appropriate Assessments Prescription** *is more confidence when explaining grades to students and parents.*

It is not uncommon for students and parents to challenge a grade simply because connections between classroom performance and grading are unclear. (Conley, 2005, p. 149)

How should teachers use formative assessments to calculate a final grade/GPA as compared to summative assessments? According to Erikson and Strommer (1991), no hard-and-fast rules about the best way to calculate grades exist, but how you grade depends on your values, assumptions, and educational philosophy (Davis, 1999). While the purpose of grades may vary from educator to educator, students ask, "Does this count for a grade?"

The Games We Play

In his article "Grading to Communicate," Tony Winger writes:

As a young teacher, I found the authority to give grades empowering. The grade was my ace in the hole, providing the leverage needed to entice students to cooperate. As time passed, it dawned on me that the manner in which I was using grades conflicted with my deeper purposes as an educator. . . . I wanted my students to wonder, to understand, and ultimately to be changed. Many of them simply wanted a good grade.

Students reported that they see their schoolwork as a game they play for grades—a game that at best treats learning as incidental, and at worst distracts students from making meaning. One student referred to this grade game as academic bulimia. Students stuff themselves with information only to regurgitate it for the test, with little opportunity for the thoughtful engagement that would produce deep understanding and growth. (2005, para. 2)

The ***reality*** is that students who play games for grades "lose out" on learning!

A. Teacher: *I always believed that the purpose of assessment was to determine report card grades. Now I know the purpose of formative grades is to modify instruction and "provide feedback to students as they progress toward a goal. If this feedback is of a high quality, improvement in student performance can result. Summative processes have more of a gate-keeping function" (Butler, 2001, para. 6).*

Dr. Foster: *From this understanding, which of these functions and purposes of grades closely reflect your values and educational philosophy?*

Table 7.9

Functions and Purposes of Grades
2009 Ken O'Conner, *How to Grade for Learning*
What counts for grades are the performances that students give to demonstrate the knowledge, skills, and behaviors they have acquired as the result of instruction and practice. These demonstrations usually happen at or near the end (however arbitrarily one defines *the end*) of a unit, a course, or a grading period. (p. 131)
2009 Rick Stiggins, "Assessment FOR Learning in Upper Elementary Grades"
Assessments become far more than merely one-time events attached onto the end of teaching. They become part of the learning process and keep students posted on their progress and confident enough to continue striving. (p. 420)
2005 Tony Winger, "Grading to Communicate"
The purpose of grades is to assess and promote learning. A low grade simply communicates a learning gap. (para. 24)
2005 Mark Conley, *Connecting Standards and Assessment through Literacy*
Good assessment should showcase a student's growth and achievement—both the journey and the destination—to provide a more comprehensive picture of what a student has achieved and what it took to get there. (p. 14)
1974 Michael Scriven, cited in "Grading Practices" by Barbara Gross Davis (1999)
Grades serve other purposes. Scriven (1974) identified at least six functions of grading: • To describe unambiguously the worth, merit, or value of work • To improve the ability of students to identify good work and improve their discrimination skills or self-evaluation of work submitted • To stimulate and encourage good work by students • To communicate the teacher's judgment of the student's progress • To inform the teacher about what students have and haven't learned • To select people for rewards or continued education (para. 2)

A. Teacher: *I believe assessments should be more than one-time events that promote learning, reflect the students' performances, and demonstrate the knowledge, skills, and behaviors acquired as the result of instruction and practice. Dr. Scriven's functions of grading are least reflective of my values and assessment philosophy; Dr. Conley's description of good assessment is most reflective.*

Final grades should provide an overall picture of students' growth and achievement and include both formative and summative assessments.

I am ready for you to show me how to weigh formative and summative assessments when I calculate final grades.

Dr. Foster: *When I compute a final letter grade for a course of study, I include both formative* (**practice**) *and summative* (**performance**) *assessments. The formative assessments that I group together include weekly practice grades, quiz scores, and other content-specific formative results. The performance components include test grades, project scores, and other content-specific summative results. "A grade that is separated into distinct components on the basis of key learning becomes a meaningful communication—to students and parents" (Winger, 2005, para. 14).*

Each component is worth a specified percentage of the overall letter grade, and I combine the grades for the components according to the predetermined weight of each to compute the overall grade (para. 17). To determine the specified percentage of the final grade for the formative and summative assessment components, I use the school's Grading Scale for Mastery (see Figure 7.9).

As 60% represents a passing grade, I count practice as 60% of the final grade. Performance accounts for the remaining 40%. As I value practice and want students to focus more on learning rather than grades, practice has a higher percentage.

Figure 7.9

Grading Scale for Mastery		
Grade	Percent	4.0 Scale
A	90–100	3.5–4.0
B	80–89	2.5–3.4
C	70–79	1.5–2.4
D	60–69	0.5–1.4
F	0–59	0–0.4

A. Teacher: *If I used the passing grade percentage for formative assessments, I think my students would more likely do the practice. If they would do the practice, they would most likely be able to do the performance—pass tests.*

Dr. Foster: ▭ **Supplement O: Grade Book Magic** *provides more information about the grading process. (Select* **Supplements** *page at www.classroommanage mentblues.com, then* **K–P** *for* **Supplement O***.)*

Let me give you a quick overview of how to calculate each component and the final grade. Read these inserts: (1) "Analyze This! Formative Assessments;" (2) "Analyze This, Too! Summative Assessments;" and (3) "In the Final Analysis! Final Grades."

Analyze This! Formative Assessments

Each week, I enter the weekly **practice** grades, quizzes, and other content-specific formative assessments from the Practice Record Sheet into the grade book and electronic grade book. At the end of the term, I average each component and convert the weekly practice grades to percentages using a conversion table for practice based on the school's Grading Criteria for Mastery (see below). **Analyze this** example!

In Practice
Dr. Foster

In the following example, **Practice** represents **60%** of the final grade. To determine the weight of each practice component, I base the decision on my values and assessment philosophy. I specify the value of student learning for Weekly Practice at **30%**, Quizzes at **10%**, and Other (writing drafts) at **20%**.

Grade Book

% of Final Grade	Weekly Practice						30	Quizzes			10	Other			20	60
English Term 1 **Practice 60%** Formative Assessments	Week 1	Week 2	Week 3	Week 4	Week 5	Week 6	Ave 4.0 Scale	Practice	Nouns	Verbs	Complex Sent.	Quizzes	*Narr. 1 Draft	*Sh. Story Draft	*Narr. 2 Draft	Other	Final Practice
Able, Annie	3	3.5	4	4	3	3	**3.4**	**88**	75	85	80	**80**	75	85	82	**81**	**84**

* **Narr.**=Narrative **Sh. Story**=Short Story

Conversion for Practice

Grade	4.0 Scale	Percent
A	4	95
	3.5	90
B	3	85
	2.5	80
C	2	75
	1.5	70
D	1	65
	0.5	60
F	0	50

Annie Able

Step 1: Average the weekly practice 4.0 scale grades.
$(3 + 3.5 + 4 + 4 + 3 + 3) ÷ 6 = 3.4$

Step 2: Convert the **Weekly Practice** average using the Conversion for Practice table.
$3.4 = 88\%$

Step 3: Average the **Quiz** scores.
$(75 + 85 + 80) ÷ 3 = 80\%$

Step 4: Average the **Other** formative assessments.
$(75 + 85 + 82) ÷ 3 = 81\%$

Step 5: Calculate the **Final Practice Grade** by weighting each component using the % of Final Grade. For example, Weekly Practice is **30%**, so count that score **3** times.
$(88 + 88 + 88 + 80 + 81 + 81) ÷ 6 = 84\%$

Use a calculator, spreadsheet, or electronic grade book to compute the final grade for **practice**. **Supplement O: Grade Book Magic** has more information about grading. (Choose **Supplements** at *www.classroommanagementblues.com*, then **K-P** for **Supplement O**.)

A. Teacher: *If I use weekly practice grades to encourage my students to evidence learning, be on task, and support others throughout a unit of study, I will also have fewer grades to calculate at the end of the grading period. I really like this!*

Analyze This, Too!
Performance Assessments

I enter **performance** grades for tests, projects, and other content-specific summative assessments in the grade book and electronic grade book throughout the grading period. At the end of the term, I average each component based on the school's Grading Criteria for Mastery. **Analyze this** example, **too!**

In the following example, **Performance** represents **40%** of the final grade. To determine the percentage of the final grade for each performance component, I based the decision on my values and assessment philosophy. I determined the value of student learning for Tests at **15%** and Writing at **25%**.

Grade Book

% of Final Grade	Tests			15	Other			25	40
English Term 1 **Performance 40%** Summative Assessments	Nouns	Verbs	Complex Sentences	**Tests**	Narrative 1	Short Story	Narrative 2	**Other**	**Final Performance**
Able, Annie	85	90	90	**88**	90	95	95	**93**	**91**

Annie Able

Step 1: Average the grades for **Tests**.
   $(85 + 90 + 90) \div 3 = 88\%$

Step 2: Average the grades for **Other** assessments.
   $(90 + 95 + 95) \div 3 = 93\%$

Step 3: Calculate the **Final Performance Grade** by weighting each component using the % of the Final Grade—Weigh **Tests** 1.5 and **Other** 2.5.
   $(88 \cdot 1.5) + (93 \cdot 2.5) \div 4 = 91\%$ or
   $132 + 232.5 = 364.5 \div 4 = 91\%$

Use a calculator, spreadsheet, or electronic grade book to compute the final grade for **performance**. **Supplement O: Grade Book Magic** has more information. (Select **Supplements** at *www.classroommanagementblues.com*, then **K-P** for **Supplement O**.)

In the Final Analysis! Final Grades

The formula I use to calculate final grades in its simplest form is (**f** + **s** = **g**), the sum of formative and summative assessments. **In the final analysis**, a more precise formula is (**f** • w_f) + (**s** • w_s) ÷ (w_f + w_s) = **g** (the letter "w" represents the **w**eight of each component).

In Practice
Dr. Foster

Practice (**f** formative assessments) represents **60%** of the final grade and a weight of 6. **Performance** (**s** summative assessments) represents **40%** of the final grade and a weight of 4. To calculate Annie's final English grade, follow the steps below.

Grade Book

% of Final Grade	30	10	20	**60**	15	25	**40**	**100**		
English Term 1 **Final Grade 100%** Formative + Summative Assessments	Practice	Quizzes	Other - Drafts	**Final Practice**	Tests	Other - Writing	**Final Performance**	**Final Grade**	GPA	Letter Grade
Able, Annie	88	80	81	**84**	88	93	**91**	**87**	3.2	B

Grading Scale for Mastery

Grade	Percent	4.0 Scale
A	90–100	3.5–4.0
B	80–89	2.5–3.4
C	70–79	1.5–2.4
D	60–69	0.5–1.4
F	0–59	0–0.4

Annie Able

Step 1: Multiply the **Final Practice** grade times 6, representing 60% of the final grade.
(84 • 6) = 504

Step 2: Multiply the **Final Performance** grade times 4 representing 40% of the final grade.
(91 • 4) = 364

Step 3: Add the sum of the final **Practice** and **Performance** grades and divide by 10.
(504+ 364) ÷ 10 = 86.8 = 87%

Step 4: Convert the **Final Grade** to a GPA and letter grade using the Grading Scale for Mastery.
87 = 3.2 = B

In the final analysis, Annie's final **performance** grade was higher than her final **practice** grade. Her **test** score was higher than her **quiz** score.

Use a calculator, spreadsheet, or electronic grade book to compute final grades. **Supplement O: Grade Book Magic** has more information about grading. (Select **Supplements** at *www.classroommanagementblues.com*, then **K-P** for **Supplement O**.)

A. Teacher: *I have a basic understanding of how to assess student learning and calculate final grades, but I still have one concern and a few more questions.*

My concern is the reaction I might get from administrators and parents about the use of the grading practices you shared.

Dr. Foster: *I have received only positive responses. Many educators and I agree that principals affirm grading practices that vary from traditional practices when teachers provide a rationale aligned with research-based practice. Parents are also supportive if they understand how it helps their children learn (Leahy, Lyon, Thompson, & Wiliam, 2005).*

A. Teacher: *That makes sense. With the information provided, I am confident that I will be able to explain how my practices evidence sound education theory and practice.*

Could you explain why homework is part of the weekly practice grade rather than a separate component in the grade book?

Dr. Foster: *I value homework, but as we discussed in our session on the* **High Expectations Prescription** *I am not always sure the grade reflects the student's work—often it is the work of a parent or someone else. Students who have parents who help with the homework get higher grades than students who do the work on their own— by his or her choice or because no one is at home to help. When homework is one part of the weekly practice grade,* **in-class** *practice that I can observe counts more than out-of-class practice.*

> Be sure all students have equal access to the resources and equipment needed to succeed. That may mean that each student has access to necessary materials provided at school or at home. If circumstances beyond their control keep them from succeeding, that's not fair. (Stiggins, 2005, p. 143)

A. Teacher: *My next question is about extra credit. How did you deal with students and parents who beg for extra credit at the end of the grading period to get the grade they want?*

Dr. Foster: *I* ***did not*** *give extra credit at the end of the grading period to raise a grade. I added challenging questions or tasks to some assignments throughout the grading period for extra points. I added these points to the assignments when assessed rather than at the end of the grading period. I urged students to avail themselves of these opportunities and go beyond expectations for higher grades.*

Students and parents received my policy about extra credit the first week of school—"Extra! Extra! Read All About It!"

Extra! Extra! Read All About It!

One question I did **not** hear from my students at the end of a grading period was, "*May I have extra credit to bring up my grade?*" Students and parents alike already knew the answer because they **read all about it** the first week of school, along with the other information about academic and behavioral expectations.

In Practice
Dr. Foster

From the desk of Dr. Foster

Students **WILL NOT** receive extra credit at the end of the grading period to raise a grade.

Students **WILL** receive opportunities for extra credit throughout the grading period.

Students **SHOULD** take advantage of these opportunities.

Dr. Foster

Early in my career, I gave extra credit at the end of each grading period to students who wanted to raise their grades. Many times the request came from parents.

I learned more from extra credit than my students. **I learned . . .**

- Some students did not apply themselves throughout the grading period and wanted a quick fix.
- If one student received it, they all wanted it.
- It was **extra** work for me. I had to come up with something that was challenging enough to be worthy of the extra points.
- It took **extra** time for me to grade the extra credit in addition to calculating final grades at the end of the term.

I added challenging questions or tasks to some assignments throughout the grading period for **extra** points. I added the **extra** points to these assignments when I assessed the assignments, not when I calculated the final grade. **My students learned** "extra" meant **extra** for them, not for me.

A. Teacher: *Thank you. Every student has the potential to succeed and reach his or her potential if teachers use your strategies. Did any of your students get F's?*

Dr. Foster: *A few of my upper elementary and middle school students did earn F's the first grading period. t had the impression that I was a pushover and thought that I would not give them an F on their report card, even if they earned it. They wanted to test me.*

Once students understood that I followed through, they earned passing grades in each of the other grading periods. It takes time to build trust. You might review authenticity in the **High Expectations Prescription** *(see pages 87–90).*

> It is through our actions that others may observe who we are and what values and beliefs we hold. This transparency is one of the relational aspects of authenticity and it fosters trust . . . This trust can become the foundation of the teacher's credibility for the learners. Unfortunately, many of us have observed and participated in classes in which the teacher's behavior did not match their words; in my experience, this has made it difficult, if not impossible, to believe anything that the teacher offered. (Glickman, 2005, para. 11).

A. Teacher: *Again, I see how one prescription can influence another.*

I understand that it may take time for some students to trust the grading practices you prescribe, but what should teachers do when a student refuses to attempt a task during practice?

Dr. Foster: *We will discuss student behavior in more detail in our next session, but I will give you two quick tips now.*

Tip 1: **Be patient—something is better than nothing is!** When a student makes no attempt at a practice task, ask him or her to *choose* the part of the task they want to do for a passing practice grade. Once finished, expect the student to be on task—do nothing or more of the practice task. **Note:** It is unacceptable to bother other students! If they want to do something, it *has* to be the practice task or another agreed-upon task.

Tip 2: **Be patient—build upon success!** It is most difficult to get a student to take the first step! Once students do one thing, they tend to do more. **Remember:** You can reach your destination one-step at a time.

A. Teacher: *I will try these tips and work on my patience!*

Dr. Foster: *Nothing succeeds like success for you and your students. "Nothing Succeeds Like Success!" is a success story for one of my students and me.*

Nothing Succeeds Like Success!

Before the first day of school, a teacher declared, "You won't be able to get Ronnie to do **anything**! He sleeps all the time!" When I observed that Ronnie was asleep, I was ready for the challenge. As a firm believer that **nothing succeeds like success**, I was determined to get him to do something!

On the first day of school, I noticed Ronnie was asleep. He was not a bother to anyone, so I let him sleep. Once the others students started to work on a diagnostic assessment, I walked over to Ronnie's desk.

I asked Ronnie to wake up. He stirred and asked, "What?"

"Everyone is working on this assignment." I pointed to the paper on his desk and asked, "Is there anything on this page you know how to do?"

Ronnie pointed to a few of the exercises. I smiled and said, "Great! Do those, then you can go back to sleep."

He looked surprised and questioned, "That's all I have to do?"

"Yes, unless you want to do more."

Ronnie finished the exercises and laid his head down. He watched to see if I was going to make him do something else. I did not.

I succeeded on day one. Ronnie did **something**, and I took the first step to build Ronnie's trust.

Each day Ronnie did more work and eventually did not sleep in class.

The *reality* is that nothing succeeds like success—one day at a time.

A. Teacher: *I would guess students who trust you and understand how you calculate grades would say they earned grades. Do you ever "give" grades?*

Dr. Foster: *If a student was one or two percentage points away from the next grade and had improved or met expectations throughout the grading period, I "gave" the higher grade. I always explained to students why I added the points. They understood that I would not "give" points the next time. If a student could meet the expectations in one grading period, he or she could meet them in the next grading period.*

I never regretted this practice on a one-time basis. The students continued to get higher grades in later grading periods because they knew I recognized the effort they had evidenced. "Make the Grade" is about a teacher who did not believe a student should receive points he did not earn.

Make the Grade

To make something, combine ingredients and follow directions to completion. The same applies for **make the grade**.

When I was an elementary school principal, Ms. Maker requested that I attend a meeting with Scott and his mother about his low spelling grade. We all agreed on a plan to help Scott improve his spelling grade.

I checked with Ms. Maker and Scott once a week to see if he followed directions and received a better spelling test grade. The resounding answers were, "Yes!"

At the end of the grading period, I went to Ms. Maker and asked what grade he received for spelling on his report card. I was shocked to hear he had earned an F. She went on to say that, even though he got higher grades on all his tests and had done everything we had asked him to do since our meeting, Scott's grade was an F—one point from a passing grade.

The *reality* is that no matter what Scott learned about spelling and how to improve his study habits, he did not make the grade.

A. Teacher: *Grading can have a positive and negative effect on student learning and success in school. Even though I feel more confident in my ability to assess student learning and performance appropriately, grading is a heavy burden.*

Dr. Foster: *When you take all the responsibility for assessment, it **is** a heavy burden. If you get your students to become owners of their learning, it is possible that they share the responsibility for learning (Leahy, Lyon, Thompson, & Wiliam, 2005).*

"In their 1998 synthesis of research, Black and Wiliam reported that formative assessment produced significant learning gains" in schools where students "were the primary users of formative assessment information" and engaged in self-assessment (Chappuis, 2005, para. 2). Yet, "student self-assessment is one kind of formative assessment that is frequently overlooked" (Bingham, Holbrook, & Meyers, 2010, p. 59).

Dr. Foster: *Let's take a short break, then we will finish our session with a discussion of reflection. This kind of self-assessment is the last active ingredient in the* **Appropriate Assessments Prescription***.*

Active Ingredient	 Reflection

Self-assessment encourages **reflection**, the fifth active ingredient in the **Appropriate Assessments Prescription**. Reflection is the "vehicle for critical analysis, problem-solving, synthesis of opposing ideas, evaluation, identifying patterns and creating meaning—in short, many of the higher order thinking skills that we strive to foster in our students" ("TAP," 2000, p. 1). Without reflection, learning ends "well short of the re-organization of thinking that 'deep' learning requires" (Ewell, 1997, p. 9).

> *By three methods we may learn wisdom:*
> *First by reflection, which is noblest;*
> *Second, by imitation, which is easiest;*
> *and third by experience,*
> *which is the bitterest.*
>
> **Confucius**
> (551 BCE–479 BCE)

How does the ability to reflect affect student achievement? In "Student Self-Evaluation: What Research Says and What Practice Shows," Rolheiser and Ross state that "self-evaluation plays a key role in fostering an upward cycle of learning" (n.d., para. 13). Students achieve increasingly better results when they set higher goals, commit personal resources, and systematically review performance to improve their future performance ("Assessment Terminology," 2002).

Dr. Foster: *From what you have learned about assessment in this session, explain the difference between self-assessment, self-evaluation, and reflection.*

A. Teacher: *Self-assessment occurs when a person uses formative assessment to monitor his or her own progress toward goals and objectives throughout the learning process. Self-evaluation takes place when a person uses summative assessment to make a judgment about his or her own performance after learning experiences.*

I think reflection is the thinking that happens before, during, and after a learning process.

Dr. Foster: *Self-assess, or reflect, on your explanations of these terms as I present more information about the role of reflection in the learning process.*

Although giving information is important, Brazilian educator Paulo Freire agrees with thinkers like John Dewey and Alfred North Whitehead that the transmission of mere "facts" should not be the goal of education. Learners need to actively process and reflect on information transmitted through different media inside and outside the classroom.

> Learning is both an active and reflective process. Though we learn by doing, constructing, building, talking, and writing, we also learn by thinking about events, activities, and experiences. This confluence of experiences (action) and thought (reflection) combines to create new knowledge. Both action and reflection are essential ingredients in the construction of knowledge. (TAP, 2000, p. 1)

In the article "Paulo Freire and Education for Critical Consciousness," Freire defined the process of combining action and reflection *praxis*—a set of practices informed by reflection ("TAP," 2000). "Our actions are not random or haphazard but informed and deliberate and we are aware of why we do what we do" (p. 1).

A. Teacher: *I am **not** always aware of why I do what I do in the classroom.*

Dr. Foster: *It is difficult to extract thought (reflection) from experiences (action) because "we are often 'parallel processing'—reflecting upon activities even as we are in the midst of doing or experiencing them. Because learning is so often subconscious" we do not realize until we stop to think about a particular activity, why we've done what we've done or that "we've actually gained new knowledge or understanding" ("TAP," p. 1).*

Look at the "Ten Steps for Lifelong Learning and Problem Solving" chart from our **High Expectations Prescription** *session.*

 *With this new information, explain why the heading **Praxis** has been added to the first column of the chart.*

Table 7.10

Praxis Practices informed by reflection	Ten Steps for Lifelong Learning and Problem Solving		
Frame	**Step 1**	*Focus*	State the vision, goal, or problem.
	Step 2	*Research*	Gather information.
Process Information	**Step 3**	*Interpret*	Analyze information and clarify the vision, goal, or problem.
	Step 4	*Predict*	Consider outcomes, resources, and obstacles.
	Step 5	*Brainstorm*	Generate objectives, hypotheses, or possible solutions.
Decide	**Step 6**	*Choose*	Make decisions, establish timelines, and determine evaluation methodology.
Plan	**Step 7**	*Design*	Develop action plans and monitoring and assessment systems.
Implement	**Step 8**	*Act*	Put plans in action and fine-tune.
Learn from Experience	**Step 9**	*Evaluate*	Verify and value assessment results.
	Step 10	*Transfer*	Reflect on a future vision, goal, or problem.

From Bellanca & Fogarty, 1986; Covey, 1991; Dewey, 1973; Elias & Tobias, 1990; Gagné, 1985; Polya, 2004; Priestley, McGuire, Flegg, Hemsley, & Welham, 1978; Russo & Schoemaker, 1989; Silva, 1990; "The steps," 1987; and Whetten & Cameron, 1991—see references on page 384

A. Teacher: *Reflection, whether conscious or subconscious, happens **as** you actively frame, process information, decide, plan, implement, and learn from experience. These practices are more effective for goal attainment and solving problems when informed by reflective thinking. Of all these practices, I have the least amount of knowledge about how reflection informs the practice of learning from experience.*

Dr. Foster: *From your self-assessment, let's explore metacognition and transfer, two reflective-thinking behaviors that foster **learning from experience**. The general definition of **metacognition** is thinking about thinking (Pierce, 2004). Reflective thinking extends and **transfers** the knowledge or skills learned in one context to a new context (Donovan, Bransford, & Pellegrino, 1999).*

How does transfer enhance present and future learning? Sousa (2006) calls transfer the most powerful and least understood principle of learning. Transfer **when** learning is "the effect past learning has on the processing and acquisition of new learning" (p. 136). Transfer **of** learning is the degree to which the learner applies new learning to future situations (p. 136).

A. Teacher: *So when I activate the prior knowledge of my students, I help them take what they have learned and make sense of or connect to what they are learning.*

Dr. Foster: *The hope is that the transfer is positive. "The quality of transfer that occurs during new learning is largely dependent on the quality of the original learning" (p. 141).*

> Transfer is the core of problem solving, creative thinking, and all other higher mental processes, inventions, and artistic products (Sousa, 2006, p. 135). . . . Michelangelo, DaVinci, and Edison were able to transfer a great deal of their knowledge and skills to create magnificent works of art and invention. Their prior learnings made greater achievement possible. (p. 137)

 Do you think rote learning facilitates transfer?

A. Teacher: *I don't think so. When I memorized something for a test, I soon forgot it. So even if I knew it for the test, I wouldn't be able to transfer it to new learning in the present or future.*

Dr. Foster: *Research confirms that when students processed "information more thoroughly for meaning, there was a high degree of transfer to new situations" (Sousa, 2006, p. 141). "Without this type of extended processing, knowledge that students initially understand might fade and be lost over time" (p. 58).*

Two of the teaching-for-transfer techniques suggested in *How the Brain Learns* are bridging and hugging. Simulation games help students "practice new roles in diverse situations" and are examples of hugging—the new instruction is kept "as close as possible to the environment and requirements that the students will encounter in the future" (p. 159). Brainstorming ways to apply new learning in other situations is an example of bridging (Sousa, 2006). (Read "Can You Relate?" for another example of bridging.)

Can You Relate?

Dr. Robert J. Marzano (2007), among others, suggests that teachers and students create metaphors and analogies to bridge or deepen understanding of new knowledge. These tasks require the examination of similarities and differences. **Can you relate** to these examples?

In Practice
Dr. Marzano

"On the surface, Frederick Douglass and Helen Keller have little in common" (p. 76). This **metaphor** example illustrates how they share common characteristics at an abstract level.

Metaphor Example		
Element 1	**Common Abstract Characteristics**	**Element 2**
Frederic Douglass		*Helen Keller*
Was a slave as a young boy.	Had a rough beginning.	Got sick as a baby, which left her deaf and blind.
Learned to read and write anyway.	Achieved goals even when difficult.	Learned how to read Braille, and write; also went to college.
Wrote books and gave speeches against slavery.	Worked to help other people who suffered like him/her.	Through her speech tours and writing, she inspired others to overcome their disabilities.

"Creating **analogies** is the process of identifying the relationship between two sets of items" (pp. 76–77). Can you see how they relate?

Bone is to skeleton as word is to _____.

Martin Luther King, Jr. is to civil rights as _____ is to women's rights.

Rhythm is to music as _____ is to _____.

Bury My Heart at Wounded Knee is to Native Americans as _____ is to _____.

Excerpted from *The Art and Science of Teaching* by Robert J. Marzano, 2007

For more information about tasks **you can relate** to that highlight how to identify similarities and differences and deepen understanding of new knowledge read chapter 3 in *The Art and Science of Teaching* by Robert J. Marzano.

A. Teacher: *I understand that reflection informs the transfer of skills and content knowledge to new learning and other contexts. How does transfer connect to the use of self-assessment?*

Dr. Foster: When s*tudents actively engage in well-designed self-assessment tasks, they experience a deep understanding of content and value learning activities (Munns & Woodward 2006). A deeper understanding and transfer of knowledge and skills are possible when students use self-assessment effectively.*

A. Teacher: *Maybe older students can self-assess **effectively**. Are elementary students too young to assess their own learning?*

Dr. Foster: *"Elementary students aren't too young to use self-assessment. . . . [They] become able to engage in self-assessment as their metacognitive abilities—their awareness of their thought processes, strategies, and skills—develop" (Bingham et al., p. 59). The more students are aware of these metacognitive processes, strategies, and skills, "the more they can control such matters as goals, dispositions, and attention" (Pierce, 2004, para. 2).*

What is the role of metacognition within the learning process? "Developing the metacognitive awareness of students through self-assessment is at the heart of powerful, effective, and transformational teaching" (Bingham et al., 2010, p. 60). Metacognition is the internal dialogue that helps learners build the skills to monitor learning, predict learning outcomes, and self-regulate—make changes and adapt strategies if they perceive they are not working (Donovan, Bransford, & Pellegrino, 1999; Halter, n.d.).

A. Teacher: *I think metacognition would affect attribution and self-efficacy.*

Dr. Foster: *Explain your thinking.*

A. Teacher: *Self-efficacy is a reflection of a student's belief he or she will reach learning goals. He or she may perceive ability and/or effort to be the reason for success.*

When students think about whether they can or cannot learn something or why they were able or not able to achieve something, they are thinking reflectively, or using metacognition.

Dr. Foster: *You made connections among the active ingredients of the* **Appropriate Assessments** *and* **High Expectations Prescriptions** *and evidenced high-level metacognitive abilities.*

Edward Vockell, in *Educational Psychology: A Practical Approach*, affirms that "Metacognition has been described as a conscious awareness of one's own knowledge and the conscious ability to understand, control, and manipulate one's own cognitive processes" (2001b, para. 9). To be most effective, these skills must become overlearned and automatic—require little activity in working memory (para. 10).

> *Small is the number of people who see with their eyes and think with their minds.*
> **Albert Einstein**

A. Teacher: *From what I've learned, I don't see how these metacognitive processes, skills, and strategies would become automatic without practice from an early age.*

Dr. Foster: *Because you recognize that students should learn metacognitive strategies, you have taken the first step. The second step is to recognize that students of all ages can learn these strategies.*

Here are the typical steps learners go through when they learn a metacognitive skill (Vockell, 2001b, para. 11).

Table 7.11

Steps to Learning a Metacognitive Skill

Step 1: Learners or teachers establish a reason to believe that there would be some benefit to knowing how to apply the process, strategy, or skill.

Step 2: Learners focus their attention on what someone else models or what happens during a metacognitively useful personal experience.

Step 3: Learners use internal dialogue about the metacognitive process. This self-talk enables them to:

- Understand, encode, and practice the process;
- Obtain feedback and make adjustments about their effective use of the process; and
- Transfer the process to new situations beyond those already used.

Step 4: Learners use the process automatically, without thinking about it.

Dr. Foster: *To review, let's use elaboration— a metacognitive strategy that has proven to promote deep understanding and retention. To* **elaborate,** *students create examples, make analogies, and explain relationships between concepts (Pierce, 2003).*

 Tell me **which step** *you are on for elaboration.*

A. Teacher: *I am on* **Step 4** *for the creation of examples and explanations about relationships between concepts. As for analogies, I am on* **Step 1.** *I know the benefits, but I have had little or no useful personal experience.*

> *The person who understands what the better ways of thinking are and why they are better can . . . change his own personal ways until they become more effective; until, that is to say, they do better the work that thinking can do and that other mental operations cannot do so well.*
>
> **John Dewey**
> (1859–1952)
>
> From *How We Think* (1973), p. 3

Dr. Foster: ✓ *Look at "The Attributes of Autonomy" in Table 7.12 and finish as many of these analogies as you can.*

Autonomy is to **reflection** as _____ is to _____.

Autonomy is to _____ as **reflection** is to _____.

Table 7.12

The Attributes of Autonomy			
Abilities **Autonomous Learners . . .**	Self-Regulatory Mechanisms	Attitudes & Capabilities	Maslow's Needs
• Display the belief that they can achieve goals and solve problems	Self-Concept	Positive Identity	Self-Esteem
• Rely more on their own past successes than the verbal comments of others	Self-Efficacy		
• Set goals and develop action plans or plan personal learning activities • Make decisions and choices	Self-Direction	Proactive Behavior	Cognition
• Act independently and exert control over their environment • Seek support, but can function well without it • Interact with others and give support	Self-Control		
• Monitor learning activities • Evaluate progress and make changes • Learn how to learn from their successes and failures	Self-Assessment	Reflective Learning	Self-Actualization
• Cope with new and unforeseen situations • Overcome temporary motivational setbacks	Self-Talk	Multiple Intelligence: **Intrapersonal**	

From Benard, 1993; Landau & Gathercoal, 2000; Little, 2003; McCarthy, 1998; and Pajares, 2002

A. Teacher: *I really had to think!*

Autonomy is to reflection as <u>high expectation</u> *is to* <u>appropriate assessment</u>.

Autonomy is to <u>coping</u> *as reflection is to* <u>thinking</u>.

Autonomy is to reflection as <u>self-talk</u> *is to* <u>self-assessment</u>.

A. Teacher: *At the beginning of our discussion about metacognition, you said that it would transform student learning. It has definitely transformed the way I think about teaching. I am anxious to learn strategies to use in my classroom.*

Dr. Foster: *You have reached the top of the "ladder of metacognition" identified by Dr. Robert Swartz and Dr. David Perkins. Read "Learning to Climb" to discover the steps students must take when they think about and make decisions.*

Learning to Climb

Dr. Robert Swartz and Dr. David Perkins, the authors of *Teaching Thinking: Issues and Approaches*, identified four levels of thought on a "ladder of metacognition" (1989). **Learning to climb** to the top is possible for all students, even those in elementary school (Bingham, Holbrook, & Meyers, 2010, p. 60).

Reflection
Strategic
Aware
Tacit

Reflective use: The individual monitors his or her thinking throughout the decision-making and ponders how to proceed and how to improve.

Strategic use: The individual organizes his or her thoughts and actively uses a series of strategies to reach a decision.

Aware use: The individual's decision-making is conscious.

Tacit use: The individual makes decisions without thinking.

What can you observe students doing each step of the way? (Bingham et al., p. 61)

- **Tacit**—When students, experienced in the mechanics of writing, edit an essay for punctuation
- **Aware**—When students learn that good social scientists take observation notes and mimic that action
- **Strategic**—When students use webs, maps, and outlines to judge the relevance and promise of their ideas
- **Reflective**—When students use rubrics to plan their work, to think through possible challenges, or to think into new discoveries

---

Learning to climb to the top of any formation requires us to take one-step at a time—whether we are the one who climbs or the one who provides the support as others climb to the top. "By setting tasks at an appropriate level and prompting children to think about what they are doing as they successfully complete these tasks, adults can help children become independent and successful thinkers" (Vockell, 2001b, para. 18).

Dr. Foster: *Before we talk about how to integrate reflection in the lessons you teach, I want to present the last formula in the* **Appropriate Assessments Prescription***.*

The formula has its origin in the work of Paulo Freire who believed reflection results "in 'critical consciousness' in which learners become actors, not observers, and authors of their own decisions" ("TAP," 2000, p. 1).

Action + Reflection = Learning

The ideal learning environment provides sufficient time for both action and reflection. Given the pressure to cover the curriculum and prepare students for state exams, "we often must end an activity without giving students some formal or informal means of discussing what they have learned. Thus, an opportunity for the meaning making (the introspection of reflection) is lost, and true learning is not fully actualized" (p. 2).

> When teachers and parents try to help students, it is important not to do too much thinking for them. By doing their thinking . . . adults or knowledgeable peers may make them experts at seeking help, rather than expert thinkers. (Vockell, 2001b, para. 18)

A. Teacher: *I admit that I thought my job as a teacher was to get students to learn and do the work I assign—reflection was not part of the equation (tacit use).*

I thought reflection was internal dialogue; now I see that it is also social dialogue. As you have done with me throughout our sessions, I need to make sure (aware use) I give my students opportunities to exercise their interpersonal and intrapersonal multiple intelligences and their thoughts and ideas to help them "internalize and link thought to action" (p. 2).

I will be able to move my students up the "ladder of metacognition" to strategic and reflective use if I am more reflective and add transfer and metacognitive strategies to my repertoire as I plan units and daily lessons.

Dr. Foster: *You have evidenced* **reflection***. To actualize the learning fully, you will need to put your plans in* **action***, evaluate the results of your actions, and transfer what you have learned to future actions—learn from experience.*

A. Teacher: *My students think all the time, but it is not what they should be thinking about in the classroom. How do I turn their thinking to learning?*

Dr. Foster: *You need to understand what your students can accomplish; create a safe learning environment where students' have confidence in your professionalism and integrity (Clark, 2004); and provide appropriate strategies and activities throughout the lessons you teach.*

> Practitioners build up a collection of images, ideas, examples and actions that they can draw upon. Donald Schön, like John Dewey (1973, p. 123), saw this [repertoire] as central to reflective thought. (Smith, 2001, para. 6)

If you told your students to stop thinking, could they do it? To see what John Dewey thinks, read "A Penny for Your Thoughts" from his book **How We Think***.*

A Penny for Your Thoughts

 All the time we are awake and sometimes when we are asleep, something is, as we say, going through our heads. When we are asleep we call that kind of sequence "dreaming." We also have daydreams, reveries, castles built in the air, and mental streams that are even more idle and chaotic. To this uncontrolled coursing of ideas through our heads the name of 'thinking' is sometimes given.

It is automatic and unregulated. Many a child has attempted to see whether he could not 'stop thinking'— that is, stop this procession of mental states through his mind—and in vain. More of our waking life than most of us would care to admit is whiled away in this inconsequential trifling with mental pictures, random recollections, pleasant but unfounded hopes, flitting, half-developed impressions. Hence it is that he who offers 'a penny for your thoughts' does not expect to drive any great bargain if his offer is taken; he will only find out what happens to be 'going through the mind' and what 'goes' in this fashion rarely leaves much that is worthwhile behind.

Excerpted from *How We Think* by J. Dewey, 1973, p. 3

Is this or is this not a laughing matter?

Which learner characteristics and elements in the learning environment influence a students' ability to reflect on learning? "It is often difficult to encourage reflection among the learners" (Clark, 2004, para. 5). If students lack the motivation to do reflective tasks, teachers should examine the characteristics of the learners and the learning environment.

Because reflection includes internal and social dialogue, teachers must look at the physical environment, as well as the interpersonal environment. Gustafson and Bennett (1999) found that a poor **physical environment** for reflection is one with "competing stimuli (e.g., televisions, personal conversations, ambient noise, poor ventilation, high or low temperature, uncomfortable furniture)" (Clark, 2004, para. 12).

A. Teacher: *As a student, I remember how difficult it was to pay attention.*

Dr. Foster: *Research "speaks of the need to establish 'active and passive' space—places where students can reflect and retreat from others to work quietly and intrapersonally, as well as places for active engagement and interpersonal learning" ("TAP," 2000, p. 3).*

A. Teacher: *This sounds great, but I have a limited amount of classroom space.*

On reflection, this could be a topic for a class meeting. I am sure my students would have better ideas than I do about how to maximize our learning space. (Review class meetings on pages 102–103.)

To encourage reflection, teachers should consider the **interpersonal environment** they create in the classroom. The findings of researchers Hatton and Smith (1995) suggest that "engaging with another person in a way that encourages talking with, questioning, or confronting, helped the reflective process by placing the learner in a safe environment in which self-revelation can take place" (Clark, 2004, para. 19).

> For students to feel comfortable sharing their views honestly and openly (reflection rather than recitation), they must feel that their opinions are valued and will not be ridiculed or minimized. ("TAP," 2000, p. 3)

A. Teacher: *This makes sense. I have learned more about teaching and learning from my dialogues with you than from the books or articles I have read on my own. With your encouragement and questions, I have become more reflective and have made positive changes in my classroom from my experiences.*

Donald A. Schön, author of *The Reflective Practitioner: How Professionals Think in Action* (1983), drew on the philosophy of John Dewey and went beyond to develop a theory of learning. He argued that "not all actions lead to learning: only when action is informed by reflection and, in turn, informs reflection, is one able to learn and refine one's knowledge" (Richmond, 1997, p. 6).

Change? Are You Talkin' to Me?

Language about change is talk about very little change, trivial in relation to a massive unquestioned stability; it appears formidable to its proponents only by the peculiar optic that leads a potato chip company to see a larger bag of potato chips as a new product.

From the opening passage of *Beyond the Stable State* by D. A. Schön, 1973

The reality is that "talk about change is as often as not a substitute for engaging in it" (Richmond, 1997, p. 2).

Gustafson and Bennett (1999) identified motivation, breadth of content knowledge, and skill and experience as **learner characteristics** that can affect reflective behavior (Clark, 2004). When teachers assign reflective tasks, they should remember these research findings:

- Skill and experience develop over time.
- Breadth of content knowledge is directly proportional to the ability to reflect on a topic.
- Both internal and external sources of motivation affect the quality of reflection (para. 7–9).

> *The whole of science is nothing more than a refinement of everyday thinking.*
> **Albert Einstein**

A. Teacher: *How do I begin to help my students become reflective thinkers?*

Dr. Foster: *According to Graham Nuthall (1999), "narratives or stories involve both visual and dramatic instructional techniques" and have a retention rate between 57% and 77% after one year (as cited in Marzano, 2007, p. 32). In* **How We Think***, Dr John Dewey provides a narrative that may help you visualize the reflective thinking process—read "What Were You Thinking?"*

What Were You Thinking?

In *How We Think* John Dewey (1973) describes two phases of reflective thinking. It "involves (1) a state of doubt, hesitation, perplexity, mental difficulty, in which thinking originates, and (2) an act of searching, hunting, inquiring, to find material that will resolve the doubt, settle and dispose of the perplexity" (p. 12).

A man traveling in an unfamiliar region comes to a branching of the road. Having no sure knowledge to fall back upon, he is brought to a standstill of **hesitation** and suspense. Which road is right? And how shall his **perplexity** be resolved? There are but two alternatives: he must either blindly and arbitrarily take his course, trusting to luck for the outcome, or he must discover grounds for the conclusion that a given road is right. Any attempt to decide the matter by thinking will involve **inquiring** into other facts, whether brought to mind by memory, or by further observation, or by both. The perplexed wayfarer must carefully scrutinize what is before him and he must cudgel his memory. He looks for evidence that will support belief in favor of either of the roads—for evidence that will weight down one suggestion. He must climb a tree; he may go first in this direction, then in that, looking, in either case, for signs of a signboard or a map, and *his reflection is aimed at the discovery of facts that will serve this purpose.*

Excerpted from How We Think by John Dewey, 1973, pp. 13-14

What were you thinking? In situations like this, do you most often seek other information before you make a decision, or do you just take your chances and hope you have chosen the right path?

The **reality** is that "in the suspense of uncertainty, we metaphorically climb a tree; we try to find some standpoint from which we may survey additional facts, and getting a more commanding view of the situation, decide how the facts stand related to one another" (p. 14).

A. Teacher: *This narrative caused me to think about my own thinking when confronted with a problem.*

Sometimes I take the time to think about the problem I need to solve in the classroom, set goals, and plan a course of action. Many times, I am impatient or respond to problems without thinking. At still other times, I make decisions on the spot. I do not think I do this blindly.

> *We only think when we are confronted with problems.*
> **John Dewey**
> (1859–1952)

A. Teacher: *The more experiences I have had with difficult situations, the more I have to draw upon to make tough decisions on the spot.*

> Even when a child (or a grown up) has a problem, it is futile to urge him [or her] to think when he [or she] has no prior experiences that involve some of the same conditions. (Dewey, 1973, p. 16)

Now I understand why students and my own children make poor decisions—they lack the experiences or knowledge.

I can tell them to stop and think (reflect) before they decide what to do, but I now see how important it is for me to model my thought processes and provide opportunities for students to set goals and solve problems in my classroom.

Dr. Foster: *How can you help your own children and the students you teach develop the thinking needed to solve problems and achieve goals?*

A. Teacher: *I remember we talked about inquiry-based learning in our session about the* **Active Engagement Prescription** *(see page 133). For assessment tasks, I recall our discussion about the assessment task rubric of Joseph Mills, Jr. (see page 141). Levels III, IV, and V require one or more solution pathways.*

In Dr. Dewey's narrative, thinking begins in forked-road situations. So I need to present dilemmas, questions, or problems that have many alternative solutions and outcomes (Dewey, 1973).

Dr. Foster: *Dr. Dewey also says, "There is no single and uniform power of thought, but a multitude of different ways in which specific things—things observed, remembered, heard of, read about—evoke suggestions and ideas that are pertinent to a problem or question and that carry the mind forward to a justifiable conclusion" (p. 55).*

A. Teacher: *After giving students something perplexing, the next step is to have them work through the "Ten Steps for Lifelong Learning and Problem Solving" to become informed by the practices and solve the problem or achieve their learning goal (see page 113). The more they reflect when they use these practices, the more automatic the processes will become.*

Dr. Foster: *Every practice (**action**) informed by **reflection** has the potential to help learners achieve goals, solve problems, and transfer the **learning** to new contexts.*

> *We cannot solve our problems with the same thinking we used when we created them.*
> **Albert Einstein**

 What dilemmas, questions, or problems would best promote reflection—facts, questions, hypothetical situations, or real-life problems the students might encounter?

A. Teacher: *Real-life problems would be best. If I couldn't think of a real-life problem, my next choice would be a hypothetical situation that interests the students.*

I would also have my students keep a journal.

Dr. Foster: 📁 **Supplement P: Learning Journal** *will help you effectively implement learning journals in your classroom to promote problem solving and lifelong learning. (Select the **Supplements** page at www.classroommanagementblues.com, then **K–P** for **Supplement P**.) You will also find resources for other reflective activities.*

Caution—for activities following practical experiences to be reflective, they should direct problem solving or goal achievement (Clark, 2004).

A. Teacher: *Now I understand why you had me keep a **Praxis Journal**. After each session, you had me think about a professional goal or problem, make an action plan, put the plan in action, and evaluate the effect my actions had on me as a teacher and on my students as learners. Finally, I had to think about what I would do in the future.*

Students also need time to think before, during, and after teaching and learning experiences, sometimes collaboratively and at other times individually (Collaborative Research Model," n.d.; "Reflection," 2001; "TAP," 2000). They need to evaluate the thinking processes they use to determine which strategies work best and apply the information about how they learn as they approach future learning ("Reflection," 2001).

> The notion of reflection-in-action . . . is sometimes described as "thinking on our feet." It involves looking into our experiences, connecting with our feelings, and attending to our theories in use. It entails building new understandings to inform our actions in the situation that is unfolding. . . . We can link this process of thinking on our feet with reflection-on-action. This is done later—after the encounter. . . . The act of reflecting-on-action enables us to spend time exploring why we acted as we did, what was happening . . . and so on. In so doing we develop sets of questions and ideas about our activities and practice. (Smith, 2001, para. 2, 5)

How much time should I give my students to reflect on each lesson?

Dr. Foster: 📁 **Supplement K: Unit and Lesson Design** *provides an explanation of how to use formative and summative reflections throughout the lessons and units you design. Guidelines provide an explanation of how much time to spend on reflective tasks. Even 3–5 minutes can increase learning and retention. (Select the **Supplements** page at www.classroommangementblues.com, and then **K–P** for **Supplement K**.)*

For examples of reflections that might be used throughout a lesson, read "What's on the Menu?"

What's on the Menu?

Think about each lesson as a *meal*. **What's on the menu?** Students respond to reflections at the beginning about what they will learn (*appetizers*) and reflections at the end to wrap up or think about what they learned (*desserts*). Reflections about content are *soups and salads*, and reflections during practice and/or performance activities serve as *entrées*.

In Practice
Dr. Foster

Appetizers	Entrées
Attention-Getters	**Practices—Performances**
Opening Reflections • What in my prior knowledge will help me with what I am to learn/do? • How will I know I have succeeded?	*Formative Reflections* • How well am I progressing? • Am I able to explain to others what I have learned?
Soups & Salads	Desserts
Presentations & Interactions	**Wrap-Ups**
Content Reflections • What information is important to remember? • What did I learn?	*Formative or Summative Reflections* • What challenges did I face? • What have I learned that will help in other situations?

Just as **what's on the menu** and how much time you have to eat **vary** from meal to meal, the types of **reflections** and the appropriate amount of time for reflections vary from lesson to lesson. Find out more about planning reflections before, during, and after activities in **Supplement L: Unit and Lesson Design**. (Select the **Supplements** page, at *www.classroommanagementblues.com*, then **K–P** for **Supplement L**.)

A. Teacher: *I know the "power of self-reflection" can deepen student learning (Chappuis, 2005, para. 27), but I have concerns about my students assessing and evaluating their own work. Will they take advantage of the situation and give themselves higher scores no matter the quality of their performance?*

Researchers have found that students, especially older ones, might take advantage of the opportunity to evaluate their own work "if left to their own devices. But, when students are **taught** systematic self-evaluation procedures, the accuracy of their judgment improves. Contrary to the beliefs of many students, parents, and teachers, students' propensity to inflate grades decreases when teachers share assessment responsibility and control" (Rolheiser & Ross, n.d., para. 40). Teacher involvement in student self-evaluation provides direct knowledge about whether individual students are on an upward or downward path toward achieving learning goals and objectives (para. 15).

What can teachers do to facilitate student-involved assessment FOR learning? Motivation and achievement are enhanced when students learn how to make effective judgments about their work and are given time to develop appropriate skills (Rolheiser & Ross, n.d.). Students achieve more because they focus more attention on objectives and assessment criteria. In addition, self-assessment provides valuable diagnostic information teachers would otherwise lack (para. 41), helps teachers and students perceive ability levels, and enhances student motivation (Coombe & Canning, n.d.; Rolheiser & Ross, n.d.).

Dr. Foster: *The choice for you and other teachers is not whether students evaluate their own work (they will regardless of the feedback) but whether you will attempt to teach them how to do so effectively (Rolheiser & Ross, n.d., para. 15). Dr. Rolheiser and Dr. Ross offer a four-stage model for teaching student self-evaluation (para. 17–20). Read about this model in "Don't Upstage Your Students."*

Don't Upstage Your Students

Teachers are the directors on the classroom stage. The students are the star performers! Each has a role to play in the success of the production—learning. Students need to trust the teacher's direction, and the teacher needs to allow the students to act, or learn. **Don't upstage them**.

In Practice
Dr. Rolheiser
Dr. Ross

Four-Stage Model to Teach Student Self-Evaluation

STAGE 1:   Allow students to *define the criteria* used to judge their performance.

STAGE 2:   Teach students how to *apply the criteria* to their own work.

STAGE 3:   Give students *feedback* on their self-evaluations and promote discussions about differences in data.

STAGE 4:   Help students develop productive *goals and action plans* to improve performance.

Don't upstage your students! "Don't ever do what the learner can do; don't ever decide what the learner can decide" (Vella, 2002, p. 16). Student self-evaluation has the potential to increase performance dramatically! For more strategies that promote self-assessment, see the **Resources** provided at *www.classroommanagementblues.com*. (Select the **Communication** page, then **Self-Evaluation**.)

Stiggins (2005) agrees with other educators that "the greatest potential value of classroom assessment is realized when we open the process up and welcome students in as full partners during their learning" (p. 23). Rolheiser and Ross offered a four-stage model (see page 206), and Stiggins outlined other ways to engage students in self-evaluation (see Table 7.13).

> Students who participate in the thoughtful analysis of quality work to identify its critical elements or to internalize valued achievement targets become better performers. When students learn to apply these standards so thoroughly that they can confidently and competently evaluate their own and each other's work, they are well on the road to becoming better performers in their own right. (Stiggins, 2008, p. 23)

Table 7.13

Ways to Engage Students in Self-Evaluation

- Develop assessment exercises.
- Offer comments on how to improve a test.
- Suggest possible assessment exercises.
- Help devise scoring criteria (Stage 1).
- Create scoring criteria on their own (Stage 1).
- Apply scoring criteria to the evaluation of their own performance (Stage 2).
- Think about how the assessment and evaluation affect their own academic success (Stage 3).
- Explore how their own self-assessment relates to the teacher's assessment and to their own academic success (Stages 3 and 4).

From Rolheiser & Ross, n.d. and Stiggins, 2005

A. Teacher: *When it comes to grading, the traditional thinking of students is that teachers are "out to get them." If I work with my students and gaps exist between their assessment and mine, we would more likely be able to resolve the discrepancies in a positive way as a team.*

Should self-evaluation be restricted to easy tasks and only my best students?

Dr. Foster: *Researchers have found that self-evaluation has a positive effect on student performance—particularly for difficult tasks and among high-need learners (Rolheiser & Ross, n.d.).*

A. Teacher: *Earlier we said elementary-age children have the ability to use self-assessment. Are they old enough to discuss assessment with teachers?*

Dr. Foster: *"The amount and nature of an assessment discussion with students will obviously vary with their age. It is, however, important that students are involved with assessment at an early age. This will help them to develop an assessment vocabulary and their ability to self-assess" (O'Conner, 2009, p. 189).*

A. Teacher: *Teaching my students about assessment will take time and timing, but if the collaboration produces higher achievement gains it will be worth it. I want to implement self-assessment and self-evaluation in my classroom.*

Dr. Foster: *You are aware of the benefits and the challenges. Not only do students need time to learn how to evaluate themselves effectively, "teachers need considerable time to work out how to accommodate an innovation that involves sharing control of a core teacher function with their existing beliefs about teacher and learner roles" (Rolheiser & Ross, n.d., p 55).*

> Timing is critical so that students see that assessment is integral, not just an add-on, to learning. (O'Conner, 2009, p. 189)

 Summarize what you have learned about self-assessment.

A. Teacher: *"When students are collaborators in assessment, they develop the habit of self-reflection. They learn the qualities of good work, how to judge their work against these qualities, how to step back from their work to assess their own efforts and feelings of accomplishment, and how to set personal goals" (Reif, 1990; "Why is," 1997, para. 1; Wolf, 1989).*

I was on target at the beginning of our discussion about self-assessment and self-evaluation. A person does use formative self-assessment to monitor his or her own progress toward goals and objectives during the learning process; and a person uses summative self-assessment to make a judgment about his or her own performance after the learning process.

I was close to the target about reflection, or thinking before, during, and after a learning experience. Reflection is a complex process that informs our actions and affects metacognition and the transfer of learning to new situations.

It will take time for me to transfer what I have learned about reflection and self-assessment in my classroom. I have learned enough to know I need to learn more.

The more students write the more I will have to assess.

Dr. Foster: *For teachers to assess thinking, students have to write.*

Books, articles, and websites are available at www.classroommanagementblues.com to help reduce paper overload and implement reflection and self-assessment. Fulwiler and Young offer a few suggestions in "Can You Buy into This?"

> Assessment is not just the measurement of learning; it is in itself an integral part of learning . . . The purpose of assessment is not merely to gather information . . . [but] to foster improvement (Frye, 1999, para. 49)

Can You Buy into This?

Telling a teacher to "use writing as a thinking tool in a large or small class may be like trying to sell someone an alpine ski ticket in southern Florida" ("Write-to-Learn," n.d., para. 63). **Can you buy into this?** You might, but I am sure you would have some **questions** "before being convinced of the pedagogical effectiveness of writing in a large or small class" (para. 63).

In Practice
Dr. Fulwiler
Dr. Young

How is writing a thinking tool?

Research on writing "has clearly indicated that carefully crafted writing assignments engage higher order thinking skills, allowing students to move beyond mere knowledge and comprehension skills into application, analysis, synthesis, and evaluation" (para. 62). Fulwiler and Young (2000) explain, "We write to ourselves as well as talk with others to objectify our perceptions of reality; the primary function of this 'expressive' language is not to communicate, but to order and represent experience to our own understanding. In this sense language provides us with a unique way of knowing and becomes a [thinking] tool for discovering, for shaping meaning, and for reaching understanding" (p. x).

How the heck am I supposed to grade all those papers?

"Writing-to-learn (WTL) activities are short, impromptu or otherwise informal writing tasks that help students think through key concepts or ideas. . . . Often, these are limited to less than five minutes of class time or are assigned as brief, out-of-class assignments" ("Write-to-Learn," n.d., para. 64). Most WTL activities are not graded—they provide formative assessment data. Many options exist to check understanding (e.g., look at five-ten every day or every other day, skim quickly to identify what the students may need help with, highlight "good ideas" in one color and "come back to this idea again" in another, or have students select a few for feedback, and many more) (para. 65–68).

What are some writing-to-learn activities I could use in my classroom?

- Ask students to write their own "exam" questions.
- Give the beginning or end of a paragraph, story, problem and have students write what follows or leads up to the statement.
- Ask students to think through a concept and create a metaphor or analogy.
- Stop and ask students to write when they need to focus attention, assimilate information, or articulate a question. (para. 76–81).

"The prospect of not grading—or not even collecting—writing assignments may go seriously against our best teacherly instinct. . . . That we don't have time to grade papers . . . should not interfere with students' potential to learn through writing" (para. 71). If you **can you buy into this**, find more activities and **Resources** at *www.classroom mangementblues.com*. (Select **Assessments**, then locate **Write-to-Learn**.)

Dr. Foster: *For closure, look at this diagram of a learning cycle. Explain the roles of expectancy, practice, evaluation, attribution, and reflection in this cycle of learning.*

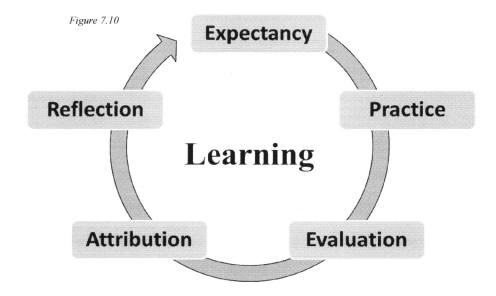

Figure 7.10

A. Teacher: **Expectancy**   *What the learner thinks he or she can do*

Practice   *What the learner does to learn what is expected*

Evaluation   *How well the learner meets expectations*

Attribution   *Why the learner believes he or she succeeds or fails to learn what was expected*

Reflection   *How the learner thinks he or she will be able to transfer learning to meet future expectations*

Dr. Foster: *You have demonstrated that you understand* **IT**—*the components of this learning cycle.*

A. Teacher: *With my understanding of the active ingredients of the* **Appropriate Assessment Prescription**, *I was able to explain* **IT** *simplistically. I know* **IT** *is a more complex process.*

Dr. Foster: **IT** *is complex. Read about the IT factor in "IT Is NO Laughing Matter!"*

IT Is NO Laughing Matter!

"Simon Cowell, [one of the original *American Idol* judges], periodically remarks about the "it" factor when assessing contestants. It seems to be one of those nebulous, undefined and subjective attributes one either has or doesn't have. And it falls into the category of you-know-it-when-you-see-it. He's right. You do know it when you see it and that's true in the workplace [and classroom] too" (Russell, 2006, para. 1).

I've got IT! I've got IT!

Students want to succeed and aspire to be great! Russell (2006) says

> The desire for greatness I'm referring to is tied to the seeds of possibility sprouting through their talents and abilities. You see, . . . [students] with the 'it' factor desire to live their life's potential. They aren't out to win. They're out to become the unique person they are, to the fullest extent of their gifts. It's that desire that fuels their drive, motivation and persistence. It's that desire that keeps them learning and growing and stretching. It's that desire that makes them exceptional. (para. 4)

Dr. Foster: *When learners "experience an accumulation of unsuccessful experiences, they can begin to infer that they are incapable of learning. As doubt builds, here too it begins to feed on itself, and another self-fulfilling prophesy begins to play out" (Stiggins, 2009, p. 419). Students begin to question: Can I learn this, or is IT too hard for me? Is IT worth the effort that I am going to have to expend to get IT? Is trying to learn IT worth the risk that I might fail again?*

A. Teacher: *We have covered so much content in this session. Is there something you can give me that will make **IT** easier to see, understand, and retain?*

Dr. Foster: *I hope the chart for **R$_x$3 Appropriate Assessments** pulls **IT** together for you (see Table 7.14). The chart includes the questions teachers need to ask to design instruction and those students need to ask to be successful. You will also see how these components align with the **P • e = p** formula and the active ingredients of the **Appropriate Assessments Prescription**.*

As they begin their schooling, young learners are quite inquisitive, eager to read their first chapter book and excited to discover their place in the world. But many students' innate curiosity is stifled by an education system that too often values compliance over creativity, taking tests over testing theories, memorizing over understanding, and high grades over learning. (Winger, 2005, para. 26)

Table 7.14

Rx 3 Appropriate Assessments			
Instructional Design	**Metacognition**	**Active Ingredients**	**Assessments** P • e = p
What is **IT** that students need to know or do? **Objective/Task** *Standards-based and connected to prior learning*	How difficult is **IT**? Have I done **IT** before? Is **IT** on the standardized test?	**Expectancy** Enhance **potential**: provide relevant tasks connected to prior knowledge, use rubrics, and reduce test/grade anxiety	**Diagnostic and Formative Assessments** Foster *motivation* through **e**mpowerment
What will **IT** take for students to succeed? **Criteria** *Expectations Dispositions*	Do I have what **IT** takes to succeed? How do I feel about **IT**?	**Attribution** Enhance **potential**: assess dispositions, avoid excessive competition, and reduce the fear of making mistakes	
How will **IT** be graded? What is **IT** worth? **Value** *Grades Incentives*	How will **IT** be graded? Am I motivated to do **IT**?	**Practice** Enhance **potential**: maintain a non-threatening environment, assess effort appropriately, assign a higher value for learning, and follow through	**Formative Assessments** Foster *learning* through **p**ractice
Did the students learn **IT**? Does **IT** need modification or reteaching? **Assessment for Learning** *Documentation*	Have I learned **IT**? How focused and motivated am I to learn **IT**? What can I do to improve **IT**?	**Reflection** Enhance **potential**: provide opportunities for students to think and self-assess	
How well did the students learn **IT**? Have the students retained **IT**? **Evaluation of Learning** *Tests and Grades*	How well did I learn **IT**? What did I do that helped me learn **IT**? What have I learned that will help me apply **IT** to other situations?	**Evaluation** Enhance **potential**: help students attribute success to practice	**Summative Assessments** Foster *success* through **P**erformance

A. Teacher: *The chart helped pull everything together for me! I am ready to use the assessment strategies you have presented.*

Dr. Foster: *Carefully read about the supplements for the **Classroom Management Blues** found at www.classroommanagementblues.com before you use them to enhance the effectiveness of the **Appropriate Assessments Prescription**. As you find other information, be aware that different prescriptions, active ingredients, and supplements will blend with this prescription to increase **EACH** student's performance and reduce test anxiety. I recommend that you implement the supplements as suggested on this **Implementation Checklist**.*

R$_x$ 3 Implementation Checklist

Select the *Supplements* tab at *www.classroommanagementblues.com*
to obtain detailed explanations, step-by-step instructions,
and blackline masters for *Supplements K–P*.

📁 **Supplement K—Unit and Lesson Design**
Use the Lesson Design Menu to develop one lesson, then one unit with multiple lessons.

📁 **Supplement P—Learning Journal**
Begin with learning journal entries for achieving a goal, then for solving a problem.

📁 **Supplement L—"Win-Win" Classroom Competitions**
Play one or more games to enhance learning.

Implement these supplements at the beginning of the year or grading period.

📁 **Supplement M—Practice Book or Primary Practice Folder**
Have students do practice activities and exercises as well as reflect about learning in a practice book or primary practice folder, and reduce paper overload.

📁 **Supplement N—Practice Record Sheet**
Use this record sheet to document student learning during practice and other activities such as participation in class discussions.

📁 **Supplement O—Grade Book Magic**
Follow the tips to calculate an overall or final grade with different weights for the formative and summative components.

Concluding Remarks

The **Appropriate Assessments Prescription** alone will not prevent or cure the ***Classroom Management Blues***, but the potential for a cure will increase when you repeat the strategies for the **Appropriate Assessments**, **High Expectations**, and **Active Engagement Prescriptions**. In the next session, learn how the **Trustworthy Behavior Prescription** can help you create and maintain a safe learning environment where students become self-disciplined.

Dr. Foster: *Look at the* **Appropriate Assessment Prescription** *and note the caution.*

Use the prescription as needed, begin with small doses to foster student learning. With consistency, you will achieve the desired effects of more trust and respect, increased learning, and improved behavior.

POPHAM'S PHARMACY
333 Success Street
Any Town, USA

Date Filled: First Day in the Classroom
Discard After: Retirement

 0003

Prescription for **APPROPRIATE ASSESSMENTS**

Patient's Name: **A. Teacher**

Patient's Address: **103 Practice Parkway — Any Town, USA**

Use **APPROPRIATE ASSESSMENTS** *as needed* to foster student learning.

Doctor: *Barbara G. Foster*

Active Ingredients
- **Expectancy**
- **Attribution**
- **Practice**
- **Evaluation**
- **Reflection**

SIDE EFFECTS: More trust and respect, increased learning, and improved behavior

CAUTION: May reduce test anxiety   **Unlimited Refills**

Resources—Access More Information

Learn more about critical and creative thinking, paper overload, unit and lesson design, prior knowledge, reflection, Write-to-Learn, self-evaluation, and rubrics on the ***Classroom Management Blues*** website. Choose **Resources**, then **Assessments** at *www.classroommanagementblues.com* for a list of books, articles, websites, and other resources.

Praxis Journal—Take Steps toward a Cure

Write responses to these prompts and questions before the next session:

- **Review the** *Appropriate Assessments Prescription* **and reflect on what you have learned.** How do formative and summative assessments affect student learning?
- **Based on what you have learned in this session, set a goal and develop a plan.** How do you plan to achieve your goal and solve one or more related problems?
- **Implement and evaluate your plan.** How did your actions affect you as a teacher and your students as learners?
- **Reflect on future goals and actions.** What will you do in the future?

STEP TWO: **TAKE PRESCRIPTIONS**

KOUNIN'S PHARMACY

444 Behavior Boulevard
Any Town, USA

Date Filled: First Day in the Classroom
Discard After: Retirement

 0004

Prescription for **TRUSTWORTHY BEHAVIOR**

Patient's Name: A. Teacher

Patient's Address: 104 Consequence Circle — Any Town, USA

Encourage **TRUSTWORTHY BEHAVIOR** and support
self-discipline *throughout the school day.*

Doctor: *Barbara G. Foster*

Active Ingredients
- **Principles**
- **Rules**
- **Consequences**
- **Documentation**
- **Procedures**

SIDE EFFECTS: More trust and respect, increased learning,
and improved behavior

CAUTION: May empower learners

Unlimited Refills

Session 8

Session 8

Encourage Trustworthy Behavior

Effective teaching and learning can take place only in a harmonious learning environment. Instead of a three-ring circus, imagine a classroom that resembles a symphony of learners rehearsing for a show.

Matthew A. Kraft
Ringmaster to Conductor

Through principled practice, teachers can empower learners, support self-discipline, and encourage **trustworthy behavior**. With consistent use of preventive, corrective, and supportive procedures and effective documentation, you can create a safe learning environment where ALL students have the opportunity to succeed.

 trust·wor-thy [trŭst′wûr *th*ē] *adj.*

Deserving of trust or confidence; dependable; reliable

Random House Dictionary

A. Teacher: *I have learned how the* **Active Engagement**, **High Expectations**, *and* **Appropriate Assessments Prescriptions** *can have a positive effect on student learning and behavior. Does that mean I don't need rules?*

Dr. Foster: *You do need to establish rules and high expectations for behavior. "Spoken and unspoken rules guide how we interact with" and treat one another (Marzano et al., 2005, para. 1).*

 Only one of the active ingredients in the **Trustworthy Behavior Prescription** *is rules. Look at the prescription (on the opposite page), and think about the other active ingredients.*

A. Teacher: *I have established rules, consequences, and procedures, but documentation is not one of my strengths. I am not sure what principles have to do with behavior management.*

Many of my students misbehave, so I know I need to make some changes!

Dr. Foster: *The first step at "The Heart of Change" is a sense of urgency (Kotter & Cohen, 2002). It sounds like you are ready to begin the change process!*

In *The Heart of Change* (2002), Kotter and Cohen advocate a systematic approach to transform organizations. Their "model suggests that successful change is most often achieved by following a rolling eight-step process" (Cohen, 2005, p. 2). Table 8.1 shows the steps outlined in *The Heart of Change Field Guide: Tools and Tactics for Leading Change in Your Organization* and modified for classroom teachers (pp. 3–5).

Table 8.1

Eight-Step Process for Change	
Step 1: **Increase Urgency**	Heighten energy and motivation; reduce fear
Step 2: **Build Guiding Teams**	Become focused, committed, and enthusiastic; model "right" behavior; hold everyone in the classroom accountable
Step 3: **Get the Vision Right**	Create a clear, inspiring, and achievable picture of a learning community; describe important behaviors needed to be successful so that strategies and main performance assessments can be created to support the **vision**
Step 4: **Communicate for Buy-In**	Deliver candid, concise, heartfelt messages to create the trust, support, and commitment needed to achieve the **vision**
Step 5: **Enable Action**	Break down barriers that can hinder students who want to make the **vision** work; identify ineffective procedures
Step 6: **Create Short-Term Wins**	Reenergize everyone to achieve visible, timely, and meaningful performance improvements and demonstrate progress
Step 7: **Don't Let Up**	Be persistent; monitor and measure progress; do not declare success prematurely
Step 8: **Make It Stick**	Recognize, reward, and model new behavior; embed it in the fabric of the classroom; make the change "the way we behave"

A. Teacher: *Step 1 reminds me to apply **Active Engagement** to heighten motivation and use **Appropriate Assessments** to reduce fear. In our session on **High Expectations**, I learned about Step 2—team building in a learning community. Now I see why these were the first prescriptions we discussed in our sessions. What is not clear is the emphasis on vision throughout the change process.*

Dr. Foster: *"A shared urgency for change may push people into action, but it is the vision that steers them in the right direction" (Cohen, 2005, p. 63). Dr. Sprick and his associates say, "When you know where you are headed, you can guide students toward their own success" (1998, p. 7).*

> *Nature uses only the longest threads to weave her patterns, so that each small piece of her fabric reveals the organization of the entire tapestry.*
> **Richard P. Feynman**
> American physicist and teacher

Dan S. Cohen (2005) says *vision is* "a compelling, motivating picture of the future" (p. 64). A good vision (1) motivates and coordinates the actions of people in the right direction; (2) clarifies the behaviors that must be encouraged, eliminated, and maintained; and (3) defines important performance indicators needed for success (pp. 64, 68).

A. Teacher: *I do have a vision of how I want my students to behave, but how do I make it happen?*

Dr. Foster: *I will walk you through the process. We will discuss **principles**, or standards of conduct needed for success; **rules**, **consequences**, and **documentation** based on these principles; and **procedures** to articulate, implement, and sustain your vision.*

Active Ingredient	🍎 Principles

The first active ingredient in the **Trustworthy Behavior Prescription** is **principles**. While Covey (1992) defines principles as guidelines that specify the parameters "within which results are to be accomplished" in contracts between individuals (p. 213), Sprick, Garrison, and Howard (1998) refer to these behaviors as "Guidelines for Success" in school and life.

> 📄 **prin·ci·ple** [prĭn′sə-pəl′] *n.*
>
> 1. a standard of personal conduct
> 2. an underlying or guiding theory or belief
>
> *The Collins English Dictionary*

A. Teacher: *I'm confused. What is the difference between rules and guidelines for success?*

Dr. Foster: *Rules require responsibility and pertain to behaviors that have consequences. "Bring books and other learning materials to class" is a rule. "Be responsible" is an example of a guideline for success—a behavior for lifelong success.*

A. Teacher: *That makes sense. Guidelines for success are goals, and rules are behavioral objectives.*

Dr. Foster: *Yes. Principles relate to guidelines for success. When you think about what is appropriate and focus on "the why of teaching" you use "principled practice" (Smagorinsky, 2009, p. 20).*

A. Teacher: *Tell me more about principles and principled practice.*

> *Correct principles*
> *are like compasses:*
> *they are always pointing the way.*
> *And if we know how to read them,*
> *we won't get lost, confused,*
> *or fooled by conflicting*
> *voices and values.*
>
> **Stephen R. Covey**
> *Principle-Centered Leadership*

What are some examples of principles that teachers might consider for their classroom? Stephen R. Covey (1992) asserts that principle-centered leadership is the key to personal and organizational effectiveness. He identifies four main principles that would apply to classroom teachers: trust, trustworthiness, empowerment, and alignment (see Table 8.2).

> The traditional science of my training told me to isolate the pieces, to remove the complexity. But new science told me to hold true to those things that I believe, to the principles that have made my teaching a joyous profession. (Maas, 2005, p. 38)

Table 8.2

Principles of Principled-Leadership	
Trust	the interpersonal foundation of all effective relationships that result in trustworthiness at the personal level
Trustworthiness	personal integrity and competence
Empowerment	management style that unleashes the potential of people and fosters innovation and initiative through self-supervision
Alignment	resolve and commitment to the organizational vision based on principles

A. Teacher: *I can see how these principles might apply to adults in organizations. Do they really work for teachers and students?*

Dr. Foster: *The principles of principled-leadership **are** high expectations for behavior, but they do apply to teachers and students. Dr. Dan Cohen says you can engage people to break down the "barriers that hinder people from trying to make the vision work . . . and by identifying processes that are ineffective" (2005, p. 4). Later we will address how Dr. Stephen Covey's principles drive the development and implementation of classroom procedures and processes.*

A. Teacher: *Could you give me an example from a real classroom teacher?*

Dr. Foster: *Jeffrey Maas, an elementary teacher, has described the five guiding principles that helped him understand, organize, and manage the learning in his classroom.*

In "Principled Practice: New Science for the Classroom," Jeffrey Maas (2005) says his principles can be "found in the first minute of the first day to the farewells on the last hour of the year, from small assignment to the grandiose project" (p. 10). He embraces, articulates, and remains focused on his principles rather than "traditional reward/punishment regimes" (p. 31). Maas believes learning is more powerful when:

>   . . . it is owned by the participants of the community.

>   . . . it is a social activity.

>   . . . it is reflective and inquiry based.

>   . . . it is based on standards (p. 11).

> *Important principles may, and must, be inflexible.*
> **Abraham Lincoln**

A. Teacher: *Principles differ from person to person.*

Dr. Foster: *They do vary. Think about the behaviors for the* **High Expectations Prescription** *(see Table 8.3), and read about the* **MegaSkills** *of Dr. Dorothy Rich that can empower learners in "Em-power the Inner Engines of Learning."*

Table 8.3

High Expectations		
Strategies Skills	**Active Ingredients** Values	**Behaviors** Guidelines for Success
Set Goals	**Efficacy**	Be a goal setter.
Model		Be a role model.
Monitor	**Authenticity**	Be equitable.
Communicate		Be respectful.
Build Trust	**Community**	Be trustworthy.
Inspire Teamwork		Be a team player.
Empower	**Autonomy**	Be a decision maker.
Self-Regulate		Be disciplined.
Self-Talk	**Resiliency**	Be affirming.
Problem Solve		Be a problem solver.

Em-power the Inner Engines of Learning

Dr. Dorothy Rich (2007) identified twelve **MegaSkills**, or inner engines of learning. These beliefs, behaviors, and attitudes can **em-power** learners to achieve in school and in life (para. 1). These are her **MegaSkills**.

Confidence: I feel able to do it.

Motivation: I want to do it.   **Perseverance:** I complete what I start.

Effort: I am willing to work hard.   **Common Sense:** I use good judgment.

Responsibility: I do what is right.   **Initiative:** I move into action.

Caring: I show concern for others.   **Teamwork:** I work well with others.

Focus: I concentrate on my goals.   **Problem Solving:** I put what I know
Respect: I am courteous.   and what I can do into action.

Say **"Start Your Engines!"** and **em-power** your students to develop the *MegaSkills*, or inner engines of learning, to maximize their potential.

A. Teacher: *Many skills (strategies), values, and behaviors (guidelines for success) in the* **High Expectations Prescription** *were those listed by Stephen Covey, Jeffrey Maas, and Dorothy Rich.*

Dr. Foster: *Which principles do these lists have in common?*

A. Teacher: *Dr. Covey lists trustworthiness as one of his key principles that equates with the* **MegaSkill** *"Responsibility, and "Be trustworthy," a behavior of the* **High Expectations Prescription***. If only I could get my students to take responsibility for their own learning and behavior.*

I think another common principle is empowerment. It is one of Dr. Covey's key leadership principles, one of the strategies for the **High Expectations Prescription***, and a catalyst for the inner engines of learning (MegaSkills). Maas focused on learning and asserted the power of ownership in the learning process.*

> *Response-ability* is the ability to choose our response to any circumstance or condition. When we are response-able, our commitment becomes more powerful than our moods or circumstances and we keep the promises and resolutions we make. . . . And as we deal well with each new challenge, we unleash within ourselves a fresh capacity to soar to new heights. (Covey, 1992, p. 49)

Empowerment is the natural result of trustworthiness (Covey, 2004). It "enables people to identify and unleash their human potential. In other words, empowering enthrones self-control, self-management, and self-organizing. . . . It taps into passion, energy and drive" (p. 253).

Dr. Foster: *Please explain what you have learned about principles.*

A. Teacher: *Principles are standards that guide behaviors in the classroom and life. I like Stephen Covey's four key principles because they connect to MegaSkills and the High Expectations' Guidelines for Success.*

Dr. Foster: *Give me an example.*

A. Teacher: *Take empowerment. Students can be empowered to develop each MegaSkill. As for the High Expectations' Guidelines for Success, being a goal setter, decision maker, and problem solver are behaviors that would empower students to succeed in school and beyond.*

Dr. Foster: *Is there anything else you would like to know about principles?*

A. Teacher: *Yes. I am not sure what alignment means.*

Dr. Foster: *Let me clarify the term as it relates to mission, vision, and values.*

How do principles align with mission, vision, and values? The purpose of an organization (school or classroom) is its mission. "A mission statement . . . embodies deeply held values and is based on timeless principles" (Covey, 1992, pp. 184–185). Values are the important traits or qualities evidenced in behaviors and used to set goals and make decisions. Vision is a mental picture of what an organization hopes to look like in the future. "Without a destination in mind, you may arrive at a place you don't want to be" (Sprick et al., 1998, p. 9). To be effective, principles, mission, vision, and values must remain in alignment—in balance and harmony.

 a·lign·ment [ə′l ī n mənt′] *n.*

1. proper or desirable relation or coordination of components
2. integration or harmonization of aims, practices, etc. within a group
3. identification with or matching of the behavior, thoughts, etc. of another person

The Collins English Dictionary

Mission Accomplished!

Mountain View Whisman School District in Mountain View, CA, and Cumberland County Schools in Fayetteville, NC, affirm that establishing a mission statement helps define a purpose for the teacher and students in the learning environment. Classroom mission statements should align with the mission of the school and district.

In Practice

Mr. Lee

Here are some steps to create a classroom mission statement that tells your story in less than 30 seconds:

- Have students brainstorm why they attend school (purpose) and how they will achieve these goals (actions).
- Write the mission statement in which students' ideas have been included.
- Post the statement with the signatures of the students and teacher.
- Review the statement with the class regularly.

Our Class Mission Statement

We, the students in Mr. Lee's second class, pledge to respect others. We also pledge to work hard by studying, asking questions, and doing our work. Our class will strive to make good choices. We accept responsibility as students of Roosevelt School.

Inspire your students to say, **"Mission accomplished!"** every day in the classroom. See more classroom examples at http://www.elemedu.ccs.k12.nc.us/Resources/Mission_Statements/Sample-Page.htm. For tips about how to create a mission statement for your classroom, use **Supplement Q: Mission, Vision, Principles, and Values.** Locate **Supplements** at *www.classroommanagementblues.com,* then **Q–V** for **Supplement Q.**

A. Teacher: *I understand how the classroom mission, vision, and value statements must work together and align with principles.*

Dr. Foster: *To show that you understand, think of a metaphor that explains these complex concepts.*

A. Teacher: *A quilt is a good example. The **mission**, or purpose, of a quilt is to provide warmth and a sense of security. The selection of images that form a pattern of what the designer wants the quilt to look like when it is finished represents the **vision**. The underside represents the **principles** that form the quilt's foundation. The threads that hold the quilt together are the **values**.*

Dr. Foster: *You have the ability to develop metaphors to demonstrate your understanding!*

A. Teacher: *I comprehend the terms, but I could use more information about how to develop mission, vision, and value statements with my students.*

Dr. Foster: 📁 **Supplement Q: Mission, Vision, Principles, and Values** *will help you identify principles and create the mission, vision, and value statements with your students. (Select* **Supplements***, then* **Q–V** *at www.classroommangementblues.com to find* **Supplement Q***.)*

> *Principles and rules are intended to provide a thinking man with a frame of reference.*
> **Karl von Clausewitz**
> *Prussian military strategist*

Active Ingredient	🍎 Rules

The next active ingredient in the **Trustworthy Behavior Prescription** is **rules**. These standards of conduct play an important role to realize the shared classroom vision and create a positive and safe learning climate. Wayson (1985) states that the ultimate "purpose for having rules is to teach good behavior. . . . [and] create a stable, predictable environment. Children and adults need a certain amount of stability so they can feel secure enough to be able to control their own behavior" (para. 2).

A. Teacher: *As a student and teacher, I have always thought of rules and their punishments as negative strategies to control classroom behavior.*

Dr. Foster: *The origin of discipline is from Latin **disciplina**, which means teaching and learning. Teachers should teach rules and provide consequences not punishments.*

A. Teacher: *The first step toward transforming classrooms is to heighten motivation and reduce fear (Cohen, 2005). We teachers should strive to create a safe learning environment—not use rules and punishments to cause students to fear us.*

Dr. Foster: *"Psychologists have found that, if children obey rules not because they believe they are reasonable, but simply to avoid punishment, they are less likely to internalize such rules and less likely to follow them without such a threat" (Staub, 1979, p. 7).*

How can teachers help students be accountable, take ownership, and realize the classroom vision? Once teachers create a mission statement and shared vision with input from students, they establish classroom rules. Teachers and students identify ideal future behaviors and "determine which current behaviors need to be encouraged and which need to be eliminated" (Cohen, 2005, p. 69).

When teachers design classroom rules with input from students, researchers say the collaborative process reduces behavior problems and "promotes mutual respect, cooperation, self-discipline, and personal responsibility" (Staub, 1979, p. 7). To initiate collaboration is challenging but possible.

> When a teacher concerned about maintaining control leaves for a few minutes or is absent, the class is likely to erupt into chaos. "It is in classrooms . . . where participation is valued above adult control that students have the chance to learn self-control—and are more likely to keep working when the teacher . . . isn't around." (Kohn, 1993, para. 77)

Controlling Interest

Jennifer Wagaman (2009) says teachers should allow students to help create class rules, but a teacher should decide which rules he or she wants first. This way, teachers have a **controlling interest** in the ownership of the classroom rules.

In Practice
J. Wagaman

Teachers should select rules in **general categories** rather than specific rules, "unless there is a specific rule that must be included" (para. 4). Wagaman offers two examples:

- ■ **Respect others**   ■ **Safety first**

Without knowing the teacher's general categories, students brainstorm ideas for class rules on the first day of school. The teacher writes each suggested rule on the white board or SmartBoard, and later, places the students' rules under his or her general class rules. For example:

- ■ **Respect others**
  - Take turns talking
  - Do not hit

"If there is a specific important rule that the students did not mention, the teacher is welcome to prompt them. . . . That is the beauty of brainstorming—everyone needs to contribute and no ideas are stupid" (para. 9).

Collaborate with students about classroom rules that promote trust and a commitment to realize the shared classroom vision. In this win-win situation, the teacher gains student buy-in, but retains **controlling interest**.

At the beginning of each school year, a teacher should help students understand that discipline is important and show students that she or he is a disciplined person. "Teachers must not just talk about something but do something to gain the respect of students" (Gayagay, n.d., para. 3). When students trust a teacher, it is easier to instill discipline and classroom rules (para. 3).

Dr. Foster: *Teachers must model the "right" behavior and hold themselves and their students accountable to realize the classroom vision (Cohen, 2005).*

A. Teacher: *I need to remember to set a good example for my students.*

From what you have shown me, I believe I could be successful if I share the creation of classroom rules with my students.

Are there guidelines I need to follow to develop effective rules?

Dr. Foster: *There is much consensus among educators about how to make sure your rules are effective. I will share some ways with you now.*

What are some guidelines to help develop effective rules? "One way to look at rules is as a way of communication between the teacher and the class. In setting and enforcing rules, a teacher can convey expectations and values, while students communicate in turn through how they respond to the rules" (Louwerse, 2000, para. 5). To be effective, rules must be clearly understood, reasonable, and consistently enforced (Louwerse, 2000; Wayson, 1985).

> If we value "participation, equality, inclusiveness and social justice," (Hargreaves & Fullan, 1998, p. 13), then our classrooms and schools need to be places where students share leadership and responsibility for learning. (Rolheiser & Ross, n.d., para. 10)

In *How the Brain Influences Behavior: Management Strategies for Every Classroom* (2009), Sousa suggests that teachers post classroom rules to remind students of expectations—cognitive reinforcers. Sprick, Garrison, and Howard (1998) agree that teachers post rules in a prominent place and recommend the following guidelines to create effective rules:

- Keep the number of rules to no more than six.

- State rules positively, if possible.

- Describe the observable behavior.

- Think about misbehaviors most likely to happen (pp. 76–77).

"A big mistake teachers make is having a list of rules and assuming that a quick explanation is good enough" (Seganti, 2008, p. 38). To be effective, teachers should teach rules and "plan on repeatedly teaching the details of any somewhat subjective rules for at least the first two to three weeks of school" (Sprick et al., 1998, p. 77). "By the Seat of Your Pants" illustrates why a quick explanation about rules is not enough.

> It isn't easy to make clear rules. For example, when teachers go into the room and say, "Be good," there is no clarity to that at all. . . . first because [it] isn't clear and second . . . because the children have to depend upon the teacher to tell them whether they are "good" or "bad." (Wayson, 1985, para. 7)

By the Seat of Your Pants

Do not learn by the seat of your pants! Take the time and my advice to teach classroom rules and share, or role- play, examples and nonexamples.

A common rule is "Be in your seat when the bell rings." You might assume that students would understand what this means. I learned the hard way that students are creative in circumventing rules.

Without teaching the rule, students might stand in their chairs, sit backwards, or even sit somewhere in the room other than at their own desks. If this were to happen, you should praise the student's creativity. Then, teach students the correct way to be in their seats when the bell rings. Once taught, it becomes the expectation.

Sometimes learning by the seat of your pants can tickle your funny bone—sometimes, not!

A. Teacher: *What are the rules you used in your classroom?*

Dr. Foster: *Here are the general rules that worked for me.*

1. Respect adults.
2. Respect other students.
3. Use appropriate language and voice level.
4. Be a team player.
5. Stay on task.
6. Take care of school and personal property.

 What do you notice about these rules?

A. Teacher: *You followed the guidelines: no more than six, observable, stated positively, and most likely misbehaviors.*

They are general. This means I would have to clarify with input from my students about the behaviors that would fall under each rule.

> Not only do students need to take more collective responsibility within the learning *community*, there is an expectation that they maximize their full potential by making choices about and taking responsibility for their own learning and behavior. (Benson, 2003; Wisniewska, 1998)

Dr. Foster: *You have grasped the important understandings about how to establish rules.*

Dr. Foster: *You can learn more about how to establish rules on the **Classroom Management Blues** website. (Select **Resources** at www.classroommanagementblues.com, and then choose **Behavior** and **Rules**.)*

Now, let's shift our conversation to the selection of consequences.

Active Ingredient	 Consequences

"The teacher's task is to help students make good choices by making clear the connection between student behavior" and **consequences**—the third active ingredient in the **Trustworthy Behavior Prescription** (Emmer, 1986, p. 7). This active ingredient is strongly linked to autonomy—one of the active ingredients in the **High Expectations Prescription**.

What is the function of consequences in the classroom? With the effective use of consequences, teachers can create and maintain a positive learning environment where students can learn to do what is right without rules or without supervision. Teachers can achieve these goals if they help students become autonomous and develop "a sense of self and the concept of respect for themselves and others" (Hatfield, n.d., para. 2).

> *Good discipline is more than just punishing or laying down the law. It is liking children and letting them see that they are liked. It is caring enough about them to provide good, clear rules for their protection.*
>
> **Jeannette W. Galambos**
> *Early childhood education specialist*

Red Light—Green Light

In "A Green Light for Common Sense," Craig Whitlock (2007) tells about "a German community where thousands of cars and big trucks barreled along the two-lane main street, forcing pedestrians and cyclists to scamper for their lives" (para. 1). No matter the number of safety crossings, speed traps, and other remedies, nothing helped.

The citizens of Bohmte, Germany, used a traffic management approach known as "shared space." They tore up the sidewalks, removed curbs, erased street markers, and abandoned nearly all traffic regulations to "force people to rely on common sense and courtesy instead" (para. 2).

Without traffic lights and lane markers, drivers paid more attention to the people and vehicles on the road and drove more carefully. They expected 95% fewer accidents, as had been the result in the town of Haren, Netherlands.

The *reality* is that a "red light" reminds us to stop and think about others and a "green light" signals us to move forward, to create a shared space.

A. Teacher: *I would love to have students who were self-disciplined and trustworthy so I could do more teaching and deal less with misbehavior.*

Dr. Foster: *On the first day of school, ask your students if they would like to be in a classroom where there were no rules, everyone received respect, and students could make their own decisions.*

A. Teacher: *My students would like this classroom, but they need rules.*

Dr. Foster: *Trustworthy behavior and self-discipline are high expectations, and most students need support in the form of effective consequences to create a "shared space" of autonomous, self-disciplined learners.*

What role do punishments play in the classroom?

A. Teacher: *Punishments should change student behavior, but I find that they do not change behavior or create a shared space. They create a threatening environment.*

I thought consequences were the same as punishments.

> As a result of rules that focus on . . . punishments, teachers and administrators tend to be viewed and to behave more as disciplinarians than as educators, and therefore spend a disproportionate amount of time policing rather than teaching. (Schimmel, 1997, p. 3)

Dr. Foster: *It depends upon how teachers use them. Here are a few differences.*

Table 8.4

Consequences—Proactive	**Punishments—Reactive**
• Usually identified in advance	• Often given spontaneously
• Mutually understood—assigned unemotionally	• Often given in anger—adversarial
• Chosen by students—empowering	• Done to students—threatening
• Promote calm	• Promote anger

A. Teacher: *I have never thought of punishments in this way. I have much to learn about how to use consequences effectively.*

How can consequences empower students to become self-disciplined? In *Shouting Won't Grow Dendrites,* Marcia Tate (2007) asserts that teachers use ineffective discipline methods because habits are hard to break and the ineffective methods sometimes work, so "teachers believe that if they are persistent, the methods will work again" (p. 102). Effective teachers develop consequences in collaboration with students, use different consequences to meet the individual needs of students, and vary consequences to maintain interest and motivation.

If teachers develop classroom rules with students, teachers should use student input about consequences as well (Sprick et al., 1998; Wagaman, 2009). As Jennifer Wagaman recommends for rules, teachers should identify a general hierarchy of consequences ahead of time. Through teacher-student collaboration, students then brainstorm ideas for consequences that are "instructive and aimed at helping students learn to conduct themselves with greater personal responsibility" (Charles, 2010, p. 163).

As students may rely on ineffective consequences they have experienced in other classes, a teacher should discuss the effectiveness of the consequences proposed, but may need to make suggestions and get student feedback. After generating ideas, the teacher makes connections to the hierarchy of consequences he or she has identified in advance.

A. Teacher: *You mentioned that effective consequences should meet the individual needs of students. Does this mean I should use different consequences with students?*

Dr. Foster: *As students vary in their degree of self-control, some need more support than others do. "Give yourself permission to use different consequences with students. Consistency with individual students is more important than always following the same consequence with every student in the class all the time" ("Strategies," 2001, p. 2).*

A. Teacher: *Won't students complain that they want to be treated the same?*

Dr. Foster: *"Actually most students will not complain once the teacher explains that some students require different consequences" (p. 2). Everyone in the classroom benefits when students behave appropriately!*

Consequences that vary every two to four months help maintain student interest and motivation. "No matter how good your reinforcement system, a lack of variety usually results in diminishing returns" (p. 2).

Another way to vary consequences and empower students is to use guided choice—by offering students two or three options from which to choose. Marvin Marshall asserts that guided choice is one way a teacher can intervene to activate internal motivation and raise student responsibility when students misbehave (Marshall, 2011).

A. Teacher: *So consequences are important, but positive interactions with students are more important?*

Dr. Foster: *"Appropriate use of negative consequences . . . is one of the most critically important skills in establishing and maintaining a well-disciplined but **positive** classroom" ("Strategies," 2001, p. 2).*

> Effective teachers use about four times as many positive consequences as negative ones (80% positive to 20% negative). Positive consequences result in higher effort and pride, better teacher-student relationships, better student-student relationships, and, in time, more self-control. ("Strategies," 2001, p. 1)

A. Teacher: *How can the use of consequences create a positive classroom?*

Dr. Foster: *Before I share the **Consequence Hierarchy and Behavior Support System** I used in my classroom, read "Pressure Points" to learn how the brain reacts to positive interactions.*

Pressure Points

When Marcia L. Tate (2007) teaches a *Worksheets Don't Grow Dendrites* course, she engages participants in an activity that **points** to the body's reaction to **pressure** when the brain is thinking both positively and negatively (p. 101).

Partner A asks Partner B to extend his or her dominant arm out to the side. While the arm is extended, Partner A pushes down on the arm and asks Partner B to resist while thinking of something positive in his or her life, something that makes him or her feel good, or something that makes him or her smile. The arm typically stays strong and the partner cannot pull the arm down no matter the pressure.

Partner A then asks Partner B to think of a time when he or she was upset, angry, or stressed and repeats the procedure. The arm invariably goes down. Partners reserve roles and repeat the procedure.

Point 1:   When the brain is thinking positively, the arm stays raised because of the body's ability to perform appropriately when the brain has confidence and is thinking good thoughts.

Point 2:   When thinking negatively or threatened, the brain prepares the body to defend itself. With less blood flow to the brain, one is not able to think at higher levels, and the body does not perform appropriately.

When stressed, angry, or under **pressure**, both teachers and students are not able to make the best decisions. This reality **points** to the importance of how teachers and students think about positive and negative consequences. Better decisions will result when everyone understands that consequences can help students learn to behave appropriately and responsibly.

In *How the Brain Influences Behavior: Management Strategies for Every Classroom*, Sousa (2009) explains that brain studies show happiness and sadness activate different parts of the brain. Happiness activates the frontal lobe where the brain processes information, while sadness activates the limbic area where the brain processes emotions (p. 181).

> Happiness . . . is designed to evaporate. If the pleasure that comes from a particular achievement never ended, then we would not need to do it again. (Sousa, 2009, p. 182)

There is research evidence that the chemical dopamine found in the prefrontal cortex is a "neurotransmitter important in aspects of happiness and closely associated with moving toward some sort of goal, such as being successful in school and in personal relationships" (Sousa, 2009, p. 182). When students do things that make them happy, dopamine increases the likelihood that they will do those things again.

> Researchers found that trustworthiness was positively correlated with happiness and negatively correlated with anger and sadness (Winston, Strange, O'Doherty, & Dolan, 2002) . . . These findings mean that students are much more likely to trust a teacher who is happy—and who, by extension, provides an environment where the students are happy—than a teacher who is not. (Sousa, 2009, p. 181)

A. Teacher: *How does happiness relate to consequences?*

Dr. Foster: *Everyone in the classroom would be happier if everyone made better choices. To achieve this goal, consequences should involve reflection and support from peers, teachers, parents, administrators, and other school personnel.*

Which consequences help students follow classroom rules and become self-disciplined? Without a well-defined continuum, or hierarchy of consequences, teachers often substitute "consequences with verbal discipline, resulting in discipline with emotion rather than with reason" ("Strategies," 2001, p. 2). Marvin Marshall developed a hierarchy of social development and says that once students understand the hierarchy, their attention turns to self-control and social responsibility" (as cited in Charles, 2010, p. 181). Marshall says a hierarchy of consequences

> [Effective teachers] know that while consequences may stop misbehavior short term, it is the positive interactions with students that change behavior in the long run. (Tate, 2007, p. 102)

- Helps students realize they constantly make choices,
- Raises awareness of individual responsibility,
- Fosters internal motivation to behave responsibly,
- Serves as an inspiration to improve,
- Encourages mature decision making,
- Promotes self-management, and
- Empowers students to analyze and correct their own behavior (p. 181).

A. Teacher: *Could you give me an example?*

Dr. Foster: *An example of an **ineffective** hierarchy of consequences would be "If you call out twice, your mother will have to come to school" (Seeman, 2000, para. 12). In this example, the teacher would take few steps before the student receives a severe consequence. Contacting a third party should occur as late as possible in your hierarchy. Parents and administrators should receive the hierarchy ahead of time so they know when the teacher will contact them to support the student in making better choices.*

Dr. Foster: *To help my students become self-disciplined, I created a **Consequence Hierarchy and Behavior Support System** based on the Chinese proverb "One beam cannot support a house." The beams that must be in place to support a [school] house include peers, teachers, other school personnel, parents, and administrators (see Figure 8.1). You will learn about the hierarchy and support system in this session. (Find more detailed information about 🗁 **Supplement R: Consequence Hierarchy and Behavior Support System** on the **Classroom Management Blues** website. Select **Supplements** at www.classroommanagement blues.com, then **Q–V** to locate **Supplement R**.)*

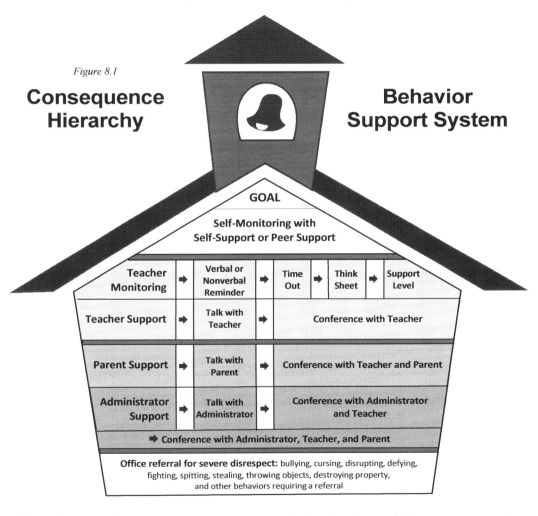

Figure 8.1

Consequence Hierarchy

Behavior Support System

GOAL

Self-Monitoring with Self-Support or Peer Support

Teacher Monitoring	➡	Verbal or Nonverbal Reminder	➡	Time Out	➡	Think Sheet	➡	Support Level
Teacher Support	➡	Talk with Teacher	➡	Conference with Teacher				
Parent Support	➡	Talk with Parent	➡	Conference with Teacher and Parent				
Administrator Support	➡	Talk with Administrator	➡	Conference with Administrator and Teacher				

➡ Conference with Administrator, Teacher, and Parent

Office referral for severe disrespect: bullying, cursing, disrupting, defying, fighting, spitting, stealing, throwing objects, destroying property, and other behaviors requiring a referral

A. Teacher: *Could you give me a more detailed explanation of the consequences in your hierarchy and support system?*

Dr. Foster: *Gladly. (See Table 8.5 on the next page.)*

Table 8.5

Brief Explanations of the Consequence Hierarchy Terms	
Reminder	Students receive verbal and nonverbal reminders from a teacher or peer to support a change in behavior or get back on task. (See more on page 268.) **Time** 5–10 seconds during instruction, a transition, or another activity
Time Out	The student thinks about the answers to these questions about his or her behavior. What rule was broken? How did the behavior affect you and others? What will you do in the future? (Select the **Supplements** page at *www.classroommangementblues.com*, then **Q–V** for **Supplement S** to learn more information about **Time Outs and Think Sheets**.) **Time** 30–60 seconds after class or during a **preferred activity**—one the student prefers. *Note:* Preferred activities (e.g., recess, a game, computer time, learning center, earned free time, before or after school) vary from student to student.
Think Sheet	The student reflects on the rule(s) broken and writes/dictates the answers to questions about his or her behavior. What rule was broken? How did the behavior affect you and others? What will you do in the future? (Select **Supplements**, then **Q–V** for **Supplement S: Time Outs and Think Sheets**.) **Time** 5–10 minutes during a preferred activity
Talk Recitation, instruction, discussion, or dialogue	The student talks with the teacher, parent, administrator, or other support personnel about the effectiveness of the consequences to achieve behavioral goals and discusses the next steps if the misbehavior continues. The teacher or student may contact the parent by phone, letter, email, or text and discuss behaviors, consequences, and future actions. (Select **Supplements** at *www.classroommangementblues.com*, then **W-Z** to locate **Supplement X: Discussion and Dialogue Prompts**.) **Time** 2–5 minutes during a preferred activity or after class
Conference	The student has a collaborative problem solving conference and dialogues with one or more supporting persons (teacher, parent, other school personnel, and/or administrator. (Select the **Supplements** page at *www.classroommangementblues.com*, then **W-Z** for **Supplement Y: Conference Guidelines and Protocols**.) **Time** 20–60 minutes during a preferred activity or before/after school

Dr. Foster: *What do you think about these consequences?*

A. Teacher: *First, I like the use of positive words like "support" and "reminder." Most hierarchies have a warning rather than a reminder. A warning is more of a threat, while a reminder can empower students to choose a different behavior.*

Dr. Foster: *A reminder may be verbal or nonverbal and take only 5–10 seconds during instruction, a transition, or another activity. In the first week or more of school, my students learned to recognize the reminders I frequently used to get them back on task. (See a list of the reminders I used in my classroom on page 268.)*

Here are some things to remember when you give a reminder or provide a consequence.

- **Before:** *Remain calm, and do not take students' responses personally.*
- **When giving a reminder or consequence:** *Use a respectful tone.*
- **After:** *Say, "Thank you," or nonverbally acknowledge (e.g., smile, thumbs up) when students correct their behavior.*

*If a reminder or other consequence is **not** effective for your students, do not use it. Modify it, or choose another option.*

*When I designed my **Consequence Hierarchy and Behavior Support System**, I did not include **specific** consequences (e.g., time out **during recess**). This kept students guessing and allowed the opportunity to choose the most effective consequence for a class or individual student. When a student had a time out during recess and it did not change classroom behavior, I tried another preferred activity until I found the one that worked for that student. As options varied, a student did not know which consequence he or she would receive for a misbehavior. Students are more likely to follow rules when the specific consequence is unknown.*

Wait a Second!

Research results have shown that an increase in "wait time from three to six seconds, accompanied by a high-order question, results in students responding with more thoughtful answers" (Wong & Wong, 1998, p. 31). If teachers and students **wait *more than* a second** before they respond, the responses and actions will be more thoughtful and responsible!

Keep the preferred activities for consequences a mystery! When students have to **wait *more than* a second** and consider the consequence they will receive for misbehavior, it is more forbidding than knowing what will happen. The *reality* is that the unknown is worrisome for students.

Dr. Foster: *When a consequence is not specific, it also allows students to choose a consequence they believe will be most effective. Guided choice gives them ownership in the success of the consequence. Again, if the consequence is not effective, you or the student must choose another consequence.*

A. Teacher: *I see how it would make students think when they are unsure of the consequence. Is a time out of 30 to 60 seconds effective?*

> To get leverage you must be able to take away something of value to a student (or give something of value as a reward) as a consequence. What does every student (and pretty much every human being) value? Their time. (Seganti, 2008, p. 22)

Dr. Foster: *Sit quietly and do not talk or do anything for 30 seconds, then 60 seconds.*

A. Teacher: *Wow! It seemed like a long time!*

Dr. Foster: *It seems even longer to students when they have to miss a preferred activity. For middle or high school students, 30 seconds to 60 seconds after class is a long time when they want to talk with friends between classes.*

*What else did you notice about the **Consequence Hierarchy and Behavior Support System**? (See page 233.)*

A. Teacher: *I noticed that the ultimate goal is for students to be at the **Self-Monitoring with Self- or Peer-Support Level**.*

What do students do at this level?

> According to Self-Determination Theory . . . people experience a sense of autonomy when they can realize their personal goals, values and interests. . . . [Researchers] state that the cluster of autonomy-supportive actions includes behaviours such as providing choice, encouraging self-initiation, minimizing the use of controls, and acknowledging the other's perspective and feelings. (Assor, Kaplan, & Roth, 2002, p. 262)

Dr. Foster: *Students set goals, self-monitor and document their behavior, and assess goal attainment. They may choose support from a peer.*

*You will learn more about Self-Monitoring with Self- or Peer Support later in this session and on the **Classroom Management Blues** website.*

A. Teacher: *In your **Behavior Support System**, students receive many opportunities to succeed with the support of the teacher before contacting a parent or administrator.*

Dr. Foster: *For time outs and conferences, I collaborated with students, used different consequences to meet individual needs, and varied consequences to help each student achieve their behavioral goals. The same was true for rewards and other incentives. We will discuss these positive consequences later in this session.*

Dr. Foster: *else have you discovered about consequences?*

A. Teacher: *Consequences require students to analyze and reflect on their behavior, as well as talk to and/or meet with supportive persons to come up with a behavior support plan to encourage appropriate behavior. Time outs, talks, and conferences occur during a time valued by the student—during a preferred activity, after class, or before/after school.*

How often did your students move to the parent and administrator levels?

Dr. Foster: *Only a few students a year moved to these levels. I did not want them at the parent level because some parents did not follow through or were more punitive than supportive.*

During the four years before I took a position in higher education, only one student moved to the administrator support level. The principal was supportive of the student and me. Read "Chill Out in the Office!" to learn how the student's behavior improved with the principal's support.

> Teachers do not generally want to give control to their students. . . . The amount of control that teachers have in the class is often seen by the administration as a measurement of the quality of a teacher. Administrators are usually happy if a teacher never sends a student to the office and interprets this as proof that the teacher is in control and must be doing a good job (Edwards, 1994; Taylor, 1987; Van Tassel, 2005)

Chill Out in the Office!

 I exhausted all the strategies and consequences I could think of to help Sam control his temper. We finally came up with a plan, with the support of the principal, to help him "**chill out**" in the office when he was angry or became aware that he was about to become angry.

I duplicated a hall pass with Sam's name and this message: "I am on my way to the office to chill out." When he brought me the pass, I only had to sign and date it.

After he presented the pass to the secretary, he sat in a designated chair until he calmed down. If the principal saw Sam, she praised him for coming to the office to chill out.

The ***reality*** is that Sam learned to trust the principal and me to help him calm down and gain control as he **chilled out in the office**.

Dr. Foster: *Principals are less likely to see a student in the office for misbehavior if he or she has a positive relationship with the student. The principals I have worked with knew my students did not appear in the office until I had exhausted other interventions.*

> The involvement of your administrator . . . can have a powerful impact on a difficult student. Your administrator may not only be able to provide stronger, more effective consequences, but more importantly, he or she can also provide unique motivation and help to develop a positive relationship with this student. (Canter & Canter, 1993, p. 229)

There are times when a student must be referred to the office immediately for behaviors defined in the student handbook (e.g., bullying, fighting, carrying a weapon). When other behaviors like disrupting, defying, and pushing become severe, these documented behaviors may result in a referral without moving through the **Consequence Hierarchy and Behavior Support System***. These referrals are at your discretion. (Learn more about office referrals for severe disrespect in* **Supplement R: Consequence Hierarchy and Behavior Support System***. Select* **Supplements** *at www.classroommanagementblues.com, then* **Q–V** *to locate* **Supplement R***.)*

A. Teacher: *I think the consequence hierarchy might work, but how do I keep track of all the levels and consequences?*

Dr. Foster: *After we talk about positive consequences (rewards and other incentives), I will show you how I monitored and documented misbehaviors and consequences.*

How should teachers use rewards to help students follow classroom rules and become self-disciplined? To create a climate for change, the last step is to recognize and reward self-management behaviors to "make them stick" (Cohen, 2005). (See page 218.) The ultimate goal is to help students "internalize positive behaviors so that they will not need a reward. Eventually, self-motivation will be sufficient to induce them to perform the desired behavior, and outside reinforcement will no longer be necessary" (Jacobson, n.d., para. 5).

> **in·cen·tive** [ĭn-sĕn′tĭv] **n.**
> A motivating influence; stimulus serving to incite to action
>
> *The Collins English Dictionary*

A. Teacher: *Isn't intrinsic motivation better than extrinsic motivation?*

Dr. Foster: *"Maybe. Nobody really knows. . . . Most behaviors are the result of a complex mix of both intrinsic and extrinsic motivation" (Sprick et al., 1998, p. 344).*

According to Dr. Sprick and others, extrinsic motivation is most effective when students need structure. The level of structure depends on the orchestration needed to assure that students will be successful.

Here are some class motivation systems for high, medium, and low structure (Sprick et al., 1998, pp. 355–386). (See Table 8.6.)

Table 8.6

Structured Motivation Systems	
Low Structure	Goal setting (teacher-guided for some students or a class)
Middle Structure	Lottery or raffle tickets, team competitions, and self-evaluation of one behavior (e.g., calling out, off task)
High Structure	Preferred activities for a behavior record-keeping system/behavior support system, whole class points, economic simulation (e.g., play money for jobs, fines, purchasing privileges)

Dr. Foster: *Begin the school year with highly structured rewards or a combination of incentives for high and middle structure. Consider goal setting when students are at the Self-Monitoring with Self- or Peer-Support Levels of the* **Consequence Hierarchy and Behavior Support System.** *Be careful not to use highly structured*

> When students are exhibiting desired behaviors, using high-powered rewards may slightly reduce their willingness to work without rewards. (Sprick et al., 1998, p. 344)

rewards when students intrinsically meet your expectations. If less structured methods fail or seem likely to fail to motivate students to behave responsibly, consider the use of more structured rewards (Sprick et al., 1998).

Here are some rewards and incentives I have found to be effective.

Table 8.7

Rewards	Celebrations	Privileges	Affirmations
• Extra points for a test or quiz • Extra time or special activity at the end of class or week • Donated prizes or certificates from businesses • Inexpensive toys, school supplies, books (prize box, class store, auction) • Extra credit • Time to talk after class	• Approved Apparel Day (e.g., hats or caps, sunglasses, backwards, dress up, opposites) • Song, dance, or performance by the teacher or students • Play celebration music: "Celebration" by Kool and the Gang; "I Just Want to Celebrate" by Rare Earth • Accomplishment banner or billboard at values.com	• Stay in at recess and play a game with a friend • Choose a class job • Sit with a friend • Use the teacher's or another special chair • Teach something to the class • An extra day to turn in homework or project • Assist the teacher in selecting class activities/materials	• Positive phone call, email, letter, or text to a parent • Attention, praise, thanks (privately) • Personal note from the teacher • Trophy, ribbon, certificate • Applause, thumbs up, high five, pat on the back • Congratulations from principal or counselor for goal achievement

From "List," n.d.; Bafile, 2003; "Constructive," n.d.; Sprick et al., 1998; Tate, 2007; and Wright, 2005

Celebrate Good Times, Come On!

In *Shouting Won't Grow Dendrites*, Marcia L Tate (2007) says, "The brain loves celebrations (p. 91). Here are some ways teachers and students can celebrate good times for academic, personal, and behavioral accomplishments (pp. 93–94):

- **Standing O.** Stand on tiptoes and form an "O" with arms raised above the head.
- **Round of Applause!** Softly clap hands together while moving hands around in a large circle.
- **Kiss your brain!** Take the dominant hand and place it on the lips and then on the top of the head.
- **Outstanding.** Make a baseball umpire's signal for an "out" and then stand up.
- **Silent Clap.** Take the forefingers of both hands and gently clap them together. There should be no sound at all.

Doug Lemov (2010) refers to the following celebrations as "props" (pp. 164–165):

- **The Roller Coaster!** Raise hands at 45 degrees, say "chug, chug, chug" as if going to the top of the roller coaster, and shout "woo, woo, woo," as if going over three humps.
- **The Home Run!** Toss up an imaginary ball and swing with an imaginary bat. Watch it soar out of sight, and then make crowd noise for a few seconds.

Laugh with your students, and **celebrate good times! Come on!**
The release of dopamine in the brain will move everyone to achieve goals!

A. Teacher: *I believe most of the rewards, celebrations, privileges, and other incentives would work for elementary and middle school classrooms, but not for high school.*

Dr. Foster: *What do you think would work for older students if they need middle- or high- structure?*

A. Teacher: *Private affirmations would be better than public for older students. I think they would like extra points, time at the end of class to talk, or to sit with a friend.*

Dr. Foster: *In general, I agree with the incentives you listed for older students. However, you would be surprised about the recognitions and rewards older students would like when asked.*

When I lecture to my senior high students, I set a timer for 10 minutes. When the timer dings, I pull a popsicle stick with one of the celebrations on it and they have to get up and do it. It breaks up the monotony, and it gets their brains to stay focused. When I started this they rolled their eyes . . . a lot, but now they can't wait for the timer to go off to see what they get to do. (Gibbon, 2009)

A. Teacher: *I do not see "no homework" passes on the list.*

Dr. Foster: *Let me share a few issues I have with some common classroom incentives: no homework passes, lunch with the teacher, and music during independent work time. Be careful with lunch with the teacher; if not used sparingly, you will find that you have no time for yourself during the school day.*

Teachers should use music routinely when students work on their own because music has a positive effect on the brain. Students could earn the privilege to select the instrumental music.

No homework passes send the message that homework has no value. If it does not matter whether some students do the homework, why should any student have to do it? Instead, give passes for a reduced assignment or an extra day to turn in homework or a project.

A. Teacher: *Is there anything else I need to know about effective rewards and incentives?*

Dr. Foster: *Remember that some of the celebrations, rewards, privileges, and affirmations are appropriate for individual **and** classwide recognition.*

*You should also think about **when** to provide rewards and other incentives.*

Teachers designate a specific time when a reward is to be given (e.g., in a specific number of minutes, end of a class or week). At other times, a student or the class should be surprised with an intermittent reward, celebration, privilege, or affirmation for self-management behaviors. "The key is to use these celebrations as sparingly as possible, but as frequently as needed (and always unpredictably) to keep students proud and excited about their achievements" (Sprick et al., 1998, p. 221).

> High school teacher Tory Klementsen told *Education World*," I think that when rewards are used variably, when they are of value, and when they are given for showing responsibility, they can have a very positive impact." (Bafile, 2003, para. 14)

Dr. Foster: *To create a climate for change, Step 7 is "Don't Let Up" (Cohen, 2005, p. 4). (See page 218.) "[Teachers] need to stay focused and demonstrate that they are not easing the pressure to achieve the vision" (p. 164). If you use the Consequence Hierarchy and Behavior Support System consistently and provide appropriately structured rewards and incentives, your students will be successful.*

*(Select **Resources** at www.classroommanagementblues.com, then **Behavior** and **Rewards** to learn more about rewards and incentives.)*

A. Teacher: *I understand how positive and negative consequences can support my students and achieve our shared vision, but I am still concerned about how to keep track of everything!*

Dr. Foster: *Let's take a break; then I will explain how I monitored and documented student behavior.*

Active Ingredient   🍎 Documentation

Administrators expect teachers to make decisions **about** student learning and behavior from an analysis of classroom data. Decisions based on these data help create the ideal learning conditions for students ("Introduction," n.d.). This calls for good **documentation**, the fourth active ingredient in the **Trustworthy Behavior Prescription**. Record keeping, or documentation, matters when teachers assess whether the teaching, learning, and behavior management strategies used are effective and help realize the shared classroom mission and vision.

> A formal data-based decision making process can help us identify important variables related to our teaching faster and more efficiently than relying on our memory to recall important events. This is especially true for teachers who often deal with many challenges that require their attention simultaneously. ("Introduction," n.d., para. 1)

Dr. Foster: *How do you document student behavior in your classroom?*

A. Teacher: *I hate to admit it, but my documentation is composed of office referrals—copies of the forms students take to the office after they get three checks on the board next to their name.*

Despite my good intentions to write down the reasons for the checks students get, I do not follow through at the end of each class or after school because I am tired, or I cannot remember what misbehaviors the checks represent.

Dr. Foster: *Students want their teachers to forget to record their behavior. If teachers forget or do not keep a written record of misbehaviors, students continue to misbehave and take a chance that they will not receive a consequence.*

A. Teacher: *Do I have to write everything down?*

Dr. Foster: *What you document depends on the level of structure needed to assure that students are successful in your classroom. The level of structure depends on the grade level, school climate, number of students in the class, and number of students identified with special needs or chronic behavior problems (Sprick et al., 1998).*

*Students on the Self-Monitoring with Self- or Peer-Support Level of the **Behavior Support System** require low structure and document their own behavior. You must document the behavior of those students who require higher structure to help them achieve their behavioral goals.*

A. Teacher: *If I understand correctly, students may need more structure at the beginning of the year with possibly less structure later in the year. An elementary classroom might need more structure than a high school class, and some students might need more structure than others might.*

I hope you will show me an efficient system that I can implement consistently to improve my students' behavior.

How can teachers monitor and document student behavior in ways that promote trustworthy behavior and self-discipline? A behavior support system aligned with principles, values, and a shared vision should focus on how to help students become trustworthy and self-disciplined. Teachers need to collect and analyze data to validate the effectiveness of the procedures, consequences, and incentives used in the classroom to support student success.

> Documenting behavior may seem to be too burdensome or time-consuming, but it is a necessary tool in addressing behavior . . . and securing necessary assistance. ("Documenting," n.d., para. 4)

Dr. Foster: *Before I explain the system I used in my classroom, I want you to reflect on some concepts from previous sessions to establish the groundwork for our discussion.*

*Let's focus first on how a behavior support system can help **all** students succeed.*

 Do you remember this formula from our session on appropriate assessments?

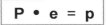
$$P \bullet e = p$$

A. Teacher: *Yes. **Practice** times **empowerment** equals **performance***

*When teachers **empower** students to do the **practice**, they are more successful on the **performance** assessment.*

Dr. Foster: *How does the same formula apply to behavior management?*

A. Teacher: *When teachers empower students to practice appropriate behaviors, they become trustworthy and self-disciplined. Practice involves learning from mistakes.*

Dr. Foster: *Exactly. "Everyone who has ever made a mistake and learned from it knows that they remember what they learn from mistakes much longer than what comes easily to them. By creating a classroom environment where mistakes are seen as opportunities to learn, students develop a sense of trust in being able to learn even when the learning is 'hard'" (Hatfield, n.d., para. 5).*

A. Teacher: *This makes me think of the principles we discussed earlier: trustworthiness, trust, empowerment, and alignment. The behavior support system aligns with these principles and gives students a sense of trust that I will create a safe environment where they feel empowered to learn trustworthy behaviors.*

Dr. Foster: *We also discussed the **expectancy times value** theory of motivation.*

 Can you explain how this theory relates to student motivation?

A. Teacher: *Of course! For a student to be motivated to do an assignment or assessment, he or she must value grades and have a high level of expectancy for success.*

Dr. Foster: *Again, your ability to make connections between the **Appropriate Assessments** and **Trustworthy Behavior Prescriptions** is impressive.*

Dr. Foster: *A behavior support system works best when students have a high level of expectancy that they can follow the classroom rules and will receive valued rewards and incentives to become self-disciplined and trustworthy.*

One last point before we move on: students know what you value by what you reward.

A. Teacher: *Because I value autonomy, I need to reward and recognize students when they demonstrate self-regulatory behaviors like self-control.*

Dr. Foster: *Absolutely. As you make decisions about how to monitor student behavior and document progress toward trustworthy behavior and self-discipline, be sure to follow these guidelines.*

Table 8.8

Behavior Support System Guidelines

- Maintain a clear vision aligned with principles—one that creates high expectations for each student;

- Keep in mind that your goal is to provide much support to help each student succeed; and

- Remember your role as coach and cheerleader, someone who gets students excited about learning and behaving in the classroom (Stein, 2010, p. 84).

When a student or class needs structure, how can teachers effectively monitor and document misbehaviors, consequences, and corrected behaviors? The ultimate goal of a behavior support system is to empower students to become trustworthy and self-disciplined. To achieve this goal and others in life, Jay White offers some reasons why teachers *and* students should harness "The Power of Writing Things Down." According to White (2009), when people write something down:

- They process emotions, see problems in a different light, and work toward solutions;

- The information becomes lodged, or fixed in long-term memory;

- Accountably is encouraged; and

- It allows a look back at past experiences.

> A teacher who manages students provides structure and organization in the classroom, but a teacher who leads students gives them hope for the future. (Stein, 2010, p. 86)

To monitor and keep a record of student behavior, Sprick and others (1998) propose that teachers use record sheets and code misbehaviors with lower case letters (t—talking at the wrong time) and positive traits with capital letters (R—Respectful). Behaviors can be recorded daily or weekly on a seating chart (pp. 257–260). (Read "De-code Behaviors.")

De-code Behaviors

Teachers can use daily or weekly behavior record sheets to document appropriate and inappropriate behaviors. See how often these behaviors happen and discover patterns the teacher used to **de-code** the **behaviors** on these seating charts (Sprick et al., 1998, p. 251). One is a daily record for students by subject; the other is for each day of the week.

Elementary (Daily)	
Rdg	t
Math	o ◯
L.A.	t t
Sci	
Health	R R
Name	*Rachel*

Middle-High School (Weekly)	
M	d d t
T	o o o
We	◯ ◯
Th	C C C
F	d
Name	*Miguel*

Codes:

◯ – On task   o – off task
R – Respectful   d – disruptive
C – Cooperative   t – talkative

Use or modify this system to document and **de-code behaviors** in your classroom. Select **Supplements** at http://www.classroommanagementblues.com, then **Q–V** for **Supplement T: Behavior Record Sheets**.

Dr. Foster: *Instead of a seating chart, I used a weekly* **Behavior Record Sheet** *to document misbehaviors. (Select* **Supplements** *at www.classroommanagementblues.com, then* **Q–V** *to download* 🗁 **Supplement T: Behavior Record Sheets***.)*

           The six rules I posted on the wall were positive statements (see page 227) and written as misbehaviors at the top of the **Behavior Record Sheet** *(see Figure 8.2 on the next page). Here is an example of a rule reworded as a misbehavior.*

                Rule—Respect adults

                Misbehavior—Was disrespectful to an adult

           I used the CHAMPs acronym at the top of the **Behavior Record Sheet** *to communicate my expectations for* **C***onversation,* **H***elp,* **A***ctivity,* **M***ovement, and* **P***articipation during instruction and transitions. (Visit http://www.state.kyus/ agencies/behave/bi/cmtips.htm for classroom management tips from* **CHAMPs: A Proactive and Positive Approach to Classroom Management***.)*

Dr. Foster: *Use this portion of a* **Behavior Record Sheet** *(Figure 8.2) to answer the following questions:*

1. *What were Annie's misbehaviors on Monday?*
2. *When Dan was not on task, what did he do?*
3. *Who was on the Self-Monitoring with Self- or Peer-Support Level?*
4. *Who was on the Parent-Support Level?*

Figure 8.2

Behavior Record Sheet

1	Was disrespectful to an adult—**N**otes	4	Was not a team player —**N**otes	Conversation—Talked at an inappropriate time Help—Demanded attention inappropriately (e.g., out of seat without permission, called out)	
2	Was disrespectful to another student —**N**otes	5	Was not on task— See **CHAMP**s in the box to the right	Activity—Did not follow directions in/out of class	
3	Used inappropriate Voice level or Language	6	Damaged personal or school property— **N**otes	Movement—Did not move appropriately in/out of the classroom (e.g., running in the hallway) Participation—Was not paying attention	

Week of Sep 5	**Monday**		**Tuesday**		**Wednesday**	
Student SL – Support Level	**SL**	**Behaviors**	**SL**	**Behaviors**	**SL**	**Behaviors**
1 Apple, Annie	T	2 3_V 2_N	T	3_V 2_N 5_C 5_H 5_H	P	
2 Best, Bernie	T	2 2	T	2	T	
3 Capable, Chris	S		S		S	
4 Dependable, Dan	T	2_N 3_L 2_N 5_A 5_A	P	2_N 3_L	P	

A. Teacher: *Annie was disrespectful to other students and used an inappropriate voice level. Dan did not follow directions. While Chris was at the Self-Monitoring with Self- and Peer-Support Level, Dan and Annie were on the Parent Support Level.*

I see that the letters represent specific behaviors (e.g., V represents—Voice Level, L represents—Language). Could you explain Notes?

Dr. Foster: *Sometimes I made Notes about a student's behavior if I thought I might forget, or need detailed information to conference with the student, a parent, or an administrator. There will be an explanation later about where I recorded this information.*

A. Teacher: *I am still concerned about the time it will take to write everything down.*

Dr. Foster: *The more descriptive your codes, the less you have to write. If you consistently document misbehaviors and follow through with consequences and incentives, your students will follow rules more and you will have fewer misbehaviors to document.*

Dr. Foster: *Look at the **Consequence Hierarchy and Behavior Support System** (see Figure 8.3). I have added "Other Support" as a student might need another level of support from school personnel or community members (e.g., counselor, special education teacher, social worker).*

Figure 8.3

Consequence Hierarchy and Behavior Support System								
GOAL	➡	**Self-Monitoring with Self-Support or Peer Support**						
Teacher Monitoring	➡	**Verbal or Nonverbal Reminder**	➡	**Time Out**	➡	**Think Sheet**	➡	**Support Level**
Teacher Support	➡	**Talk with Teacher**	➡	**Conference with Teacher**				
Parent Support	➡	**Talk with Parent**	➡	**Conference with Teacher and Parent**				
Other Support (e.g., counselor, special education teacher)	➡	**Talk with Other Support Person**	➡	**Conference with Teacher and Other Support Person**				
Administrator Support	➡	**Talk with Administrator**	➡	**Conference with Administrator and Teacher**				
➡ **Conference with Administrator, Teacher, Parent, and Other Support**								
Office referral for severe disrespect: bullying, cursing, disrupting, defying, fighting, spitting, stealing, throwing objects, or destroying property, and other behaviors requiring a referral								

Dr. Foster: *Here is a brief description of how to use the **Behavior Record Sheet** with the **Consequence Hierarchy and Behavior Support System**. (Select the **Supplements** page at www.classroommanagementblues.com, then **Q–V** to locate 📂 **Supplement R: Consequence Hierarchy and Behavior Support System** for detailed information about how to implement this system.)*

*After a **Reminder**, record the rule number for the misbehavior on the **Behavior Record Sheet**—the consequence is a **Time Out** during a preferred activity. A student completes a **Think Sheet** for the second recorded misbehavior. With a third misbehavior, the student **Talks with the Teacher**. After the fourth misbehavior and a **Conference with Teacher**, the student moves from the Teacher Support Level to the Parent Support Level. (Review consequences on page 234.)*

For a student who chronically misbehaves, the teacher follows the student's IEP or the behavior support plan developed in a conference with the student and one or more supportive persons (e.g., teacher, parent, counselor, special education teacher, administrator).

. Dr. Foster: *If a student moves beyond the Teacher Support Level to Parent, Other, or Administrator Support during the week, he or she remains on that support level until the beginning of the next week.*

*In an elementary or self-contained classroom, students start **every day** on the Teacher Monitoring and Support Level, unless they are on the Self-Monitoring with Self- and Peer-Support Level. Students who change classes throughout the school day continue through the hierarchy during the course of the week.*

 Let's check your understanding.

*Look at the information for Dan on a **Behavior Record Sheet** (below) and refer to the **Consequence Hierarchy and Behavior Support System** (on the previous page). Explain Dan's support level and consequences on Thursday for **2** disrespecting a student, **5_H** calling out an answer, and **5_A** not following directions.*

Figure 8.4

Behavior Record Sheet					
Week of Sep 12	**Thursday**		**Friday**		
Student SL – Support Level	SL	**Behaviors** Circle – Corrected Behavior	SL	**Behaviors** Circle – Corrected Behavior	
4 Dependable, Dan	A	②⑤$_H$ 5_A	A	2_N	

A. Teacher: *Dan will remain on the Administrator Support Level for the rest of the week. He will return to the Teacher Monitoring and Support Level on Monday.*

*He was disrespectful to another student, so the first consequence on Thursday was a **Time Out**. He then called out without raising his hand and completed a **Think Sheet**. With the third misbehavior (not following directions), Dan would have had to **Talk with the Administrator**.*

I noticed that you added circles to the Behavior Record Sheet to document "Corrected Behaviors." I want my students to correct their behavior, but I never documented corrections.

Dr. Foster: *When students have the opportunity to correct their behavior, it creates "a classroom where mistakes are seen as opportunities to learn" (Hatfield, n.d., para. 5). Have students ever said that you notice when they do something bad, and not when they do something good?*

A. Teacher: *Yes. Parents say this, too. I do notice "good" behavior, but I don't have documentation to prove it. This would be helpful!*

Dr. Foster: *My students earned a reward or special activity at the end of the week if they did not have a number or corrected all their misbehaviors—that is, circled by the end of the week.*

Dr. Foster: *To get a number circled a student had to correct the specific misbehavior recorded. If a student was disrespectful to another student, I recorded a "2." Later, when the student showed respect to that student, I circled the number. Only in special cases did I circle a number soon after recording the misbehavior; however, this may be necessary with younger students at first.*

A. Teacher: *I would have to make a conscious effort to notice corrected behaviors. If students perceive that I will not circle numbers, they will not make the corrections.*

Dr. Foster: *When students correct a behavior, the consequence **does not** change. It **does** give students the opportunity to earn the reward or special activity at the end of the week. Corrected misbehaviors also soften the response when a student has to talk with a parent or the administrator about his or her behavior.*

*Students have until the end of the week to correct their misbehaviors. They do not have to correct the behavior on the day the misbehavior occurred. (For more information about correcting behaviors, select **Supplements** at www.classroom managementblues.com, then **Q–V** to locate 🗁 **Supplement R: Consequence Hierarchy and Behavior Support System**.)*

Students would ask me what behaviors they needed to correct and would remain focused on the classroom rules they needed to correct. Read "Correct Me if I Am Wrong!" to find out why I began this practice in my classroom.

Correct Me if I Am Wrong!

I don't remember the year I began to give students the opportunity to correct their misbehaviors. I do remember what sparked the idea!

It was Monday morning, and one of my students received a warning, broke a rule, and received her first number within the first 15 minutes of the school day. Despite the consequences, she received three more numbers in the next 30 minutes.

Within 45 minutes, I had spent more time dealing with her misbehaviors than teaching. I asked her if she wanted to earn the reward at the end of the week.

She replied, "It doesn't matter! I never get it any way!"

I realized she was right. So I told her if she would correct her misbehaviors by the end of the week, she would receive the reward.

By the end of the day, she and all the other students had corrected all their misbehaviors. We were **all** on our way to having the best week we had had all year!

Correct me if I am wrong. The ***reality*** is that everyone
in class receives a reward when students correct misbehaviors.

A. Teacher: *What if a student does not value the reward or special activity at the end of the week?*

Dr. Foster: *The reward or special activity remained a mystery. If students knew what the reward or activity was to be on Friday, they might not strive to achieve the goal. The students and I mutually agreed upon possible rewards and special activities before implementing the system.*

A. Teacher: *What if I have one or more students with special needs?*

Dr. Foster: *These students may focus on one or two rules for the reward or special activity and have a special plan for the other rules.*

A. Teacher: *Won't students complain that this is not fair?*

Dr. Foster: *To be equitable, everyone in the classroom could have an individualized behavior support plan—even the teacher. Read "Turnabout Is Fair Play."*

Turnabout Is Fair Play

In Practice

Dr. Foster

Students and teachers alike have behaviors they need or want to change. As team members in the learning community, we need to trust and support each other to change these behaviors. As **turnabout is fair play**, I had a consequence hierarchy and behavior support system, too.

For the first week or two, we practiced using my Consequence Hierarchy and Behavior Support System. We role-played and stopped when a misbehavior occurred to discuss the process of recording a number. I provided reminders and explained consequences. The students set goals, self-monitored behaviors, took time outs, and completed think sheets.

Before we put the system into effect, we discussed my Teacher Behavior Support System. I would identify a behavior I "really" wanted to work on, like using "wait time" or asking questions before calling out a student's name.

On a whiteboard or bulletin board, I posted the rule I needed to follow and a place to record a check (✓) when the rule was broken. We discussed what my consequences would be each time I broke the rule and the reward we would share if I corrected my misbehaviors by the end of the week.

I taught the students how to remind me respectfully when I broke the rule and corrected my behavior. We role-played and practiced how they would respond and do the record keeping.

Turnabout means you will let someone do something you do because it is fair. This **turnabout is fair play** strategy promotes trust and commitment toward the shared classroom vision. In this win-win situation, everyone receives support in the learning community; it promotes "all for one and one for all."

A. Teacher: *I understand how your behavior support system would work when students misbehave, but I have questions about the Self- and Peer-Support Levels?*

Dr. Foster: *When a student had no misbehaviors or fewer than three corrected misbehaviors each week for at least two weeks, students advanced to the Self-Monitoring with Self- and Peer-Support Level. The need for structure is less for these students at this level (see Figure 8.5).*

Figure 8.5

Behavior Support System	Need for Structure				
	Low ⟶				High
	Level S Self- or Peer Support	**Level T** Teacher Support	**Level P** Parent Support	**Level O** Other Support	**Level A** Administrator Support

A. Teacher: *Once students are on Level S, do they ever return to Teacher Support?*

Dr. Foster: *Yes. Whether students are on the Self-Monitoring with Self- and Peer-Support Level or not, teachers are responsible for students' behaviors. You would continue to record the misbehaviors and corrected behaviors of all students. The consequences for the misbehaviors are the responsibility of the student, but they must be observable by the teacher. Students may take a time out, do a think sheet, or follow their personal action plan to improve behavior. If a third misbehavior is recorded, the student moves to Level T—Teacher Support.*

A. Teacher: *I think students would want to strive to stay at Level S, but I still have questions about how students will monitor and document their own behavior.*

Dr. Foster: *Before I provide the details, let me clarify the terms "Self-Support" and "Peer Support."*

How do trustworthy and self-disciplined students monitor and document their own behavior?
Learners have the ability to control their impulses and the potential to make consistent, accurate, proactive, positive, and reflective judgments about their own behavior. To become trustworthy and self-disciplined, students must have the opportunity to learn how to support themselves and their peers.

Independent or self-supported learners do not rely on the teacher to tell them what to do, they are responsible for how they think, learn, and behave. Although teachers might assume that independent learning means that students work alone, working alone does assure the development of independent learning skills (Broady & Kenning, 1996).

 self-sup·port [self-sə-ˈpȯrtʹ] *n.*

The supporting and maintaining of oneself without reliance on outside assistance

Random House Dictionary

The characteristics of independent and dependent learners represent the opposite ends of a learner independence continuum (see Table 8.9). "Most learners would be somewhere in between the two extremes" (Mynard & Sorflaten, 2002, para. 4).

Table 8.9

Independent Learners	Dependent Learners
Are self-reliant	Rely heavily on the teacher
Can make informed decisions	Cannot make decisions
Are aware of their strengths and weaknesses	Do not know their own strengths and weaknesses
Plan their learning and set goals	Do not know the best way to learn something
Are intrinsically motivated to make progress in learning	Do not set learning goals and will only work when teachers offer extrinsic motivators like grades or rewards
Often reflect on the learning process and their own progress	Do not reflect on how well they learn and the reasons for success or failure

A. Teacher: *Because the ability to set goals, be resourceful, and make thoughtful choices are self-management behaviors, independent learners can take responsibility for their own behavior in many of the same ways as they do their learning.*

Students can set behavioral goals, make plans and decisions, monitor progress, and reflect on their own progress. This reminds me of the Ten Steps for Lifelong Learning and Problem Solving and learning journals we talked about in the **Appropriate Assessments Prescription**.

Dr. Foster: *You are a model of independent thinking and reflection!*

Students on the Self-Monitoring with Self- or Peer-Support Level make their own decisions. They may keep a learning journal; use behavior contracts, forms, and records sheets you provide; or design their own record-keeping system.

Review how to set goals (on pages 83–84), and use 📂 **Supplement P: Learning Journal** *at all support levels for students to set goals, monitor behavior, and document goal attainment. In* 📂 **Supplement U: Self-Management Record Sheets**, *you will find forms that students can use to monitor self-management behaviors. (Select* **Supplements** *at www.classroommanagementblues.com, then* **K–P** *for* **Supplement P** *and* **Q–V** *for* **Supplement U.***)*

A. Teacher: *Do students at the Self-Monitoring with Self- and Peer-Support Level receive the same reward or special activity at the end of the week as the students on the teacher, parent, and administrator support levels?*

Dr. Foster: *As self-directed learning refers to "the degree of choice that learners have within an instructional situation" (Grow, 1996, para. 4), self-supported students may choose to participate or choose an alternate reward or activity with teacher approval.*

 What could you do if a student is not successful the first time he or she is on the Self-Monitoring and Self-Support Level?

A. Teacher: *The student might want peer support from a student who has been successful at the self-monitoring level.*

Now that I think about it, a student might choose peer support when he or she first advances to Level S. I could also make this suggestion during my talk or conference with the student.

> Self-control . . . is the capacity to control one's impulses, both to stop doing something that is unnecessary (even if one wants to continue doing it), and to start doing something that is necessary (even if one does not want to do it). (Sousa, 2009, p. 45)

Dr. Foster: *Your thinking is consistent with mine about peer support. Students may appear to be self-directed learners and turn out to be highly dependent, or may have the knowledge and ability, but "not be experienced or motivated enough to continue on their own" (Grow, 1994, para. 4).*

Another option for students is to request the opportunity to work with a partner at the Teacher-Support Level to see if they can meet the Self-Monitoring with Peer-Support Level expectations. The peer support should continue until they are confident enough to be successful on their own.

A. Teacher: *I understand better what students would do at Self-Support Level S to document behavior and progress toward goal attainment, but tell me more about peer support.*

To Parsons and Blake (2004), peer support is an umbrella term for a wide range of activities, and they offer synonyms for these activities: peer listening, peer befriending, buddy systems, circle of friends, peer mentoring, peer advocacy, peer education, and peer tutoring. Peer support is a voluntary activity that takes place between those of a similar age, role, or background, and it "enables those who participate to gain life skills and supports their emotional development" (para. 2).

> Developing independent learning abilities is not about letting students work alone, it is about assisting students to develop skills which will help them to become good learners; to take responsibility for learning and to be able to apply these skills to any new learning situation. The road towards independence is often a long and rocky one and learners need considerable support. (Mynard & Sorflaten, n.d., para. 21)

Dr. Foster: *I like the way Michele Heisler describes peer support. Her model is to help people self-manage diabetes, but applies universally to self-monitoring many behaviors.*

Heisler says there is "strong evidence for the benefits of . . . self-management programs that combine discussion of key self-management issues participants are facing, peer exchange and support, and behaviorally based approaches to strengthen participants' . . . problem solving skills, and efforts to set and follow through on specific behavioral goals" (2007, p. 217).

She goes on to say, "Peers are especially effective as leaders for self-management programs. As people who are themselves living with. . . . [the same] conditions, they serve as excellent role models for participants" (p. 215).

A. Teacher: *This makes sense, and, as you stated earlier, students need to be taught how and when to provide the support.*

Dr. Foster: *Yes. Students must learn and be empowered to practice peer support to be effective and successful.*

A. Teacher: *Once my students understand the expectations of Level S: Self-Support or Peer Support, I think they will want to move to that level quickly.*

This creates high expectations for students, and I know I will need to be a cheerleader to excite them about reaching this level.

> The energy and excitement that you invest in the system, and in acknowledging student successes, should be concentrated on "Look at what you did" rather than "Look at what you get." By keeping your focus on the students' improved growth, maturity, progress, and so on, you increase the chances that the students will begin working less for the "reward" and more for their sense of satisfaction in meeting expectations successfully. (Sprick et al., 1998, p. 351)

How can students be empowered to learn self-management behaviors? Teachers can teach students the behaviors expected of them to be trustworthy and self-disciplined. These self-management behaviors are values-based and components of autonomy, authenticity, community, resiliency, and reflection.

> Students are responsible for their own motivation and for monitoring their own behavior. Teachers should not lift these responsibilities off the students' shoulders. The role of the teacher is to teach students how to monitor themselves. (Kay & Kay, 1994)

A. Teacher: *I see more and more connections among the prescriptions you have already given me. Self-management and trustworthiness are from the* **High Expectations** *and* **Appropriate Assessments Prescriptions.**

Dr. Foster: *Many elements of the active ingredients in each prescription interconnect with the* **Trustworthy Behavior Prescription**—*common principles and values hold them together. (Review autonomy on pages 105–111 and reflection on pages 191–208.)*

Dr. Foster: *This table shows the self-regulatory mechanisms and self-management behaviors that correspond to the abilities of autonomous learners.*

Table 8.10

High Expectations for Student Behavior		
Self-Regulatory Mechanisms	**Abilities** An autonomous learner . . .	**Active Ingredients** Self-Management Behaviors
Self-Concept	• Displays the belief that he or she can achieve goals and solve problems	**Authenticity** • Is positive and hopeful • Has a sense of humor
Self-Direction	• Sets goals and develops action plans or plans personal learning activities • Makes decisions and choices	**Autonomy** • Sets goals • Makes action plans • Generates possible cognitive solutions
Self-Control	• Acts independently and exerts control over his or her environment • Seeks support, but can function well without it • Interacts with others and gives support	**Community** • Is proactive • Affirms and supports others • Generates possible social solutions
Self-Talk	• Copes with new and unforeseen situations • Overcomes temporary motivational setbacks	**Resiliency** • Is resourceful • Persists to achieve goals • Bounces back from negative situations
Self-Assessment	• Monitors learning activities • Evaluates progress and makes changes • Learns how to learn from his or her successes and failures	**Reflection** • Monitors and corrects behaviors • Is responsible • Makes thoughtful choices

From Benard, 1993; Landau & Gathercoal, 2000; Little, 2003; McCarthy, 1998; and Pajares, 2002

A. Teacher: *As I look through the self-management behaviors in this table, I realize that I should model and be more proactive, positive, and hopeful about my students.*

Dr. Foster: *To change your behavior, awareness is the first step.*

Marvin Marshall, an experienced teacher, counselor, and administrator, believes the best way to establish discipline is to activate internal motivation and raise student responsibility. He says that this can be achieved if teachers (1) articulate clear behavioral expectations, (2) empower students to reach them, (3) infuse positivity in all aspects of teaching, and (4) promote a desire to do the right thing instead of pushing for obedience (as cited in Charles, 2010, p. 175).

A. Teacher: *There is the word "empower" again. Tell me more!*

Dr. Foster: *Dr. Marshall and I agree that one of the best ways to empower students is to teach the behaviors expected and have the students practice until they can do them automatically—**P**ractice times **e**mpowerment equals **p**erformance.*

*To empower my students, I recorded the self-management behaviors observed each week when students faced a challenge on a **Self-Management Record Sheet** (see Figure 8.6). Here is part of the record sheet with six of the self-management behaviors from "High Expectations for Student Behavior" (on page 255). ▭ **Supplement U: Self-Management Record Sheets** contains more self-management behaviors and detailed information about how to document these behaviors. (Select the **Supplements** page **U** at www.classroommanagement blues.com, then **Q–V** for **Supplement U**.)*

Figure 8.6

1	Was positive and hopeful (had a sense of humor)	4	Persisted to achieve goals
2	Set goals and made action plans	5	Reflected and made thoughtful choices and decisions
3	Monitored and corrected behavior	6	Generated possible cognitive or social solutions

Self-Management	Week of Sep 5		Week of Sep 12		Week of Sep 19	
Student SL – Support Level	**SL**	**Behavior** When faced with a challenge	**SL**	**Behavior** When faced with a challenge	**SL**	**Behavior** When faced with a challenge
1 Apple, Annie	**T**	2 4	**T**	6c 2 3		

Dr. Foster: *My students suggested that we have a celebration when the class reached the goal of 100 behaviors on the **Self-Management Record Sheet**. I posted the count on the whiteboard or bulletin board. Until the class no longer needed the system, I increased the goal after each celebration to keep students challenged and motivated.*

> [A] goal of Win-Win Discipline is to help students learn to control themselves responsibly in various situations. Thus, to the extent feasible, teachers should give students an opportunity to resolve problems on their own and display responsible behavior. (Charles, 2010, p. 162)

Dr. Foster: *Another strategy that empowers students to evaluate and document their self-management behaviors is **teacher-supported** whole class self-monitoring. Read "Class Self-Monitoring Is So Cool!" to learn how one teacher used whole class self-monitoring in his classroom.*

Whole Class Self-Monitoring Is So Cool!

Fred Roemer (n.d.) calls his students "The Polar Bears" because they are **so cool**. He uses whole class self-monitoring to help them learn self-control, constructive introspection, and honest self-reporting. Mr. Roemer shared the steps he followed to implement whole class self-monitoring in his classroom.

In Practice
Mr. Roemer

Teachers who use the whole class self-monitoring should:

- **Adjust the class schedule so students can examine their behavior during behavior checks evenly spaced throughout the day and transition times.**
  Mr. Roemer says to begin with 30-minute intervals between checks.

- **Decide on an audible or visual cue to signify the behavior check.**
  Mr. Roemer suggests the use of an alarm on a computer or kitchen timer set at 30-minute intervals.

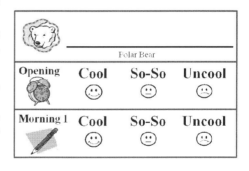

- **Create a record sheet for students to track personal behavior.**
  Shown is the top part of Mr. Roemer's tracking sheet. He strongly advocates that teachers praise accurate self-reporting, not behavior, during behavior checks.

- **Have a short discussion about personal behaviors and those of their classmates in objective terms.**
  When introducing the system, Mr. Roemer recommends that students concentrate on honest self-reporting without being judgmental of behavior, positive or negative.

- **Develop a plan for withdrawal from the system.**
  Mr. Roemer explains, "Either plan for using self-monitoring for a set length of time, or plan for gradually exempting appropriate students from conduct sheet and behavior sheets until the whole class no longer needs them." (para. 12).

Mr. Roemer thinks this strategy is **so cool** because "it works." Make tracks to his website at http://www.pb5th.com/selfmoni.shtml for 15 hints, tips, and much more. "In my experience, the rewards you receive later—a relaxed, functioning classroom and mature, responsible students" (para. 32).

A. Teacher: *Why is whole class monitoring at the teacher support level?*

Dr. Foster: *The main difference between self-monitoring and whole class self-monitoring is that a teacher schedules "behavior breaks" for the whole class to evaluate and document behaviors at the same time.*

A. Teacher: *If I use whole class self-monitoring and the record sheet to document self-management behaviors, I am confident that I will empower some students to be more responsible. Students on the Self- or Peer-Support Level could use the* **Self-Management Record Sheet** *to monitor their own self-management behaviors.*

Dr. Foster: *You will find* **Self-Management Record Sheets** *at www.classroommanagement blues.com. (Select* **Supplements***, then* **Q–V** *for* **Supplement U***.)*

A. Teacher: *What should I do when my whole class misbehaves?*

When misbehaviors are classwide, how can teachers help students get back on task? A variety of strategies is available to help teachers handle classwide misbehavior and get students back on task. The need for structure is the primary factor teachers must consider when they choose a classwide system to help students become trustworthy and autonomous.

A. Teacher: *I admit I tend to raise my voice when my whole class seems out of control. Some students may be on task, but they are difficult to see when chaos breaks out.*

Dr. Foster: *I've been there. When this happened to me, I could not get all the numbers written down fast enough on the* **Behavior Record Sheet** *before some of the students would begin to follow the rules. Then, I could not remember who should receive a number. In addition, the students with numbers received consequences while those students who should have had a number recorded got by without a consequence.*

My goal was for the whole class to self-monitor and document their academic progress and behavior. Until then, the class remained on the Teacher Support Level of the **Consequence Hierarchy and Behavior Support System***.*

 If your class is on the Teacher Support Level, what should you do first if misbehavior is classwide?

A. Teacher: *So you want me to use the same* **Consequence Hierarchy and Behavior Support System** *(on page 233) for classwide misbehavers. The first step would be to give the class a reminder. For example, I might write Rule 5 (stay on task) on the board, point to the rules, or hold up my hand showing all five fingers.*

Dr. Foster: *Yes, everyone wins when the class gets back on task with a reminder—no one would have to deal with consequences. If most of the students get on task after the reminder, record a "5" for the few who do not. If there are still too many misbehaviors to record, provide the mutually agreed upon signal that the class will have time out for one minute during a preferred activity or at the end of class.*

The time for the time out would increase for every minute it took the class to get back on task. You would establish these corrective procedures with the students during the first week of school.

Dr. Foster:  *Tell me the sequence of consequences you would use after a reminder and time out signal if misbehavior continues to be classwide.*

A. Teacher: *I would have the students do a think sheet. If the classwide misbehavior continued, I would have a class meeting (Talk with the Teacher) to come up with a mutually agreed upon solution. (Review class meetings on pages 102–103.)*

Dr. Foster: *Your responses are proactive. Be sure to clarify, make decisions about, and practice the reminders and sequence of consequences before you try to implement a classwide system for misbehavior.*

You will get more information about whole class and personal reminders when we discuss procedures—the last active ingredient in the **Trustworthy Behavior Prescription**. *Read "Time Is Golden" to learn about an effective strategy to reward positive classwide behavior.*

Time Is Golden

According to Stella Mcintyre, "golden time" is a strategy to reward positive classwide behavior with free minutes at the end of a lesson or class. This **time is golden** for classes at all grade levels that need a more immediate reward system.

"Once the students understand the system, I find that I have [gotten] through everything I've planned and still have time left at the end of the lesson for golden time" (Mcintyre, n.d., para. 5). Once implemented, students "stay within the boundaries of expected behavior [and] an effective learning atmosphere has been achieved" (para. 6–8, 11). I recommend:

- Clarify the learning objective and components of the lesson;
- Divide the lesson into smaller segments of about 20 minutes or even less to maintain the students' concentration;
- Tick off each lesson component once it has been completed so that students know they have made progress through the lesson; and
- Incorporate feedback at the end of the lesson so students can reflect.

Time is golden for both teachers and students when the reward system results in more time for teaching and learning. This strategy can be the first step to achieve these timely goals.

A. Teacher: *Golden time aligns well with the transitions or off-task time recommended between 20-minute teaching and student-learning episodes to "increase the degree of focus when students return to task" (Sousa, 2006, p. 123). In addition to routine tasks, a story about the learning, or brain-breaks for 2–3 minutes would be effective to help students stay focused when they return to a task or instruction.*

Dr. Foster: *Another way to recognize classwide self-management behaviors is to use a system of tally points or to spell out a special activity or celebration letter-by-letter on the board (e.g., s-p-e-c-i-a-l a-c-t-i-v-i-t-y, c-e-l-e-b-r-a-t-i-o-n).*

A. Teacher: *I am familiar with the use of point systems to recognize positive class and small group behaviors. It doesn't go well when one or two students keep the whole class or a small group from earning points.*

Dr. Foster: *Here is my philosophy for resolving this situation. If one or two students can keep a class or small group from earning points, these students can earn class or group points if they behave appropriately with positive peer support. Ellen, for example, might earn the class or group a point for being in her seat and on the right page. I teach the students how to respectfully support her to be successful. Before long, everyone wants Ellen on his or her team.*

When students learn how to give peer support, everyone becomes more self-disciplined and trustworthy.

A. Teacher: *I like the systems you have described, but I am still concerned about the time needed to monitor and document students' support levels, misbehaviors, consequences, and self-management skills, as well as the practice and assessment grades for the content I teach.*

Dr. Foster: *I put my documentation system on a clipboard.* 🗁 **Supplement V: Clipboard Management** *will help you handle academic and behavioral data collection and record keeping. You will learn how to set up a clipboard and electronic tablet management system in* **Supplement V**. *(Select the* **Supplements** *page at www.classroommanagementblues.com, then* **Q–V** *for* **Supplement V**.*)*

Here is an example of the components that make up a clipboard management system for a self-contained elementary classroom. (See Figure 8.7 on the next page.)

- *Daily **lesson plans** on top*

- *A **seating chart** for the substitute teacher or to code behaviors and other student information (see page 245)*

- *A Behavior Record Sheet to record numbers for **misbehavior***

- *The Self-Management Record Sheet to record numbers for self-management behaviors that demonstrate **self-Control***

- *A Practice Record Sheet for each class or content area (e.g., **Reading, Math, English**)*

- *A page with index cards or file labels to record **notes** about misbehaviors, self-management behaviors, and learning objectives—an explanation of how to make this page is included with* **Supplement V: Clipboard Management** *at www.classroommanagementblues.com*

- *A **plastic sleeve** with post-its, passes, stickers, and so on*

Figure 8.7

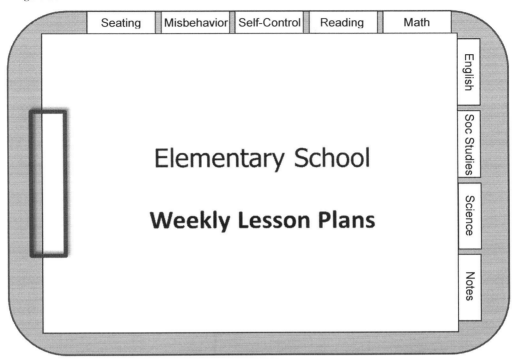

Dr. Foster: *A middle or high school teacher could use a clipboard for each class (e.g., Period 1, Period 2). Here is an example of the components that make up the clipboard management system with more than one class on the same clipboard. (See Figure 8.8 on the next page.)*

- *Daily **lesson plans** on top*

- *A Practice Record Sheet behind the tabs for **Period 1** and **Period 2***

- *A **seating chart** for each class that can be used by a substitute teacher or to code behaviors and other student information (see page 245)*

- *A Behavior Record Sheet to record numbers for **misbehavior***

- *The Self-Management Record Sheet to record numbers for self-management behaviors that demonstrate **self-Control***

- *A page with index cards or file labels to record **Notes** about misbehaviors, self-management behaviors, and learning objectives—an explanation of how to make this page is included with **Supplement V: Clipboard Management** at www.classroommanagementblues.com*

- *A **plastic sleeve** with post-its, passes, and so on*

Figure 8.8

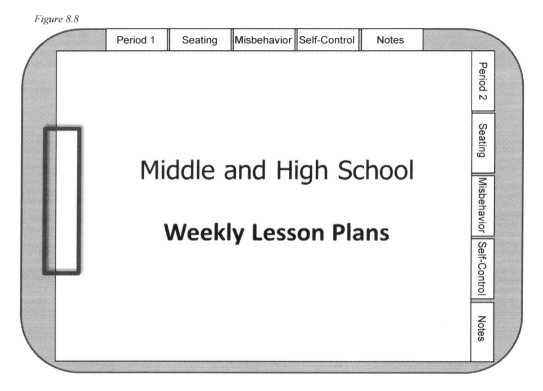

A. Teacher: *How can I teach with a clipboard in my hand?*

Dr. Foster: *You will have to get used to it, but it is a habit well worth developing because IT WORKS!*

If you put the clipboard down, just ask, "Where is my clipboard?" Students will check themselves to see if their behavior is appropriate. When you hold the clipboard, students think you might write down a number for a misbehavior even if you only want to look at your lesson plan.

A. Teacher: *If you say it works, I will try it!*

Dr. Foster: *The last active ingredient we will discuss in this session is **procedures**.*

> Teachers must think carefully about how they mete out discipline so that it is fair, consistent, and provides students with the knowledge that there are consequences for their actions. This does not mean that students need to feel "punished" as much as it means that students develop an awareness of their own self-control. Teachers have the responsibility of showing students that their daily choices matter in a way that is positive and not vilifying. (Hatfield, n.d., para. 1)

Active Ingredient	🍎 Procedures

To create and maintain a safe learning community, teachers must consistently use well-defined **procedures**, the last active ingredient in the **Trustworthy Behavior Prescription**. According to Harry and Rosemary Wong (1998), procedures require instruction—explanations, modeling, practice, and reinforcement to become habits.

> *Habit is a cable;*
> *we weave a thread of it each day,*
> *and at last we cannot break it.*
> **Horace Mann**
> American education reformer

A. Teacher: *You know I value time. If I have to explain, model, practice, and reinforce every procedure, will there be any time left to teach?*

Dr. Foster: *Think about how much instructional time is lost when you deal with misbehaviors throughout the school day because students do not do what you expect of them.*

A. Teacher: *I get it! If I explain, model, practice, and reinforce procedures, my students will be empowered to meet my expectations, and there will be more time for teaching and learning.*

Dr. Foster: *You **have** it! You and your students need procedures for everything do throughout the school day. We will focus on preventive, supportive, and corrective procedures in this session. Readings and resources to implement other procedures will be available on the **Classroom Management Blues** website. (Select **Resources** at www.classroommanagementblues.com, then **Behavior** and **Procedures**.)*

Spend most of the first two weeks of the school year teaching students to follow preventive, supportive, and corrective procedures so that they are better able to learn (Wong & Wong, 1998). **Preventive** procedures minimize misbehavior so students can learn in a safe learning community. Teachers use **supportive** procedures to encourage trustworthy behavior and empower students to take responsibility for their actions. Finally, **corrective** procedures stop misbehavior and help students behave in a more responsible manner (Charles, 2010).

> Student achievement at the end of the year is directly related to the degree to which the teacher establishes good control of the classroom procedures in the very first week of the school year. (Wong & Wong, 1998, p. 4)

Which *preventive* procedures can minimize misbehavior to create a safe learning community? "The most effective way to deal with misbehavior is to prevent it in the first place" (Tate, 2007, p. 3). Students like and respect teachers who create a safe learning environment, use preventive procedures, and plan proactively to accomplish the following purposes (shown on the next page):

- Deliver brain-compatible lessons that reduce behavior problems and increase academic achievement;

- Create a psychologically and physically safe learning environment that includes appropriate lighting, music, aromas, and seating; and

- Develop appropriate rituals, celebrations, consequences, and parental support;

- Deal with chronic behavior problems that conventional classroom management practices do not alleviate (Tate, 2007, p. xiii).

A. Teacher: *It is okay if my students like me, but I would prefer respect!*

Dr. Foster: *Respect is possible when you consistently implement preventive procedures and strategies in your classroom. "Get with It! describes a few of these strategies.*

> *If your students like you, there is nothing they won't do **for** you! If your students don't like you, there is nothing they won't do **to** you.*
> **Marcia L. Tate**
> *Shouting Won't Grow Dendrites*

Get with It!

According to the Dr. Jacob Kounin's research results, the technique used to manage behavior is most crucial, not the personality of the teacher ("Discipline," 2011). **Get with it**, and use these proactive teacher **behaviors** to prevent misbehavior in your classroom (Wuest, 1999; "Discipline," 2011).

- *Prevent* misbehavior **with** planned routines and clear directions for **transitions** between activities in a lesson.
- Maximize active participation, maintain **group focus**, and *prevent* misbehavior **with** effective grouping.
- **With** detailed lesson plans, the class can move along at a brisk pace. **Momentum** or lesson flow *prevents* misbehavior.
- **Withitness** *prevents* misbehavior when the classroom arrangement ensures every student is always in sight.

Get with it, and see how lesson plans that flow, groups that remain focused, transitions that have clear routines and directions, and room arrangements that make sure everyone is always in sight can keep misbehaviors to a minimum in your classroom.

Tate (2007) offers teachers a theoretical framework for proactive management that aligns with brain research and the research results of Jacob Kounin (pp. 2–3). The main concepts of the brain researchers Tate cites include:

- Change the state (feeling moments) of a student's brain—social interaction, music, and lighting variations (Jensen, 2003)
- Provide daily routines that students follow consistently (Tileston, 2004)
- Plan backwards—start where you expect to end up (Guskey, 2001)
- Design valuable lessons so students experience success—students who succeed seldom misbehave (DiGiulio, 2000)

A. Teacher: *These concepts are familiar; they are preventive procedures for the strategies found in the **Classroom Management Blues** prescriptions!*

Dr. Foster: *Give me some examples.*

A. Teacher: *Misbehavior diminishes when I follow the procedures for lesson planning, peer teaching, and "quality grouping" to actively engage my students in the learning process. (Review **Active Engagement** pages 53–61.)*

*When I establish zero tolerance for put-downs, help students set goals, and have class meetings, I can inspire my students to learn and behave appropriately. (Review **High Expectations** pages 75–103.)*

*I can create a non-threatening learning environment, promote on-task behavior, increase the expectancy for success, and prevent misbehavior when I follow the procedures for effective practice, win-win competitions, formative assessments, and learning episodes that challenge all students. (Review **Appropriate Assessments** pages 157–172.)*

Dr. Foster: *Can you name some preventive procedures for strategies we discussed earlier in this session for the **Trustworthy Behavior Prescription**?*

A. Teacher: *I can prevent or at least diminish misbehavior if I use whole class self-monitoring and give students the opportunity to share in the development of the classroom mission, vision, and rules.*

Dr. Foster: *The procedures for the strategies you described have the potential to prevent misbehavior, as do consequences. Students are more likely to follow classroom rules if they know you will consistently follow through with established consequences for misbehavior. Consequences may also be supportive, empower students to become self-disciplined, and encourage trustworthy behavior.*

What are some *supportive* procedures that encourage trustworthy behavior and empower students to become self-disciplined? Proactive teachers have supportive procedures in place to help students take responsibility for their actions. With this support, students stay on task and achieve at high academic levels.

Dr. Foster: *One **supportive** procedure that can help you and your students respond proactively is the use of a verbal and nonverbal reminder. This is the first level of **teacher** support and monitoring (see Figure 8.9).*

Figure 8.9

Consequence Hierarchy and Behavior Support System						
GOAL	➡	**Self-Monitoring with Self- Support or Peer Support**				
Teacher Monitoring	➡	**Verbal or Nonverbal Reminder**	➡	**Time Out**	➡	**Think Sheet**

Dr. Foster: *You must have the attention of the student or class for a reminder to be effective. Read about one of my favorite whole class attention getters in "Class! Yes!"*

Class! Yes!

To get the attention of my class, I used Jeff Battle's whole brain teaching attention-getter **Class! Yes!** Battle used to be a teacher who called for his class to get quiet, only to have a few comply. He would ask again, a bit louder, and feel his blood pressure rise. Here is how he gets the attention of his class now.

To get my classes' attention I simply say "Class?" and then they reply "Yes!" Next is the catch, the hook that makes this fun, and gets them invested in it in a way that has them look at me and grin rather than continue their conversations.

When I say "Class!" and they say "Yes!" they have to say it the way I say it. If I say "Classity-class-class!" they have to say "Yessity-yes-yes!" If I say it loudly, they have to respond loudly. If I whisper, they respond in a whisper. They have to match my tone and intensity. (Battle, n.d., para. 7–8)

When you need to get the attention of your class, use **Class! Yes!** When your class seems out of control, use **Class! Yes!** Go to http://www.wholebrain teaching.com/ to see Mr. Battle model this strategy and learn more whole class teaching strategies.

Dr. Foster: *Once I had my students' attention, I used a reminder like **The ZIPPER Strategy**. Read "Zip It!" to learn about this self-reflection strategy for individual student or whole class misbehavior that has the potential to stop misbehavior.*

Zip It!

To get the attention of my class, I would use Jeff Battle's whole-brain teaching attention-getter **Class! Yes!** Then, I would use a nonverbal reminder like "closing a ZIPPER" or a verbal reminder to "**Zip It!**" to signal my class to use "The ZIPPER Strategy" that teaches appropriate self-reflection in emotionally charged situations (Sousa, 2009, p. 52).

The **ZIPPER** Strategy

Z	Zip Your Mouth	Stop and take a deep breath!
I	Identify the Problem	What do I need? What is the problem?
P	Pause	Take a moment to calm down and reflect.
P	Put Yourself in Charge	Take control of my actions.
E	Explore Choices	What can I do?
R	Reset	Pick an option.

As with any procedure or strategy, you can make modifications to better support your students. Dr. Marie Sanders, an education consultant, suggested these modifications to "The ZIPPER Strategy" for older students.

Z	Zip Your Mouth	Stop and take a deep breath!
I	Identify the Problem	What do I need? What is the problem?
P	Pause—Put Yourself in Charge	Take a moment to calm down. and reflect
I	Inventory Options	What can I do?
T	Take Control	Pick an option.

When your class seems out of control, use **Class! Yes!** Then remind them to **Zip It**—stop, identify the problem, pause, take control of their actions, explore choices, and choose an option. Visit the www.wholebrainteaching.com/ website and learn more whole class teaching strategies.

A. Teacher: *The ZIPPER Strategy is a procedure I should model for my students. Everyone should think before we act inside and outside the classroom.*

Dr. Foster: *Think about how many seconds it takes to implement a nonverbal and verbal reminder.*

Table 8.11

Reminders	Nonverbal	Verbal
Universal	• Pause. Take deep breaths and silently count to ten. • Pause. Make eye contact. Show a rule number with your fingers. • Point to mission, vision, or rules posted in the classroom.	• Pause. Take deep breaths and count to ten. Then ask, "Where's my clipboard?" • Point to a graphic (e.g., ZIPPER, vision statement, rules chart) and state the appropriate behavior.
Whole Class	• Use an attention-getter, then an agreed-upon nonverbal signal—use a motion (e.g., close a ZIPPER) or point to a picture (e.g., ZIPPER). • Stop. Wait. Look at your watch. If the class does not comply, count the seconds and write them on the board for *time out* . . . 30 seconds, 1 minute, and so on, until the class is attentive and ready to learn.	• Say, "Attention, class" with clockwise arm motion overhead. • Use the Class, Yes attention-getter, and then state the expected behavior or use ZIPPER. • Say, "Class, #" (rule #). • Ask, "Where's my clipboard?" • Say, "I see (Name's) book is out." • Recognize someone behaving appropriately and say, "I see (Name's) (insert appropriate behavior)."

Individual	• Agree on a private cue or signal to get the student back on task.
	• While you continue teaching:
	  - Stand close to the student (physical proximity).
	  - Lightly pat the top of the desk to signal to get back on task.
	  - Hand a pencil to the student.
	  - Calmly open the student's book.
	  - Supportively touch shoulder.
		• Ask privately, "What are you supposed to be doing?"
		• State privately the expected behavior "I expect you to be (insert appropriate behavior)."
		• While you continue teaching, mention the student's name: "I want all of you, including Rosa, to solve this problem," or say, "Rosa, # 3," for Rule 3.

From Battle, n.d.; Canter & Canter, 1993; Sousa, 2009; Sprick et al., 1998; and Tate, 2007

A. Teacher: *Reminders take only a few seconds. It takes several minutes to respond to misbehaviors and provide consequences.*

What is the most effective procedure a supportive teacher can use to respond to student misbehavior?

Dr. Foster: *The most effective procedure is to pause and say nothing for a few seconds. When teachers or students pause, it gives everyone time to calm down and think about what they do and say in response to a person or situation.*

Craig Seganti, a middle and high school teacher, deals with manipulative, irrelevant comments by just looking at the student and not saying anything. He explains that silence can also be a very powerful manipulation destroyer because there is no real answer to a manipulative question (2008, p. 126).

Supportive procedures like silence and wait time empower students to think about how to behave or correct their behavior. Read about the results of these practices in "Stay with It!"

Stay with It!

Withitness is Dr. Jacob Kounin's most notable technique. Teachers with this ability communicate by their actions that they *see* everything that happens in the classroom. **Stay with it** and use these supportive **behaviors** to empower your students to correct their misbehaviors on their own.

- **With** the **overlapping** ability to handle distractions, move toward a student who is off task, make eye contact, and give "the look" while still teaching; or work with one or more students and give a personal reminder to another student. When you are able to maintain lesson **smoothness** despite any diversions, students know you have **withitness** so they choose to behave.

- **With** class alerting (give a verbal or nonverbal cue or reminder, noticeably scan the room frequently and systematically, or ask a question to check understanding), **group focus** and on-task behavior can be regained.

- **With** encouragement for one student "doing the right thing," the **ripple effect** might empower other students to do the right thing.

Stay with it, and see how supportive behaviors like **withitness** can have a **ripple effect** on **group focus** and promote self-discipline.

From "Discipline Theorists," 2011;
"Kounin Model," 2002; and Wuest, 1999

Dr. Foster: *Let's review.*

> *Minimize misbehavior with preventive procedures like class meetings and "quality grouping" to create a safe learning community. Communicate withitness, give reminders, and use other supportive procedures to empower students to think about and take responsibility for their actions.*
>
> *If students do not take responsibility for their actions despite the preventive and supportive procedures in place in your classroom, use corrective procedures to stop misbehavior, teach appropriate behavior, and help students behave in a more responsible manner (Charles, 2010).*

How can *corrective* procedures help students behave more responsibly? Spencer Kagan, originator of Win-Win Discipline, believes that all participants "win" when a discipline system is used to help students develop responsible behavior. To achieve this goal, Kagan says students, teachers, parents, and administrators must (1) work together on the **same side**; (2) cooperate to propose **collaborative solutions** to discipline problems; and (3) have a **shared vision** of learned responsibility—the wish for students to behave appropriately and practice self-management skills and behaviors (Kagan, 2002, para. 20).

A. Teacher: *Corrective procedures would be the consequences (i.e., time out, think sheet, parent contact, and conference) in the* **Consequence Hierarchy and Behavior Support System**.

Figure 8.10

Consequence Hierarchy and Behavior Support System						
GOAL	➡	**Self-Monitoring with Self-Support or Peer Support**				
Teacher Monitoring	➡	**Verbal or Nonverbal Reminder**	➡ **Time Out**	➡ **Think Sheet**	➡ **Support Level**	
Teacher Support	➡	**Talk with Teacher**	➡ **Conference with Teacher**			
Parent Support	➡	**Talk with Parent**	➡ **Conference with Teacher and Parent**			
Other Support (e.g., counselor, special education teacher)	➡	**Talk with Other Support Person**	➡ **Conference with Teacher and Other Support Person**			
Administrator Support	➡	**Talk with Administrator**	➡ **Conference with Administrator and Teacher**			
➡ **Conference with Administrator, Teacher, Parent, and Other Support**						
Office referral for severe disrespect: bullying, cursing, disrupting, defying, fighting, spitting, stealing, throwing objects, or destroying property, and other behaviors requiring a referral						

A. Teacher: *When students learn to take responsibility for their actions, everyone benefits, or wins, in the classroom. Time outs and think sheets are consequences that encourage students to reflect on their actions and consider alternative ways to correct their behavior. (Review page 234.)*

> Thinking win-win is a frame of mind and heart that seeks mutual benefit and mutual respect in all interactions. (Covey, 2004, p. 152)

Dr. Foster: *When teachers, parents, other support personnel, and administrators dialogue and conference with students, the goal is to work together toward a shared vision—to help students learn to behave responsibly. Everyone collaborates to find solutions to behavior problems—another element of Dr. Kagan's Win-Win Discipline. (Review page 270.)*

We will discuss how to effectively dialogue and conference with students, parents, administrators, and colleagues in the next session. You **can** *learn to promote collaborative interactions in meetings to establish corrective procedures to help students behave in a more responsible manner.*

How Do We Collaborate?

It is really simple!

All we do is take everything we were doing last year and call it "collaboration."

(Friend & Cook, 1992, p. 5)

A. Teacher: *You make it sound easy. Students do not like to talk with administrators or teachers about their behavior any more than with their parents. Personally, a meeting with parents is not one of my favorite things to do, either.*

Kagan's elements of Win-Win Discipline point to the definition and characteristics of collaboration as defined in Friend and Cook's book, *Interactions: Collaboration Skills for School Professionals.* "Interpersonal collaboration is a style of direct interaction between at least two co-equal parties voluntarily engaged in shared decision making as they work toward a common goal" (1992, p. 5).

A. Teacher: *Students, teachers, families, and administrators can identify and work toward a common goal. All parties must voluntarily consider each other as co-equals and be willing to share decision making and accountability. (See "Collaboration" on pages 319–326.)*

Dr. Foster: *According to Dr. Covey, principle-centered leaders believe in empowerment trustworthiness, trust, and alignment. (Review page 220.) You can lead by modeling these principles in your interactions with students, parents, and administrators. "People then come to know for themselves how respected, appreciated and valued they are. Why? Because their opinions are sought. Their input is respected. Their unique experience is valued. They are genuinely involved" (2004, p. 127).*

A. Teacher: *As our common goal is to empower students to take responsibility for their actions, everyone, including the students, must trust and respect each other as we share ideas, decision making, and accountability. I set the tone, parameters, and guidelines for dialogues and conferences to determine the corrective procedures to help the student succeed.*

You have high expectations for me to be the leader and coach!

Dr. Foster: *I believe you will succeed! Keep **everyone** focused on the goal!*

A. Teacher: *All these meetings and conferences will be time consuming! I know what you will say about this!*

Dialogue and conferences will take time at the beginning of the school year, but as the year goes on, my students will stay on task, become self-disciplined, and rely less and less on me and others to correct them.

Dr. Foster: *I could not have said it better! As a bonus, administrators and parents will be supportive of you and your students.*

A. Teacher: *I believe in your behavior support system, but I need some examples of what to say and tips for conducting effective collaborative problem-solving conferences with students, parents, and other school personnel to develop behavior support plans for my most challenging students!*

> Some students misbehave mainly because they have not established any trusting relationships with their parents, peers, or adults. Teachers who take the time to establish meaningful and trusting relationships with troubled students often find that behavior problems decrease significantly. (Sousa, 2009, p. 114)

Dr. Foster: *When you use* 📁 **Supplement Y: Conference Guidelines and Protocols** *and* **Effective Communication Prescription**, *interactions with students, parents, and administrators will be less intimidating and more productive.* 📁 **Supplement Z: Classroom Management Plans and Checklists** *offers helpful tips to design and implement classroom management and behavior support plans for challenging students. (Select* **Supplements** *at http://www.classroommanagementblues.com, then* **W–Z** *for* **Supplements Y** *and* **Z**.*)*

Let me share with you the behavior support plan for Sam, a challenging student I had a few years ago. Read about him in "Play It Again, Sam!"

Play It Again, Sam!

Sam was a challenging and troubled student. He was the only one who reached the Administrator Support Level on my **Consequence Hierarchy and Behavior Support System** (see page 247). He often lost his temper and bothered other students; no one wanted to sit next to him. When supportive and corrective procedures were only effective for short periods during the first weeks of school, I had to come up with an behavior-improvement plan to help everyone in the classroom be successful in the months ahead.

In Practice
Dr. Foster

No wonder Sam was angry. The community held his family in low esteem, and Sam had a similar reputation at school. Although I already knew his family struggled financially, he shared his family situation with me during one of our problem-solving conferences. We talked about what he could and could not control at home and at school.

I wanted Sam to know that he was a person of value and capable of learning and controlling his behavior, so we came up with a special plan for him to earn points for guitar lessons during lunchtime. When he maintained appropriate behavior and corrected his misbehaviors for incrementally longer periods, he earned points. His goal was to learn to play the guitar my husband and I purchased for him; then he would be able to take it home at the end of the school year.

How did the other students react? You would think the students would be upset because Sam was getting special treatment, but they supported and encouraged him as he got his temper and other misbehaviors under control. With fewer classroom disruptions, everyone was happier and more successful.

From day one, my students knew that I believed each one of them was special and would receive different consequences to support their learning and development. They knew they were equally important to me, and I would do what was necessary to help each of them be successful in the classroom.

It was a challenge, but we did not give up. Not only did Sam learn to play the guitar, he played as his classmates sang a song at a program one evening with his family and members of the community in attendance. After the song, the pride on Sam's face brought tears to my eyes as the crowd and students applauded his performance.

My students and I learned a lot that year about valuing and supporting one another. Together we made a difference in the life of a challenging and troubled student. When Sam heard "**Play it again, Sam!**" he knew he was capable and worthy of respect.

A. Teacher: *I see that consequences can be corrective and supportive; we do not have to threaten students. That is not to say that students will enjoy receiving a consequence, but they will learn to "deal with it" and strive to achieve self-control within their learning environment.*

Deal With It!

Deb Wuest (1999) says that teachers who have **with**itness "intervene early and quickly in dealing with misbehavior" (para. 5). When teachers see misbehavior, they must stop and **deal with it** immediately!

- **With** providing a supportive consequence and following through, this causes a **ripple effect** that positively influences the behavior of other students.

- **With** accountability through record keeping—both teacher—and student-maintained (e.g., checklists, task cards), **group focus** continues and students stay on task.

- **With** intervening early and quickly to correct misbehaviors, lesson maintain **smoothness** after an interruption.

When you see misbehavior, do not wait—**deal with it!** If you use corrective procedures, you will see a **ripple effect** that positively influences on-task behavior, **group focus**, and lesson **smoothness**.

From "Kounin Model," 2002; and Wuest, 1999.

Some educators believe that Kounin's "suggestions are of less help in supportive discipline and almost no help at all in the techniques of corrective discipline, where misbehavior must be stopped and redirected positively" ("Kounin Model," 2002, para. 14). As with other procedures and strategies, teachers can modify Kounin's techniques to be more positive and supportive. He gave one example of a ripple effect in which the teacher gives a *reprimand* ("I see a few people who may have to stay in after class to finish."), but a teacher could change the words and instead offer a *reminder* ("I see many of you are working to finish up before class ends.").

A. Teacher: *I have definitely changed my thinking about how to be more proactive and positive when I address misbehaviors. I learned to put names on the board when students misbehave. Now I see how degrading and ineffective this public display is to empower students to be more responsible.*

My plan is to take Dr. Cohen's advice to "let go of the past," create a safe and positive learning environment for my students, and replace this practice with what I have learned about preventive, supportive, and corrective procedures and strategies.

> The fear and stigma of public punishment must not be underestimated. I have asked persons 60 to 70 years-old to recollect school experiences. The majority of those memories are negative ones—punishments handed out by teachers in front of children a half century before (Gartrell, 1987, p. 10).

Dr. Foster: *As we conclude our discussion of procedures, I want to share the 90% and 10% rule. During the first few weeks of school, you should "spend 90% on describing rules more completely and installing procedures more systematically and 10% on actual teaching. The reason is that students will learn better and remember the material when they know what is expected of them in terms of how they should behave in the classroom" (Sasson, 2007, para. 3). With consistent use of the 90% and 10% principle of teaching rules and procedures, you are less likely to have serious classroom management problems (para. 1).*

A. Teacher: *I have learned so much about the development and implementation of principles, mission and vision statements, rules, consequences, ways to document and support self-discipline, and procedures. I am anxious to get started!*

> *Trust is the fruit of the trustworthiness of both people and organizations.*
> **Stephen R. Covey**
> *The 8th Habit:*
> *From Effectiveness to Greatness*

Great teachers establish guidelines (**principles**) that communicate high expectations, identify behaviors to be encouraged (**rules**), find ways to hold everyone accountable and recognize responsible behavior (**consequences**), utilize a system to monitor and assess performance (**documentation**), and implement processes (**procedures**) that create classrooms that encourage trustworthy behavior and empower students to become self-disciplined. The **active ingredients** of the **Trustworthy Behavior Prescription** represent the common understandings of Covey's areas of commitment to win-win agreements, Cohen's eight-step process that leads to successful change, Marzano's questions for successful instructional design, and Sprick, Garrison, and Howard's structure for responsible behavior. (See Table 8.12 for a synthesis of these concepts.)

Table 8.12

Rx 4 Trustworthy Behavior			
RESEARCH Covey (1992) *Principle-Centered Leadership*	Sprick, Garrison, & Howard (1998) *CHAMPs*	Cohen (2005) *The Heart of Change Field Guide*	Marzano (2007) *The Art and Science of Teaching*
Areas of commitment for win-win agreements	**Structure for responsible behavior**	**Eight-step process leading to successful change**	**Questions for successful instructional design**
PRINCIPLES *Guidelines—* parameters within which results are to be accomplished (principles and policies)	*Guidelines for success*—traits, attitudes, and behaviors for the classroom and throughout life	*Get the Vision Right*— identify behaviors required for success	What will I do to *establish and communicate* learning goals and *high expectations* for all students?
RULES *Desired results—* what is to be done (goals and objectives)	*Long-range goals* —instructional and behavioral	*Build Guiding Teams*— model "right" behavior *Get the Vision Right*— identify behaviors that must be encouraged, eliminated, and maintained	What will I do to *set up classroom rules*?
CONSEQUENCES *Consequences—* what does and will happen as a result of evaluation	*Corrective consequences and reward systems*	*Increase Urgency*— reduce fear *Build Guiding Teams*— hold everyone accountable *Make-It-Stick*— recognize and reward responsible behavior	What will I do to *maintain* classroom *rules* and *celebrate success*?
DOCUMENTATION *Accountability—* performance standards, evaluation, and methods of measuring progress	*System for* assuring expectations are met and *monitoring* specific, observable, behavioral *expectations*	*Get the Vision Right*— describe important performance indicators to determine success *Don't Let Up*— monitor and measure progress *Create Short-Term Wins*—demonstrate that progress is occurring	What will I do to *recognize and acknowledge adherence to* classroom *rules and procedures*? What will I do to *track* student *progress*?
PROCEDURES *Resources—* support to help accomplish the results	*Encouragement procedures*	*Increase Urgency*— heighten motivation *Communicate for Buy-in*—create trust, support, and commitment *Enable Action*—identify effective processes	What will I do to *establish classroom procedures* and *maintain effective relationships* with students?

Dr. Foster: *Carefully read about the supplements at www.classroommanagementblues.com before using them to enhance the effectiveness of the* **Trustworthy Behavior Prescription***. As you find other information, be aware that different prescriptions, active ingredients, and supplements will blend with this prescription to encourage trustworthy behavior and empower **all** students to become self-disciplined.*

I recommend that you implement the supplements for this prescription as outlined on the **Implementation Checklist***.*

R$_x$ 4 Implementation Checklist

Select the *Supplements* page at
www.classroommanagementblues.com
to obtain detailed explanations, step-by-step instructions,
and blackline masters for *Supplements Q–V.*

*Implement the following supplements as applicable
at the beginning of the year or grading period:*

🗀 **Supplement Q—Mission, Vision, Principles, and Values**
Create mission and vision statements aligned with principles and values
to maintain focus on academic and behavioral goals and objectives

🗀 **Supplement R—Consequence Hierarchy and
Behavior Support System**
Implement the hierarchy to monitor behavior and provide support and
consequences to empower students to achieve academic and behavioral
goals and objectives

🗀 **Supplement S—Time Outs and Think Sheets**
Use time outs and think sheets to encourage students to reflect on their
actions and consider alternative behaviors

🗀 **Supplement T—Behavior Record Sheets**
Keep a record of misbehaviors and corrected misbehaviors to support
students as they become trustworthy and self-disciplined

🗀 **Supplement U—Self-Management Record Sheets**
Recognize and reward self-management behaviors to promote autonomy
and resiliency

🗀 **Supplement V—Clipboard Management**
Use a clipboard to handle academic and behavioral data collection
and record keeping

Concluding Remarks

The **Trustworthy Behavior Prescription** alone will not prevent or cure the *Classroom Management Blues*, but the potential for a cure or prevention will increase if used along with strategies of the **High Expectations**, **Active Engagement**, and **Appropriate Assessments Prescriptions**. In the next session, learn how to use the **Effective Communication Prescription** to help build relationships with students and parents to assure that all students reach their full potential.

Dr. Foster: Look at the **Trustworthy Behavior Prescription** and note the caution.

Encourage **Trustworthy Behavior** and support self-discipline throughout the school day to create and maintain a safe learning community where students learn to behave responsibly. With consistency, you will achieve the desired effects of more trust and respect, increased learning, and improved behavior in your classroom.

KOUNIN'S PHARMACY

444 Behavior Boulevard
Any Town, USA

Date Filled: First Day in the Classroom
Discard After: Retirement

 0004   Prescription for **TRUSTWORTHY BEHAVIOR**

Patient's Name: A. Teacher

Patient's Address: 104 Consequence Circle — Any Town, USA

Encourage **TRUSTWORTHY BEHAVIOR** and support self-discipline *throughout the school day*.

Doctor: *Barbara G. Foster*

Active Ingredients
- Principles
- Rules
- Consequences
- Documentation
- Procedures

SIDE EFFECTS: More trust and respect, increased learning, and improved behavior

CAUTION: May empower learners   **Unlimited Refills**

Resources—Access More Information

Learn more about discipline, self-direction, rules, principles, rewards and other incentives, peer support, procedures, monitoring, and documentation at the *Classroom Management Blues* website. Select the **Resources** page at *www.classroommanagementblues.com*, then **Behavior** for a list of books, articles, websites, and other resources.

Praxis Journal—Take Steps toward a Cure

Write responses to these prompts and questions before the next session:

- **Review the *Trustworthy Behavior Prescription* and reflect on what you have learned.** How do student self-monitoring and self-discipline affect student learning?
- **Based on what you have learned in this session, set a goal and develop a plan.** How do you plan to achieve your goal and solve one or more related problems?
- **Implement and evaluate your plan.** How did your actions affect you as a teacher and your students as learners?
- **Reflect on future goals and actions.** What will you do in the future?

STEP TWO: **TAKE PRESCRIPTIONS**

VYGOTSKY'S PHARMACY

555 Communication Circle
Any Town, USA

Date Filled: First Day in the Classroom
Discard After: Retirement

 0005

Prescription for **EFFECTIVE COMMUNICATION**

Patient's Name: **A. Teacher**

Patient's Address: **105 Respect Road — Any Town, USA**

Maintain **EFFECTIVE COMMUNICATION** *as directed*
with students, families, and other educators.

Doctor: *Barbara G. Foster*

Active Ingredients

- **Advocacy**
- **Feedback**
- **Dialogue**
- **Collaboration**
- **Professionalism**

SIDE EFFECTS: More trust and respect, increased learning,
and improved behavior

CAUTION: May increase parent involvement   **Unlimited Refills**

Session 9

Maintain Effective Communication

We consider every behavior that someone displays in the presence of someone else as communication, and therefore we assume that in the presence of someone else one cannot not communicate.

Wubbels, Brekelmans, van Tartwijk, and Admiral
*Interpersonal Relationships between
Teachers and Students in the Classroom*

Successful teachers **direct** every aspect of the classroom environment and effectively communicate what students are to learn and how they should **act** toward one another. Through effective communication with your students, their parents or caregivers, other educators, and members of the community, you can build relationships that foster student learning and promote appropriate behavior.

 com·mu·ni·cate [kə-myōo′nĭ-kāt′] *v.*

1. to have an interchange, as of ideas

2. to express oneself in such a way that one is readily and clearly understood

*The American Heritage Dictionary
of the English Language*

Dr. Foster: *Look at the* **Effective Communication Prescription** *(on the opposite page). This prescription is essential when you apply* **Active Engagement**, *repeat* **High Expectations**, *use* **Appropriate Assessments**, *and encourage* **Trustworthy Behavior**.

Communication is the common language (verbal and nonverbal) needed to transfer knowledge and feelings from one person to another. According to Lev Vygotsky, social interaction plays a primary role in the development of cognition, and "all the higher functions originate as actual relationships between individuals" (1978, p. 57).

*The relationship
is the communication
bridge between people.*

Alfred Kadushin
Social-work educator

A. Teacher: *It is through social interaction (dialogue) that I have learned about the complexities of each prescription. I look forward to our conversation about the other active ingredients of the* **Effective Communication Prescription**.

A. Teacher: *The caution for the prescription is a concern, but I hope to become more confident and competent in my ability to involve and communicate with parents. I know I have a lot to learn.*

Dr. Foster: *Then let's begin.*

If people were to look into your classroom, what would your words, actions, and interactions with students communicate?

A. Teacher: *I can't help but think of metaphors and similes. It would be like an audience at a play. They would see the actors on the stage and carefully chosen props.*

In my classroom, observers would see many books, inspirational quotations of famous people on my bulletin boards, and desks positioned to allow partner and small group discussion.

Dr. Foster: *Your classroom communicates that you inspire your students through the words of successful people and value books and peer teaching.*

A. Teacher: *I am comfortable with what my classroom communicates, but I am not as confident about what I say and how I interact with my students. Like the actors on stage, I would like some rehearsals before opening my door to critics or an audience.*

Dr. Foster: *You have better communication skills than you think. Without too much control, it is my job as the director to advise, inspire, coach, and encourage you, the actor, to move from your current skill level to perform at a higher level of effectiveness.*

A. Teacher: *I recognize your reference to Lev Vygotsky's* **Zone of Proximal Development***. With your guidance, I will become a more effective communicator.*

Dr. Foster: *Let's set the stage. Our focus in this session will be advocacy, collaboration, feedback, dialogue, and professionalism—the active ingredients in the* **Effective Communication Prescription***. In our roles as director and actor, together we will make all the creative pieces come together for the performance— the ability to communicate effectively with colleagues, parents, other educators, and the community to empower students to learn and succeed.*

Throughout this session, I will direct your attention to dialogue from film to give your brain a break.

> *Effective communication is the key, and it's one thing I had to learn— to talk to the actors. I was so involved with the visual and technical aspects that I would forget about the actors.*
>
> **Steve Buscemi**
> American actor, writer, and film director

Effective communication in the classroom occurs when teachers send and receive purposeful messages that support student learning. When teachers are advocates for students (send purposeful messages) and actively listen to students (receive purposeful messages), students "feel significant, confident, respected, and responsible" (McLeod, Fisher, & Hoover, 2003, pp. 68–69).

Active Ingredient	🍎 Advocacy

Advocacy is the first active ingredient in the **Effective Communication Prescription**; for teachers, it is the active support of students. To be perceived as authentic, every verbal and nonverbal behavior must communicate the belief that every student has the potential to learn. To achieve this goal, teachers booster, champion, and provide students with genuine encouragement.

> 📄 **ad·vo·ca·cy** [ăd′və-kə-sē] *n.*
>
> Active support, esp. of a cause
>
> **Synonyms:** encouragement, championing, boosterism
>
> *The Collins English Dictionary and Thesaurus of the English Language*

A. Teacher: *I think I communicate my belief that every student can learn, but it may only be my perception.*

Dr. Foster: *That is why advocacy is so important. It calls for more than words or beliefs; it calls for actions—specific behaviors.*

Imagine the booster section at a ball game. How does the behavior of the boosters differ from other people who attend the game to support a team?

A. Teacher: *Some spectators may sit quietly, but not the boosters. To support their team, they make themselves known by their cheers and demonstrative gestures.*

If I communicate effectively, there is no question about my support of students and their potential to learn.

How do teachers verbally advocate for student learning and success? Effective communicators focus the message, understand where the audience is coming from, and make it clear that the message is important ("Interpersonal Communication," n.d.). Whether the goal is to inform, instruct, motivate, persuade, direct, or do something else, the message must be specific and relevant to the listener.

Dr. Foster: *The goal of advocacy is to express caring and support of students to empower them to learn and succeed beyond their wildest dreams (Edwards, 2010).*

My father was a farmer. I watched him plant seeds with the hope they would grow to produce quality vegetables. Without his care and support, his crops would fail.

The same is true for teachers who are student advocates. Without care and support, students would be unable to learn and succeed. Read how Darius Krider changed his thinking about students in "The Seeds We Sow."

The Seeds We Sow

In his article "Teachers as Social Advocate Leaders," Darius Krider (2008) wrote about the plethora of problems that adversely affect the ability of students to learn and the paradigm shift he experienced. The way he thought about his students changed from how he viewed them as problems to a view of them as students with problems.

In American society, we have a system that sows seeds unevenly, which leaves some land barren and unproductive. While the dominant group is cultivated by having their needs met, others are truncated in their growth. Knowing the kind of unequal results this system produces in our children's education should suggest the need for a novel approach in leadership among educators. I recommend an egalitarian approach in which educators are social advocates for students and promote equal education for all.

To be social advocates for students, teachers first must have a perspective that values all students, particularly "disadvantaged" and "at-risk" students. According to the great educational thinker Paulo Friere, in his book *The Pedagogy of the Oppressed*, teachers enforce and reinforce a mindset in oppressed students to accept a subservient position in life by teaching them at the lowest level. Teachers should view all students as having the ability to learn at high levels, no matter their background.

That is why a paradigm shift is needed among teachers. I speak from experience . . . I was also one of those students for whom I am now advocating. The conditions that they live in I, too, lived in and conformed to as a boy. Fortunately, I was able to escape because I had advocates—not necessarily social advocate teachers—although I did not realize it at the time.

Excerpted from "Teachers as Social Advocate Leaders" by D. Krider, 2008

The ***reality*** is that teachers can become advocates who
sow the seeds of hope and success.

Dr. Foster: *Remember to "sow seeds evenly" and strike a balance among advantaged and disadvantaged, males and females, and gifted and those with challenges.*

A. Teacher: *I have heard many stories about "students who succeeded against all odds because a teacher or other adults believed in them and expressed that belief both verbally and nonverbally" (p. xvii). Can you give me some verbal examples? (See Table 9.1 on the next page.)*

Table 9.1

Messages That Support Student Learning and Success

In *Inviting Students to Learn: 100 Tips for Talking Effectively with Your Students,* Edwards (2010) says students need to know they are valued. Tell students how important they are, and they will come to believe that they are important. This builds powerful, trusting relationships. (p. 5)	• You are truly a special class! As you move forward, it will be fun to see all the exciting and powerful things you do with your lives. • It's a joy and a privilege to have the opportunity to work with you!
In *The Art and Science of Teaching,* Marzano (2007) states that to establish and maintain effective relationships with students, teachers must provide guidance, work as a team with students, and control, both academically and behaviorally. (p. 149)	• We are a team here and succeed as a team. I have a stake personally in the success of each one of you. • You can count on me to give clear directions for your learning and behavior.
In *The Key Elements of Classroom Management,* McLeod, Fisher, and Hoover, (2003) assert that students perceive teachers as more understanding, caring, fair, and helpful when they make positive statements. The message students get is that they are worthy and capable. (pp. 65, 69)	• You carefully thought through the issues under discussion. • You acted with the most noble purpose possible in the current situation. • You acted with the best intentions.
In *Succeeding with Difficult Students,* Canter and Canter (1993) stress that difficult students expect teachers to give up on them. However, proactive teachers consistently show that they care and will do everything in their power to help students succeed—no matter how difficult the problem. (p. 33)	• I care about you, and I will do everything in my power to help you succeed. (p. 36) • I want you to be successful in my class. I know you can do the work. The next time you believe that the work is too hard, let me know and I'll find a way to give you more help. (p. 46)

In what ways do effective teachers use nonverbal messages to communicate a belief that all students can learn? Teachers may say "I believe in you" or "I know you can do this," but if their nonverbal behaviors (e.g., facial expressions, body language) say otherwise, students do not perceive them as genuine or trustworthy. People communicate up to 90% of what they say and feel through their actions, not their words (Hansen, 2011, p. 7). As most teachers are not aware they exhibit low expectations for some students and not others, teachers must consistently monitor these behaviors (Hansen, 2011; Windle & Warren, 2006).

Wubbels, Brekelmans, van Tartwijk, and Admiral (1999) assert, "Spoken and written language are well equipped for the communication of content, but the communication of interpersonal relationships is particularly the domain of nonverbal behavior" (p. 159). They classified the most important nonverbal aspects of teacher behavior in five channels:

> Studies have found that teachers engage in affirming nonverbal behaviors . . . with students more frequently when they believe they are dealing with high-ability students than when they believe they are interacting with "slow" students. (Bamburg, 1994, para. 8)

1. Space (the teacher's use of proximity and space in the classroom)
2. Body (position and movement of the trunk, the arms, and the head)
3. Face (different expressions)
4. Visual behavior (duration of time the teacher looks at the students)
5. Voice (the noncontent aspects of speech) (pp. 159–160).

Voice tone, pitch, and pacing account for 38% of what others perceive and understand (Windle & Warren, 2006). Some points about voice are:

- Rapid and higher pitched speech tends to denote anger and/or excitement.
- Low and monotone speech usually signifies boredom.
- Abrupt speech evidences feeling defensive. (para. 1)

A "Bitter" Pill to Take

Mr. Bitterman taught in the classroom next to mine. At lunchtime one day, I overheard him say, "Fred doesn't know it, but I can't stand him! I keep him in the back of the room so I don't have to look at him."

Lunch left a bitter taste in my mouth that day. I can imagine how difficult it was for Fred to take Mr. Bitterman *every* day.

The ***reality*** is that students know when teachers dislike them.

A. Teacher: *I've known a few teachers who don't like their students, and they don't seem to care who knows it. The climate they create cannot possibly be conducive to learning.*

How would you suggest I monitor my nonverbal behaviors toward students so that they do not perceive me as a teacher who dislikes or is out to "get" them?

Dr. Foster: *To be authentic, be honest with yourself about your actions.*

Dr. Foster: *Think of a challenging student whose absence from class might be a relief to you. Then complete this self-assessment exercise. Check the boxes that best describe the frequency of your nonverbal interactions.*

Figure 9.1

Supplement W: Nonverbal Interactions—Self-Assessment

When _____ approaches you or your desk, how often do you . . .
        Name

- **Smile acceptingly**   Often ☐ Not Sure ☐ Not Often

When _____ talks to you or answers a question, how often do you . . .
        Name

- **Give positive nods**   Often ☐ Not Sure ☐ Not Often

- **Maintain approving eye contact**   Often ☐ Not Sure ☐ Not Often

- **Lean gently forward giving full attention**   Often ☐ Not Sure ☐ Not Often

When you give instructions or ask questions, how often do you . . .

- **Stand or sit near _____ arms/legs uncrossed**   Often ☐ Not Sure ☐ Not Often
                      Name

From Cotton, 2001 and Jones & Jones, 2001

A. Teacher: *Do you need to see what I've checked?*

Dr. Foster: *I do not. It is more important for you to reflect as I explain the significance of your responses.*

*If **all** your responses are **Often**, you **most likely** pay attention to and demonstrate warm, open, friendly, and responsive interactions toward the student (Cotton, 2001). These are signs that you hold high expectations for and like the student. As you identified him or her as a challenging student, the problems you have may be about the behavior management issues we discussed in our session on trustworthy behavior.*

*If **three or more** responses are **Not Sure**, video your interactions with the student and complete the exercise again.*

*If even **one** response is **Not Often**, it is an indication that you pay less attention to and **may** have lower expectations for the student. Make a conscious effort (set a goal) to interact with the student to increase a **behavior** for which you checked **Not Often**. Write the behavior or behaviors you need to exhibit toward the student on your lesson plan as a reminder to monitor your behavior.*

A. Teacher: *Let me see if I understand. My students are more likely to feel valued and accept the high expectations I have for them if I openly smile and make eye contact (Gazin, 2004). If I follow through with these nonverbal interactions, I'll see a positive change in students after a reasonable about of time.*

Dr. Foster: *"A positive attitude can truly work wonders because students intuitively sense that the teacher has a genuine interest and belief in them" (para. 10).*

Complete 🗁 **Supplement W: Nonverbal Interactions—Self-Assessment** *for other students and you will begin to recognize when you use effective body language to help **all** your students learn and succeed. (Select **Supplements**, then **W–Z** at www.classroommanagementblues.com to download the blackline master of the self-assessment—**Supplement W**.)*

A. Teacher: *To be an advocate requires that I be in a positive emotional state to communicate verbally and nonverbally with students, families, colleagues, other educators, and the community to build effective professional relationships.*

Is there anything else I can do to improve my relationships with students?

What can advocates of student learning and success do to establish and maintain professional relationships with students? Students infer the meaning of a teacher's intentions from the teacher's behavior (Wubbels et al., 1999). "Teacher behavior, then, is the language of relationships. Students 'listen' to every behavior made by the teacher as a statement of the type of relationship the teacher wants, even when the teacher's actions have no such intent" (Marzano, 2007, p. 152).

This emotional component of the effective teacher-student relationship can foster a sense of cooperation and concern (Anderman & Wolters, 2006; Perry, Turner, & Meyer, 2006). Smiling and enthusiasm are two behaviors that can have positive effects on teacher-student relationships, as well as on student engagement and achievement (Bettencourt, Gillett, Gall, & Hull, 1983; Gettinger & Kohler, 2006; Moskowitz & Hayman, 1976; Rosenshine & Furst, 1973).

A. Teacher: *This is consistent with what I learned in the preceding session.*

- *There is a positive correlation between trustworthiness and happiness. Effective teacher-student relationships need trust.*

- *Smiling and enthusiasm are positive behaviors that can activate the frontal lobe where information is processed.*

Are there other things I can do to improve my professional relationship with students?

Dr. Foster: *Here are several action steps that communicate an appropriate level of cooperation and concern (Marzano, 2007, pp. 154–158). (See Table 9.2.)*

Table 9.2

Action Steps to Foster Cooperation and Concern	
Step 1: Know Something About Each Student	• Use an interest survey. Find **Supplement G: About Me Survey** at www.classroommanagementblues.com. • Ask for appropriate information at parent-teacher conferences.
Step 2: Engage in Behaviors that Indicate Affection for Each Student	• Greet students at the door. • Attend an after-school function of those students who feel alienated. • Develop a schedule to interact in a friendly way with a few students each day.
Step 3: Bring Student Interests into the Content and Personalize Learning Activities	• Ask students to construct metaphors and analogies. • Integrate student interests from **Supplement G**: **About Me Survey** in lessons. • Give students opportunities to do preferred-learning activities. Find **Supplement E: Surveys for Preferred Learning Styles, Conditions, and Activities** at *classroommanagementblues.com*.
Step 4: Engage in Physical Behaviors that Communicate Interest in Students	• Engage in nonverbal behaviors that show an interest in students. Find **Supplement W: Nonverbal Interactions— Self-Assessment** at *classroommanagementblues.com*. • Look interested in what students have to say.
Step 5: Use Humor when Appropriate	• Laugh at yourself. • Keep a book of jokes or cartoons handy.

Action steps from *The Art and Science of Teaching* by R. J. Marzano, 2007, pp. 154-157

A. Teacher: *I have learned these and many other strategies for* **High Expectations** *and other prescriptions that apply to* **Effective Communication***.*

Dr. Foster: *Think about these strategies: "What do you believe about yourself as a teacher and your ability to have an impact on the lives of the students you teach? Do you believe that you have the skills to help students in becoming everything they want to become?" (Edwards, 2010, p. 3).*

A. Teacher: *If I am truly dedicated (not acting), I can make a difference and be an advocate for student learning and success!*

The teaching strategies I choose and the language I use about myself, my students, the subject matter I teach have a profound effect on my interactions with students (Edwards, 2010).

Dr. Foster: *The language you use **does** affect the relationship between you and the students whose behavior you want to strengthen, or change (McLeod et al., 2003).*

Dr. Foster: *As advocates for student learning and success, teachers can help motivate students to develop a positive attitude toward themselves, the content they are learning, and their ability to succeed (Edwards, 2010; Wlodkowksi, 1984).*

"Positive messages from someone the student detests are not likely to have much effect!" (McLeod et al., 2003, p. 98). The stronger (not closer) the teacher-student relationship, the more effective positive messages will be to empower learners.

Active Ingredient	 Feedback

Master teachers provide quality **feedback**, the second active ingredient in the **Effective Communication Prescription**. Oral, written, and other feedback is the information teachers give students about past learning and behavior that may influence future learning and behavior (Seashore, Seashore, & Weinberg, 1992). It starts with the intention of the teacher to empower students to learn and succeed. In *What Did You Say? The Art of Giving and Receiving Feedback*, Seashore and others say, "One thing that gets in the way of our good intentions is our lack of skill, but if the intentions are not good in the first place, sharpening the feedback skills is like sharpening a weapon" (p. 139).

> Better relationships empower both parties. Therefore, I want to improve our relationship because the better my relationships, the more I am empowered. (Seashore, Seashore, & Weinberg, 1992, p. 140)

" I " Empower " You "

When a teacher uses "I" messages, he or she controls students. When a teacher uses "You" messages, students become empowered to take responsibility for their behavior, learning, and success (McLeod, Fisher, & Hoover, 2003).

In Practice

McLeod, Fisher & Hoover

Examples of positive messages that empower students include:

- "You are certainly able to get started quickly."
- "You must feel proud of your success on the test. Your practice paid off."
- "You have a real knack for adding personal examples to your writing."
- "You are working so hard at determining importance as your read. You must notice the difference it is making in your comprehension." (pp. 99–100).

When teachers use "you" messages rather than "I" messages, they say **"I" empower "you"** to take responsibility for your own learning, be proud of your accomplishments, and realize success is under your control. Feedback promotes "an internal locus of control" and serves as a scaffold until students can assume responsibility on their own (p. 100).

Why does specific, purposeful, and authentic feedback empower students to learn and succeed? To Tauber (1998), teachers who offer inspirational, affective feedback and informational, cognitive feedback to students for whom they hold high expectations get more from these students. "Research provides evidence that teachers often do talk with *good* students as if they were active, self-regulated learners" but tell other students what to do (Brookhart, 2008, p. 35).

Behaviorists like Thorndike (1913) and others considered positive feedback "positive reinforcement" and called negative feedback "punishment." In the last 20 years, researchers have focused on the characteristics of effective feedback, feedback in context, and the student's role in the feedback process. "Results show that feedback is not always effective because the message sent is filtered through the students' perception (influenced by prior knowledge, experiences, and motivation) as it becomes the message received" (p. 3).

> If we think of ourselves in a negative light, a "positive" message may be perceived quite negatively. The meaning of feedback is again determined by the receiver, so "positive" and "negative" cannot be meaningfully applied to the feedback, but only to the receiver's reaction. (Seashore, Seashore, & Weinberg, 1992, p. 99)

A. Teacher: *I always feel uncomfortable when I give feedback on student work. I do not remember learning about how to provide effective feedback. I give the kind of feedback my teachers gave me over the years—"Good job" or "Many errors."*

Dr. Foster: *It can be emotionally draining and time consuming if you lack the knowledge and skill to give effective feedback. Your "script" and that of your students should read "What knowledge and skills do I aim to develop? How close am I now? What do I need to do next?" (Brookhart, 2008, p. 1).*

A. Teacher: *I want to learn how to give effective feedback on student work that will empower my students to learn and succeed. I know I should not use positive and negative terms when I refer to feedback. What else can I do?*

Dr. Foster: *You are on the path to mastering the art of giving effective feedback.*

To master the art of giving effective feedback, Edwards (2010) and others recommend that teachers stay completely away from inferences and judgments both positive and negative about student work, the person who gives and receives the feedback, and other issues related to students (Brookhart, 2008; Ellison, Hayes, Costa, & Garmston, 2008; Seashore et al., 1992). They recommend that you avoid statements like these:

- "You're so smart." (judgment about the student receiving feedback)
- "I enjoyed your presentation." (inference about person giving feedback)
- "I liked the way you entered the room." (judgment about other issues)
- "That was an excellent report." (judgment about student work)
- "You cited 48 authors in your report. You must have worked really hard." (inference about student work)

A. Teacher: *I use similar statements all the time. How can I avoid these kinds of statements when I have to grade student's work and give grades?*

Dr. Foster: *That is a valid question. Researchers investigated the effect of grades and descriptive comments on learning and motivation (Butler & Nisan, 1986). They affirm what many teachers and Dr. Susan Brookhart have observed if a paper is returned with both a comment and a grade. "Many students will pay attention to the grade and ignore the comment. The grade 'trumps' the comment. . . . Descriptive comments have the best chance of being read as descriptive if they are not accompanied by a grade" (Brookhart, 2008, p. 8).*

A. Teacher: *From what I have learned so far in this session and in our session on appropriate assessments, I should give more feedback on practice and formative assessments as these do not receive an evaluativefgrade. If the feedback is "for" learning, students can use the comments to learn and succeed on summative assessments on which they receive a grade as feedback.*

> Research does suggest students will be more interested in their grade than in the feedback, which is why practice work should not be graded. (Brookhart, 2008, p. 36)

Dr. Foster: *"As you progress toward your goal . . . notice how you instinctively apply your new learning and understanding" (Edwards, 2010, p. 48).*

A. Teacher: *I am amazed at how your choice of words makes me feel. Where can I find more examples of better ways to phrase my comments?*

Dr. Foster: *Adverbs are powerful and can encourage and create pride in accomplishments. The example is from **Inviting Students to Learn: 100 Tips for Talking Effectively with Your Students** by Dr. Jenny Edwards. (Find Dr. Edwards book on the **My Bookshelves** page of the **Classroom Management Blues** website. For more information and other resources about effective feedback, select **Resources** at www.classroommanagementblues.com, then **Communication** and **Feedback** .)*

A. Teacher: *Now I know some of the characteristics of ineffective feedback. What are some of the characteristics of effective feedback?*

Ellison, Hayes, Costa, and Garmston (2008) found that teachers, who make judgments, provide information about the person giving the feedback, and use inferences as feedback reduce the students' ability to assess their own work. Students benefit from undisputable data and can make their own judgments and inferences. Along with data, teachers should ask reflective questions to guide students to think about and process the data (Edwards, 2010, p. 70; Ellison et al., 2008). (See Table 9.3 for some examples of effective and ineffective feedback.)

Table 9.3

Effective and Ineffective Feedback		
Providing Data *Effective*	**Reflective Questioning** *Effective*	**Making Inferences** *Ineffective*
You stood in five different spots during the five minutes you presented.	What were some of the things that you wanted to communicate with the audience from each of the different spots?	You stood in five different spots during the five minutes as you presented to the group. *You must have been nervous.*
You cited 48 authors in your report.	What were some of the strategies you used to obtain and read that many authors?	You cited 48 authors in your report. *You must have worked really hard.*
You said that it took you 60 hours to prepare the final report.	What were some of the strategies that you used to focus on the project to finish it?	You said that it took you 60 hours to prepare the report. *You went to a lot of trouble to put the project together.*

From *Inviting Students to Learn: 100 Tips for Talking Effectively with Your Students* by J. Edwards, 2010

Dr. Foster: *Sometimes the lessons learned come from the stories and experiences of others—like Goldilocks.*

Lessons From Goldilocks

Teachers can learn some **lessons from Goldilocks** and Dr. Susan M. Brookhart about how specific to make their feedback: not too narrow, not too broad, but just right! Learn how Dr. Brookhart learned this lesson.

"I had given back an extensive paper to a student at the end of one marking period. I had read it with "pen in hand" and had almost absentmindedly corrected all his mechanical errors. The class had the opportunity to redo these paper for credit, and he did—but all he did was make the editing changes I had marked for him. It annoyed me to give him credit for work that I had done. . . . For about 10 minutes of correction work, he "revised" a major project. I won't do that again!" (Brookhart, 2008, p. 33)

The ***reality*** or moral of this sad fable is: go for conceptual feedback—do not do the work for the student. "Give suggestions that are specific enough so that the student can take concrete next steps" (p. 34).

Hattie and Timperley (2007) identified feedback about the **task** and **task processing** as effective feedback (see Table 9.4). While feedback about **self-regulation** can be effective to the degree that it enhances self-efficacy, feedback about the person does not contain information that can further learning and implies that achievement is something beyond the student's control (Brookhart, 2008).

Table 9.4

Feedback about the Task	Feedback about Task Processing
Information about . . . • Errors or format • Depth or quality of the work in relation to learning targets (often against criteria) • Directions to get more information • Misconceptions	Information about . . . • The method used • Strategies used • Other possible strategies • The relationship between what was done and the quality of the performance
Examples . . . You should include more information . . . You can find out more by . . . Look again at the format directions.	Examples . . . Why was your answer wrong? What strategies could you have used to improve the quality?
NOTE: This feedback may not transfer to learning other tasks.	NOTE: When possible, describe task and process as well as their relationship.

From Brookhart, 2008 and Hattie & Timperley, 2007

A. Teacher: *That was helpful! I have learned that to be effective.* **I must be observant**, *so that my feedback follows verifiable observations, not inferences.* **I must be clear**, *and not add to potential misunderstandings.* **I must be flexible**, *able to reframe my feedback in a form my students can understand and accept. Finally,* **I must practice** *and learn from my mistakes (Seashore et al., 1992).*

Dr. Foster: *"Even though this seems a little bit difficult right now, you will be surprised and delighted at just how quickly you have mastered it [the art of giving effective feedback 'FOR' learning]" (Edwards, 2010, p. 77).*

Here are a few more tips (see Table 9.5, "Strategies for Giving Effective Feedback 'FOR' Learning").

Table 9.5

Strategies for Giving Effective Feedback "FOR" Learning	
Cotton, 2001; Jones & Jones, 2001;and "Coaching for Success," 1987	• Give specific, supportive, and sincere suggestions for improvements when work does not meet standards. • Provide encouragement for attempts on challenging tasks. • Use a checklist to assure every student receives supportive feedback with the same frequency.
Brookhart, 2008	• Give descriptive, formative feedback, not evaluative feedback, while students are still mindful of the learning target and there is still time for them to act on it—something they are still striving for, not what they have already done. • Comment on as many strengths (performances based on specific criteria) as weaknesses (suggestions for improvement). • Compare a student's work with established criteria and sometimes with his or her own past performance—not with the work of other students—especially on wall charts and displays.

If Walls Could Talk

In one of my first parent-teacher conferences, a mother said something that I have never forgotten. She asked me to look at the chart I had on the wall that had stars for students who received 100s on their spelling tests. She said, "How do you think my son feels every day he enters the room and sees that he has no stars?"

My intention was to motivate students to study for spelling tests, but the messages to students were, "I only value 100s, not learning." and "Some students are smarter than others." The feedback to students was not "FOR" learning.

The **reality** is that charts and other evidence of student performance displayed on classroom walls *do* talk to students. They may tell students that achievement is beyond their reach or control.

A. Teacher: *Again, it reminds me that students perceive different messages from the physical classroom environment.*

I understand that even if I think that my communications are clear, I cannot control how my students choose to perceive them. I can control the amount and quality of the feedback I choose to provide. Can you give me some suggestions to make better choices?

Dr. Foster: *When teachers can use strategies that address the amount and quality of written, oral, and other types of feedback, they are able to increase the probability that the student perceives the feedback as intended.*

How can teachers determine the appropriate delivery method, amount, and type of feedback that empowers learners? The most difficult decision for teachers is how much feedback to give because their natural instinct is to "fix" everything—to achieve every learning goal perfectly (Brookhart, 2008). "For real learning, what makes the difference is a usable amount of information that connects with something students already know and takes them from that point to the next level" (p. 12). Neugebauer (1983) says feedback should be in small doses and on a timely basis.

> To overload a person with feedback is to reduce the possibility that he may use what he receives effectively (Lehner, 1978)

In *Grading Students' Classroom Writing: Issues and Strategies,* Speck (2000) "advises teachers not to give more feedback than the student wrote (which can be an indication of the student's literacy level), as it can be overwhelming. Long comments . . . [may not give] the student good enough direction as to where to begin making revisions" (as cited in Reesor, 2002, p. 253). Even when feedback is supportive and specific, it may not help students if it is too short. Responses that are abrupt (e.g., "Rewrite this) or contain one word (e.g., "Good") do not provide enough information for students to understand what the teacher intends by the comment (Underwood & Tregidgo, 2006, p. 88).

Dr. Foster: *Nevertheless, in many instances a single word can act as a catalyst for reflection, or internal feedback experiences (Seashore et al., 1992). Just as one picture can be worth a thousand words, "with the right timing, one word may be worth a thousand pictures" (p. 173).*

> One-word feedback is process feedback, as opposed to content feedback. Content feedback is packed with information from you to me, while process feedback simply invites me to notice my automatic pilot. Ultimately, the most powerful effect of any feedback is to create a reflection— a reflection that allows me to use my own capacity to look at myself in the mirror. (Seashore, Seashore, & Weinberg, 1992, p. 176)

A. Teacher: *Because?*

Dr. Foster: *Exactly. How can your use of the word "because" be so effective?*

It invites me to reflect or do an instant replay in my own mind of what I have just said.

A. Teacher: *Just as my word choice **caused** you to think, one word can give just the right amount of support to empower my students to think.*

Dr. Foster: *Here is what Dr. Brookhart says you should know and consider when you make decisions about the right amount of feedback to give:*

- *The topic in general .and specific learning targets (objectives)*

- *Typical developmental learning progressions for the topic and learning targets (objectives)*

- *Individual students (2008, p. 12)*

A. Teacher: *Let me see if I understand. To help students take the next step toward a learning target, or objective, I need to know about my students, what I want them to learn, and what comes next. "For some students, simply getting clarity and improvement feedback on one point would be sufficient, whereas others can handle more" (p. 12). Maybe, "selecting two or three main points about a paper for comment" would be just right (p. 13).*

My next question is, "How do I know whether to give written, oral, or other forms of feedback?"

It is ineffective to give more written feedback than a student writes. It is best to deliver comments orally if many words are necessary to make clear what the student needs to do to move toward the learning target (Brookhart, 2008; Underwood & Tregidgo, 2006). Another consideration would be the students' ability to read, especially younger children (Brookhart, 2008). In this situation, the best way to give feedback would be to talk privately with the students.

> Some kinds of assignments lend themselves better to written feedback (for example, reviewing and writing comments on students' written work); some, to oral feedback (for example, observing and commenting as students do math problems as seatwork); and some, to demonstrations (for example, helping a kindergarten student hold a pencil correctly). Some of the best feedback can result from conversations *with* the student. (Brookhart, 2008, p. 15)

A. Teacher: *Maybe oral feedback about an individual student's work is best, but I do not have the time to talk with every student about everything he or she needs to do.*

Dr. Foster: *"If the same message would benefit a group of students, providing feedback to the class or group can save time and also serve as a minilesson or review session. . . . Or you can pull a group aside to give some feedback while others are doing something else" (p. 17).*

Dr. Phil Race urges teachers to find a balance between feedback processes that make the best use of our time as teachers and deliver high learning payoff—more student learning. To see what this looks like in practice, read "It's a Balancing Act."

It's a Balancing Act

In *Using Feedback to Help Students Learn*, Phil Race provides the advantages and disadvantages of written, face-to-face, and electronic feedback, as well as feedback in print. He urges us teachers to find a balance between the feedback processes that deliver high learning payoff and "other feedback processes [that] are highly efficient in terms of our time" (n.d., p. 10).

In Practice
Dr. Race

Codes Written on Students' Work	Whole Group Debriefing Session

Rather than write individual feedback directly onto student's work, write a code (a letter, a number, or a symbol), and alongside compile a "glossary of codes" on paper, overhead, or presentation slides to use when you debrief the work with the whole group. In the debriefing, a teacher can go through each of the important codes, clarify what the code means, and answer students' questions. (pp. 7–8)

Advantages: This process saves much time and energy as the teacher writes each common feedback comment once. As limited space is available on student work, detailed comments can be provided to address common errors and misunderstandings. In addition, students get their work back "without it being covered with threatening feedback markings." (p. 7)

Disadvantage: The process of debriefing can bore students who made few errors or had misunderstandings. Provide a handout of the coded feedback and discuss those most relevant to the whole group, or provide the oral feedback in small groups while the other students work on something else. (p. 7)

While some feedback like one-to-one, face-to-face feedback delivers high learning payoff (more learning), face-to-face communication with a large group of students is highly efficient (saves time). **It's a balancing act** to think about processes that both have a high learning payoff and are highly efficient. Codes written on students' work and debriefed in a whole-group session is a balanced process.

Well-Balanced?

First Man: *So what's your story? You, the poor kid that never got to go to Exeter or Andover?*

Second Man: *Despite my privileged upbringing, I'm actually quite well-balanced. I have a chip on both shoulders.*

These lines are from the film *A Beautiful Mind* (2001), based on the life of John Forbes Nash, Jr., a Nobel Laureate in economics. The movie, a moving love story, provides a revealing look at mental illness.

Retrieved from www.moviequotes.com

Dr. Foster: *The goal is to balance processes with "**high learning payoff**" and "**efficiency**," not a balance between oral and written feedback. "If you circulate while students are working on assignments, you can provide them with immediate feedback about their performance. You can catch errors, assist them with problems, and affirm correct, thoughtful work" (Weinstein & Mignano, 2003, p. 190).*

 If a teacher circulates while students work on assignments, would this describe high learning payoff, efficiency, or both?

A. Teacher: *It would be high learning payoff **and** efficiency. If I were unable to monitor and provide feedback while students work on assignments, I would need to check the written "assignments once they've been submitted and return them to students as soon as possible" (p. 190). Immediate feedback would have a positive effect on student learning, and I would have fewer papers to grade after school.*

When I do need to give written feedback, what do you suggest?

Underwood and Tregidgo (2006) reviewed research studies, described best practices, and made recommendations about how to improve student writing through effective feedback. They "learned that in order for students to benefit from feedback, they have to (1) notice it, (2) accept it, and (3) understand what to do with it" (p. 75). This requires that the feedback be readable, non-threatening, and easy to link to the exact part that needs work (Race, n.d.).

Brookhart (2008) offers several ways to deliver written feedback: on the work, usually close to the evidence; on annotated rubrics or an assignment cover sheet; or on a combination of the two. "If comments are descriptions of some specific detail on a paper, it helps to put them right next to what they are describing, perhaps in the margin nearby" (p. 36). Otherwise, teachers should place all the comments at the beginning or end of the paper. For long, written assignments, annotated rubrics and cover sheets are effective.

A. Teacher: *I am familiar with rubrics. What is an "annotated" rubric?*

Dr. Foster: *Most rubrics list the criteria but do not provide a place for other comments. Here is an example of an annotated rubric.*

Figure 9.2

Collaborative Work Skills Rubric

Problem Solving You gave others in the group the opportunity to suggest solutions before you offered your solutions.	Actively looks for and suggests solutions to problems.	Refines solutions suggested by others.	Does not suggest or refine solutions, is willing to try out solutions suggested by others.	Does not suggest or refine solutions and is not willing to try solutions suggested by others.

From "Collaborative Work Skills Rubric" at http://rubistar.4teachers.org

A. Teacher: *That makes sense. I just leave a space at the beginning or end of the rows to add comments, or feedback.*

What goes on the cover sheet?

Dr. Foster: *Though it varies from assignment to assignment, a cover sheet should contain assessment criteria, point values, and a place for comments.*

Here is part of a lab report cover sheet.

Figure 9.3

Name _____ Date _____

Class _____ Total Points _____

Lab Report Evaluation

Criteria	Points	Comments
Introduction (15 points) Background information on topic is clear, accurate, and sufficient. Purpose of the lab or hypothesis is clear, in proper form.		
Method (15 points) Description of materials is clear, accurate, and complete. Description of procedures is clear, accurate, and complete.		
Results (15 points) Data display (tables, graphs) is appropriate, clear, and complete. Text describes what happened in the lab.		
Conclusions (15 points) Discussion of results is according to the hypothesis or lab purpose. Discussion includes a description of limitations of findings and sources of error.		

From *How to Give Feedback to Your Students* by S. M. Brookhart, 2008, pp. 20–22

A. Teacher: *Would it not be a good idea for students to brainstorm important qualities and criteria to help develop the rubric or cover sheet for an assignment?*

Dr. Foster: *The feedback given to students on rubrics and cover sheets that students help develop would almost certainly be beneficial. They would most likely pay more attention to it, accept it, and know what to do with it (Underwood & Tregidgo, 2006).*

Though the ability to decide criteria for assignments will vary with age, it is important for students at an early age to be involved with assessment. "This will help them to develop an assessment vocabulary and their ability to self-assess" (O'Conner, 2009, p. 189).

A. Teacher: *I know how to give effective feedback, but I still need practice. I am confident in my ability to determine the appropriate delivery method, amount, and type of feedback to empower my students to use it to improve their work and to self-assess.*

Is there anything else I need to think about when I give feedback to help my students learn and succeed?

Dr. Foster: *Think back to our first session. What were Bloom's Domains of Educational activities?*

A. Teacher: *The three domains were cognitive (knowing), psychomotor (doing), and affective (feeling). So I need to explore the feelings of my students.*

Dr. Foster: *The feelings of your students do matter. "Communication . . . is not so much a matter of intellect as it is of trust and acceptance of others, of their ideas and feelings" (Covey, 1992, p. 117).*

> We will learn that unless there are good feelings between people, they will find it almost impossible to reason together because of emotional barriers. We will learn that fear is a knot of the heart and that to untie this knot we must improve our relationship. (Covey, 1992, p. 117)

What are the barriers to effective communication and feedback? "Barriers are the distractions, prejudices, judgment calls, and preconceived notions about a person and the value of his [or her] message" that lead to poor relationships and prevent people from understanding the full message (Shafir, 2003, p. 43). Semantic barriers include external barriers, differences in language, distractions within the learning environment, and internal barriers that come from within the person ("Interpersonal Communication," n.d.). According to Rebecca Z. Shafir (2003), "Getting through the fog of distractions and personal biases to allow the message to be heard is a challenge. . . . When we are aware of our obstacles, we are then better able to deal with them" (p. 48).

Teachers must set the stage for effective communication and feedback in the classroom. Threats, harsh comments, and sarcasm must be eliminated as they produce chemical imbalances and place the brain in survival mode ("Concept to Classroom," 2004; Elder, n.d.; Seashore et al., 1992; Sousa, 2006; Sousa, 2009; Tate, 2007). Aggressive behavior may be triggered or make it nearly impossible to get and keep a student's attention.

A. Teacher: *I remember from our session on high expectations that teachers should establish a goal of zero tolerance for put-downs from anyone in the classroom to create a non-threatening environment (see pages 96–97).*

Dr. Foster: *Zero tolerance for put-downs is one way to create and maintain a nonthreatening learning environment. Teachers can also increase the probability that students will understand and accept what is communicated if they do not shout, interrogate, criticize, preach, or give commands ("Coaching for Success," 1987; Cotton, 2001; Jones & Jones, 2001).*

> *Let's have an intelligent conversation here:*
> *I'll talk and you listen.*
> **Waterworld**
> American film—1995

A. Teacher: *I hear you. When I am angry or upset, I should wait until I calm down and have my feelings under control before I make comments or give feedback (Neugebauer, 1983).*

In *Positive Discipline in the Classroom*, Nelsen, Lott, and Glenn (1997) described the difference between encouragement and praise. Encouragement inspires and invites students to change for themselves. Praise expresses a favorable judgment and invites students to seek approval from and change for others. According to Haim Ginott (1965), a child therapist and psychologist, evaluative praise invites dependency discourages self-direction and self-control.

> People learn in a supportive environment. That's the nature of human beings. So if you want a child to learn, you have to give them a lot of support and a lot of encouragement. You can't threaten a child . . . into learning. (Hirsch, 2001, para. 11)

Dr. Foster: *"Good boy for raising your hand" is an example of evaluative praise. Instead, "teachers should use expressions of appreciation for effort, improvement, or accomplishment like 'Thank you for raising your hand'" (p. 220).*

A. Teacher: *"Good boy" sounds like something I would say to my dog. I should use adjectives like "good" to describe a behavior, not the student.*

Students who succeed in the classroom want to hear praise. I will need to help them accept and understand how encouragement and supportive feedback are more empowering.

Dr. Foster: *One of your strengths is your ability to come up with an action plan to deal with difficult situations. You recognize how important it is to create a positive and supportive learning environment where students are encouraged and empowered to learn and succeed.*

A. Teacher: *Aren't there times when criticism is needed?*

Dr. Foster: *Although it is best to provide constructive criticism in private, public criticism is acceptable in a nonthreatening learning environment "where 'mistakes' are recognized as opportunities to learn—for you as well as your students" (Brookhart, 2008, p. 59).*

Dr. Foster: *What would you think if a teacher told students they did a good job to help their self-esteem, but most of their answers were wrong?*

A. Teacher: *This would **not** be helpful, positive, or truthful. The students might believe incorrect facts or concepts are correct, think the teacher is stupid not to have noticed, or believe that work of any quality is acceptable (Brookhart, 2008, pp. 34–35).*

> Tone refers to the expressive quality of the feedback message, and it affects how the message will be "heard." The tone of a message is conveyed by word choice and style; these are much more than just linguistic niceties. (Brookhart, 2008, p. 33)

Dr. Foster: *Research suggests that many students would prefer constructive criticism to feedback with an exaggeratedly positive tone. Teachers can establish or eliminate semantic barriers to effective communication by their tone and choice of words.*

Are You Tone Deaf?

Our tone "can override the overt meaning of our words and sour our communication in an instant" (Denton, 2007, pp. 14–15). People who are tone deaf cannot hear differences between tones without training and education. Can you hear the differences between tone and word choice in teacher language? To find out if you **are tone deaf**, do this exercise.

In Practice
Dr. Denton

---

(1) Which of these tones would be respectful and enable a student to stay on task?
(2) Which one would convey a lack of confidence that the student will ever do the right thing?

Tone A: "What should you be doing right now?" asked matter-of-factly.

Tone B: "What should you be doing right now?" asked with a sigh.

Match the tones with these meanings: (3) "I want forgiveness for my mistake," (4) "I'm reminding you to mind your manners," and (5) "You're being rude."

Tone C: "Excuse me," in a warm, matter-of-fact tone.

Tone D: "Exxxx-cuuussse meeee" using a singsong voice drawing out the syllables.

Tone E: "Excuse me!" with emphasis on the second syllable of "excuse."

Teachers "can try on and practice new words, phrases, tones, and pacings to replace any ineffective language patterns" they use (p. 10). In *The Power of Our Words: Teacher Language that Helps Children Learn,* Paula Denton describes a language change process and offers tips that can help teachers learn better language to become better teachers and students, better learners.

A. Teacher: *My mother used to say, "It is not what you say. It is how you say it."*

Dr. Foster: *"Our tone conveys an enormous amount about how we're feeling and what we're truly thinking, perhaps even more than our actual words" (Denton, 2007, p. 14). Be mindful of those students unable to detect tone; they may react inappropriately to what you say.*

> ✓ *Check your answers with these for the In Practice "Are You Tone Deaf?"*
> (1) A   (2) B   (3) C   (4) E   (5) D

A. Teacher: *I was able to choose the right words and tones, and I have the ability to eliminate semantic barriers, maintain a non-threatening learning environment, and address external barriers to teaching and learning. What can I do to eliminate judgments, preconceptions, and prejudices inside me that impede effective communication?*

Dr. Foster: *We might not be able to eliminate these internal barriers, but we can listen to "get a better understanding of why we don't connect with certain individuals and why some persons have trouble connecting with us" (Shafir, 2003, p. 51).*

In *The Zen of Listening: Mindful Communication in the Age of Distraction*, R. Z. Shafir (2003) describes some of the "great walls" (e.g., status, physical appearance, personal agendas, past experiences) that prevent effective communication (see Table 9.6). Walls are easy to identify, but one must apply mindful listening to conquer barriers and reduce their influence (p. 69).

> *Talking to you is like talking to a wall.*
> **Circle of Iron**
> American film—1979

Table 9.6

Great Walls of Communication	How to Begin to Conquer Barriers
Status (e.g., teacher/student, rich/poor, doctor/patient)	Acknowledge that every person has valuable insights and opinions to share by virtue of life experiences
Gender, race, age prejudice, physical appearance	Recognize that there are more able-bodied people with communication handicaps than people with physical handicaps
Negative **past experiences**	Try not to let past experiences contaminate the present
Our **personal agendas**	Sit back and make an effort to listen—when it is time to speak, make a connection between the other person's interests and yours
Negative self-talk	Do not proclaim deficiencies, even silently, as it chips away at self-confidence, increases anxiety, and reduces the ability to focus on the message and the messenger

From *The Zen of Listening: Mindful Communication in the Age of Distraction*
by R. Z. Shafir, 2003, pp. 54, 58, 63, 67

A. Teacher: *We talked about positive self-talk in our session on high expectations. Even though I know that I can face challenges and achieve more through positive self-talk, my instinct is to think that I cannot overcome these great walls.*

To help me handle complex concepts in other sessions, you shared a metaphor. I hope you have one to help me conquer these barriers.

Dr. Foster: *You can improve your ability to actively listen to people you want to connect with if you "get into their movie" (Shafir, 2003).*

Active listening is when you think about what the speaker says to make sure you understand and then provide feedback to clarify what you don't understand ("Interpersonal Communication," n.d.).

The more you concentrate on the speaker's ideas and feelings and get into other people's movies, the more you will notice how much better people respond to you (p. 93). Reflective listening is active listening.

> Good movies have a way of drawing us into the characters' consciousness, values, and lifestyle. We, the audience, empathize with the characters, often to the point of feeling their fear or sadness. We leave the theatre with the thought that our connection with the characters, at least in a small way, has changed our lives. Our mood and our scope of understanding have been altered by forgetting ourselves for a while to view another's perspective. (Shafir, 2003, p. 81)

 How do you feel when someone actively listens to you?

A. Teacher: *I feel like my opinion counts—as if someone cares about me. It also makes me feel important (Shafir, 2003, p. 91). So it is my job to be empathetic and non-evaluative when I listen to my students so they will feel important, confident, respected, and responsible (McLeod, Fisher, & Hoover, 2003, p. 69).*

"For active listening, you must stop thinking your own thoughts and force yourself to listen to what the speaker is saying" ("Interpersonal Communication," n.d., p. 86). This means that the listener must clarify, paraphrase, acknowledge, summarize, and frame what the speaker says ("Interpersonal Communication," n.d.; McLeod et al., 2003).

> *Let your heart guide you. It whispers, so listen carefully.*
> **The Land Before Time**
> American film—1988

A. Teacher: *I could use some clarification of these terms.*

Dr. Foster: *Here are a few examples and a description of these active listening strategies (see Table 9.7).*

Table 9.7

Active Listening Strategies		
Strategy	**Description**	***Examples***
Clarify	Assure the message is fully understood	*Let me see if I understand . . .* *Would you give me an example . . .*
Paraphrase	Use the speaker's words to show the message is understood	*What I think you are saying is . . .* *In other words . . .*
Acknowledge	Show the message is understood and appreciated	*I appreciate that . . .* *I understand that you believe . . .*
Summarize	Briefly restate the main ideas or conclusions	*So we discussed . . .* *We've agreed that . . .*
Frame	Test whether the speaker is open to hearing other ideas	*We seem to agree . . .* *I can see your point . . . but . . .*

From "Interpersonal Communication," n.d. and McLeod et al., 2003

Dr. Foster: *We have discussed much information about feedback. Let's make sure you understand the main ideas.*

 Which active listening strategy do I want you to demonstrate?

A. Teacher: *You asked me to **summarize** the main ideas and conclusions from our conversation about feedback.*

- *The first thing I learned was that judgments are ineffective. Effective feedback "FOR" learning provides data and reflective questions about the task or task process so students can improve and assess their own work.*

- *I learned that I should give feedback in small doses, and the amount and type of feedback given depends on the topic, the next step toward a learning target, and the needs of individual students.*

- *I know that I need to create and maintain a positive, nonthreatening learning environment, choose my words carefully, and use a tone that gives students the best chance to pay attention to, accept, and use the feedback given.*

- *I need to be an active and reflective listener. I must "get into the movies" of my students so they feel respected and connected with me.*

- *Face-to-face feedback has the highest learning payoff, but I need to balance this delivery method with other, more efficient methods.*

- *Finally, I need to be an active listener.*

Dr. Foster: *You do understand. More important, you are consciously aware of the skills you need to practice to maintain effective communication to help your students use feedback to learn and succeed.*

As the ability to communicate clearly and effectively is one of the 21st-century skills for lifelong learning and success in life, students must learn effective sending and receiving skills. According to Trilling and Fadel (2009), students should be able to:

- Articulate thoughts and ideas effectively—use oral, writen, and nonverbal communication skills in several forms and contexts;

- Listen effectively to decipher meaning, knowledge, intentions, values, and attitudes;

- Use communication for a range of purposes (e.g., to inform, instruct, motivate, persuade);

- Utilize multiple media and technologies, and know how to assess their impact as well as judge their effectiveness; and

- Communicate effectively in adverse environments (e.g., multilingual) (p. 55).

A. Teacher: *As students spend so much of their time using technology, face-to-face communication is essential for student learning and success in the 21st century. I need to be an effective communicator and model the interactions and language I want my students to use (p. xxi).*

Dr. Foster: *You have been an active listener throughout this session. Let's take a break before we discuss dialogue.*

> Children learn both verbal and nonverbal communication strategies by imitating parents, teachers, and other significant people in their lives. However, most American parents converse with their children for only about 38 minutes per week. In contrast, teachers might communicate with children for up to seven hours each weekday. (Hansen, 2011, p. 7)

Active Ingredient   🍎 Dialogue

The next active ingredient in the prescription for **Effective Communication** is **dialogue**—from the Greek word dialogos. *Dia* is Greek for "through" and means "between or among" in Latin. In his booklet "On Dialogue," David Bohm says dialogue ("the word between us") broadly refers to speaking, thinking, and reasoning (as cited in van den Heuvel, 1996, para. 1–3). Dictionaries equate "dialogue" with conversation and discussion, but Alexander (2005), Bohm and Peat (2000), Fisher (2009), and others make distinctions among the different kinds of talk—all "exchanges (and series of exchanges) where one individual addresses another individual and the second individual replies" (Littleton & Howe, 2010, p. 1).

📄 **di·a·logue** [dī-ə-lŏg] *n.*

- conversation between two or more people

- an exchange of opinions on a particular subject; discussion

- the lines spoken by characters in a literary or dramatic work

The Collins English Dictionary

How does dialogue compare with other kinds of talk? Robert Fisher (2009) divides talk into five broad categories: telling, questioning, conversation, discussion, and dialogue. In an international study across five countries, Alexander (2005) found that teachers used **discussion** and **dialogue** less frequently than the following kinds of talk:

- **rote**—*drilling* facts, ideas, and routines through constant repetition;

- **recitation**—*questioning* that tests or stimulates recall of what had been taught earlier, or to cue students to work out the answer from clues in the question; and

- **instruction/exposition**—*telling* students what to do, and/or imparting information, and/or explaining facts, principles, or procedures (p. 12).

> The so-called "recitation script" of closed teacher questions, brief recall answers and minimal feedback which requires children to report someone else's thinking rather than to think for themselves . . . is remarkably resistant to efforts to transform it (Alexander, 2005, p. 2). When recitation starts . . . remembering and guessing supplant thinking. (Nystrand, Gamoran, Kachur, & Prendergast, 1997, p. 6)

A. Teacher: *Drilling, questioning, and instructing may not be dialogue, but I think these techniques do play important roles in the classroom.*

Dr. Foster: *"Exposition or lecturing, when well done, can be cognitively challenging and form a basis for thinking . . . dialogue . . . [and] discussion" (Fisher, 2009, p. 6). Questioning can also "scaffold and facilitate genuine dialogue" (p. 7).*

If You Ask Me

When asked whether her teacher was a good teacher, one child replied, "No, because she never tells you what you don't already know."

Another complained, "The teacher does all the talking. She's not interested in what we think."

A third commented, "I dread getting things wrong so I keep quiet." (Fisher, 2009, p. 2)

The ***reality*** is that many teachers do not assess what students
know or ask students for their opinions.

 Look at the distinctive elements among conversation, discussion, and dialogue in this chart (see Table 9.8 on the next page).

Table 9.8

Kinds of Talk		
Conversation "Let's talk"	**Discussion/Debate** "Let's discuss/debate this"	**Dialogue** "Let's think together"
• Is a cooperative exchange of thoughts and ideas when each person takes turns speaking and listening • Seeks equilibrium • Can be about deep matters and human concerns, and is informal, less structured, aimless, carefree, and effortless • Is an important way for human beings to make meaning and relate to others through a casual interplay of ideas with acceptance of what each person says	• Is a teaching strategy • Is a disciplined, systematic exchange characterized by assertions, challenges, and counter-assertions where participants are "mutually responsive" to diverse opinions • Means debate about a topic • Involves the expectation that knowledge and critically informed understanding will come from testing arguments and evidence, analyzing ideas, and exploring values	• Is a learning tool • Is an unpredictable, collaborative exchange where partners engage critically and creatively with each other's ideas and build on these ideas to resolve a problem • Aims at disequilibrium • Involves seeking to reach a common understanding through statements and suggestions offered for joint consideration • Relinquishes teacher control

From Brookfield & Preskill, 1999; Fisher, 2009; and Luxford & Smart, 2009

A. Teacher: *It seems that the distinctive elements among conversation, discussion, debate, and dialogue relate to purpose. To build trust, one or more students and I could have a conversation about something of mutual interest. To get students to think critically about a dilemma or controversial topic, we could have a thoughtful discussion. To solve a problem, one or more people (teachers, students, parents, colleagues, support personnel, administrators) could have a dialogue to build on each other's ideas to reach a common understanding about an action plan.*

Dr. Foster: *Effective teachers need a "repertoire of approaches" to select from based on the fitness for a specific purpose in relation to the learner, the content, and/or the context (Alexander, 2005, p. 11).*

A. Teacher: *Conversation is easier—but we all need to work on our ability to listen, be receptive to different viewpoints, think about what is heard, and give others wait time to think (p. 13).*

> **A. Teacher:** *Would you share some guidelines for thoughtful discussion and dialogue? My students would benefit from learning to think critically and creatively.*

What can teachers do to facilitate and support thoughtful discussion? Teachers should spend just as much time when they plan as when they facilitate a discussion. A thoughtful discussion requires that teachers make sure students are fully informed about the topic, model elements of effective discussion, assign different roles, determining appropriate questions and problems, vary group size, and keep student and teacher talk in balance as much as possible (Brookfield & Preskill, 1999).

> **A. Teacher:** *I realize what I thought was discussion was only a closed question and answer session in which my students remembered or guessed. They did not have to think.*
>
> *Thoughtful discussion seems complicated. How do you suggest I get started?*

> **Dr. Foster:** *Let me remind you that lecturing, "when done well, can form a basis for thinking, dialogue, and discussion (Fisher, 2009; Shor & Friere, 1987).*
>
> *Do you remember the retention percentages for lecture and discussion?*

> **A. Teacher:** *I remember that the retention rate for discussion is 50% after 24 hours and 5% for lecture. If teachers actively engage students throughout a lecture, they will retain more. (See page 52.)*

Three of Jane Vella's 12 principles and practices to begin, maintain, and nurture dialogue are consistent with the prerequisites for thoughtful discussion outlined by Brookfield and Preskill in their book *Discussion as a Way of Teaching*. Two of these principles include **teamwork** and **engagement** of the learners in learning the content (Vella, 2002). Teachers can use these practices to nurture dialogue and thoughtful discussion through engagement and teamwork.

- Pose questions at the beginning to frame the talk

- End with a series of teacher or student generated unanswered questions

- Introduce deliberate one minute periods of reflective silence every 20 minutes

- Provide other deliberate perspectives (e.g., assertions, counter-assertions)

- Identify personal assumptions, subject them to critical scrutiny, and share how they might be investigated

- Have students participate in *buzz groups* made up of three or four students who discuss an issue that arises or questions that require judgments about the relative merit, relevance, or usefulness of the information presented (Brookfield & Preskill, 1999). (Read "What's All the Buzz About?" on page 312 for more information about buzz groups.)

Vella's third principle is to establish **clear roles** and **role development**. Teachers should assign different conversational roles so students can see that expressing a point of view is one way to add to a discussion. Alternate roles give tentative students opportunities to speak and keep talkative students from dominating the discussion (Brookfield & Preskill, 1999). (Read "Select a Cast of Characters" for examples of conversational roles.)

Select a Cast of Characters

The actors in a play or the people in a story or an event make up the cast of characters. Brookfield and Preskill (1999) recommend that teachers **select a cast of characters** for class discussions (pp. 115–116). The roles that students play help them hone their listening and discussion skills.

Discussion—The Event

Cast of Characters

*Narrator: This character introduces the topic of conversation and draws on personal ideas and experiences as a way to help others get into the conversation about the problem, dilemma, or theme.

Reflective analyst: This character keeps a record of the conversation's development and gives a summary every 20 minutes or so that focuses on shared concerns, issues the group avoids, and emerging common themes.

*Protagonist: This character listens for helpful tips, resources, and suggestions that the other characters have voiced as they discuss how to work through a problem or situation. The protagonist keeps a record of the ideas and reads the record before the event ends.

*Antagonist: This character listens carefully for any emerging consensus and then formulates and expresses a contrary view. This keeps groupthink in check and helps participants explore a range of alterative interpretations.

Detective: This character listens attentively for unacknowledged, unchecked, and unchallenged biases for culture, race, class, or gender that emerge in conversation and brings them to the groups' attention.

Theme spotter: This character identifies themes left unexplored that might form a focus for the next event.

*Referee: This character listens for judgmental comments that may be offensive, insulting, and demeaning and that contradict ground rules for respectful conversation generated by group members.

These *characters were renamed, but retain the original characters' roles' in the discussion.

When teachers **select a cast of characters** and assign different roles, students become more tolerant of other viewpoints and better able to articulate assertions and counter-assertions. Learn more techniques, suggestions, and applications in *Discussion as a Way of Teaching* by Brookfield & Preskill (1999).

A. Teacher: *I can better support thoughtful discussions in my classroom if I assign different roles and model elements of effective discussion.*

You mentioned the use of different group sizes as well as appropriate questions and problems. I apply what I have already learned about Quality Grouping, higher-order thinking questions, and problem-based learning.

Dr. Foster: *They do apply. Remember to use* **Supplement A: Quality Grouping** *to determine the composition of discussion groups. (Select* **Supplements***, then* **A–F** *at www.classroommanagementblues.com to locate* **Supplement A***.)*

You may also want to consider buzz groups. Read to find out "What's All the Buzz About?"

What's All the Buzz About?

Brookfield and Preskill (1999) recommend that teachers use *structured* **buzz** groups to change the pace and format of discussions. **What's all the buzz about?**

Students have about 20 minutes to answer as many questions as they can about the reading or lecture and record their answers in writing. Groups could have the option to explore a theme of mutual interest for the reading or lecture.

According to Bruffee (1993), teachers should make assignments short and manageable, have students analyze a text, limit assignments to a couple of pages or just one paragraph, and provide genuinely puzzling questions with many possible answers. Students back up responses by referring to specific examples from the text or their experience (Brookfield and Preskill, 1999).

The way students report to the large group can take many forms. Students can share one or two insights, summarize the themes explored, address a challenging question that emerged, or offer frequent themes and concepts (p. 107–108).

Whole class discussions can be stimulating and productive for short periods of time. "Even if discussion gets off to a good start in a large group, it makes sense eventually to divide students into small groups" (p. 104). Brookfield and Preskill (1999) say that large group discussions

- Inhibit the participation of some individuals, allowing the most socially confident and aggressive to dominate;
- Perpetuate the inequalities of class, race, and gender that exist in the larger society; and
- Lead to tedium and a reluctance to speak up about issues that may include self-disclosure (p. 104).

Dr. Foster: *Problem-based learning and many higher-order thinking questions can effectively perpetuate discussion in large and small groups. Teachers might ask students to synthesize, hypothesize, or consider cause-and-effect (Brookfield & Preskill, 1999). (Select* **Supplements** *at www.classroommanagementblues.com, then* **A–F** *and find* ☐ **Supplement D: HOT Questions Starters.***)*

☐ **Supplement X: Discussion and Dialogue Prompts** *has questions and other prompts that will help you sustain momentum during thoughtful discussions and dialogues. Some of the questions might ask students to support their answer, give more evidence, clarify their response, or link to another response or question (Brookfield & Preskill, 1999; Elkind & Sweet, 1997). (Select* **Supplements** *at www.classroommanagementblues.com, then* **W–Z** *for* **Supplement X.***)*

A. Teacher: *I will be able to facilitate and support more thoughtful discussions and creative dialogue if I use different problems, questions, prompts, and groups. This may require more time to plan, but my students and I will be more engaged in the learning process.*

Mind Your P's and Q's

The question: What are the important tools we need to support in a 21st-century approach to learning and teaching? **The answer**: good teachers, the Internet, cell phones, educational games, tests, and quizzes, educational funding, and loving parents (Trilling & Fadel, 2009, p. 89). But **mind your p's and q's** because problems and questions are even more important!

p's *Problems* and the invention of their possible solutions

q's *Questions* and the process to uncover their answers

The ***reality*** is that the most powerful learning tools ever devised are questions and problems. "The learning power of the right question at the right time has been celebrated through recorded history . . . [by] philosophers, [and] education theorists [who] have placed questioning and inquiry at the heart of learning and understanding" (p. 90). Throughout time, passionate and tireless persistence to find solutions to perplexing problems has been the motivator for "tool making, invention, religion, laws, science, engineering, business, and the evolution of virtually all our modern technologies and societal institutions" (pp. 90–91). Learn more by reading Trilling and Fadel's *21st Century Skills: Learning for Life in Our Times.*

Dr. Foster: *In a discussion about "an issue involving right and wrong, it is important to guide the students to the right conclusions rather than allowing them to think that whatever they conclude is okay. The art is in asking questions that help them arrive at the right conclusions on their own" (Elkind & Sweet, 1997, para. 19).*

Treasure Hunt

A father confides in his lazy sons that he buried a treasure in the field. The sons dig through the entire field but find nothing. When they have almost given up and concluded that their father has lied to them and that there was no treasure, it occurs to them that because they have already dug through the field, they might as well plant something. That is what they do. They sell the produce and earn a fortune. Finally, they understood their father's message: there truly was a treasure buried in the field.

If the father had set working the field as the immediate goal for them, they would never have made the fortune, because the fortune could only arise as a by-product of their efforts. And their understanding that there is a treasure in the field is the result of the process they were engaged in (Simenc, 2008, p. 328).

Excerpted from "The Status of the Subject in the Classroom Community
of Inquiry by M. Simenc, 2008

The *reality* is that it is not possible to teach children values in a direct manner. To simply explain a certain value and ask them to accept it will not assure they will act on it.

Dr. Foster: *"Both discussion and dialogue facilitate exploratory talk, where partners engage critically and creatively with each other's ideas. . . . Dialogue is creative because it is about improving and making connections between ideas and concepts that you have not thought of connecting before" (Fisher, 2009, p. 9).*

A. Teacher: *This is what I have experienced through my dialogues with you in each of our sessions. I want to learn more to help my students learn through creative dialogue. What do you recommend?*

How do teachers promote and support creative dialogue? According to Alexander (2006), Hattie (2008), and Fisher (2009), dialogues may inhibit cognition and learning and be limited, repetitive, or dull. When dialogues are open-ended, stimulate new ideas, and allow for different opinions (i.e., critical viewpoints), they have the power to enable cognition and learning. In *Creative Dialogue: Talk for Thinking in the Classroom*, Fisher (2009) lists some behaviors associated with creative dialogue that are not attributable to traditional student teacher interactions. To promote creative dialogue, teachers should have a shared agenda, engage in cooperative enquiry, and encourage children to ask questions. When dialogue is imaginative, exploratory, reflective, and persuasive, it becomes more creative (p. 11).

Wear More Than One Hat

To facilitate cognition and creative thinking, dialogues must allow for different viewpoints and stimulate new ideas. Edward de Bono, a medical doctor, developed the six hat thinking system in which people wear a metaphorical hat when they discuss or dialogue about a topic. He says everyone can do creative thinking. "Just as the ability to use the reverse shift is part of every driver's driving ability, the ability to use creative thinking should be part of every thinker's thinking skill" (1995, p. 14).

Six Hat Thinking System

White Hat	**Information** Be factual.	I know . . .	• Cover information, facts, and figures • Define information needs and gaps • Ask questions
Red Hat	**Feelings** Be emotional.	I feel . . . Others may feel . . .	• Introduce feelings and emotions usually supported by logic • Provide an intuition without
Black Hat	**Weaknesses** Be logical negative.	It's not . . .	• Make logical judgment statements and provide cautions • Point out why a suggestion does not fit the facts, the available experience, the system in use or the policy to be followed
Yellow Hat	**Strengths** Be logical positive.	It's good . . .	• Find reasons why something will work and why it will be beneficial • Look forward to the results • Find something of value in what happened
Green Hat	**New Ideas** Be creative.	It's possible . . .	• Offer other options, proposals, provocations, and changes • Propose something interesting
Blue Hat	**Thinking About Thinking** Be metacognitive.	We could think . . .	• Provide an overview • Discuss the process • Look at the thinking about the subject

From "Exploring Patterns of Thought . . . Serious Creativity" by E. de Bono, 1995, pp. 12–18

Individuals may make statements under the protection of the hat they have. They may also ask someone to switch hats to say something using a different hat or to make someone change their thinking. "An individual can ask a whole group to adopt a hat for a limited period of time" (e.g., "What we need is three minutes of green hat thinking") (p. 15).

Creative thinking is not limited to artists, designers, and inventors (p. 14). Inspire students to **wear more than one hat** when they dialogue with one another.

Students can be encouraged to develop dispositions that support creative dialogue and thinking if teachers model them in their teaching. Brookfield and Preskill (1999) identify appreciation, mindfulness, hospitality, deliberation, mutuality, and humility as dispositions that create a safe learning environment, promote democratic processes, and foster mutual growth (pp. 9–16). (See Table 9.9.)

> From Socrates to Dewey and Habermas, educative dialogue has represented a forum for learners to develop understanding by listening, reflecting, proposing, and incorporating alternative views. For many philosophers, learning through discussion has also represented the promise of education as a foundation for democracy. (Michaels, O'Connor, & Resnick, 2008, p. 283).

Table 9.9

Dispositions FOR Creative Dialogue and Thinking in the Classroom

Hospitality	the willingness to encourage others to participate, take risks, and show strongly held opinions
Mindfulness	the willingness to listen and focus attention on others' words
Humility	the willingness to admit errors in judgment and the limitations of one's knowledge and experience
Deliberation	the willingness to offer arguments and counterarguments supported by evidence, data, and logic
Appreciation	the willingness to let others know their comments, insights, and observations are respected
Mutuality	the willingness to devote oneself to the learning of others as much as one's own learning

Shift into Reverse

A creative person can drive creative dialogue if he or she will **shift into reverse** and "consider the opposite of what has been thought, said, or done before. Some of our ideas may be wrong and sometimes the reverse of what we think might be true" (Fisher, 2009, p. 55). To discover new solutions to a problem or strategies to resolve a situation, people can look at a problem or situation in a different way.

In Practice

Robert Fisher

Students can look at a problem or situation from another angle if they turn it "around, inside out, backwards, or upside-down" (p. 55). For example, you might ask: "What can I do to make _____ better?" Reverse this and ask, "What can I do to make _____ worse?" The rearrangement of information can inspire new ideas.

For more ideas to drive creative dialogue, read Dr. Robert Fisher's book *Creative Dialogue: Talk for Thinking in the Classroom.*

When teachers teach dialogic skills through dialogue, they also teach about dialogue (Fisher, 2009). Dialogic skills include the ability to listen actively, ask better questions, challenge positively, and use technology for learning to solve problems, build on and extend ideas, and collaborate with others to reach agreement (Fisher, 2009; Luxford & Smart, 2009). Many resources support the development of these skills to promote democratic processes and foster mutual growth. (Select **Resources** at *www.classroommanagementblues.com*, then **Communication** and **Dialogue**.)

A. Teacher: *We have already dialogued about how to listen actively and ask better questions. When it comes to challenging positively, I think students would "be confident in expressing and justifying their own viewpoints and in challenging the viewpoints and listening to the justifications of others" (Luxford & Smart, 2009, p. 49) in a safe learning environment where everyone is mindful, hospitable, and respectful of the comments and insights of others.*

Dr. Foster: *Why do you think positive challenges in a safe environment would extend understanding?*

A. Teacher: *If the environment is not safe, students will not challenge and reject views in a constructive way or justify their own views. Dialogue extends understanding. So if ideas are accepted without challenge, there would only be a series of monologues (Barnes & Todd, 1995).*

Dr. Foster: *What would happen if students master the skill of positive challenge and transfer it beyond the classroom?*

A. Teacher: *You have taught me about dialogic skills through dialogue. That is why you ask "positive challenge" questions.*

I am up to the challenge! Here is my answer.

If students master the skill of positive challenge, the environment beyond the classroom may not be safe for them to transfer the skill. "Not all adults are comfortable with children who challenge albeit positively" (Luxford & Smart, 2009, p. 50).

Without the questions, I would have just accepted that this skill would have a positive effect on student learning. Now I understand that I must help my students understand when it is appropriate and safe to use this skill with adults and other children beyond the classroom.

Dr. Foster: *Learning through dialogue can be risky, and like the phrase "no pain, no gain," a teacher must be willing to tolerate disequilibrium, difficulties, and some discomfort to achieve worthwhile goals. Confidence and the ability to negotiate these and other challenges will increase for you and your students with practice. When creative dialogue "works there will be a forward movement, sometimes in odd directions and with unexpected outcomes" (Fisher, 2009, p. 200).*

Students Say the Funniest Things

Teacher: *Why are you late, Frank?*

Frank: *Because of the sign.*

Teacher: *What sign?*

Frank: *The one that says, "School Ahead, Go slow."*

Teacher: *Donald, what is the chemical formula for water?*

Donald: *H I J K L M N O!!*

Teacher: *What are you talking about?*

Donald: *Yesterday you said it's H to O!*

Teacher: *Harold, what do you call a person who keeps on talking when people are no longer interested?*

Harold: *A teacher!*

Retrieved from http://www.lotsofjokes.com/classroom_dialogue.asp

For dialogue and other forms of communication to work, "students must take their knowledge and express it in a variety of clear and effective formats to fit the demands of the situation and of society" (Lemov, 2010, p. 47). Research shows that children exchange few words (less than six) during group talk and seldom extend the ideas of other children (Fisher, 2009; Luxford & Smart, 2009). In our high-tech "world beset by problems and strife caused by the failure of communication there can be no task more important than teaching children how to . . . think, talk, and listen" (Fisher, 2009, pp. 195, 200).

> *What we've got here is a failure to communicate.*
>
> **Cool Hand Luke**
> American Film—1967

A. Teacher: *Earlier you said the use of technology is dialogic. Isn't using technology replacing dialogic interactions with teachers, parents, and even peers?*

Dr. Foster: *Children are "dialogue-deprived" and should be required to use proficient grammar and complete sentences when they discuss, make requests, and answer questions (Fisher, p. 195). Read "Knock! Knock!" to see how this can be done to help students become more proficient in the use of grammar and complete sentences.*

Knock! Knock!

Who's there?

Scholar.

Scholar who?

A scholar who can use a complete sentence

In Practice
Doug Lemov

He is not joking! Doug Lemov, author of *Teach Like a Champion: 49 Techniques that Put Students on the Path to College*, stresses how important it is for students to use complete sentences to enter college, write papers once there, and interview with potential employers after graduation. "The complete sentence is the battering ram that knocks down the door to college" (2010, p. 47). He offers several methods to help students build complete sentences when they answer with a fragment or one word.

One method is to provide the first words of a complete sentence (p. 48).

Teacher:	James, how many tickets are there.
James:	Six.
Teacher:	There are . . .
James:	There are six tickets in the basket.

Another method is to remind students before or after an answer (p. 49).

Teacher:	Who can tell me in a complete sentence what the setting of the story is?
Student:	Los Angeles in 2013
Teacher:	Complete sentence.
Student:	The setting is the city of Los Angeles in the year 2013.

Knock! Knock!   *Who's there?*

Teachers.   *Teachers who?*

Teachers who "strive to give students the maximum amount of practice building complete sentences" (p. 48)

Learn more techniques in Doug Lemov's *Teach Like a Champion: 49 Techniques that Put Students on the Path to College*

Dr. Foster: *Rather than use computers to run educational software, explore the Internet for useful data, or compose better homework assignments, students play games and chat online with friends—activities that do not have a positive effect on educational performance. Research shows a correlation between high educational performance and moderate computer use. Poor performance is associated with frequent and little computer use (Fisher, 2009, p. 195).*

A. Teacher: *I agree that frequent computer use leaves little or no time for students to read books, dialogue with parents and peers, and interact socially in other ways. As a parent and teacher, I know very little about how to help children navigate the cyber-culture.*

Dr. Foster:  *With a shift toward the impersonal use of technology, how can teachers use technology to further dialogic learning?*

A. Teacher: *I do not know where to begin.*

Dr. Foster: *Let me get you started. You could have students record the first writing draft or learning activity to discuss with a partner, response group, or class (Fisher, p. 196).*

A. Teacher: *I like that idea. I could also have my students use the digital video cam to record a dialogue and use it to reflect on or evaluate the process as well as the content, like Fisher suggests.*

*I was able to **build on and extend the idea** about the use of technology FOR learning. My students need to learn this dialogic skill.*

As the world becomes more dependent on technology, we need to "make dialogue and human relationships a top priority at home and at school" (p. 196).

Dr. Foster: *A teacher's ability to sustain positive human relationships is dependent on effective communication and the ability to dialogue and collaborate with others. Collaboration, a 21st-century skill, does not happen in isolation; it requires dialogue.*

> When we do not use dialogue and instead ask learners to be passive, they do indeed learn. They learn how to be passive. . . . They learn that they have no power, except to obey. (Vella, 2002, p. 25)

Active Ingredient   🍎 Collaboration

The ability to collaborate with others is a dialogic skill expected of professionals in the 21st century. According to Marilyn Friend (2007), **collaboration**, the fourth active ingredient in the **Effective Communication Prescription**, refers to the style or approach to interactions among individuals who plan and solve problems together in a supportive and mutually beneficial relationship ("Stepping Stones," 2007).

What is the difference between collaboration and cooperation? Collaboration is "More Than 'Making Nice'" (Pappano, 2007). When people successfully combine their efforts to help each other, they create something greater than the sum of their individual energies (Brookfield & Preskill, 1999). Friend (2007), Trilling and Fadel (2009), and Kozar (2010) agree that collaboration has the following characteristics:

> *The fact is what we're doing could be construed as . . . collaboration with the enemy. . . . Must we build them a better bridge than they could have built for themselves?*
>
> **The Bridge on the River Kwai**
> British film—1957

- *Interactions* between at least two co-equal parties are **voluntary**.

- At least one common *problem, goal, or need* is of **mutual** importance.

- *Parties* **share** *responsibility* to make decisions, complete tasks associated with a collaborative activity, and actively engage in the synthesis of information through dialogue in which participants strive to compromise, accommodate, negotiate, and support each other's opinions, needs, talents, ideas, and solutions.

- **Parity** is present in decision making. Individual *contributions* are equally valued.

- Each party **shares** *material and human resources*.

- Everyone **shares** *accountability* for successes and failures.

Dr. Foster: *As it is difficult for every characteristic to be evidenced all the time when people plan and solve problems together, true collaboration is rare (Brookfield & Preskill, 1999; Pappano, 2007).*

A. Teacher: *It is probably rare because people like me do not know what it means!*

*Is an activity **voluntary** if it is required? In September, our principal required us to collaborate. We had to "jointly write new curricula and document collaboration in logs turned into her every two weeks. Each log entry included an outline of topics for teachers to talk about, with room to summarize the discussion. Topics to be covered included goals and objectives for the week or unit, common assessments and individual teacher assessments used, instructional strategies, and lesson design, as well as adjustments to instruction from a shared evaluation of assessment results" (Pappano, 2007, p. 2).*

Dr. Foster: *People may be required to collaborate, but the interactions among the participants are **voluntary**. You probably know people who attend meetings and pretend to be team players, but they choose to not cooperate or collaborate.*

A. Teacher: *It is like the idiom, "You can lead a horse to water, but you can't make it drink." People have the opportunity to do something, but you cannot force them to do it if they do not want to.*

Dr. Foster: *To get everyone to choose to collaborate willingly, people must find at least one problem, goal, or need of **mutual** importance. It has to be specific and important enough to maintain **shared** attention and commitment (Friend & Cook, 1992, p. 7).*

A. Teacher: *I think everyone would agree to spend time, energy, and other **human resources** on students and student learning.*

Dr. Foster: *To remain focused on student learning is a **common** goal and **shared** responsibility for teachers, students, families, and other school professionals (Pappano, 2007).*

A. Teacher: *I have been on lots of committees where we start out focused on student learning but in the end, we make decisions less effective for students' learning and more convenient for the teachers.*

Dr. Foster: *Could you give me an example?*

A. Teacher: *The principal in my school requires us teachers to adjust instruction based on **shared** evaluation of assessment results. Research shows that when teachers adjust instruction based on assessment data student learning improves, but some teachers do not want to document or share assessment results with other teachers. Many do not want to share **materials or human resources**. Still others do not want to share responsibility for the **success or failure** of a collaborative activity.*

I get frustrated when I try to collaborate with teachers who put their own self-interest above the common good. What do you recommend?

Dr. Foster: *After we clarify the key characteristics of collaboration, I will share guidelines to help students, colleagues, and families improve their ability to collaborate. Select the **Resources** page, then **Communication and Collaboration** at www.classroomman agementblues.com for books, articles, and other resources to improve collaboration in your classroom and school.*

> **Lloyd:** *Nobody thought we could do this. Nobody thinks it'll work, do they?*
>
> **Diane:** *No. But you just described every great success story.*
>
> **Say Anything . . .**
> American film—1989

A. Teacher: *I am unfamiliar with the term **parity**.*

Dr. Foster: ***Parity** means "equality in value or standing" (Dictionary.com Unabridged). When people engage in a collaborative activity, each person's contributions may not be the same as those of other team members, but they are equally valued.*

A. Teacher: *Then the "p-a-r" in **par**tners would represent people in relationships where each person has **parity**! In a collaborative relationship, the contributions of each partner would be valued equally.*

Smooth Sailing in Partnerships

Walther-Thomas, Korinek, McLaughlin, and Williams (2000) developed *Stepping Stones to Success II Collaboration: Working Together for All Students* for the Virginia Department of Education. The collaborators on this document remind teachers that good partners:

P lan together routinely

A ddress classroom concerns proactively

R eceive ongoing administrative support

T hrive on challenges

N urture a sense of community

E valuate student performance

R eflect on practice and strive for improvement

S upport each other

To develop successful partnerships, Michael Massey of the Royal Institute of International Affairs offers tips that were prepared in collaboration with participants at the SEED 2007 Annual Partnerships Forum and Practitioners' Workshop in South Africa.

- Develop a realistic and achievable mission and shared purpose
- Have patience—it takes time to clarify goals, build trust and respect, set and manage expectations, and understand the interests of each partner
- Be flexible and prepared for change
- Communicate effectively
- Set priorities for activities and establish roles and responsibilities
- Share decision making and evaluate performance regularly
- Address shortcomings and handle conflicts constructively

There may be some rough seas, but **smooth sailing in partnerships** is possible when people learn to work in collaboration with one another.

Dr. Foster: *Partners value the contributions of each person equally. Partners in a collaborative relationship have **equal power**, or standing, in the decision making as they "work together on a specific collaborative activity even though they do not have parity in other situations" (Friend & Cook, 1992, p. 6).*

If you say to one flower, "Grow," but you water another, the first one won't grow. If you say, "Let's work as a team," but then think independently and authoritatively and make a lot of unilateral, arbitrary decisions, you won't build a team. (Covey, 2004, p. 248)

A. Teacher: *Can people work on par with a supervisor or someone who has power over them? Teachers might not voice their opinions in a meeting with a principal if they believe there could be negative consequences. A parent might remain silent in a parent-teacher conference if he or she believes there could be ramifications for their child. Fear of repercussions is another reason I think true collaboration is rare. People do not trust each other.*

We talked about how to build trust in our session on high expectations. I am confident in my ability to build trust with my students and their families to improve our chances to collaboratively achieve goals and solve problems. Many of the same techniques might help me work with some teachers but be more challenging with others.

Dr. Foster: *Trust is one of the keys that opens the door to collaboration; another key is respect. "Only after a period of time in which trust, and subsequently respect, are established can school professionals [as well as parents, and students] feel relatively secure in fully exploring collaborative relationships" (Friend & Cook, 1992, p. 9).*

A. Teacher: *As creative dialogue and true collaboration both need a safe environment; the strategies for one would work for the other. How do you suggest I begin?*

Dr. Foster: *Use the strategies found in* 📁 **Supplement Y: Conference Guidelines and Protocols** *to create a safe environment for dialogue and collaboration. (Select* **Supplements** *at http://www.classroommanagementblues.com, then* **W–Z** *and find* **Supplement Y**.*) Think of collaboration as a dance. As the interactions among partners must be voluntary, supportive, and mutually beneficial,* ***invite*** *colleagues, other school professionals, parents, and students to dance, or collaborate, with you.*

Shall We Dance?
American film—2004

John: *To dance you need a partner. My partner is right here. . . .*

Beverly: *I don't know how.*

John: *Yea, you do . . .*

Beverly: *I don't know the steps.*

John: *I'll teach you.*

The ***reality*** is that **parents** may find it hard to talk with someone at school because they did not feel safe at school when they were a student or they may not want hear about their child's grades or behavior.

Shall We Dance?
American film—2004

The *reality* is that "despite compelling evidence indicating that working collaboratively represents best practice, **teachers** in many schools continue to work in isolation. Even in schools that endorse the idea of collaboration, the staff's willingness to collaborate often stops at the classroom door" (DuFour, 2004, p. 9).

The *reality* is that "we grade our **students** based on their individual effort and results, so when we ask learners to work in groups, it may contradict the structure they are used to and become a major challenge, both emotionally and cognitively" (Kozar, 2010, p. 17).

The *reality* is that students, families, and other teachers will accept the invitation to collaborate if they feel safe and valued as equal partners. Teachers who know the steps can take the lead.

I could dance with you until the cows come home.
On second thought, I'd rather dance with the cows
until you come home.

Duck Soup
American film—1933

A. Teacher: *You make it sound like everyone will want to collaborate with me if I follow the guidelines and protocols for collaborative conferences or meetings. I can't believe there won't be conflict.*

Dr. Foster: *Challenges, complacency, and conflict often happen when people work together. Some people even become defiant.*

When teachers plan and solve problems together, how can they address conflict and other challenges? To prevent complacency and maintain commitment, educators should review and discuss the benefits, successes, lessons learned, progress toward goals and objectives, and specific reasons for the collaborative activity regularly at conferences or team meetings (Cohen, 2005). As no formal hierarchies exist between collaborating partners, there is the potential for conflict. To resolve conflict, the key is "to get the issue out on the table so that it is visible" (p. 46). This way it does not become more difficult to resolve.

A defining dimension of collaboration that captures both the potential dynamism and frustration implicit in collaborative endeavors is the reality that partners share a dual identity: They maintain their own distinct identities and organizational authority separate from a collective identity. This reality creates an intrinsic tension between *organizational self-interest* . . . and a *collective interest*. (Thomson, Perry, & Miller, 2007, p. 4)

Friend and Cook (1992) suggest that for teams to resolve conflict they must negotiate professionally, communicate effectively, and problem-solve collaboratively. Covey (2004) also recommends collaborative problem solving; he calls it a search for the Third Alternative. "The Third Alternative isn't my way, it isn't your way—it's better than a compromise . . . [it's] the middle way—a higher middle position that is better than either of the other two ways, like the tip of a triangle" (p. 187).

A. Teacher: *The idea of the Third Alternative sounds good in theory, but not everyone interacts collaboratively when it comes to conflict.*

Dr. Foster: *Everyone has one or more preferred conflict management styles—each has strengths and weaknesses. Here is a description of the styles identified by Thomas-Kilmann (1974) and situations in which each would be most appropriate.*

Table 9.10

Conflict Management Styles	
Competitive	Force— use power when decisions must be made quickly and a person is perceived to have more responsibility than others to make decisions
Avoidance	Withdraw— ignore temporarily when there is not enough time to address the conflict or when it is extremely serious or emotionally laden
Accommodating	Smooth— set aside personal needs when the conflict issue is relatively unimportant or it will resolve the conflict quickly (inappropriate for those who feel powerless or taken advantage of)
Compromising	Share— give and take when there is limited time to manage the conflict or with competitive individuals (may lead to more conflict)
Collaborative	Problem-solve—when there is ample time and the other defining characteristics like trust and commitment are present

From "Cultivating Collaborative Cultures," n.d.; Friend & Cook, 1992; and Thomas & Kilmann, 1974

Dr. Foster: *You need to know your preferred conflict management style or styles and recognize the styles of those with whom you work. To determine these styles, use the Thomas-Kilmann Conflict Mode Instrument. You may purchase the instrument or find it in the book **Interactions: Collaboration Skills for School Professionals**. To download the instrument online, select the **Resources** page at www.class roommanagementblues.com, then **Communication** and **Collaboration**.*

A. Teacher: *I would rather compromise or use collaborative problem solving to work through a conflict than battle over it, withdraw, or give in!*

Dr. Foster: *How you respond will set the tone for conflict resolution. Use the ground rules to initiate collaborative problem solving in ▢ **Supplement Y: Conference Guidelines and Protocols** when you work with other teachers and conference with students and their parents or caregivers. (Select **Supplements** at www.classroom managementblues.com, then **W–Z** for **Supplement Y**.)*

Dr. Foster: *In which classroom situations will you and your students work in collaboration with one another?*

A. Teacher: *My students and I will collaborate when we create our class mission and vision statements (page 223), establish rules (page 224), and determine rewards and individual consequences (page 238). I will also provide opportunities for my students to collaborate in class meetings (page 103) and quality groups (page 53).*

Dr. Foster: *What do you need to do for these collaborative activities to be successful?*

A. Teacher: *I must communicate effectively, build trusting relationships, and model collaborative interactions. When we participate in these activities, my students will learn the same skills needed to work with others to achieve goals and solve problems, no matter the profession they choose in the future.*

Dr. Foster: *In any profession, it is not about mindless precedent ("This is how I have always done it") or personal preference ("This is how I like to do it") (DuFour, 2011, p. 59). It is about "How can we do it?"*

With the shift from a "document-focused work style to a people-focused work style" in the 21st-century workplace, collaboration and communication skills are just as important as academic skills ("Building Strong Team," n.d., para. 4). The expectation is for professionals to communicate clearly and work interdependently to achieve common goals and solve problems (Trilling & Fadel, 2009).

Communication is one of the basic competencies of teachers and other professionals. "Indicators of communication competence are: interaction involvement, conflict resolution style, and team-work attitudes" (Bjekic & Zlatić, 2006, p. 164).

*This leads us to a discussion of professionalism, the last **active ingredient** in the* **Effective Communication Prescription**.

Active Ingredient	Professionalism

Professionalism, the last active ingredient in the **Effective Communication Prescription**, can foster trust and respect, increase student learning, and reduce behavior problems. According to Sprick, Garrison, and Howard (1998), "Effective teachers understand that it is important for them to behave in a way that communicates their professionalism" (p. 25). The National Education Association expects teachers to fulfill their commitment to students and the profession.

pro·fes·sion·al·ism *n.*
[prə-fĕsh′ ə-nə-lĭz′ əm]

The conduct, aims, or qualities that characterize a profession or a professional person

Merriam-Webster

To achieve these commitments, Sprick, Garrison, and Howard (1998) urge teachers to demonstrate professionalism at all times and maintain a vision of themselves as professionals. Teachers are considered professional, when they

- Engage in ongoing professional development and reflect on teaching practices,

- Respect the confidentiality of students and colleagues,

- Actively solve problems,

- Work collaboratively with colleagues,

- Act in a professional manner, and

- Present a professional appearance (pp. 25–28).

> It can be argued late into the night as to whether teaching is a profession or not. We maintain that it is, but only for teachers who perform as professionals. (Wong & Wong, 1998, p. 293)

In the 2009 *Phi Delta Kappa/Gallup Poll*, Americans responded to questions about the personal qualities they would look for in a teacher, if experience and training were similar. They ranked professionalism and enthusiasm #1 (Bushaw & McNee, 2009, p. 15).

Dr. Foster: *You have evidenced professionalism in these professional development sessions with me. You have learned how to communicate enthusiasm (see page 288), be a problem solver (see page 113), collaborate with others (see page 321), and reflect on teaching practices (see page 191). We will wrap up this session with a discussion of personal appearance, professional conduct, and confidentiality.*

A. Teacher: *I question the connection between my personal appearance and professionalism, but I want to hear what you have to say about professional conduct and confidentiality.*

> *Oh, you are something special, you are something special . . .*
> *THANK YOU!*
> *Ah, it's your professionalism that I respect.*
>
> **Little Shop of Horrors**
> American film—1986

What are the legal issues related to the confidentiality of information about students and colleagues? The Family Educational Rights and Privacy Act (FERPA) is a federal law that protects the privacy of student educational records and assures parents and eligible students the right to access records (see Table 9.11). Only school personnel with a "legitimate educational interest" have permission to view student records and information from discipline records without prior parental or eligible student consent. Legitimate educational interest requires that the information pose a "significant risk to the safety or well-being of that student, other students, or other members of the school community" ("Confidentiality Issues," 2010, para. 1).

Table 9.11

Legal Terms Related to FERPA and Confidentiality

Directory information	Information not considered harmful or an invasion of privacy that may be released without consent (i.e., student's name, participation in sports, dates of attendance is permitted—a social security number; ethnicity, race, and/or nationality; gender are not. *Note:* Parents/eligible students must receive notice, and may request a privacy restriction.
Educational records	Records maintained by an institution (or by any party acting for the institution directly related to a student) that includes information in any medium (i.e., handwriting, print, audio and video tapes, film, e-mail); admissions and biographical information; grades, test scores, papers, schedules, recorded communications, disciplinary records, financial records, and so on. *Note:* Institutions may release records if they remove all personally identifiable information. Sharing personal notes with another person or placing them in an area where others may view them makes personal notes educational records. The use of e-mails and faxes does not guarantee confidentiality.
Eligible student	A student 18 years old or attending a school beyond high school
Legitimate educational interest	Requirement to obtain access to educational records—paper or electronic. *Note:* Institutions must use "reasonable methods" to assure only teachers and other school officials (e.g., outside service providers) who "need to know" have permission to education records. Curiosity is not a legitimate educational interest.

From "FERPA Information," n.d.; "Section-by-Section Analysis," 2008; and Van Dusen, 2004

A. Teacher: *To fulfill my professional commitment to students, I must respect and uphold the dignity and work of students, maintain the confidentiality of information about students, and communicate information only when prescribed by federal or state law ("Regulations," 2010, para. 5).*

I have heard my colleagues talk about students in the hallway and teachers' lounge. According to FERPA, teachers should not use personally identifiable information about the student when they talk with someone or if others can hear who do not have a "legitimate educational interest" in the information.

Dr. Foster: *Discussions in hallways, teachers' lounges, and other places inside and outside the school "may borderline on being unprofessional . . . Regardless of the behavior of others, maintain your high level of professional behavior" (Sprick et al., 1998, p. 26).*

A. Teacher: *What if someone violates FERPA?*

Dr. Foster: *The Family Policy Compliance Office with the Department of Education in Washington, DC, investigates a school district or postsecondary institution when a parent, eligible student, school official, or some other party (not a parent or eligible student) files a complaint ("Section-by-Section Analysis," 2008, p. 14). A confirmed school district or postsecondary institution violation could lead to a loss of federal funds if the institution does not make mandated corrections in a reasonable period of time ("FERPA Information," n.d.). "A willful or unauthorized disclosure could constitute just cause for disciplinary action" (para. 16).*

Find more about FERPA and confidentiality on the **Classroom Management Blues** *website. (Select* **Resources** *at www.classroommanagementblues.com, then* **Communication** *and* **Professionalism** *to locate books, articles, and other related resources.)*

A. Teacher: *What about respect for confidentiality of collegial information?*

Dr. Foster: *Be aware of federal and state laws for confidentiality and other school related issues. "Unnecessary disclosure of information in which the employee has a reasonable expectation of privacy may result in employer liability in tort for invasion of privacy or intentional infliction of emotional distress" ("Privacy in the Workplace," 2004, para. 2).*

"Maintain confidentiality of information concerning colleagues and dispense such information only when prescribed or directed by federal or state law or professional practice" ("Regulations," 2010, para. 7). The Code of Ethics of the National Education Association includes the obligation to not knowingly make false or malicious statements about colleagues ("Code of Ethics," 1975).

A. Teacher: *I have not heard about the arrest of any teacher for not respecting the confidentiality of students or colleagues, but I do not want to be the first one. Just as I would not want my colleagues to put me down or talk behind my back, I should keep information about them private unless there is significant risk to the safety or well-being of that person, students, or other members of the school community ("Confidentiality issues," 2010; Sprick et al., 1998).*

I am more aware of my professional and legal responsibilities about what I say about students and other school professionals, but I do not see how what I wear is a reflection of my professionalism.

> *We're all prisoners of each other's gossip, killed by each other's whispers.*
> **Peyton Place**
> American film—1957
>
> ———
>
> *I want my gossip from the horse's mouth, not the tail.*
> **The Big Knife**
> American film—1955

Dr. Foster: *"Make no mistake, we judge others by their dress, and they judge us too. . . . In an ideal world, viewed through rose-colored glasses, it would be wonderful to be accepted for ourselves alone, not our appearance. In the real world, however, our all-too-visible selves are under constant scrutiny" (Wong & Wong, 1998, p. 51).*

> Students need to know that we value them. By communicating the value we hold for students, we can help them to appreciate themselves and feel powerful and accepted. As a result of our telling them how important they are, they will come to believe that they are important. . . . One way to communicate students' value is by dressing well. (Edwards, 2010, p. 5)

How does personal appearance influence the perception of professionalism? Research results show that what teachers wear affects respect, credibility, acceptance, and authority (Wong & Wong, 1998). Teachers who possess these traits are able to foster trust and respect, increase student learning, and reduce misbehavior more effectively.

A. Teacher: *Although respect, credibility, acceptance, and authority mean more to me than dressing professionally, it would be the easiest way to communicate that I am a creditable professional who has authority and is worthy of respect and acceptance.*

Dr. Foster: *You are much better off if you make the way you "dress work for you than to allow it to work against you" (p. 52). What counts is how students, parents, administrators, and the larger community perceive you.*

A. Teacher: *I want my students, their parents, administrators, and the larger community to perceive me as a professional, but schools have very different dress codes—some mandated by the district, others established by the teachers themselves. In one school, the administrator expects teachers to wear designer or almost designer clothing to "fit" in with the neighborhood. In another school with lots of discipline problems, teachers wear t-shirts, tanks, spaghetti straps, shorts, flip-flops, and baggy clothes. We cannot wear these clothes in our school, but we can wear blue jeans on Friday ("What IS Professional Dress?" 2011).*

I have observed that more behavior problems occur when teachers wear jeans or students do not wear uniforms. Everyone is more relaxed and less focused on teaching and learning. On reflection, I need to rethink wearing blue jeans and see if it makes a difference in my classroom.

> *You may want to re-think your wardrobe a little.*
>
> **Erin Brockovich**
> American film—2000

A. Teacher: *Is there clothing that is both comfortable **and** professional?*

Dr. Foster: *For a physical education teacher "who frequently provides demonstrations to students, wearing nice workout clothing is probably perfectly reasonable" (Sprick et al., 1998, p. 28). You could wear black jeans rather than blue jeans. Here are more tips to maintain an appropriate level of casualness and formality.*

Table 9.12

Guidelines for a Professional Appearance
Clothing • Clean career clothing in good condition (avoid clingy tops, rump-hugging bottoms, dressing like teenagers) • Pressed, neat, tailored shirts and pants; suits, jackets, and sweaters for men as well as women, and ties for men (establishes authority) • Sleeves (considered more put-together and mature) • Bright colors (elementary) or soft muted tones (secondary)
Shoes • Comfortable with arch support and padding for the balls of your feet as well as your heels (e.g., no tennis shoes except for field trips, jog-a-thons) • Sensible flats, low heels (avoid trendy high-heels) • Closed-toed shoes in case of getting accidentally stepped on
Other • Tasteful make-up (avoid daring hues) • Simple, classic, and a small amount of jewelry (don't chance an accident or the loss of meaningful jewelry)

From "How to Dress Like a Teacher," n.d.; Lewis, n.d.; and Wong & Wong, 1998

A. Teacher: *My students wear uniforms, so I think they would be receptive to me dressing appropriately for school. They would see that I value them and the profession.*

Dr. Foster: *What suggestions do you have for new teachers who find themselves in schools where teachers do not wear professional attire?*

A. Teacher: *I think it would be very difficult for new teachers to not dress like everyone else because they want acceptance from their colleagues. We should dress professionally and be leaders, role models, and mentors for new teachers.*

Dr. Foster: *The way you act demonstrates your professionalism.*

What is a teacher's professional code of conduct? There is no unifying code of conduct for teachers in the United States, but those adopted by states and local school boards are similar to those of the Association of American Educators (AAE) and the National Education Association (NEA). As stated by the AAE, the code of ethics is "designed to help educators create a nurturing environment for students" (para. 3). According to the NEA, the expected behaviors of teachers center on a commitment to the student and the profession (Wilson, 2010).

States and school districts define the professional manner expected of teachers as they interact with students, families, colleagues, and communities. The National Council for Accreditation of Teacher Education calls these verbal and nonverbal behaviors *professional dispositions* (attitudes, values, and beliefs). Two of these dispositions are fairness and the belief that all students can learn ("Professional Standards," 2008).

> The manner in which an educator carries himself or herself is a reflection of one's classroom, school, community, and educational system. Conduct is a representation of how well one takes care of himself or herself, from aesthetics to language and behavior. . . . Conduct also includes one's ability to initiate and maintain quality communication with all the parties involved in education. ("Role of Teacher Professionalism," n.d., para. 6)

Dr. Foster: *What are some of the professional dispositions expected in your state and school district?*

A. Teacher: *My school district expects us to show appreciation for diversity and a commitment to teaching all students; arrive on time and accept responsibilities; seek and accept constructive feedback from others to improve performance; and behave ethically when interacting with students, families, colleagues, and the community ("Professional Dispositions," n.d.).*

> All learned occupations have a definition of professionalism, a code of conduct . . . [with] at least three common elements. First is an expectation of selflessness: that we who accept responsibility for others . . . will place the needs and concerns of those who depend on us above our own. Second is an expectation of skill: that we will aim for excellence in our knowledge and expertise. Third is an expectation of trustworthiness: that we will be responsible in our personal behavior toward our charges. (Gawande, 2009, p. 182)

Dr. Foster: *No matter the state or school district, teachers who violate the code of professional practice and conduct may receive a public or private reprimand and possibly suspension or revocation of teacher certification.*

A. Teacher: *How to act in a professional manner should be common sense, but a few teachers act in ways that demean the profession.*

Dr. Foster: *Dr. Steven W. Edwards gave this advice to participants at a **Safe Schools Conference** in Louisville, Kentucky: "Teach like there is a camera on you!"*

A. Teacher: *That is really good advice! With the capability of cell phones to take pictures and record video and audio, I do not want to be a teacher who acts unprofessionally and has a picture shown or a video played on 24-hour news broadcasts on a slow news day. Incidents that involve teachers do not remain local today.*

> *You will remember to smile for the camera, won't you? Say, "Cheese."*
> **The Great Mouse Detective**
> American film—1986

To Be or Not to Be a Headliner

A headliner is the star performer who gets top billing in a program or on a marquee. Teachers should want **to be a headliner** who "attains and maintains the highest possible degree of ethical conduct" (Code of Ethics, n.d., para. 3), **not to be a headliner** in local and national newspapers or online for exercising unprofessional judgment.

Student Locked in Cage: NM Teacher on Leave After Cell Phone Video Leaked

A shop teacher at a New Mexico high school has been put on paid leave after cell phone video surfaced of her locking up a student in an outdoor cage.

Santa Fe police say the 15-year-old boy was acting out in class on Jan. 7. The teacher had other students help drag the boy outside and lock him in the chain-link enclosure used for storage.

Santa Fe Police Detective Sgt. Louis Carlos tells KOAT-TV in Albuquerque that the boy can be seen waving to classmates and eventually kicks the gate to free himself. Carlos calls the video disturbing and says the female teacher could face child abuse and false imprisonment charges.

The district attorney will determine if charges are warranted.

Excerpted from "Student Locked in Cage," 2011, para. 1–4

Other examples: Teacher Guilty of Surfing Internet During Lessons
29-Year-Old Teacher Arrested for Sex with Teen Student
Teacher Arrested on Drug Trafficking Charges
1st Grade Teacher Charged with Choking Students

The ***reality*** is that some teachers choose to be headliners.

Dr. Foster: *A professional is dependable and behaves ethically. Teachers communicate professionalism when they arrive at work on time; fulfill duties without the need of reminders; attend and give full attention at faculty meetings; stay on top of attendance and grade reports; and so on (Sprick et al., 1998).*

The Great Debate

The great debate is whether teaching is a job or a profession. For some, teaching is a way to pay the bills. To them, they only have to work 180 days a year from 8 a.m. to 3 p.m. with summers off. These teachers "do not want to be professionals. It takes work and effort to be a professional. It takes time to go to conferences, read the journals, work actively on committees, and give extra help after school to students who need it" (Wong & Wong, 1998, p. 294).

The *reality* is that "the debate over whether teaching is a profession will be resolved when all teachers or at least a significant number of them" communicate professionalism (p. 293).

A. Teacher: *"All some teachers want is a job" (Wong & Wong, 1998, p. 294).*

Teaching is more than a job to me. It is my profession.

At the beginning of this session, you asked me to imagine what people would see if they looked in my classroom. I indicated that I lacked confidence about what I would communicate. Now I am confident that once I put what I have learned about advocacy, feedback, dialogue, collaboration, and professionalism into practice in my classroom, everyone will see that I am a professional who maintains effective communication with my students and others.

My confidence level is also much higher about my ability to communicate effectively with families, colleagues, other school professionals, and the community. I am not only on stage in my classroom; I am on stage in a professional role in the school and the community.

> *All the world's a stage,*
> *And all the men*
> *and women*
> *merely players.*
>
> **William Shakespeare**
> From *As You Like It*
> Act II, Scene VII

Dr. Foster: *In your role as a professional educator, think about the character traits that describe how you act and communicate in the classroom. Put an X along the spectrum from ineffective to effective (see Table 9.13 on the next page).*

Table 9.13

R$_x$ 5 Effective Communication			
Ineffective	**A Spectrum of Character Traits**	**Effective**	**Active Ingredients**
discouraging	_ _ _ _ _ _ _ _ _ _ _ _ _ _ _	inspiring	
indifferent	_ _ _ _ _ _ _ _ _ _ _ _ _ _ _	enthusiastic	**Advocacy**
negligent	_ _ _ _ _ _ _ _ _ _ _ _ _ _ _	persistent	
vague	_ _ _ _ _ _ _ _ _ _ _ _ _ _ _	instructive	
judgmental	_ _ _ _ _ _ _ _ _ _ _ _ _ _ _	informational	**Feedback**
detrimental	_ _ _ _ _ _ _ _ _ _ _ _ _ _ _	supportive	
reactive	_ _ _ _ _ _ _ _ _ _ _ _ _ _ _	proactive	
social	_ _ _ _ _ _ _ _ _ _ _ _ _ _ _	dialogical	
unthinking	_ _ _ _ _ _ _ _ _ _ _ _ _ _ _	reflective	**Dialogue**
boring	_ _ _ _ _ _ _ _ _ _ _ _ _ _ _	engaging	
competitive	_ _ _ _ _ _ _ _ _ _ _ _ _ _ _	collaborative	
disparaging	_ _ _ _ _ _ _ _ _ _ _ _ _ _ _	appreciative	**Collaboration**
avoiding	_ _ _ _ _ _ _ _ _ _ _ _ _ _ _	compromising	
unprofessional	_ _ _ _ _ _ _ _ _ _ _ _ _ _ _	professional	
unreliable	_ _ _ _ _ _ _ _ _ _ _ _ _ _ _	dependable	
biased	_ _ _ _ _ _ _ _ _ _ _ _ _ _ _	fair	**Professionalism**
ineffective	_ _ _ _ _ _ _ _ _ _ _ _ _ _ _	competent	

A. Teacher: *My self-assessment of each character trait along the spectrum indicates that I need to improve my ability to communicate effectively. My goal is to apply the active ingredients to improve my effectiveness because what I say to my colleagues, students, their parents, and other school professionals (and sometimes what I do not say) will stay with them forever (Anderson, n.d.).*

Dr. Foster: *As you apply these active ingredients, carefully read about the supplements on the **Classroom Management Blues** website. When you learn about other strategies, prescriptions, active ingredients, and supplements, blend them with this prescription to maintain effective communication.*

*I recommend that you implement the supplements for effective communication as outlined on this **Implementation Checklist**.*

R$_x$ 5 Implementation Checklist

Select the *Supplements* page
at *www.classroommanagementblues.com*
to obtain detailed explanations,
step-by-step instructions, and
blackline masters for *Supplements W–Z*.

Implement the following supplements throughout the academic year.

📁   **Supplement W—Nonverbal Interactions —Self-Assessment**
Complete the self-assessment to find out if your body language is effective for all students.

📁   **Supplement X—Discussion and Dialogue Prompts**
Use these questions and prompts to sustain momentum during thoughtful discussions and dialogues.

📁   **Supplement Y—Conference Guidelines and Protocols**
Follow these guidelines and protocols to promote effective communication and collaboration with students, parents, and other school professionals.

Concluding Remarks

The **Effective Communication Prescription** will not prevent or cure the *Classroom Management Blues*, but the potential will increase if you use the strategies for **High Expectations**, **Active Engagement**, **Appropriate Assessments**, and **Trustworthy Behavior** in your classroom. In our last session, you will learn how to continue treatment and have regular checkups to prevent a relapse.

Dr. Foster: *Look at the* **Effective Communication Prescription** *and note the caution.*

Keep using the prescription as directed to empower students to learn and succeed. With consistency, you will achieve the desired effects of more trust and respect, improved behavior, and increased learning and parental involvement.

VYGOTSKY'S PHARMACY

555 Communication Circle
Any Town, USA

Date Filled: First Day in the Classroom
Discard After: Retirement

 0005

Prescription for **EFFECTIVE COMMUNICATION**

Patient's Name: **A. Teacher**

Patient's Address: **105 Respect Road — Any Town, USA**

Maintain **EFFECTIVE COMMUNICATION** *as directed* with students, families, and other educators.

Doctor: *Barbara G. Foster*

Active Ingredients
• **Advocacy**
• **Feedback**
• **Dialogue**
• **Collaboration**
• **Professionalism**

SIDE EFFECTS: More trust and respect, increased learning, and improved behavior

CAUTION: May increase parent involvement   **Unlimited Refills**

Resources—Access More Information

Learn more about advocacy, collaboration, interpersonal communication, intrapersonal communication, conflict resolution, feedback, listening, professionalism, and parent-teacher conferences on the ***Classroom Management Blues*** website. Select the **Resources** page at *www.classroommanagement blues.com*, then **Communication** for a list of books, articles, websites, and other resources.

Praxis Journal—Take Steps toward a Cure

Write responses to these prompts and questions before the next session:

- **Review the *Effective Communication Prescription* and reflect on what you have learned.** How does effective communication affect student learning?
- **Based on what you have learned in this session, set a goal and develop a plan.** How do you plan to achieve your goal and solve one or more related problems?
- **Implement and evaluate your plan.** How did your actions affect you as a teacher and your students as learners?
- **Reflect on future goals and actions.** What will you do in the future?

STEP THREE: **PREVENT A RELAPSE**

Today's assignment:

Complete
Didactic Checkups

Session 10

Photos.com

Session 10

Complete Didactic Checkups

We're made to change, Deutschman says, because humans are great at learning. It starts with a relationship: "We can change but we need to learn from other people. We need first to start with their belief and conviction in us. We start with an emotional bond knowing they believe in us. Then we need to learn from them." In addition to the right relationship, learning takes a kind of humility and the emotional safety to fail and start again. "We have to keep becoming beginners and going through the process of learning again. Yes, it's frustrating, but it's worth it."

Joshua Freedman
A Hope for Change: Alan Deutschman on Change or Die

Like the proverb "An apple a day keeps the doctor away," the **apples**, or prescriptions, I have recommended can help you prevent and cure the ***Classroom Management Blues***. To self-monitor the effectiveness of the strategies you choose to implement in your classroom, you need frequent didactic checkups.

 di·dac·tic [dī dak′tik] **adj.**

Intended for instruction

Random House Dictionary

A. Teacher: *I want to keep the blues away. Can I do this on my own?*

Dr. Foster: *You have the ability to succeed!*

In this session, I will synthesize the information from the other sessions and provide a framework to help you self-manage your treatment. (Review Session 4 "Begin Personalized Treatment" on pages 41–49.) You will also learn coping strategies to prevent a relapse.

*You have learned about five prescriptions and their active ingredients. If you consistently repeat **high expectations** for yourself, **actively** use **trustworthy** strategies, **assess** your progress, and **communicate** with others about your successes and need for support, you will be able to prevent or cure the **Classroom Management Blues**.*

A. Teacher: *So the prescriptions we have discussed can affect **my** learning and behavior as well as the learning and behavior of my students.*

I hope I can remember everything.

Dr. Foster: *To remember, use the first letters of the prescriptions to spell out* **TEACH.**

Encourage	**T**rustworthy Behavior
Apply Active	**E**ngagement
Use Appropriate	**A**ssessments
Maintain Effective	**C**ommunication
Repeat	**H**igh Expectations

> 🗎 **teach** [tēch] **v.**
>
> **Synonyms:** coach, communicate, demonstrate, discipline, guide, enlighten, develop, instruct, inform, nurture, prepare
>
> *Roget's 21st Century Thesaurus*

A. Teacher: *The acronym* **TEACH** *will help me remember the prescriptions, but I am overwhelmed with the complexity of how to use all the active ingredients and supplements for each prescription.*

Table 10.1

 Prescriptions for the Classroom Management Blues

Trustworthy Behavior	**Active** **Engagement**	**Appropriate** **Assessments**	**Effective** **Communication**	**High** Expectations
Active Ingredients • Principles • Rules • Consequences • Documentation • Procedures	*Active Ingredients* • Brain Research • Constructivism • Higher-Order Thinking • Learning Styles • Student Interest	*Active Ingredients* • Expectancy • Attribution • Practice • Evaluation • Reflection	*Active Ingredients* • Advocacy • Feedback • Dialogue • Collaboration • Professionalism	*Active Ingredients* • Efficacy • Authenticity • Community • Autonomy • Resiliency
Supplements Q. Mission, Vision, Principles, and Values R. Consequence Hierarchy and Behavior Support System S. Time Outs and Think Sheets T. Behavior Record Sheets U. Self-Management Record Sheets V. Clipboard Management	*Supplements* A. Quality Grouping B. Jigsaw Tasks C. LTC (Learner Teacher Checker) D. HOT Question Starters E. Surveys for Preferred Learning Styles, Conditions, and Activities F. Motivation and Activity Planning Forms	*Supplements* K. Unit and Lesson Design L. "Win-Win" Classroom Competitions M. Practice Book N. Practice Record Sheet O. Grade Book Magic P. Learning Journal	*Supplements* W. Nonverbal Interactions—Self-Assessment X. Discussion and Dialogue Prompts Y. Conference Guidelines and Protocols Z. Classroom Management Plans and Checklists	*Supplements* G. About Me Survey H. Homework Contract I. Inspiration Frames J. High Expectations Strategy Game

Dr. Foster: *In one of my favorite books, **The Art and Science of Teaching: A Comprehensive Framework for Effective Instruction**, Dr. Robert J. Marzano wrote, "Teaching is a complex endeavor involving many interacting components. Just as an airplane pilot consults a comprehensive checklist before every takeoff as a way of reminding herself of the complexities of flying, so too should a teacher remind himself of the complexities of teaching on a daily basis" (2007, p. 189).*

How can teachers handle the complexities of teaching? Brenda Zimmerman of York University and Sholom Glouberman of the University of Toronto study the science of complexity and propose a distinction among three kinds of problems: simple, complicated, and complex. It is simple to bake a cake from a mix, complicated to send a rocket to the moon, and complex to raise and teach children as the outcomes are uncertain (Gawande, 2009, p. 49).

> There is no disputing the importance of experience. It is not enough for a surgeon [or teacher] to have the textbook knowledge. . . . One needs practice to achieve mastery. (Gawande, 2009, p. 12)

A. Teacher: *If a person followed the directions on the box of a cake mix precisely, he or she could successfully make a cake every time. A parent or teacher might successfully raise or teach one child, but the next one may require an entirely different approach (p. 49).*

Dr. Foster: *Despite the uncertainty, it is possible to raise and teach children well.*

Atul Gawande, a medical doctor, says, "Knowledge has both saved us and burdened us" (p. 13). He describes two difficulties experts in medicine and other fields like teaching face in complex environments. "The first is the fallibility of human memory and attention, especially when it comes to mundane, routine matters that are easily overlooked under the strain of more pressing events" (p. 36). The second is that "people can lull themselves into skipping steps even when they remember them" (p. 36). It is nearly impossible to avoid daily mistakes, even with technology.

A. Teacher: *This disappoints me. Is there a way for teachers to manage all the complexities of teaching?*

Dr. Foster: *You need to continue to gain knowledge, build experience, and use checklists for complicated and complex tasks.*

Precise and practical checklists can help teachers and learners perform complex tasks at high levels, offer a way to verify procedures, and "provide a kind of cognitive net" that catches mental mistakes (pp. 13, 36). It is important to identify the kinds of situations checklists can help with and those they cannot (p. 48). A checklist can help the pilot know if the plane is ready to fly, but the checklist cannot fly the plane (p. 120).

Good checklists do not spell everything out. They should include between five and nine (ten at the most) "reminders of the most critical and important steps—the ones that even highly skilled professionals using them could miss" (p. 123–124). For ease of reading, the steps on good checklists have upper and lowercase text, are free from clutter and unnecessary colors, and fit on one page.

Which didactic checklists can empower teachers to manage the complexities of teaching? Teachers can use checklists to assess their knowledge, emotions, and ability levels to manage the complexities of teaching, as well as prevent or cure the *Classroom Management Blues*. The three domains of educational activities identified by Benjamin Bloom and a group of educational psychologists provide a framework for the kinds of checklists needed to solve problems, change behaviors, and achieve goals in the classroom.

Dr. Foster: *Carefully designed checklists empower you to get things right, and this gives you the power to succeed (Gawande, 2009). We will focus on four checklists to help you prevent or cure the* ***Classroom Management Blues*** *(see Table 10.2).*

Table 10.2

Didactic Checklists to Cure or Prevent the Classroom Management Blues		Bloom's Domain of Educational Activities
☑ **Checklist 1** *Warning Signs of the Classroom Management Blues* (See page 345.)	***How do I feel during the school day?*** How often do you experience warning signs of the **Classroom Management Blues**?	**Affective**
☑ **Checklist 2** *Self-Regulatory Mechanisms of Autonomous Learners* (See page 346.)	***What have I done to succeed?*** How often do you use each self-regulatory mechanism?	**Psychomotor**
☑ **Checklist 3** *Stages of Change—Prochaska, DiClemente, and Kern* (See page 347.)	***Where am I in the change process?*** At what stage of change do you find yourself?	**Cognitive**
☑ **Checklist 4** *Ten Steps for Lifelong Learning and Problem Solving* (See page 348.)	***What are my next steps?*** What do you need to do to change a behavior, achieve a goal, or solve a problem?	**Affective, Cognitive, and Psychomotor**

A. Teacher: *We talked about the information included on these checklists in other sessions. I am already familiar with what to do; I just need to do it!*

Dr. Foster: *I am confident you will do what you need to do! First, write* **Didactic Checkup** *on your calendar as you would a doctor appointment every week or two. Later, checkups every month or two will suffice to sustain the changes.*

*Today, you will complete your **first didactic checkup**. Follow the directions on each checklist and record your responses on the **Didactic Checkup Record Sheet** and progress charts (see pages 353–355). (Select the **Supplements** page at www.classroommanagementblues.com, then **W–Z** to download the **Supplement Z: Checklists**, progress charts, and Didactic Checkup Record Sheet.)*

*Now complete ☑ **Checklist 1** to assess how you feel during the school day.*

☑ Checklist 1—How do I feel during the school day?
Warning Signs of the *Classroom Management Blues*
GOAL: To **rarely** experience the warning signs—achieving a score of 10 or less

- On the Didactic Checkup Record Sheet, rate each item from 0 to 4 using the rating scale for the frequency of warning signs.
- Graph the total score and assess your progress.

Rating Scale	
0	Never
1	Rarely
2	Occasionally
3	Frequently
4	All the time

1. I have a headache during or after school.
2. I lose my temper with students.
3. I lack the energy to go to school.
4. I frown or overreact to small things.
5. I experience paper overload.
6. I feel like a failure as a teacher.
7. I am sad, disappointed, aggravated, or frustrated during the school day.
8. I blame others for what is happening in my classroom.
9. I lack the skills to cope with my teaching responsibilities.
10. I give up on or am too critical of some students.

Didactic Checkup Record Sheet

☑ **Checklist 1—How do I feel during the school day?** Rate each item from 0 to 4 using the rating scale for the **Frequency of Warning Signs**.

Item	1	2	3	4	5	6	7	8	9	10	Total
Checkup 1	3	3	4	3	4	2	4	2	3	2	30

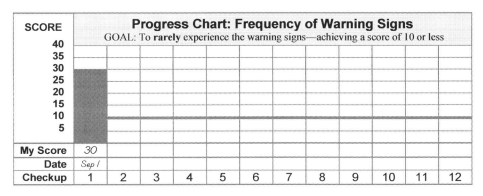

Progress Chart: Frequency of Warning Signs
GOAL: To **rarely** experience the warning signs—achieving a score of 10 or less

SCORE												
My Score	30											
Date	Sep 1											
Checkup	1	2	3	4	5	6	7	8	9	10	11	12

A. Teacher: *I have experienced many of the warning signs.*

Dr. Foster: *If you continue to use the prescriptions, you will succeed! Now complete* ☑ **Checklist 2** *to assess how much you use the self-regulatory mechanisms.*

☑ Checklist 2—What have I done to succeed?
Self-Regulatory Mechanisms of Autonomous Learners
GOAL: To **frequently** evidence self-regulatory mechanisms—achieving a score of 30 or more

- On the Didactic Checkup Record Sheet, rate each item from 0 to 4 using the Rating Scale for the frequency of using self-regulatory mechanisms inside and outside the classroom.
- Graph the total score and assess your progress.

Rating Scale	
0	Never
1	Rarely
2	Occasionally
3	Frequently
4	All the time

1. I interact with others and give support.
2. I seek support even though I can function well without it.
3. I act independently to control my environment.
4. I use self-talk to cope with new and unforeseen situations.
5. I use self-talk to overcome temporary motivational setbacks.
6. I believe I can achieve my goals and solve my problems.
7. I rely more on my own past successes than the verbal comments of others.
8. I set goals and develop action plans or plan personal learning activities.
9. I monitor learning activities, evaluate my progress, and make changes.
10. I believe I am learning from my successes and failures.

Didactic Checkup Record Sheet

☑ **Checklist 2—What have I done to succeed?** Rate each item from 0 to 4 using the Rating Scale for the **Frequency of Self-Regulatory Mechanism Usage**.

Item	1	2	3	4	5	6	7	8	9	10	Total
Checkup 1	3	2	2	2	2	2	3	1	1	2	20

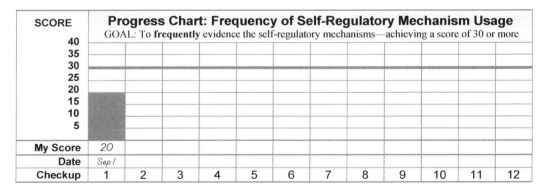

A. Teacher: *I have a lot to work on! Once I complete my first didactic checkup and develop an action plan, my score will improve. I also need to review how to use self-talk.*

Dr. Foster: *You have a good plan to improve your use of the self-regulatory mechanisms. Next, use* ☑ **Checklist 3** *to assess where you are in the change process.*

☑ Checklist 3—Where am I in the change process?
Stages of Change—Prochaska, DiClemente, and Kern
GOAL: To maintain the change and achieve transcendence

- Based on the descriptors, identify your current stage of change.
- Fill in the box on the Didactic Checkup Record Sheet for relapse or your stage of change.

Transcendence Not returning to old ways	• I no longer go back to my old behaviors. If I do, it seems abnormal. • I am not tempted to return to my old ways.
Maintenance Maintain the change	• I am on track and avoid temptations. • I remind myself of how much progress I have made. • I have acquired new skills to avoid a relapse. • I anticipate the situations in which a relapse could happen and prepare coping strategies in advance. • I understand it often takes a while to let go of old behavior patterns and practice new ones until they are second nature. • I recognize that it is normal to regress—attain one stage and fall back to a previous stage. • I re-evaluate my progress up and down these stages.
Action—Willpower Practice the change	• I believe I have the ability to change. • I use different strategies to change. • I am open to help and seek support from others.
Preparation—Determination Get ready to change	• I am committed to making a change and want information about what I need to do. • I want to know what strategies and resources are available.
Contemplation Think about change	• I know I have a problem, but I am not yet ready to change. • I weighed the pros and cons of change, but I doubt the long-term benefits will outweigh the short-term costs. • I am open to educational information, but I do not know for sure that the strategies will work perfectly.
Precontemplation Not considering change	• I do not believe I have a problem. • I do not need to change.
Relapse Resume old behaviors	• I am discouraged because I have returned to my old ways. • I am unable to recognize environmental cues and high-risk situations that tempt me.

Didactic Checkup Record Sheet

☑ **Checklist 3—Where am I in the change process?** Put a box around "relapse" **or** your level of change, then fill in the corresponding cell on the progress chart *(on the next page)*.

Transcendence	Maintenance	Action/Willpower	
Determination	Contemplation	Precontemplation	Relapse

Progress Chart: Stage of Change
GOAL: To maintain the change and achieve transcendence

Transcendence												
Maintenance												
Action—Willpower	▓▓											
Preparation												
Contemplation												
Precontemplation												
Relapse												
Date	*Sep 1*											
Checkup	1	2	3	4	5	6	7	8	9	10	11	12

A. Teacher: *Wow! When I first met with you weeks ago, I was at the **Contemplation Stage**. I knew I had a problem but was not sure if meetings with you would help. As I attended the sessions, I was at the **Preparation-Determination Stage**— I wanted strategies and resources to cure my **Classroom Management Blues**.*

*Thanks to you, I find myself at the **Action-Willpower Stage**. I know I have the ability to change and have actively begun to use the prescriptions and supplements I learned in our sessions. I look forward to the day when I maintain the changes and do not return to my old ways.*

Dr. Foster: *You deserve the credit! You were open to the help and information offered. I am confident you will be successful even if you have a few relapses along the way.*

*Think about your analysis of the other checklists and look at ☑ **Checklist 4**. Use the ten steps to write an action plan.*

☑ Checklist 4—What are my next steps?
Ten Steps for Lifelong Learning and Problem Solving

- Write an action plan in your Praxis Journal.

Frame	Step 1	*Focus*	State your vision, goal, or problem.
	Step 2	*Research*	Gather information.
Process Information	Step 3	*Interpret*	Analyze information and clarify the vision, goal, or problem.
	Step 4	*Predict*	Consider outcomes, resources, and obstacles.
	Step 5	*Brainstorm*	Generate objectives, hypotheses, or possible solutions.
Decide	Step 6	*Choose*	Make decisions, establish timelines, and determine evaluation methodology.
Plan	Step 7	*Design*	Develop action plans and monitoring and assessment systems.
Implement	Step 8	*Act*	Put plans in action and fine-tune.
Learn from Experience	Step 9	*Evaluate*	Verify and value assessment results.
	Step 10	*Transfer*	Reflect on a future vision, goal, or problem.

A. Teacher: *These are my action plan and personal learning activities.*

> ***Step 1:*** ***Focus.*** *One of my lowest scores on* **Checklist 1** *was "blaming others for what is happening in my classroom." I have learned that I am in control.* **I WILL NOT blame others for what happens in my classroom.**
>
> *Based on* **Checklist 2,** **I WILL develop an action plan and use self-talk to cope with situations in my classroom.**
>
> ***Step 2:*** ***Research.*** *I reviewed the information about Effective Communication and self-talk from the session about High Expectations.*
>
> ***Step 3:*** ***Interpret.*** *After I reviewed the information, my goals are clear.*
>
>> 1. *I WILL NOT blame* **my students** *for situations in my classroom.*
>>
>> 2. *I WILL use* **positive self-talk before class and before I respond to situations in my classroom.**
>
> ***Step 4:*** ***Predict.*** *I am more negative during the last hour of the day, and a few students "push my buttons" during this time.*
>
> ***Step 5:*** ***Brainstorm.*** *These are the objectives to achieve my goals.*
>
>> 1. *I WILL NOT verbally or nonverbally blame a student for what happens in my classroom* **more than five times in the next week.** *This is a bad habit of mine; it will be challenge.*
>>
>> 2. *I WILL tell myself something positive ("I will . . ." or "I can . . .")* **at the beginning of class, before I handle a problem situation, and throughout the last hour of the day.**
>>
>> 3. *I will affirm myself* **every time** *I use positive self-talk and catch myself before I blame a student for a classroom situation.*
>
> ***Step 6:*** ***Choose.*** *I will mark* **"Didactic Checkup"** *on my calendar one week from today, keep track of the times I meet my objectives, and write reflections in my Praxis Journal.*
>
> ***Step 7:*** ***Design.*** *I will put a tally mark next to the word* **BLAME** *on my daily lesson plan every time I recognize that I have blamed a student for a situation in the classroom. I will put a tally mark next to the word* **AFFIRM** *on my lesson plan every time I affirm positive statements I make to myself in the classroom. I will write reflections in my Praxis Journal every day after school.*
>
> ***Step 8:*** ***Act.*** *I will put plans into action and fine-tune as needed.*
>
> ***Step 9:*** ***Evaluate.*** *I will complete a* **didactic checkup** *after one week.*
>
> ***Step 10:*** ***Transfer.*** *I will reflect on whether I achieve my objectives and write a new action plan with the same goals or one or more new goals.*

A. Teacher: *It took some time to write this plan. I hope I find that the time was worth it when I assess my progress on my next* **didactic checkup.**

Dr. Foster: *I am confident that with practice, your ability to write action plans will improve (Checklist 4). You will also find that you will have more time inside and outside the classroom when you rarely show warning signs of the **Classroom Management Blues** (Checklist 1), frequently evidence each self-regulatory mechanism (Checklist 2), and maintain changes or do not return to your old ways (Checklist 3).*

In Session 8, we discussed the eight steps at the heart of change. To implement and sustain change, Dr. Cohen recommends that you "Make It Stick" (2005, p. 5). This means that you should not forget to recognize and reward yourself when you have followed through and your checkups show improvement! Read "Get Your Just Rewards" and learn how to reward yourself.

Get Your Just Rewards!

 In "Reward Yourself—You'll Achieve More Goals," Anne Wayman (2010) says it is best to write down your goals, attach a due date, and remember to reward yourself with small as well as large rewards. "When you reward yourself for achieving a goal it actually makes it a tiny bit easier to achieve the next goal" (para. 1–2). So be sure to **get your just rewards!**

The *reality* is that "rewarding yourself is just one more excellent way to train your mind to be truly self-supportive" (para. 4).

Many rewards are free or close to it. Wayman (2010) suggests a fresh cup of coffee or tea or a 10-minute call to a friend. In "19 Ways to Enhance Your Sense of Humor," Katz and Gordon ask, "What is the greatest reward?" Is it hugs from your children, chocolate, or a perfect night's sleep? The answer "that spans all people is laughter" (para. 6). They recommend these **just rewards** to live a healthier and happier life:

- *Rent a funny movie or read the comics.*

- *Sort through family photos and write funny captions.*

- *Ask a friend or coworker to tell you something funny.*

- *Download free jokes and funny true stories to your phone.*

- *Read an activity listing online or in the newspaper and choose a laugh-inducing event to attend such as a movie, a performance by a stand-up comic, or a funny play.*

A. Teacher: *I can reward myself when I succeed, but what if I have a relapse?*

What can teachers do if they experience a relapse of the *Classroom Management Blues*? Prochaska and DiClemente say most people who successfully change their behavior do not follow a straight path. "Rather than seeing oneself as a failure and letting feelings of discouragement undermine self-confidence, an analysis of how the relapse happened can be used as an opportunity to learn how to cope differently" ("Stages of Change," 2003, para. 17). People can get back on track if they learn to anticipate high-risk situations more effectively, avoid temptation, control environmental cues, and handle unexpected episodes of stress.

> What keeps me from getting discouraged when my failures outnumber my successes is to keep thinking long-term. I often must endure a lot of failures to hit the next big breakthrough. So I just plow through those failures as fast as possible. It's like a conveyor belt—there's a new success on that belt somewhere ahead, and the faster the belt moves, the sooner it will arrive. (Pavlina, 2006, para. 19)

Dr. Foster: *If you experience a relapse, "Don't let up! It is normal for people to experience one or more relapses. Persist and continue to monitor and measure your progress (Cohen, 2005). (See page 218.)*

A. Teacher: *So it is like falling off a horse—I need to get back on. That means I need to take the prescriptions, use the supplements as prescribed, and have regular checkups.*

Dr. Foster: *You **can** become resilient and bounce back! Resources are available to help you develop resiliency and enhance your ability to cope. (Select **Resources**, then **Checkups** and **Coping with Personal change** at www.classroommanagement blues.com for more information.)*

Change will not happen overnight. When you start to sing the blues, take steps to achieve your goals. Review what you have learned in each session and use the checklists to assess your progress. "Real change happens when you live on the edge of what you are capable of and achieve what you once thought was impossible" (Trivett, 2004, para. 1).

*It is possible to prevent a relapse and cure the **Classroom Management Blues**. **Supplement Z: Classroom Management Plans and Checklists** will facilitate the process. (Select **Supplements** at www.classroommanagementblues.com, then **W–Z** for **Supplement Z**.)*

Remember, other prescriptions, active ingredients, and supplements are available for you to use in conjunction with the ones I have recommended in our sessions. Find what works for you!

Concluding Remarks

You have the power to prevent or cure the ***Classroom Management Blues***! Just as your students need to practice to improve their performance, you need to practice new behaviors for several months to improve your performance in the classroom. Maintenance and a commitment to sustain the new behaviors may take years ("Prochaska," n.d.).

To handle the complexities of teaching, be disciplined; make a commitment to use the prescriptions, supplements, and checklists recommended in this book; and have regular didactic checkups.

Resources—Access More Information

Learn more about how to cope with change on the ***Classroom Management Blues*** website. Select **Resources** at *www.classroommanagementblues.com*, then ***Checkups***. For a list of my favorite classroom management books, choose the **My Bookshelves** tab.

Praxis Journal—Take Steps toward a Cure

Write your responses to these prompts:

- Explain why you want to prevent or cure the ***Classroom Management Blues***.
- Complete *Checklists 1, 2, and 3* on pages 353–354.
- For *Checklist 1*, describe how you feel (warning signs).
- For *Checklist 2*, explain what you have done, as well as the self-regulatory mechanisms you have used effectively to achieve your goal or solve a problem.
- For *Checklist 3*, state your current stage of change and explain why you expect to remain at this level or move to another level.
- Review the Progress Chart on 355 and describe the progress you have made to prevent or cure your ***Classroom Management Blues***.
- Complete **Checklist 4** on page 348 and detail your next steps.
- Mark the next didactic checkup on your calendar.

Didactic Checkup Record Sheet 1

How do I feel about school? For ☑ **Checklist 1** (on page 345), rate each item from 0 to 4 using the Rating Scale for the **Frequency of Warning Signs**. Record your scores on the progress chart below and the total score on the Progress Chart on page 355.

Item	1	2	3	4	5	6	7	8	9	10	Total
Checkup 1											
Checkup 2											
Checkup 3											
Checkup 4											
Checkup 5											
Checkup 6											
Checkup 7											
Checkup 8											
Checkup 9											
Checkup 10											
Checkup 11											
Checkup 12											

What have I done to succeed? For ☑ **Checklist 2** (on page 346), rate each item from 0 to 4 using the Rating Scale for the **Frequency of Self-Regulatory Mechanism Usage**. Record your scores on the progress chart below and the total score on the Progress Chart on page 355.

Item	1	2	3	4	5	6	7	8	9	10	Total
Checkup 1											
Checkup 2											
Checkup 3											
Checkup 4											
Checkup 5											
Checkup 6											
Checkup 7											
Checkup 8											
Checkup 9											
Checkup 10											
Checkup 11											
Checkup 12											

Didactic Checkup Record Sheet 2

Where am I in the change process? For ☑ **Checklist 3** (on page 347), determine your "Stage of Change" and put a box around the stage below and fill in the corresponding cell on page 355.

Checkup 1	Transcendence Determination	Maintenance Contemplation	Action/Willpower Precontemplation	Relapse
Checkup 2	Transcendence Determination	Maintenance Contemplation	Action/Willpower Precontemplation	Relapse
Checkup 3	Transcendence Determination	Maintenance Contemplation	Action/Willpower Precontemplation	Relapse
Checkup 4	Transcendence Determination	Maintenance Contemplation	Action/Willpower Precontemplation	Relapse
Checkup 5	Transcendence Determination	Maintenance Contemplation	Action/Willpower Precontemplation	Relapse
Checkup 6	Transcendence Determination	Maintenance Contemplation	Action/Willpower Precontemplation	Relapse
Checkup 7	Transcendence Determination	Maintenance Contemplation	Action/Willpower Precontemplation	Relapse
Checkup 8	Transcendence Determination	Maintenance Contemplation	Action/Willpower Precontemplation	Relapse
Checkup 9	Transcendence Determination	Maintenance Contemplation	Action/Willpower Precontemplation	Relapse
Checkup 10	Transcendence Determination	Maintenance Contemplation	Action/Willpower Precontemplation	Relapse
Checkup 11	Transcendence Determination	Maintenance Contemplation	Action/Willpower Precontemplation	Relapse
Checkup 12	Transcendence Determination	Maintenance Contemplation	Action/Willpower Precontemplation	Relapse

Didactic Checkup Progress Charts

Record Total Scores for Checklist 1 and Checklist 2 (see page 353).

Checklist 1

SCORE	**Progress Chart: Frequency of Warning Signs** GOAL: To **rarely** experience the warning signs—achieving a score of 10 or less											
40												
35												
30												
25												
20												
15												
10												
5												
My Score												
Date												
Checkup	1	2	3	4	5	6	7	8	9	10	11	12

Checklist 2

SCORE	**Progress Chart: Frequency of Self-Regulatory Mechanism Usage** GOAL: To **frequently** evidence the self-regulatory mechanisms— achieving a score of 30 or more											
40												
35												
30												
25												
20												
15												
10												
5												
My Score												
Date												
Checkup	1	2	3	4	5	6	7	8	9	10	11	12

Fill in the box for stage of change or relapse on Checklist 3 (see page 354).

Checklist 3

	Progress Chart: Stage of Change GOAL: To maintain the change and achieve transcendence											
Transcendence												
Maintenance												
Action - Willpower												
Preparation												
Contemplation												
Precontemplation												
Relapse												
Date												
Checkup	1	2	3	4	5	6	7	8	9	10	11	12

Epilogue

Today's assignment:

Do No Harm

Photos.com

Epilogue

Do No Harm

Just maybe I'm getting that teaching passion anew,
And amidst all the yet million things to do
I yearn for the difference I'll make in each life,
I put aside my weariness and my overwhelming strife.

Heather Skipworth Craven
Back to School Blues for Teachers

For lasting education reform, America must first look to the teachers as teachers in the classroom remain at the heart of student learning (Levine, 2000, para. 4). *You* are at the heart of student learning. When you suffer from the **Classroom Management Blues** and no longer have a passion for teaching, student learning suffers. In "What's my job? Defining the Role of the Classroom Teacher," Wiggins writes:

> The heart does not seek "fixes" but insight and understanding. When we lose heart, we need an understanding of our condition that will liberate us from that condition, a diagnosis that will lead us toward new ways of being in the classroom simply by telling the truth about who, and how, we are. Truth, not technique, is what heals and empowers the heart. (Palmer, 1997, p. 6)

> The job of being a teacher has arguably never been more challenging. But let us not conflate challenging with stressful. So much of the current real stress of teaching comes, like all stress, from a lack of conscious awareness about the point of it all, the absence of clarity and priorities, and the resultant feeling that little is in our control. (2010, p. 27)

A. Teacher: *When I began these sessions, my heart was not in it. I felt like I was failing my students. Despite being overwhelmed and feeling stressed with all the expectations of being a teacher, I did not want to quit! That is why I came to you for help.*

I am not as stressed or overwhelmed as I was at the beginning of these sessions because I am using the recommended prescriptions and supplements. My students and I trust and respect each other more every day. I am dealing with fewer behavior problems, and most of all, my students are increasingly motivated to learn.

Dr. Foster: *"Once a problem improves, people often stop doing what caused it to improve"* *(Dweck, 2008, p. 243). They feel better, so they stop taking their prescriptions.*

For a lasting cure of the ***Classroom Management Blues****, continue with the prescriptions, supplements, and checkups.*

A. Teacher: *I know I need to follow the self-help survival guidelines you have given me to prevent a relapse and cure the* ***Classroom Management Blues****.*

I do not want to lose heart again!

Dr. Foster: *Take heart! You have the knowledge, ability, and resources to cure the* ***Classroom Management Blues*** *without doing harm to yourself and your students.*

"Do no harm" is an important maxim of professional ethics for physicians. If one is not technically competent to do something, he or she should not do it (Pence, 2004). The same is true for teaching professionals. Do no harm, maintain your passion for teaching, follow through with the recommended prescriptions and supplements to remain in control of your classroom, and sustain a lasting cure for the ***Classroom Management Blues***.

References

14th Amendment. (2002). Early years. Retrieved from Museum of Natural History: http://topics.law .cornell.edu/constitution/amenmentxiv

2009 PDK/Gallup Poll. Retrieved from PHI DELTA KAPPA International: http://www.pdkpoll.org

2011 PDK/Gallup Poll. Retrieved from PHI DELTA KAPPA International: http://www.pdkintl.org/poll/ docs/pdkpoll43_2011.pdf

Advancement Project, Education Law Center—PA, FairTest, the Forum for Education and Democracy, Juvenile Law Center, and NAACP Legal Defense and Educational Fund. (2010, December). Federal policy, ESEA reauthorization, and the school-to-prison pipeline. Joint position paper retrieved from http://www.fairtest.org/files/Federal_Policy,_ESEA_Reauthorization,_and_the_ School-to-Prison_Pipeline__12_06_101.pdf

Advantages of Rubrics. (2009). Retrieved from http://www.teachervision.fen.com/teaching-methods-and-management/rubrics/4522.html

Ainley, M. D. (1998). Some perspectives on interest in learning and classroom interaction. Retrieved from http://www.aare.edu.au/98pap/ain98054.htm

Albert, L. (1996). *A teacher's guide to cooperative discipline*. Circle Pines, MN: American Guidance Service.

Alexander, R. (2005, July 12). Culture, dialogue and learning: Notes on an emerging pedagogy. *International Association for Cognitive Education and Psychology* (ACEP) 10th International Conference, University of Durham, UK. Retrieved from http://www.learnlab.org/research/wiki/ images/c/cf/Robinalexander_IACEP_2005.pdf

Alexander, R. (2010, November). Speaking but not listening? Accountable talk in an unaccountable context. *Literacy UKLA, 44*(3), pp. 103–111. Retrieved from http://www.robinalexander.org.uk /docs/UKLA.pdf

Alexander, R. J. (2006). *Towards dialogic teaching* (3rd ed.) Cambridge, UK: Cambridge University Faculty of Education: Dialogos.

Allen, Z., & Allen, R. (2005, April). A bit of apple history & folklore. Retrieved from http://www.vegpara dise.com/highestperch39.html

Ames, C. (1992). Achievement goals and the classroom motivational climate. Student perceptions in the classroom, 327–348. Hillsdale, NJ: Erlbaum.

Anderman, E. M., & Wolters, C.A. (2006). Goals, values, and affect: Influences on student motivation. In P. Alexander & P. Winne (Eds). *Handbook of Educational Psychology* (pp. 369–389). Mahwah, NJ: Erlbaum.

Anderman, L. H., & Midgley, C. (1997, June). Motivation and middle school students, Retrieved from *ERIC Digest*, ED421281: http://ceep.crc.uiuc.edu/eecearchive/digests/1998/anderm98.pdf

Anderson, A. N. (n.d.). Effective communication for good teachers. Retrieved from http://www.ehow. com/way_5244958_effective-communication-good-teachers.html

Anderson, L. W. (Ed.), Krathwohl, D. R. (Ed.), Airasian, P. W., Cruikshank, K. A., Mayer, R. E., Pintrich, P. R., Raths, J., & Wittrock, M. C. (2001). *A taxonomy for learning, teaching, and assessing: A revision of Bloom's Taxonomy of Educational Objectives* (Complete edition). New York, NY: Longman.

Anonymous. (n.d.). Questions about trying to change. Retrieved from http://gangsandkids/guestion0b. html

Aronson, E. (2005). Tips for implementation. Retrieved from *The Jigsaw Classroom*: http://www.jigsaw .org/tips.htm

Assessment Terminology: A glossary of useful terms. (2002). Prepared for: Assessing learning . . . Should the tail wag the dog? Assessing Learning Conference—9/28–30, 1995. Retrieved from http://www.newhorizons.org/strategies/assess/terminology.htm

Associated Press—Central Falls, Rhode Island. (2010, February 24). All teachers fired at underperforming school in Rhode Island. Retrieved from *foxnews.com:* http://www.foxnews.com /us/2010/02/24/teachers-fired-underperforming-school-rhode-island/

Assor, A., Kaplan, H., & Roth, G. (2002). Choice is good, but relevance is excellent: Autonomy-enhancing and suppressing teacher behaviours predicting students' engagement in schoolwork. *British Journal of Educational Psychology, 72,* 261–278. Retrieved from http://hsf.bgu.ac.il/edu/ files/eduhome/segel/avi_assor/bjep202002.pdf

Attribution Theory—Heider. (2009). Retrieved from http://www.12manage.com/methods_heider_attrib ution_theory.html

Attribution Theory—Weiner. (n.d.). Retrieved from http://tip.psychology.org/weiner.html

Bafile, C. (2003). Classroom rewards reap dividends for teachers and students. Retrieved from http://www .educationworld.com/a_curr/curr300.shtml

Baker, D. (2012). Teaching for gender difference. Retrieved from http://www.narst.org/publications/ research/gender.cfm

Baker, K. (2007). Are international tests worth anything? *Phi Delta Kappan, 89*(2), 101–104.

Baker, R. M. (n.d). A brief history of the blues. Retrieved from http://www.island.net/~blues/history.html

Bamburg, J. (1994). Raising expectations to improve student learning. Retrieved from http://www. kidsource.com/kidsource/content4/student.expectations.html#differenial#differential

Bandura, A. (1985). Passages from Albert Bandura. In *Social foundations of thought and action: A social cognitive theory.* Upper Saddle River, NJ: Prentice-Hall. Retrieved from http://www.des.emory. edu/mfp/effquotes.html

Bandura, A. (1989) Regulation of cognitive processes through perceived self-efficacy. *Developmental Psychology, 25,* 729–735.

Bandura, A. (1994). Self-efficacy. In V. S. Ramachaudran (Ed.), *Encyclopedia of Human Behavior* (Vol. 4, pp. 71–81). New York, NY: Academic Press. (Reprinted in H. Friedman [Ed.], *Encyclopedia of Mental Health.* San Diego, CA: Academic Press, 1998). Retrieved from http://www.des. emory.edu/mfp/effpassages.html#sources

Bandura, A. (1997). *Self-efficacy: The exercise of control.* New York, NY: Freeman.

Barksdale, M. A., & Thomas, K. F. (2000). What's at stake in high-stakes testing: Teachers and parents speak out. *Journal of Teacher Education, 51*(5), 384–397. Retrieved from http://www.soe.vt.edu/ elementaryed/barksdale/docs/BarksdaleThomasHST.pdf

Barnes, D., & Todd, F. (1995). *Communication and learning revisited: Making meaning through talk.* Portsmouth, NH: Boynton/Cook.

Barnett, T. (2005). Understanding problem-based learning. *Handbook of Enquiry & Problem-Based Learning.* Retrieved from http://www.aishe.org/readings/2005-2/chapter2.pdf

Barnwell, P. (2008, June 30). Could standard grading practices be counterproductive? *Education Week.* Retrieved from http://www.edweek.org/ew/articles/2008/06/30/43barnwell-com_web.h27.html

Bartel, M. (2005). Grading art. Retrieved from http://www.bartelart.com/arted/gradingart.html

Bartlett, L. (2005, August). Dialogue, knowledge, and teacher-student relations: Freirean pedagogy in theory and practice. *Comparative Education Review, 49*(3), 344–364. Retrieved from http:// www.tc.columbia.edu/faculty/bartlett/publications/pdf/49_3cer.pdf

Barton, P. E. (December, 2007). The right way to measure growth. *Educational Leadership 65*(4). Retrieved from http://www.ascd.org/publications/educational_leadership/dec07/vol65/num04/The_Right_Way_to_Measure_Growth.aspx html

Basics of Rubrics. (2007). Retrieved from www.schreyerinstitute.psu.edu/pdf/rubricbasics.pdf

Battle, J. (n.d.). Attention getter: Class-yes | First steps. *Teaching Challenging Kids 101*. Retrieved from http://www.wholebrainteaching.com/first-steps/class-yes.html

Beane, A. L. (1999). *The bully free classroom: Over 100 tips and strategies for teachers K–8*. Minneapolis, MN: Free Spirit.

Bellis, M. (2012.). Sir Isaac Newton. *Inventors*. Retrieved from http://inventors.about.com/library/inventors/blnewton.htm

Benard, B. (n.d). Resiliency requires changing hearts and minds. Retrieved from http://www.mfiles.org/mariweb/take_action/b3_resiliency_source1.html

Benard, B. (1993). Fostering resiliency. *Inventors*. Retrieved from http://www.ascd.org/readingroom/edlead/9311/benard.html

Benard, B. (1995). High expectations. Retrieved from http://www.ncrel.org/sdrs/areas/issues/students/atrisk/at6lk11.htm

Benson, P. (2003). What is autonomy? Retrieved from http://ec.hku.hk/autonomy/what.html

Bettencourt, E. N., Gillett, M. H., Gall, M. D., & Hull, R. E. (1983). Effects of teacher enthusiasm training on student on-task behavior and achievement. *American Educational Research Journal, 20*(3), 435–445.

Betterini, W. (2007). Self-esteem: Being your own cheerleader. Retrieved from http://www.wingsfortheheart.com/self-esteem-being-your-own-cheerleader.htm

Bingham, G., Holbrook, T., & Meyers, L. E. (2010, February). Using self-assessments in elementary classrooms. *Phi Delta Kappan, 91*(5), 59–61.

Bjekic, D., & Zlatić, L. (2006, October). Effects of professional activities on the teachers' communication competencies development. *Association of Teacher Education in Europe*, 31st Annual ATEE Conference, Convention Center Bernardin, Portorož, Slovenia. Retrieved from http://www.pef.uni-lj.si/atee/978-961-6637-06-0/163-172.pdf

Black, P., & Wiliam, D. (1998). Inside the black box: Raising standards through classroom assessment. *Phi Delta Kappan, 80*(2), 139–148. Retrieved from http://edu.stockholm.se/upload/Bed%C3%B6mning/Inside%20the%20Black%20Box.doc

Black, P., & Wiliam, D. (2006). Assessment for learning in the classroom. In J. Gardner (Ed.). *Assessment and Learning* (pp. 9–25). Thousand Oaks, CA: Sage.

Bloom, B. S. (1956). *Taxonomy of educational objectives, Handbook I: The cognitive domain*. New York, NY: David McKay.

Boe, J. (2005). The strangest secret. Retrieved from http://www.holistic-online.com/guided-imagery-strangestsecret.htm

Bohm, D., & Peat, F. D. (2000). *Science, order, and creativity* (2nd ed.). London, England: Routledge.

Bradshaw, R. (1991, September/October). Stress management for teachers: A practical approach. *Clearing House, 65*(1), 43–47. Retrieved from KYVL Academic Search Premier database.

Brain Research Sheds New Light on Student Learning, Teaching Strategies, and Disabilities. (2009, October 2). Retrieved from *Council for Exceptional Children:* http://staging.cec.sped.org/AM/Template.cfm?Section=Home&CONTENTID=6271&TEMPLAT=/CM/ContentDisplay.cfm

Broady, E., & Kenning, M. (1996). Learner autonomy: An introduction to the issues. In *Promoting Learner Autonomy in University Language Teaching*. The Association for French language Studies (AFSC) with the Center for Information in Language Teaching Research. London, UK: Middlesex University.

Brookfield, S. D., & Preskill, S. (1999). *Discussion as a way of teaching: Tools and techniques for democratic classrooms.* San Francisco, CA: Jossey-Bass.

Brookhart, S. M. (2008). *How to give effective feedback to your students.* Alexandria, VA: Association for Supervision and Curriculum Development.

Brooks, J., & Brooks, M. (1993). *In search of understanding: The case for constructivist classrooms.* Alexandria, VA: Association for Supervision and Curriculum Development.

Brown, E. (2006). History of Reading Instruction. Retrieved from http://www.thephonicspage.org/On%20 Phonics/historyofreading.html

Brown v. Board of Education: National Historic Site. (2008). History & culture. Retrieved from http://www.nps.gov/brvb/historyculture/index.htm

Bruffee, K. A. (1993). *Collaborative learning: Higher education interdependence and the authority of knowledge.* Baltimore, MD: Johns Hopkins University Press.

Bruner, J. S. (1964). The course of cognitive growth. *American Psychologist, 19*, 1–15.

Buck, S., Ritter, G. W., Jensen, N. C., & Rose, C. P. (2010). Teachers say the most interesting things—An alternative view of testing. *Kappan, 91*(6), 50–54.

Building Strong Team Collaboration Skills with Web 2.0 Tools. (n.d.). *Web 2.0 Teaching Tools.* Retrieved from http://www.web2teachingtools.com/team-collaboration.html

Bureau of Justice Statistics. (2010, November). Indicators of school crime. Retrieved from http://bjs.gov/index.cfm?ty=pbdetail&iid=2231

Burgess, R. (2000). *Laughing lessons: 149 2/3 ways to make teaching and learning fun.* Minneapolis, MN: Free Spirit.

Bushaw, W. J., & McNee, J. A. (2009, September). Americans speak out: Are educators and policy makers listening? The 41st Annual Phi Delta Kappa/Gallup Poll of the Public's Attitudes Toward the Public Schools in *Phi Delta Kappan, 91*(1), 9–23.

Butler, R., & Nisan, M. (1986). Effects of no feedback, task-related comments, and grades on intrinsic motivation and performance. *Journal of Educational Psychology, 78*, 210–216.

Butler, S. (2001). Assessment vocabulary. Retrieved from http://www.ncsu.edu/sciencejunction/route/professional/Assessment/assess.html

Butterfly, The. (2006). Retrieved from *PatriciaPolacco.com:* http://www.patriciapolacco.com/books/butterfly/butterfly_navigations.html

Calculating Genetic Risk. (2010). Retrieved from *Learn Genetics—Genetic Science Learning Center:* http://learn.genetics.utah.edu/content/health/history/genetic/

Campbell, G. L. (2004). Towards a strategy of prevention. *Homeless in America: The spiritual dynamics of the unmet need to belong—Exploring the root cause.* Retrieved from http://glcampbell.com/homelessnessinamerica.htm

Canter, L., & Canter, M. (1993). *Succeeding with difficult students: New strategies for reaching your most challenging students.* Santa Monica, CA: Lee Canter & Associates.

C.A.R.E: Strategies for Closing the Achievement Gaps. (2007). *National Education Association* (3rd ed.). Retrieved from http://www.nea.org/assets/docs/mf_CAREbook0804.pdf

Caring for the Whole Patient. (2009, May). Retrieved from: http://www.cancer.net/patient/Coping/Caring+for+the+Whole+Patient

Carter, S. (1994, December). Organizing systems to support competent social behavior in children and youth: Volume III, Teacher stress and burnout. *National Clearinghouse of Rehabilitation Training Materials*, ED 380 970. Retrieved from http://interact.uoregon.edu/wrrc/Burnout.html

Casey, M. (2000). Moral inspiration in the lives of racially diverse rural adolescents. Paper presented at the annual meeting of the American Educational Research Association, April 24–28, New Orleans, LA.

Center for Disability Information & Referral (CeDir). (1998). Patricia Polacco. Retrieved from http://www.iidc.indiana.edu/cedir/kidsweb/fpwdinfo.html#Patricia Polacco

Centers for Disease Control and Prevention. (n.d.). Teen birth rates declined again in 2009. Retrieved from http://www.cdc.gov/Features/dsTeenPregnancy/

Chapman, V. G., & Inman, M. D. (2009, Spring). A conundrum: Rubrics or creativity/metacognitive development? Educational Horizons, *87*(3) 198–201.

Chappuis, J. (2005, November). Helping students understand assessment. *Educational Leadership*, *63*(3), 39–43. Retrieved from ASCD: http://www.ascd.org/publications/educational_leadership/nov05/vol63/num03/Helping_Students_Understand_Assessment.aspx

Charles, C. M. (2010). *Building classroom discipline* (10th ed.). Boston, MA: Pearson Education.

Cheating Is a Personal Foul. (1999). Academic cheating fact sheet. Retrieved from http://www.glass-castle.com/clients/www-nocheating-org/adcouncil/research/cheatingfactsheet.html

Chemical Formula. (n.d.). Balancing chemical equations. Retrieved from http://www.chemicalformula.org/basic-chemistry/balancing-chemical-equations

Chickering, A. W., & Gamson, A. F. (1987). Seven principles for good practice in undergraduate education. (AAHE Bulletin). Racine, WI: The Johnson Foundation, Inc./Wingspread. Retrieved from http://www.bell.ac.uk/edu/GoodPractice/principles.htm

Children in China sickened by school pressure—study. (2010, January 20). Retrieved from *China Daily*. http://www.chinadaily.com.cn/opinion/2010-01/20/content_9349582.htm

Clark, D. (2004). Learning through reflection. Retrieved from http://www.nwlink.com/~donclark/learning/reflecting.html

CNN Justice— CNN Wire Staff. (2010, March 31). More students disciplined following girl's suicide. Retrieved from http://www.cnn.com/2010/CRIME/03/30/massachusetts.bullying.suicide/index.html

Coaching for Success. (1987). *Development Dimensions International*. Retrieved from http://www.ndted.org/TeachingResources/ClassroomTips/Coaching_for_Success.htm

Code of Ethics. (n.d.). *National Education Association—NEA Home*. Retrieved from http://www.nea.org/home/30442.htm

Cohen, D. S. (2005). *The heart of change field guide: Tools and tactics for leading change in your organization*. Boston, MA: Harvard Business School Press.

Collaborative Research Model: Student learning teams in undergraduate research. (n.d.). Retrieved from http://www.uoregon.edu/~tep/resources/crmodel/strategies/learning_through_reflection.html

Collaborative Work Skills Rubric. (n.d.). Retrieved from http://rubistar.4teachers.org/index.php?screen=CustomizeTemplate&bank_rubric_id=15&section_id=6&

Concept to classroom. (2004). Constructivism as a paradigm for teaching and learning. *Educational Broadcasting Corporation*. Retrieved from http://www.thirteen.org/edonline/concept2class/constructivism/index_sub6.html

Confidentiality issues; parental rights. (2010, August 16). *TCTA Survival Guide*. Retrieved from http://tcta.org/publications/tctas_survival_guide/confidentiality_issues_parental_rights

Conley, M. W. (2005). *Connecting standards and assessment through literacy*. Boston, MA: Allyn and Bacon.

Constructive classroom rewards: Promoting good habits while protecting children's health. (n.d.). Retrieved from www.cspinet.org/nutritionpolicy/constructive_rewards.pdf

Cook, L. (2004, April). Co-teaching: Principles, practices, and pragmatics. New Mexico Public Education Department Quarterly Special Education Meeting. Retrieved from http://www.ped.state.nm.us/seo//library/qrtrly.0404.coteaching.lcook.pdf

Coombe, C. & Canning, C. (n.d.). Using self-assessment in the classroom: Rationale and suggested techniques. Retrieved from http://philseflsupport.com/self-assessmenttechniques.htm

Cooper, B. S., & Gargan, A. (2009, September). Rubrics in education: Old term, new meanings. *Phi Delta Kappan, 91*(1), 54–55.

Cotton, K. (2001, January). *Expectations and student outcomes.* Retrieved from http://www.nwrel.org/scpd/sirs/4/cu7.html

Covey, S. R. (1989). *Seven habits of highly effective people.* New York, NY: Fireside.

Covey, S. R. (1992). *Principle-centered leadership* (First Fireside ed.). New York, NY: Simon & Schuster.

Covey, S. R. (1995, August). Think win-win for quality. *Principle-Centered Leadership.* Retrieved from http://www.qualitydigest.com/aug95/covey.html

Covey, S. R. (2004). *The 8th habit: From effectiveness to greatness.* New York, NY: Free Press.

Craven, H. S. (2005, August) Back to school blues for teachers. *Inspiring Teachers.* Retrieved from http://www.inspiringteachers.com/classroom_resources/inspirational_humorous/back_to_school_blues.html

Craven, J., & Farrow, S. (1997). Self-talk—surviving transplantation. A personal guide for organ transplant patients—Their families, friends and caregivers. Retrieved from http://www.sjhc.london.on.ca/sjh/programs/mental/survive/st6c.htm#Table%206.1

Crawford, L. (1998, Spring). Teaching community to 6th graders. *Responsive Classroom, 10*, 2. Retrieved from http://www.responsiveclassroom.org/newsletter/10_2NL_3.asp

Cultivating Collaborative Cultures. (n.d.). [PowerPoint]. Retrieved from http://woodard.latech.edu/~pleonard/epas_report_2005_06/products/5_day_wksh_pp/cultiv_coll_culture.ppt

Dalton, J., & Smith, D. (1986). Extending children's special abilities—Strategies for primary class rooms. Retrieved from http://www.teachers.ash.org.au/researchskills/nglis.htm

Davenport Community Schools. (2005). What does a 'brain-compatible' classroom look like? Instructional strategies. Retrieved from http://www.davenport.k12.ia.us/curriculum/classrooms.asp

Davis, B. G. (2002). Grading practices. Retrieved from http://teaching.berkeley.edu/bgd/grading.html

de Bono, E. (1995, September). Exploring patterns of thought . . . serious creativity. *Journal for Quality and Participation 18*(5), 12–18.

Denton, P. (2007). *The power of our words: Teacher language that helps children learn.* Turners Falls, MA: Northeast Foundation for Children.

Desrochers, C. (2000). Creating lessons designed to motivate students. *Contemporary Education, 71*(2), 51. Retrieved from KYVL Academic Search Premier database.

Dewey, J. (1973). *How we think: Revised and expanded version.* New York, NY: Houghton Mifflin.

Dewey, J. (1938). *Experience and education.* New York, NY: Simon and Schuster.

De Witt, A. (2005). The truth about affirmations. *Guided Imagery.* Retrieved from http://www.holistic-on line.com/guided-imagery-article-thetruth-about-affirmations.htm

Dialogue Education. (2010). Retrieved from http://en.wikipedia.org/wiki/Dialogue_education

Diệp, Nghiêm Thị Bích. (2009, July 2). Theoretical background of peer teaching. *Summary: What's peer-teaching.* Retrieved from http://cnx.org/content/m26497/1.1/

DiGuilio, R. (2000). *Positive classroom management* (2nd ed.). Thousand Oaks, CA: Corwin Press.

Dillon, S. (2011, August 8). Overriding a key education law. *The New York Times.* Retrieved from http://www.nytimes.com/2011/08/08/education/08educ.html?pagewanted=all

Direct instruction or learning cycle? (n.d.). Retrieved from http://www.huntel.net/rsweetland/pedagogy/theories/instructnl/drectLrnen/directOrLrnCycle.html

Discipline Theorists. (2011). The Kounin model. *Classroom management and discipline.* Retrieved from http://www.elearnportal.com/courses/education/classroom-management-and-discipline-discipline-theorists

Documenting and tracking behavior problems. (n.d.). *Managing individual behavior—Project IDEAL.* Retrieved from http://www.projectidealonline.org/classMgt_IndividualBehavior.php

Donaldson, R. (2002, September). What's wrong with schools of education? Retrieved from http://www.brainsarefun.com/Edschools.html

Donovan, S., Bransford, J., & Pellegrino, J. (Eds). (1999). *How people learn: Bridging research and practice.* National Academy of Sciences [On-line]. Available: http://www.intime.uni.edu/model/learning/refl.html

Downey, C. J., Steffy, B. E., Poston, Jr., W. K., & English, F. W. (2009). *50 Ways to close the achievement gap.* (3rd ed.) Thousand Oaks, CA: Sage.

Downing, S. (2006). Autonomy as motivator I. Retrieved from http://www.oncourseworkshop.com/Motivation008.htm

DuFour, R. (2004, May). What is a professional learning community? *Educational Leadership, 61*(8), 6–11. Retrieved from http://www.allthingsplc.info/pdf/articles/DuFourWhatIsAProfessionalLearningCommunity.pdf

DuFour, R. (2011, February). Work together but only if you want to. *Phi Delta Kappan, 95*(5), 57–61.

Dun, S. (2005). Classic chembalancer. Retrieved from http://funbasedlearning.com/chemistry/chemBalancer/default.htm

Dweck, C. S. (2008). *Mindset: The new psychology of success.* (Ballantine Books Trade Paperback Edition). New York, NY: Ballantine Books.

Education Manifesto: A Nation Still at Risk. (1998, April 30). *National Commission on Excellence in Education.* Retrieved http://www.edreform.com/index.cfm?fuseAction=document&nglishd=1548

Educational Resources. (n.d.). Howard Gardner's multiple intelligences theory. Retrieved from http://www.pbs.org/wnet/gperf/education/ed_mi_overview.html

Edwards, C. (1994). Learning and control in the classroom. *Journal of Instructional Psychology, 21*(4), 340–346.

Edwards, J. (2010). *Inviting students to learn: 100 tips for talking effectively with your students.* Alexandria, VA: Association for Supervision and Curriculum Development.

Elder, J. (n.d.). Findings about brain research and brain-friendly instructional strategies. Retrieved from http://readingprof.com/papers/5_.pdf

Elkind, D. H., & Sweet, F. (1997). Ethical reasoning and the art of classroom dialogue. Retrieved from http://www.goodcharacter.com/Article_3.html

Ellis-Christensen, T. (2009). What is a win-win situation? Retrieved from http://www.wisegeek.com/what-is-a-win-win-situation.htm

Ellison, J., Hayes, C., Costa, A., & Garmston, B. (2008). *Cognitive Coaching foundation seminar trainer's guide.* Highlands Ranch, CO: Center for Cognitive Coaching.

Emmer, E. T. (1986). *Effects of teacher training in disciplinary approaches.* Washington, DC: U.S. Department of Education, Office of Educational Research and Improvement. Retrieved from ERIC database. (ED316927)

Erickson, B. L., & Strommer, D. W. (1991). *Teaching college freshmen.* San Francisco, CA: Jossey-Bass.

Ethics of Youth, The—2008 Summary, The. (2009). Retrieved from *Josephson Institute: Center for Youth Ethics:* http://charactercounts.org/programs/reportcard/index.html

Ewell, P. T. (1997). *Organizing for learning: A point of entry.* Draft prepared for discussion at the 1997 AAHE Summer Academy at Snowbird. National Center for Higher Education Management Systems. Retrieved from http://www.intime.uni.edu/model/learning/learn_summary.html

Expectancy theory. (n.d.). Retrieved from http://changingminds.org/explanations/theories/expectancy.htm

Expectancy value theory. (2010). *University of Twente.* Retrieved from http://www.utwente.nl/cw/theorieenoverzicht/Theory%20clusters/Public%20Relations,%20Advertising,%20Marketing%20and%20Consumer%20Behavior/Expectancy_Value_Theory.doc/

Expectations. (2001). Closing the achievement gap requires multiple solutions. Retrieved from http://www.somsd.k12.nj.us/~chssocst/ssteacherinservice0402solutions.htm

FAQS and Factsheets. (2005). Retrieved from *Teacher Support Network:* http://www.teachersupport.info/

Farivar, S., & Webb, N. M. (1994). Helping and getting help: Essential skills for group problem solving. Arithmetic Teacher, *41*, 521–525.

FERPA Information. (n.d.). *JSU—Office of the Registrar.* Retrieved from http://www.jsu.edu/registrar/ferpa.html

Feigelson, S. (1998). *Energize your meetings with laughter.* Alexandria, VA: Association for Supervision and Curriculum Development.

Fisher, R. (2009). *Creative dialogue: Talk for thinking in the classroom.* Abingdon, UK: Routledge.

Flowerday, R., & Bryant, M. (n.d.). Teacher craft: Choice in the classroom. Retrieved from http://tc.unl.edu/mbryant/Choice.htm

Foster, B. G. (1995). *Feasibility or fantasy: Helping children become media literate consumers.* Doctoral dissertation. Spalding University, Louisville, KY.

Freedman, J. (2007, April). A hope for change: Alan Deutschman on change or die. Retrieved from http://www.6seconds.org/pdf/a_hope_for_change.pdf

Freedman, J. (2010, January). The six seconds EQ model [Web blog]. Retrieved from http://www.6seconds.org/blog/2010/01/the-six-seconds-eq-model/

Freedman, J., Ghini, M., & Fiedeldey-Van Dijk, C. (2005, April). White paper: Emotional intelligence and performance. Retrieved from *Six Seconds*: http://www.6seconds.org/sei/eq_success.php

Freire, P. (1972). *Pedagogy of the oppressed.* Harmondsworth, UK: Penguin Books.

Freire. P. (1978). *Pedagogy in process.* New York, NY: Seabury.

Friend, M. (2007). Collaborating for school success. Training material presented at VASSP/VFEL in collaboration with Virginia Department of Education and the College of William and Mary workshop, Williamsburg, VA.

Friend, M., & Cook, L. (1992). *Interactions: Collaboration skills for school professionals.* White Plains, NY: Longman.

Frye, R. (1999, June). Assessment, accountability, and student learning outcomes. Retrieved from http://pandora.cii.wwu.edu/dialogue/issue2.html

Fulwiler, T., & Young, A. (2000). *Language connections: Writing and reading across the curriculum.* WAC Clearinghouse Landmark Publications in Writing Studies. Retrieved from http://wac.colostate.edu/books/language_connections/language_connections.pdf/

Further word on cheating in American schools, A. (n.d.). Retrieved from http://www.gibbsmagazine.com/gibbsmagazine-www/Further%20Cheating.htm

Gallwey, W. T. (n.d.). What is the inner game? Retrieved from *The Inner Game:* http://theinnergame.com/html/whatisInnerGame.html

Gallwey, W. T. (1999). Coaching. Retrieved from *The Inner Game of Work:* http://theinnergame.com/html/IGW_ChapterExcerpts.html##

Gan, J. (n.d.). Fear of failure. Retrieved from http://www.succezz.com/MotivateYourWayToSuccess.html

Garcia, T., McKeachie, W. J., Pintrich, P. R., & Smith, D. A. (1991). *A manual for the use of the Motivated Strategies for Learning Questionnaire* (Tech. Rep. No. 91-B-004). Ann Arbor, MI: The University of Michigan, School of Education.

Gartrell, D. (1987). Assertive discipline: Unhealthy for children and other living things. *Young Children, 42*(2), 10–11.

Gawande, A. (2009). The checklist manifesto: How to get things right. New York, NY: Metropolitan Books-Henry Holt.

Gayagay, L. (n.d.). How to instill positive discipline and effective classroom rules. Retrieved from http://www.helium.com/items/1374184-how-to-instill-positive-discipline-and-effective-classroom-rules

Gazin, A. (2004). What do you expect? Retrieved from *Teacher Scholastic:* http://teacher.scholastic.com/products/instructor/Aug04_expectations.htm

Geisler, S. (2001). The formation and effects of teacher expectations on students. Retrieved from http://uwstout.edu/lib/thesis/2001/2001geislers.pdf

Generational Characteristics. (n.d.). Retrieved from http://www.dhss.mo.gov/LPHA/New2008MCHI/GenerationalDifferences_Worksheet_GalenHoff.pdf

Gettinger, M., & Kohler, K. M. (2006). Process-outcome approaches to classroom management and effective teaching. In C. Evertson, C. M. Weinstein, & C. S. Weinstein (Eds). *Handbook of Classroom Management: Research, Practice, and Contemporary Issues* (pp. 73–95). Mahwah, NJ: Erlbaum.

Gibbon, C. (2009, March 30). Classroom celebrations. *Teacher discussions, blogs, chat, social networking for teachers—ProTeacher Community.* Retrieved from http://www.proteacher.net/discussions/showthread.php?t=113659

Gibbs, J. (2006). About Tribes. *Tribes: A new way of learning and being together.* Retrieved http://www.tribes.com/about_tribes_process.htm

Gilbert, C. B. (n.d.). Standardized test accountability debate nothing new. Retrieved from http://www.associatedcontent.com/article/5850472/standardized_test_accountability_debate.html?cat=4

Glasser, W. (1997, April). A new look at school failure and school success. *Phi Delta Kappan, 78*(8), 596. Retrieved from KYVL Academic Search Premier.

Glickman, C. J. (2005, October 3). Chapter 1: Introduction. In *Sex and Shame: Authenticity in Adult Education. Electronic Journal of Human Sexuality: Vol. 8.* Retrieved from http://www.ejhs.org/volume8/Glickman1.htm

Ginott, H. (1965). *Between parent and child: New solutions to old problems.* New York, NY: Macmillan.

Global Learning Partners. (2006ba). Jane's story. Retrieved from http://www.globalearning.com/janevella.htm

Global Learning Partners. (2006b). What is dialogue education?/Switch the focus! Retrieved from http://www.globalearning.com/dialogueeducation.htm

Global Learning Partners. (2010). How dialogue education is different. Retrieved from http://www.globalearning.com/compare.htm

Glod, M. (2008, June 25). Test results improve after 'No Child' law, study finds. *Washington Post Politics, National, World & DC Area News and Headlines—Washingtonpost.com.* Retrieved from http://www.washingtonpost.com/wpdyn/content/article/2008/06/24/AR2008062401322.html

Glossary of Terms & Links. (n.d.). Guided practice. Retrieved from http://www.usu.edu/teachall/text/effective/EFFglos.htm

Goleman, D. (1995). *Emotional intelligence.* New York, NY: Bantam Books.

Graham, S. (1990). Communicating low ability in the classroom: Bad things good teachers sometimes do. In S. Graham and V. Folkes (Eds.), *Attribution theory: Applications to achievement, mental health, and interpersonal conflict* (pp. 17–36). Hillsdale, NJ: Erlbaum.

Gredler, M. E. (1992). *Learning and instruction: Theory into practice.* New York, NY: Macmillan.

Green, K. E. (2010). Student performance: The impact of teacher expectations and student-teacher relationships (Research project). Retrieved from http://www.cehs.ohio.edu/gfx/media/pdf/kelsey.pdf

Gross, A. E. & McMullen, P. A. (1983). Models of the help-seeking process. In J. D. Fisher, N. Nadler, & B. M. DePaulo (Eds.). *New directions in helping, 2,* 45–61. New York, NY: Academic Press.

Grossman, P. (2005, January/February). Teaching: From 'A nation at risk' to a profession at risk? Retrieved from http://www.edletter.org/past/issues/2003jf/nation.shtml

Grow, G. O. (1994). In defense of the staged self-directed learning model. *Longleaf Publications.* Retrieved from http://www.longleaf.net/ggrow/SSDL/SSDLReply.html

Grow, G. O. (1996). Teaching learners to be self-directed. *Adult Education Quarterly, 41*(3), 125–149. Expanded version retrieved from http://www.longleaf.net/ggrow

Gruwell, E. (1999). The Freedom Writers with Erin Gruwell. *The freedom writers' diary: How a teacher and 150 teens used writing to change themselves and the world around them.* New York, NY: Broadway Books.

Guided Imagery and Visualization. (2007). Retrieved from http://www.holistic-online.com/guided-imagery.htm

Gumbel, P. (2010, December 7). China beats out Finland for top marks in Education. *Breaking News, Analysis, Politics, Blogs, News Photos, Video, Tech Reviews.* Retrieved from http://www.time.com/time/world/article/0,8599,2035586,00.html#ixzz17XACd2S2

Guskey, T. R. (2001, Summer). The backward approach. *Journal of Staff Development, 22*(3), 60.

Guthrie, J. T. (2001, March). Contexts for engagement and motivation in reading. Retrieved from http://www.readingonline.org/articles/handbook/guthrie/

Hall, E. (n.d.). The history of the standardized test. Retrieved from http://www.ehow.com/about_53 92902_history-standardized-test.html

Halter, J. (n.d.). Metacognition. Retrieved from http://coe.sdsu.edu/eet/Articles/metacognition/start.htm

Hansen, J. (2011, Winter). Teaching without talking. *Educational Horizons, 89*, 6–11.

Hansen, J. M., & Childs, J. (1998, September). Article outline: Creating a school where people like to be. *Educational Leadership Magazine, 56*, 14–17. Retrieved from http://portfolios.valdosta.edu/dsp itts/article_outline.htm

Hargreaves, A. & Fullan, M. (1998). *What's worth fighting for out there?* Mississauga, ON: Ontario Public School Teachers' Federation.

Harmin, M. (1994). Strategies for encouraging beyond praise and rewards. *Inspiring active learning: A handbook for teachers.* Alexandria, VA: Association for Supervision and Curriculum Development.

Hatfield, L. (n.d.). How to instill positive discipline and effective classroom rules. Retrieved from http://www.helium.com/items/858542-how-to-instill-positive-discipline-and-effective-classroom-rules

Hattie, J. (2008). *Visible learning: A synthesis of over 800 meta-analyses relating to achievement.* London, UK: Routledge.

Hattie, J., & Timperley, H. (2007). The power of feedback. *Review of Educational Research, 77*, 81–112.

Hatton, N., & Smith, D. (1995). *Reflection in teacher education: Towards definition and implementation.* University of Sydney: School of teaching and Curriculum Studies. Retrieved from http://www2.edfac.usyd.edu.au/LocalResource/Study1/hattonart.html

Heider, F. (2009). Retrieved from http://en.wikipedia.org/wiki/Fritz_Heider

Heisler, M. (2007, October). Overview of peer support models to improve diabetes self-management and clinical outcomes. *Diabetes Spectrum 20*(4), 214–221. doi: 10.2337/diaspect.20.4.214

Herbert, B. (2007, October 9). High-stakes flimflam. *The New York Times—Breaking News, World News & Multimedia.* Retrieved from http://www.nytimes.com/2007/10/09/opinion/09herbert.html?_r=2

High Expectations. (n.d.). Beyond reflection: Teacher learning as praxis. Retrieved from http://www.ncrel.org/sdrs/areas/issues/students/atrisk/at6lk1.htm

Hildreth, S. (2012). Edible color wheels. Retrieved from http://www.princetonol.com/groups/iad/Files/color.htm

Hirsch, J. (2001, March) Inside the classroom: The mood inside the schools. Frontline. Testing Our Schools: Testing: in the Classroom. *Public Broadcasting Service.* Retrieved from http://www.pbs.org/wgbh/pages/frontline/shows/schools/testing/theme.html

Hoegerl, C. (2005, September). Teacher, heal thyself. *The Journal of the American Osteopathic Association 105*(9). Retrieved from http://www.jaoa.org/cgi/content/full/105/9/426-a

Hoffman, J. V., Assaf, L. C., & Paris, S. G. (2001). High-stakes testing in reading: Today in Texas, tomorrow? *Reading Teacher, 54*(5), 482–492.

Hoffman-Kipp, P., Artiles, A. J., & Lopez-Torres, L. (2003, Summer). Beyond reflection: Teacher learning as praxis. *Theory into practice, 42*(3), 248–254. doi:10.1353/tip.2003.0030

Hopper, C. H. (2009). Brain bites: What brain research says about each principle. Memory Principles [PowerPoint]. Retrieved from http://college.cengage.com/collegesurvival/hopper/practicing_colege/4e/prepare/ppt/hopper_ch04_memory_principles_expanded_classroom.ppt\

Horn, J. (2010, January 4). Schools matter: New CREDO study shows no charter school miracles for NYC. *Schools Matter.* Retrieved from http://www.schoolsmatter.info/2010/01/new-credo-study-shows-no-charter-school.html

How Standardized Testing Damages Education. (n.d.). *Fair Test: National Center for Fair & Open Testing.* Retrieved from www.fairtest.org/files/how%20standardized%20tests%20hurt%20ed.pdf

How to Dress Like a Teacher. (n.d.). *eHow | How to Videos, Articles & More - Trusted Advice for the Curious Life.* Retrieved from http://www.ehow.com/how_4494683_dress-like-teacher.html

Howey, S. C. (2009). Student motivation: Factors in student motivation. Retrieved from http://www.nacada.ksu.edu/Clearinghouse/AdvisingIssues/Motivation.htm

Hoxby, C. M. (2000). Is there a crisis? (Interview). Retrieved from http://www.pbs.org/wgbh/pages/frontline/shows/vouchers/howbad/crisis.html

Huitt, W. (2002). Social cognition. *Educational Psychology Interactive.* Valdosta, GA: Valdosta State University. Retrieved from http://chiron.valdosta.edu/whuitt/col/soccog/soccog.html

Humor—Index. (n.d.). *Humor, Fun.* Retrieved from http://www.animalliberationfront.com/Games/Comedy/Quotes%20-%20Citaten.htm

Hunter, M. (1984). Knowing, teaching, and supervising. In P. L. Hosford (Ed.), *Using what we know about teaching* (pp. 169–193). Alexandria, VA: Association for Supervision and Curriculum Development.

Hunter, M. (2004). *Mastery teaching.* Thousand Oaks, CA: Corwin Press.

Independent Test Results Show NCLB Failing (2008, January.). Retrieved from http://www.fairtest.org/independent-test-results-show-9f-failing

Interpersonal Communication. (n.d.). Retrieved from http://www.uc.edu/armyrotc/ms2text/MSL_201_L08b_Interpersonal_Communication.pdf

Introduction to data-based decision making, The. (n.d.). *Special Connections.* Retrieved from http://www.specialconnections.ku.edu/cgi-bin/cgiwrap/specconn/main.php?cat=assessment&section=ddm/main

Jackson, R. R. (2009). *Never work harder than your students & other principles of great teaching.* Alexandria, VA: Association for Supervision and Curriculum Development.

Jacobson, M. F. (n.d.). Constructive classroom rewards: Promoting good habits while protecting children's health. *Center for Science in the Public Interest.* Retrieved from http://www.cspinet.org/nutritionpolicy/constructive_rewards.pdf

Jain, S. (2009). High-stakes testing: Gaming the system or getting it right? Retrieved from http://www.parentwiseaustin.com/Archive/2009-09/High-Stakes-Testing-GamingSystem-or-Getting-It-Right

Janac, K., Kipperman, D., & Linder, D. (1997). Learning strategies matrix. Retrieved from http://edweb.sdsu.edu/courses/ET650_online/MAPPS/Strats.html

Janis, I. (1980). The influence of television on personal decision-making. In Withey, D. B., & Abeles, R. P. (Eds.). *Television and social behavior: Beyond violence and children.* (pp. 161–190). Hillsdale, NJ: Erlbaum.

Jehlen, A. (2010, October). How Finland reached the top of the educational rankings. *NEA Today.* Retrieved from http://neatoday.org/2010/07/-finland-reached-the-top-of-the-educationalrankings/

Jensen, E. (1998). Motivation and rewards. *Teaching with the Brain in Mind.* Alexandria, VA: Association for Supervision and Curriculum Development.

Jensen, E. (2003). *Tools for engagement: Managing emotional states for learner success.* Thousand Oaks, CA: Corwin Press.

Johnson, D. D., & Johnson, B. (2006). High stakes: Poverty, testing, and failure in American schools (2nd ed.). Lanham, MD: Rowman & Littlefield.

Johnson, J. (n.d.). Standardized testing: Benefits for teachers. *Helium.* Retrieved from http://www.helium.com/items/1733280-benefits-of-standardized-testing

Jones, S. (1996). The neutralization of benefits in standardized testing. Retrieved from http://eserver.org/courses/fall96/76-100g/jones/

Jones, V. F., & Jones, L. S. (2001). *Comprehensive classroom management: Creating communities of support and solving problems,* (6th ed.) Needham Heights, MA: Allyn & Bacon.

Jordan, M. (1994). *I can't accept not trying: Michael Jordan on the pursuit of excellence.* San Francisco, CA: Harper Collins.

Kagan, S. (2002, Winter). What is win-win discipline? *Kagan Online Magazine.* Retrieved from http://www.kaganonline.com/free_articles/dr_spencer_kagan/ASK15.php

Kamii, C. (1991). Toward autonomy: The importance of critical thinking and choice making. *School Psychology Review, 20,* 3.

Kara, A. (2008.). Understanding today's schools with chaos theory. *Welcome to The Fountain Magazine.* Retrieved from http://www.fountainmagazine.com/article.php?ARTICLEID=881

Katz, D. L., & Gordon, D. L. (2005). *Stealth health.* New York, NY: Reader's Digest Association. Retrieved from http://www.rd.com/family/19-ways-to-enhance-your-sense-of-humor/

Kay, R. S., & Kay, D. S. (1994). The best is within them: Propositions, principles, and strategies for teaching respect, responsibility, and excellence in the classroom. Unpublished manuscript.

Kekes, J. (1992). *The examined life.* University Park, PA: Pennsylvania State University Press.

Kemmerling, C. (2005) The pros of standardized testing. *The Astro Home Page.* Retrieved from http://astro.temple.edu/~mhicks/standardizedtestingpro.html

Kennedy, L. M., & Tipps, S. (2000). *Teaching and learning elementary math: Guiding children's learning of mathematics,* (2nd ed.). Belmont, CA: Wadsworth/Thomson Learning.

Kerachsky, S. (n.d.). Commissioner's statement: The condition of education 2010. *National Center for Education Statistics (NCES), a part of the U.S. Department of Education.* Retrieved from http://nces.ed.gov/programs/coe/statement/s8.asp

Kern, M. F. (2008). Stages of change. Retrieved from http://www.addictioninfo.org/articles/11/1/Stages-of-Change-Model/Page1.html

Klauser, H. A. (2000). *Write it down, make it happen: Knowing what you want—and getting it!* New York, NY: Touchstone.

Kohn, A. (1993, September). Choices for children: Why and how to let students decide. *Phi Delta Kappan.* Retrieved from http://www.alfiekohn.org/teaching/cfc.htm

Koretz, D. (n.d.). The use and misuse of test scores in reform debate. Retrieved from http://www.rand.org/pubs/research_briefs/RB8008/index1.html

Kotter, J. P., & Cohen, D. S. (2002). The heart of change. Boston, MA: Harvard Business Review Press.

Kounin Model. (2002.). *TeacherMatters—Classroom Management and Discipline.* Retrieved from http://www.teachermatters.com/index.php?option=com_content&view=article&id=9:kounin-model&catid=4:models-of-discipline&Itemid=4

Kozar, O. (2010). Towards better group work: Seeing the difference between cooperation and collaboration. *English Teacher Forum, 2.* Retrieved from http://exchanges.state.gov/englishteaching/forum/archives/docs/files-folder111111/48_2-etf-towards-better-group-work-seeing-the-difference-between-cooperation-and-collaboration.pdf

Kraft, M. A. (2010, April). From ringmaster to conductor. *Phi Delta Kappan, 91*(7), 44–47.

Krapp, A. (2002, June 25). An educational-psychological theory of interest and its relation to SDT. Retrieved from http://www.unibwmuenchen.de/campus/SOWI/instfak/psych/krapp/Aa-Interessepd f/Krapp02.pdf

Krapp, A., Hidi, S., & Renninger, A. (1992). Interest, learning and development. In A. Renninger, S. Hidi, & A. Krapp (Eds.). *The role of interest in learning and development.* Hillsdale, NJ: Erlbaum.

Krider, D. (2008, Summer). Teachers as social advocate leaders. *Childhood Education.* Retrieved from http://findarticles.com/p/articles/mi_qa3614/is_200807/ai_n27899134/

Krovetz, M. L. (1999, May/June). Fostering resiliency. *Thrust for Educational Leadership, 28*(5), 28. Retrieved from KYVL Professional Development Collection.

Krovetz, M. L. (2004). Resiliency and adolescents at risk: Reconceptualizing schools as communities. In *The Four Components of Resiliency.* San José State University—Module 14, Session 1 ~ Lecture Notes. Retrieved from http://alternativeed.sjsu.edu/documents/notes/mod14_1notes.pdf

Landau, B. M., & Gathercoal, P. (2000, February). Creating peaceful classroom. *Phi Delta Kappan, 81,* 450.

Larrivee, B. (2009). *Authentic classroom management: Creating a learning community and building reflective practice* (3rd ed.). Upper Saddle River, NJ: Pearson.

Launius, R. D. (n.d.). Sputnik and the dawn of the space age. *The History of Satellites.* Retrieved from http://inventors.about.com/library/inventors/blsatellite.htm

Leahy, S., Lyon, C., Thompson, M., & Wiliam, D. (2005, November). Minute by minute, day by day. *Association for Supervision and Curriculum Development.* Retrieved from http://www.ascd .org/publications/educational_leadership/nov05/vol63/num03/Classroom_Assessment@_Minute_ by_Minute,_Day_by_Day.aspx

Leavell, D. (n.d.). Authentic assessment: Using rubrics to evaluate project-based learning. [PowerPoint] Retrieved fromwww.tcet.unt.edu/weblibrary/ppt/rubric1.ppt

Lehner, George F. J. (1978, June). Aids for giving and receiving feedback. *Child Care Information Exchange.*

Lemov, D. (2010). *Teach like a champion: 49 techniques that put students on the path to college.* San Francisco, CA: Jossey-Bass.

Lesson design. (n.d.). Retrieved from http://members.tripod.com/teaching_is_reaching/lesson_design.htm

Levine, A. E. (2000, January 30). Education for lasting reform: First look to the teachers. Education. *Center for Education Reform* – Editorials. Retrieved from http://www.edreform.com/Resources/ Editorials/?Education_for_Lasting_Reform_First_Look_to_the_Teachers&year=2000

Lewis, B. (n.d.) Avoiding teacher burnout: Practical tips for avoiding burnout and renewing your commitment to teaching. *About.com: Elementary Education.* Retrieved from http://k6educators. about.com/cs/helpforteachers/a/avoidburnout.htm

Lewis, B. (n.d.). What teachers should wear—Teaching dress code—The right threads=The right classroom atmosphere. *Elementary Education—Lesson Plans and Teaching Strategies for Elementary School Teachers.* Retrieved from http://k6educators.about.com/od/classroommanage ment/a/attire.htm

Lewis, B. (2008, January 30). How should teachers dress? *Elementary Education—Lesson Plans and Teaching Strategies for Elementary School Teachers.* Retrieved from http://k6educators.about. com/b/2008/01/30/how-should-teachers-dress-2.htm

Liam, S. (2010, January 3). United Federation of Teachers recommends changes to charter school law. Retrieved from http://www.theepochtimes.com/n2/content/view/27411/

Lipton, L., & Wellman, B. (1998). *Patterns and practices in the learning-focused classroom.* Guilford, VT: Pathways. Retrieved from *Instructional Strategies for Engaging Learners*, Guilford County Schools, TF, 2002: http://its.guilford.k12.nc.us/act/strategies/walk_around_survey.htm

List of reward ideas. (n.d.). *CanTeach.* Retrieved from www.canteach.ca/elementary/classman2

Little, D. (2003). Learner autonomy and second/foreign language learning. Retrieved from http://www.lang.ltsn.ac.uk/resources/goodpractice.aspx?resourceid=1409

Littleton, K., & Howe, C. (2010). *Educational dialogues: Understanding and promoting productive interaction.* London, UK: Routledge.

Lord, A. (1999). Consciousness and the placebo effect. Retrieved from http://serendip.brynmawr.edu/bb/neuro/neuro99/web3/Lord.html

Louwerse, M. (2000, December 16). Strategies for effective classroom rules. ELTNEWS.com for Teaching English in Japan. *Kids World.* Retrieved from http://www.eltnews.com/features/kids_world/2000/12/strategies_for_effective_class.html

Lumb, A. L. (2002). Apple quert symbolism. Retrieved from http://www.wooddragonarts.freeserve.co.uk/apple_quert_symbolism.htm

Lumsden, L. (1997, July). Expectations for students. *ERIC Digest,* Number 116. ED409609. Retrieved from http://cepm.uoregon.edu/publications/digests/digest116.html

Luxford, H., & Smart, L. (2009). *Learning through talk: Developing learning dialogues in the primary classroom.* Abingdon, UK: Routledge.

Maas, J. (2005). Principled practice: New science for the classroom. In T. Hatch, D. Ahmed, D. Lieberman, M. E. White, & D. H. Pointer Mace (Eds.), *Going Public with Our Teaching: An Anthology of Practice* (pp. 270–280). New York, NY: Teachers College Press. Retrieved from http://www.goingpublicwithteaching.org/Ch20_Maas.pdf

Marker, P. (n.d.). Standards and high stakes testing: The dark side of a generation of political, economic and social neglect of public education. *The Rouge Forum.* Retrieved from http://www.rougeforum.org/MarkerOrlando.htm

Marshall, M. (2000, August). Classroom meetings. Retrieved from http://teachers.net/gazette/AUG00marshall.htmls

Marshall, M. (2011, February). Guided choices of the raise responsibility system. Retrieved from http://www.marvinmarshall.com/guided-choices-of-the-raise-responsibility-system/

Marzano, R. (1992). *A different kind of classroom: Teaching with dimensions of learning.* Alexandria, VA: Association for Supervision and Curriculum Development.

Marzano, R. J. (2007). *The art and science of teaching: A comprehensive framework for effective instruction.* Alexandria, VA: Association for Supervision and Curriculum Development.

Marzano, R. J. (2009, September) Setting the record straight on "high-yield" strategies. *Phi Delta Kappan, 91*(1), 30–37.

Marzano, R. J., Gaddy, B. B., Foseid, M. C., Foseid, M. P., & Marzano, J. S. (2005). Module 1: General classroom behavior. *Handbook for Classroom Management That Works* by Association for Supervision and Curriculum Development. Retrieved from http://www.ascd.org/publications/books/105012/chapters/Module-1@-General-Classroom-Behavior.aspx

Maslow, A. H. (1943). A theory of human motivation. *Psychological Review, 50*, 370–396. Retrieved from http://psychclassics.yorku.ca/Maslow/motivation.htm

Massey, M. (2007). Tips for developing successful partnerships. *Seed Insight: Theme 1—Starting and Growing a Venture.* Retrieved from http://www.seedinit.org/en/component/docman/doc_download/11-seed-insight-start-up-success-tips-for-partnerships.html

McBride, A. (2006, December). Landmark cases. *Brown v. Board of Education (1954).* Retrieved from http://www.pbs.org/wnet/supremecourt/rights/landmark_brown.html

McCarthy, C. P. (1998, July). Learner training for learner autonomy on summer language courses. *The Internet TESL Journal, IV*(7). Retrieved from http://iteslj.org/Techniques/McCarthy-Autonomy. html

McGarry, D. (1995). *Learner Autonomy 4: The Role of Authentic Texts.* Dublin, Ireland: Authentik.

McGhee, P. (n.d.). Team building humor strengthens a team identity or spirit. *Health, Healing and the Amuse System: Humor as Survival Training.* Retrieved from http://www.laughterremedy.com/ articles/team_building.html

Mcintyre, S. (n.d.). How to instill positive discipline and effective classroom rules. Helium. Retrieved from http://www.helium.com/items/1373618-positive-discipline-and-effective-classroommanage ment/print

McLeod, J., Fisher, J., & Hoover, G. (2003). *The key elements of classroom management: managing time and space, student behavior, and instructional strategies.* Alexandria, VA: Association for Supervision and Curriculum Development.

McTighe, J., & O'Conner, K. (2005, November). Seven practices for effective learning. *Educational Leadership, 63*(3), 10–17. Retrieved from http://www.ascd.org/publications/educational-leader ship/nov05/vol63/num03/Seven-Practices-for-Effective-Learning.aspx

Mearns, J. (2009, May). The social theory of Julian B. Rotter. Retrieved from http://psych.fullerton.edu /jmearns/rotter.htm

Mendler, A. N. (2001). *Connecting with students.* Alexandria, VA: Association for Supervision and Curriculum Development.

Metacognition. (n.d.). Retrieved from *North Central Regional Educational Laboratory:* http://www.ncrel. org/sdrs/areas/issues/students/atrisk/at7lk5.htm

Michaels, S., O'Connor, C., & Resnick, L. B. (2008). Deliberative discourse idealized and realized: accountable talk in the classroom and civic life. *Studies in Philosophy and Education, 27*(4), 283–297.

Mills, D. W. (2002). Applying what we know—Student learning styles. Retrieved from http://www.csrnet. org/csrnet/articles/student-learningstyles.html

Mills, J. L., Jr. (2008). Tiered instruction and assessments. Retrieved from *CurrTech Integrations:* http:// www.csrnet.org/csrnet/articles/studentlearningstyles.html

Mobbs, R. (2003, December). Benjamin Bloom. Retrieved from http://www.le.ac.uk/cc/rjm1/etutor /resources/learningtheories/bloom.html

Moskowitz, G., & Hayman, J. L. (1976). Success strategies of inner-city teachers: A year-long study. *Journal of Educational Research, 69*, 283–289.

Mother's Education Level. (2008). Retrieved from http://www.rikidscount.org/matriarch/documents /08%20Factbook%20Indicator%205.pdf

Mountain View Whisman School District—Mission Statement. (n.d.). *Mission Statement.* Retrieved from http://www.mvwsd.org/index.php?option=com_content&task=view&id=536&Itemid=743

Mueller, J. (2008). Rubrics. Retrieved from *Authentic Assessment Toolbox*: http://jonathan.mueller .faculty.noctrl.edu/toolbox/rubrics.htm

Munns, G., & Woodward, H. (2006). Student engagement and student self-assessment: The REAL framework. *Assessment in Education: Principles, Policy & Practice, 13*(2), 193–213.

Murden McClure, V. (Speaker.) (2011, October 17). We can do better. *Spalding University Presidential Inaugural Address.* Lecture conducted from Cathedral of the Assumption, Louisville, Kentucky.

Mynard, J., & Sorflaten, R. (2002). Independent learning in your classroom. *TESOL Arabia Learner Independence Special Interest Group.* Retrieved from http://ilearn.20m.com/research/zuinde.htm

Nation at Risk, A. (1983, April). Retrieved from http://www.ed.gov/pubs/NatAtRisk/risk.html

National Assessment of Educational Progress. (2010). NAEP Overview. Retrieved from http://nces.ed. gov/nationsreportcard/about/

National Center for Education Services. (2010). Indicators of school crime and safety: 2010. Retrieved from http://nces.ed.gov/programs/crimeindicators/crimeindicators2010/ind_11.asp

National Institute of Mental Health. (n.d.). Suicide in the U.S.: Statistics and prevention. NIH Publication No. 06-4594. Retrieved from http://www.nimh.nih.gov/health/publications/suicide-in-the-us-statistics-and-prevention/index.shtml

Neill, M. (2010, October 12). Letters—Testing a student, and a system. *The New York Times—The Opinion Pages*. Retrieved from http://www.nytimes.com/2010/10/18/opinion/l18schools.html

Neils, H. (n.d.). 13 signs of burnout and how to help you avoid it. Retrieved from http://www.assessment.com/mappmembers/avoidingburnout.asp?Accnum=06-5210-010.00

Nelsen, J., Lott, L., & Glenn, H. S. (1997). *Positive discipline in the classroom*. Rockland, CA: Prima.

Neugebauer, R. (1983, July/August). Guidelines for effective use of feedback. Child Care Information Exchange, 1–3. Retrieved from https://secure.ccie.com/library/5003201.pdf

Nichols, S. L., & Berliner, D. C. (2007). *Collateral damage: How high-stakes testing corrupts America's schools*. Cambridge, MA: Harvard Education Press.

No Child Left Behind: A Desktop Reference. (2007). Retrieved from U.S. Department of Education: http://www2.ed.gov/admins/lead/account/nclbreference/page_pg3.html

Nystrand, M., Gamoran, A., Kachur, R., & Prendergast, C. (1997). *Opening dialogue: Understanding the dynamics of language and learning in the English classroom*. New York, NY: Teachers College. Press.

O'Conner, K. (2009). *How to grade for learning K–12* (3rd ed.). Thousand Oaks, CA: Corwin Press.

Ogden, S. N. (1999). Why are you the victim of put downs? *More on Put Downs*. Retrieved from http://www.fearfreeed.com/Putdowns.htm

Oxford, R. L. (1990). *Language learning strategies: What every teacher should know*. Boston, MA: Heinle & Heinle.

Pajares, F. (2002). Overview of social cognitive theory and of self-efficacy. Retrieved from http://www.des.emory.edu/mfp/eff.html

Palmer, P. J. (1997, November/December). The heart of a teacher: Identity and integrity in teaching. *Change Magazine, 29*(6), 14–21. Retrieved from *Maricopa Center for Learning and Instruction*: http://www.mcli.dist.maricopa.edu/events/afc99/articles/heartof.html

Pangaro, L. N., & McGaghie, W. C. (2005). Evaluation and grading of students. In R. E. Fincher (Ed.), *Guidebook for Clerkship Directors* (3rd ed.). Omaha, NE: Alliance for Clinical Education—Nebraska Medical Center. Retrieved from http://familymed.uthscsa.edu/ACE/chapter6.htm

Parsons, M., & Blake, S. (2004, November). Peer support: An overview. *spotlight briefing*. Retrieved from www.citized.info/pdf/external/ncb/Final_Peer_support_aw.pdf

Patsula, P. J. (1999). Applying learning theories to online instructional design. Sookmyung Women's University, Seoul. Retrieved from http://www.patsula.com/usefo/webbasedlearning/tutorial1/learning_theories_full_version.html#bruner

Paulo Freire. (2010). Retrieved from http://www.k12academics.com/educational-philosophy/paulo-freire

Pavlina, S. (2006, January 18). Intelligent risk taking [Web blog]. Retrieved from *Personal Development for Smart People:* http://www.stevepavlina.com/blog/2006/01/intelligent-risktaking/

Payne, J. (2010). Teaching ideas: Classroom readiness. Retrieved from http://www.neighborjanepayne.com/read.php?SD=31&SS=80

Pearson, J. C., & Nelson, P. E. (1985). *Understanding and sharing: An introduction to speech communication* (3rd ed.). Dubuque, IA: William C. Brown.

Pence, G. E. (2004). Part two: Ethical theories and medical ethics. *Classic Case in Medical Ethics* pp. 10–25. New York, NY: McGraw-Hill. Retrieved from http://biology.franklincollege.edu/Bioweb/Biology/course_p/bioethics/Medical%20Ethics.doc

Perry, N. E., Turner, J. C., & Meyer, D. K. (2006). Classrooms as contexts for motivating learning. In P. Alexander & P. Winne (Eds.). *Handbook of Educational Psychology* (pp. 327–348). Mahwah, NJ: Erlbaum.

Peterson, S. W. (2004). The best medicine. Presentation to The Chicago Literary Club, March 14, 2005. Retrieved from http://www.chilit.org/Petersen4.htm

Pierce, W. (2004, November). *Metacognition: Study strategies, monitoring, and motivation.* Workshop presented at Prince George's Community College. Retrieved from http://academic.pgcc.edu/~wpeirce/MCCCTR/metacognition.htm

Pintrich, P., & Schunk, D. (1996). *Motivation in education: Theory, research & applications*, Ch. 3. Englewood Cliffs, NJ: Prentice-Hall. Retrieved from http://des.emory.edu/mfp/PS.html

Plucker, J. (2004, July). Howard Gardner. *Human Intelligence.* Retrieved from http://www.indiana.edu/~intell/gardner.shtml

Polacco, P. (2006). *The butterfly.* London, UK: Puffin.

Popham, W. J. (2007). Assessment for learning: An endangered species? *Educational Leadership—Informative Assessment, 65*(4), 70–73. Alexandria, VA: Association for Supervision and Curriculum Development.

Popham, W. J. (2008). *Transformative assessment.* Alexandria, VA: Association for Supervision and Curriculum Development.

Priestley, P., McGuire, J., Flegg, D., Hemsley, V., & Welham, D. (1978). *Social skills and personal problem solving: A handbook of methods.* Cambridge, UK: Tavistock.

Prince, A. (2005). Using the principles of brain-based learning in the classroom—How to help a child learn. Retrieved from http://www.superduperinc.com/handouts/pdf/81_brain.pdf

Privacy and the Workplace. (2004). Law and the workplace. *American Bar Association Family Legal Guide.* Retrieved from http://public.findlaw.com/abaflg/flg-12-4f-2.html

Prochaska and DiClemente's Stages of Change Model. (n.d.). Retrieved from http://www.timlebon.com/stagesofchangemodelprochaska.html

Prochaska and DiClemente's Stages of Change Model. (n.d.). *UCLA Center for Human Nutrition.* Retrieved from http://www.cellinteractive.com/ucla/physcian_ed/stages_change.html

Professional Dispositions and Teacher Preparation. (n.d.). [PowerPoint]. Retrieved from http://www.ed.psu.edu/educ/for-current-faculty-and-staff/associate-dean-undergrad/dispositions/ci-295-disposition-project/Dispositions%20Presentation.ppt

Professional Standards for the Accreditation of Teacher Preparation Institutions. (2008, February). *National Council for Accreditation of Teacher Education.* Washington, DC: National Council for Accreditation of Teacher Education.

Protecting Students with Disabilities. (2009). Frequently asked questions about Section 504 and the Education of Children with Disabilities. Retrieved from http://ed.gov/about/offices/list/ocr/504faq.html

Race, P. (n.d.). Using feedback to help students to learn. *The Higher Education Academy.* Retrieved from phil-race.co.uk/wp-content/uploads/Using_feedback

Race to the Top Fund. (2010). Retrieved from U.S. Department of Education: http://www2.ed.gov/programs/racetothetop/index.html

Raffini, J. (1993). *Winners without losers: Structures and strategies for increasing student motivation to learn.* Needham Heights, MA: Allyn and Bacon.

Rattanavich, S. (2001). Problem-based learning. Retrieved from http://tlc.buu.ac.th/personal/Problem-based_learning_paperat_Pattaya.pdfs

Ravitch, D. (2010, November 11). The myth of charter schools. *The New York Review of Books.* Retrieved from http://www.nybooks.com/articles/archives/2010/nov/11/myth-charter-schools/?pagination=false

Ravitch, D. (2011, January 26). Education perspectives: NCLB/Student testing. *Fresh Perspectives.* Retrieved from http://freshperspectives.typepad.com/education_perspectives/government/

Reesor, M. (2002). Issues in written teacher feedback: A critical review. *The English Teacher, 5*(3), 242–255.

Reflection. (2001, June). Retrieved from http://www.intime.uni.edu/model/learning/refl.html

Regulations of Connecticut State Agencies Section 10-145-d-400a. (2010, August) *Connecticut Code of Professional Responsibility for Educators.* Retrieved from www.sde.ct.gov/sde/cwp/view.asp?a=2613&q=321332

Research on causes of country differences. (2011). Programme for International Student Assessment. *Wikipedia.* Retrieved from http://en.wikipedia.org/wiki/Programme_for_International_Student_Assessment#Topical_studies

Rich, D. (2007). Introduction to MegaSkills: About MegaSkills. *MegaSkills Online Education Center.* Retrieved from http://www.megaskillshsi.org/aboutMegaSkills.html

Richmond, J. E. D. (1997). Introduction. In *Donald Schön—A Life of Reflection,* remarks at special session in honor of the memory of Donald Schön at the Conference of the Association of Collegiate Schools of Planning, Fort Lauderdale, November 6–9, 1999. Forthcoming, *Journal of Planning Literature.* Retrieved from http://the-tech.mit.edu/~richmond/professional/jplschon.pdf

Riddile, M. (2010, January 15). PISA: It's poverty not stupid. *The Principal Difference: A School Leadership Blog.* Retrieved from http://nasspblogs.org/principaldifference/2010/12/pisa_its_poverty_not_stupid_1.html

Robinson, K. (2006, June). TED and Reddit asked Sir Ken Robinson anything—and he answered. Retrieved from http://blog.ted.com/2006/06/sir_ken_robinso.php

Robinson, K. (2009, September). Why creativity now? A conversation with Sir Ken Robinson. *Educational Leadership, 67*(1), 22–26. (A. M. Azzam, Interviewer) Association for Supervision and Curriculum Development.

Roemer, F. (n.d.). Whole Class Self-Monitoring. *Mr. Roemer's Fifth Grade Polar Bears.* Retrieved from http://www.pb5th.com/selfmoni.shtml

Role of Teacher Professionalism in Education. (n.d.). *Illinois Professional Teaching Standards.* Retrieved from http://students.ed.uiuc.edu/vallicel/Teacher_Professionalism.html

Rolheiser, C., & Ross, J. (n.d.) Student self-evaluation: What research says and what practice shows. Retrieved from http://www.cdl.org/resource-library/articles/self_eval.php

Rooney, J. (2010, April). Remember the children. *Educational Leadership, 67*(7), 88–89.

Rose, M. C. (1999, August). All together now! *Instructor, 110*(22), 1. Retrieved from KYVL Academic Search Premier.

Rosenholtz, S. J., & Simpson, C. (1984). The formation of ability conceptions: Developmental trend or social construction? *Review of Educational Research, 64,* 479–530.

Rosenshine, B., & Furst, N. (1973). The use of direct observation to study teaching. In R. Travers (Ed.). *Handbook of Research on Teaching* (2nd ed., pp. 263–298). Chicago, IL: Rand McNally.

Russell, N. S. (2006). The it factor. Retrieved from *JobBank USA:* http://www.jobbankusa.com/Career Articles/Personal_Aspects/ca6706a.html

Ryan, R. M., & Deci, E. L. (2000a). Intrinsic and extrinsic motivations: Classic definitions and new directions. *Contemporary Educational Psychology, 25,* 54–67. Retrieved from http://www.idealibrary.com

Ryan, R. M., & Deci, E. L. (2000b, January). Self-determination theory and the facilitation of intrinsic motivation, social development, and well-being. *American Psychologist, 55.* Retrieved from http://www.psych.rochester.edu/SDT/theory.html

Sanders, M. M. (2002). Schools of education in selected private universities and colleges: Meeting the challenges of multicultural education in education for preservice elementary teachers (Doctoral dissertation). Retrieved from Dissertations and Theses database. (UMI No. 3078921)

Sasson, D. (2007, February 10). Effective classroom management: Strategies of teaching class rules and procedures effectively. Retrieved from http://www.suite101.com/content/effective-classroom-management-a13423

Sasson, R. (2007). Affirmations and self-talk. Retrieved from http://www.successconsciousness.com /affirmations_self_talk.htm

Sawyer, D. (Host). (2010, November 15). Educating China: See a Chinese classroom firsthand. [Television Episode]. In *ABC News and World Report with Diane Sawyer*. Retrieved from http://abcnews.go.com/WNT/video/educating-china-12165881

Schimmel, D. (1997). Traditional rule-making and the subversion of citizenship education. *Social Education*, *61*(2), 70–71. Retrieved from http://juristic-clinic.org/attachments/127_rule-making .eng.doc

Schön, D. (1983). *The reflective practitioner. How professionals think in action.* London, UK: Temple Smith.

Schroeder, B. (2006, March 4). Glossary: Effective teaching terms and links. Retrieved from http:// www.usu.edu/teachall/text/effective/EFFglos.htm

Schubart, B. (2006, March 4). What's wrong with our schools? Retrieved from http://www.schubart .com/?page_id=74

Schunk, D. H. (2000). *Learning theories: An educational perspective.* Upper Saddle River, NJ: Prentice-Hall.

Seashore, C. N., Seashore, E. W., & Weinberg, G. M. (1992). *What did you say? The art of giving and receiving feedback.* North Attleborough, MA: Douglas Charles Press.

Section-by-Section Analysis. (2008, December). *Family Educational Rights and Privacy Act (FERPA) Final Rule 34 CFR Part 99.* Retrieved from www2.ed.gov/policy/gen/guid/fpco/pdf/ht12-17-08-att.pdf

Seeman, H. (2000). Preventing your rules from falling apart. *Preventing Classroom Discipline Problems: A Classroom Management Handbook* (3rd ed.). Lanham, MD: Scarecrow Press. Excepts retrieved from http://teachers.net/gazette/MAR01/seeman.html

Seganti, C. (2008). *Classroom discipline 101: How to get control of any classroom.* Los Angeles, CA: Craig Seganti.

Sewell, A., & St. George, A. (2000). Developing efficacy beliefs in the classroom. *Journal of Educational Enquiry*, *1*(2). Retrieved from http://www.aare.edu.au/99pap/sew99301.htm

Shafir, R. Z. (2003). *The zen of listening: Mindful communication in the age of distraction* (2nd ed.). Wheaton, IL: Quest Books.

Shaunessy, E., & McHatton, P. A. (2008). Urban students' perceptions of teachers: Views of students in general, special, and honors education. *Urban Rev*, *41*, 486–503. doi: 10.1007/s11256-0080112-z

Shepherd, J. (2010, August 31). Girls think they are cleverer than boys from age four, study finds. *The Guardian*. Retrieved from http://www.guardian.co.uk/education/2010/sep/01/girls-boys-schools-gender-gap

Shepard, L. A. (2005, November). Linking formative assessment to scaffolding. *Educational Leadership*, *63*(3), 66–70. Retrieved from ASCD: http://www.ascd.org/publications/educational_leadership/ nov05/vol63/num03/Linking_Formative_Assessment_to_Scaffolding.aspx

Shor, I., & Friere, P. (1987). *A pedagogy for liberation: Dialogues on transforming education.* Westport, CT: Bergin and Garvey.

Siegle, D. (2000a). What influences self-efficacy? *Neag Center for Gifted Education/Talent Development.* Retrieved from http://www.gifted.uconn.edu/siegle/SelfEfficacy/section2.html

Siegle, D. (2000b). Help students set goals. *Neag Center for Gifted Education/Talent Development.* Retrieved from http://www.gifted.uconn.edu/siegle/SelfEfficacy/section8.html

Siegle, D. (2000c). Table of contents for self-efficacy intervention. *Neag Center for Gifted Education/Talent Development.* Retrieved from http://www.gifted.uconn.edu/siegle/SelfEfficacy/section0.html

Siegle, D. (2003, April). Influencing student mathematics self-efficacy through teacher training. Paper presented at the Annual Meeting of the American Research Association, Chicago, IL: Retrieved from http://www.gifted.uconn.edu/siegle/Conferences/AERA2003_Siegle.pdf

Simenc, M. (2008). The status of the subject in the classroom community of inquiry. *Theory and Research in Education, 6*(3), 323–336. Thousand Oaks, CA: Sage.

Simola, H. (2005). *The Finnish miracle of PISA: Historical and sociological remarks on teaching and teacher education.* Comparative Education, *41*, 455–470.

Singharath, R. (2007, October 27). Advantages and disadvantages of the rubric. Retrieved from http://epsyrubrics.wetpaint.com/page/Advantages+and+Disadvantages+of+the+Rubric

Six Change Approaches–Kotter and Schlesinger. (n.d.). Dealing with resistance to change six change approaches. Retrieved from http://www.valuebasedmanagement.net/methods_kotter_change_approaches.html

Skapinakis, P. (2003, August). Depressed? How to diagnose clinical depression; Clinical depression symptoms. *Psychology Free Online Medical Advice.* Retrieved from http://web4health.info/en/answers/bipolar-dia-depression.htm

Smagorinsky, P. (2009). Is it time to abandon the idea of "Best Practices" in the teaching of English? *English Journal—EJ Extra, 98*(6), 15–22. Retrieved from http://brn227.brown.wmich.edu/mcee/Smagorinsky.pdf

Smith, M. K. (2001, July). donald schon (schön): learning, reflection and change. Retrieved from http://www.infed.org/thinkers/et-schon.htm

SNC2P. (n.d.). Balancing chemical equations using marshmallow models. Retrieved from http://cccsnc2p.wikispaces.com/file/view/Balancing+Chemical+Equations+using+marshmallow+models.doc

Sommers-Flanagan, J., & Sommers-Flanagan, R. (2010). School-parent collaboration: A labor of love. *American School Counselor Association.* Retrieved from http://www.schoolcounselor.org/content.asp?contentid=486

Sousa, D. A. (1998, December 16). Is the fuss about brain research justified? *Education Digest, 63*(3), 10. Retrieved from http://www.edweek.org/login.html?source=http://www.edweek.org/ew/articles/1998/12/16/16sousa.h18.html&destination=http://www.edweek.org/ew/articles/1998/12/16/16sousa.h18.html&levelId=2100

Sousa, D. A. (2001). *How the brain learns: A classroom teacher's guide* (2nd ed.). Thousand Oaks, CA: Corwin Press.

Sousa, D. A. (2006). *How the brain learns: A classroom teacher's guide (*3rd ed). Thousand Oaks, CA: Corwin Press.

Sousa, D. A. (2009). *How the brain influences behavior: Management strategies for every classroom.* Thousand Oaks, CA: Corwin Press.

Speck, B. W. (2000). Grading students' classroom writing: Issues and strategies. *ASHE-ERIC Higher Education Report, 27*(3). Washington, DC: George Washington University.

Sprenger, M. (2009, September). Focusing the digital brain. *Educational Leadership, 67*(1), 34–39. Retrieved from http://www.leadlouisiana.net/documents/focusing.pdf

Sprick, R., Garrison, M., & Howard, L. M. (1998). *CHAMPs: A proactive and positive approach to classroom management for grades K–9.* Longmont, CO: Sopris West.

Stage, F. K., Muller, P. A., Kinzie, J., & Simmons, A. (n.d). Creating learning centered classrooms. What does learning theory have to say? *ERIC Digest,* ED422777. Retrieved from KYVL ERIC.

Stages of Change Model. (2003). Retrieved from http://www.addictionalternatives.com/philosophy/stagemodel.htm

Starnes, B. A. (2010, January). My mother's gravy. *Phi Delta Kappan, 91*(4), 72–74.

Staub, E. (1979). *Positive social behavior and morality, Volume II, socialization and development.* New York, NY: Academic Press. As cited in Schimmel, D. (1997). Traditional rule-making and the subversion of citizenship education. *Social Education, 61*(2), 70–71. Retrieved from http://juristic-clinic.org/attachments/127_rule-making.eng.doc

Stefanou, C. R., Perencevich, K. C., DiCintio, M., & Turner, J. C. (2004). Supporting autonomy in the classroom: Ways teachers encourage student decision making and ownership. *Educational Psychologist.* Retrieved from http://www.leaonline.com/doi/abs/10.1207/s15326985ep3902_2?journalCode=ep

Stein, L. (2010, January). Lead students—don't just manage them. *Phi Delta Kappan, 91*(4), 82-87.

Stephanie. (2008, April 25). Re: Standardized testing ruins a school's spirit [Web blog message]. Retrieved from http:/www.edutopia.org/standardized-testing-NCLB-school-suffers

Stepping stones to success II (2007). Collaboration: Working together for all students. *Virginia Department of Education.* Retrieved from http://www.doe.virginia.gov/teaching/career_resources/stepping_stones2.pdf

Sternberg, R. J. (2006). Creating a vision of creativity: The first 25 years. *Psychology of Aesthetics, Creativity, and the Arts, 1*, 2–12. doi: 10.1037/1931-3896.S.1.2 Retrieved from http://www.apa.org/journals/features/acas12.pdf

Sternberg, R. J., & Lubart, T. I. (1991). An investment theory of creativity and its development. Human Development, *34*(1), 1–31.

Stiggins, R. (2002, June). Assessment crisis: The absence of assessment FOR learning. *Phi Delta Kappan, 83*(10), 758. Retrieved from Academic Search Premier. Record 6755928.

Stiggins, R. (2005). *Student-involved assessment FOR learning* (4th ed.). Upper Saddle River, NJ: Pearson Prentice Hall.

Stiggins, R. (2008). *Student-involved assessment FOR learning* (5th ed.). Upper Saddle River, NJ: Pearson Prentice Hall.

Stiggins, R. (2009, February). Assessment FOR learning in upper elementary grades. *Phi Delta Kappan, 90*(6), 419–421.

Stone, L. (2007). Continuous partial attention. Retrieved from http://lindastone.net/qa/continuous-partial-attention/

Stoskopf, A. (2001, March 19). Reviving Clio: Inspired history teaching and learning (without high-stakes tests). *Phi Delta Kappa International.* Retrieved from http://www.pdkintl.org/kappan/ksto0102.htm

Strategies for sound discipline. (2001). *Teaching for Excellence,* (XX)6. Adapted from *Discipline with Unity* by Terry Alderman.

Strauss, V. (2006, October 10). The rise of the testing culture: As exam-takers get younger, some say value is overblown. *Washington Post—Politics, National, World & DC Area News and Headlines.* Retrieved from http://www.washingtonpost.com/wp-dyn/content/article/2006/10/09/AR2006100900925.html

Student Locked in Cage: NM Teacher on Leave After Cell Phone Video Leaked. (2011, January 19). Retrieved from http://www.huffingtonpost.com/2011/01/19/student-locked-in-cage_n_811006.html

Stumbo, C., & McWaters, P. (2011). Measuring effectiveness: What will it take? *Educational Leadership, 68*(4), 10–15.

Swartz, R., & Perkins, D. (1989). *Teaching thinking: Issues and approaches.* Pacific Grove, CA: Midwest.

TAP into Learning. (2000, Winter). Paulo Freire and education for critical consciousness. *Action + reflection = learning*, 3(2). Retrieved from http://www.sedl.org/tap

Tate, M. L. (2007). *Shouting won't grow dendrites: 20 techniques for managing a brain-compatible classroom*. Thousand Oaks, CA: Corwin Press.

Tauber, R. T. (1998). Good or bad, what teachers expect from students they generally get! ERIC document ED 426 985 in Miller, R. (2001, November). Greater expectations national panel: Greater expectations to improve student learning. *Association of American Colleges and Universities*. Retrieved from http://www.greaterexpectations.org/briefing_papers/ImproveStudentLearning.html

Taylor, B. W. (1987). *Classroom discipline: A system for getting the school administrator to see classroom discipline problems your way*. Dayton, OH: Southern Hills Press.

Taylor, R. (2002). *Taylor's human connection model*. Retrieved from http://www.gstboces.org/iss/iss/trainings/di/handouts/Product-Grid.pdf

Thomas, K. W., & Kilmann, R. H. (1974). *Thomas-Kilmann conflict mode instrument*. Mountain View, CA: Xicom.

Thomson, A. M., Perry, J. L., & Miller, T. K. (2007, December 1). Conceptualizing and measuring collaboration. *Journal of Public Administration Research and Theory Advance Access (Online)*. Retrieved from http://www.indiana.edu/~jlpweb/papers/Conceptualizing%20and%20Measuring%20Collab_Thomson_Perry_Miller_JPART_Dec%202007.pdf

Thorndike, E. L. (1913). *Educational psychology: Volume 1: The original nature of man*. New York, NY: Columbia University Teachers College.

Tienken, C. H. (2008). Rankings of international achievement test performance and economic strength: Correlation or conjecture? *International Journal of Education Policy & Leadership, 3*(4), 1–15.

Tileston, D. W. (2004). *What every teacher should know about classroom management and discipline*. Thousand Oaks, CA: Corwin Press.

Tomlinson, C. A. (2007, December). Learning to love assessment. *Educational Leadership*. Retrieved from Association for Supervision and Curriculum Development: http://www.ascd.org/publications/educational_leadership/dec07/vol65/num04/Learning_to_Love_Assessment.aspx

Travers, P. D., & Rebore, R. W. (2000). National goals for public schools announced. *Foundations of education: Becoming a teacher* (4th ed.). Boston, MA: Allyn & Bacon.

Trilling, B., & Fadel, C. (2009). *21st century skills: Learning for life in our times*. San Francisco, CA: Jossey-Bass.

Tripod Project. (2002–2003). Stage-two summary report (short version) for balanced (vs. imbalanced) teacher control and student autonomy. *Harvesting Reports and Teachers' Responses to Prompts for 2002–2003)*. Retrieved from http://www.ksg.harvard.edu/tripodproject/Stage%20Two%20Exec%20Summary%202002-03.pdf

Trivett, S. (2004). Coaching for transformation. Retrieved from http://www.changezone.co.uk/STEVE/coachingfortransformation.html

Trumbull, E., & Pacheco, M. (2005). The teacher's guide to diversity: Building a knowledge base. In *Volume 1: Human Development, Culture, and Cognition*. The Education Alliance. Providence, RI: Brown University.

Twenty Kinds of Class Meetings. (n.d.). Retrieved from Educators for Social Responsibility: http://www.ethicsed.org/consulting/meetingideas.htm

Underwood, J. S., & Tregidgo, A. P. (2006). Improving student writing through effective feedback: Best practices and recommendations. *Journal of Teaching Writing, 22*(2), 73–97. Indianapolis, IN: Indiana University Purdue.

Universal Declaration of Human Rights. (2011). Retrieved from http://www.un.org/en/documents/udhr/index.shtml

U.S. Charter Schools. (n.d.). Overview. Retrieved from http://www.uscharterschools.org/pub/uscs_docs/o/index.htm

U.S. Department of Education. (2000, July). Hard work and high expectations: Motivating students to learn. Retrieved from http://www.kidsource.com/kidsource/content3/work.expectations.k12.4.html

U.S. Department of Health and Human Services. (2009a). *Child maltreatment 2009.* Retrieved from Administration for Children and Families, Administration on Children, Youth and Families, Children's Bureau: http://www.acf.hhs.gov/programs/cb/stats_research/index.htm#can.

U.S. Department of Health and Human Services. (2009b). Results from the 2009 national survey on drug use and health: Volume I—Summary of national findings. Retrieved from Substance Abuse and Mental Health Services Administration, Office of Applied Studies: http://oas.samhsa.gov/NSDUH/2k9NSDUH/2k9Results.htm#3.1.1

van den Heuvel, W. (1996). On dialogue. Retrieved from http://www.david-bohm.net/dialogue/on_dialogue.htm

Van Dusen, W. R., Jr. (2004). FERPA: Basic guidelines for faculty and staff a simple step-by-step approach for compliance. Retrieved from http://www.nacada.ksu.edu/Resources/FERPAOverview.htm

Van Tassell, G. (2005, March.). *Classroom management.* CYC—Reading for Child and Youth Care People, 74. Retrieved from www.cyc-net.org/cyc-online/cycol-0305-classroom.html

Vella, J. K. (2002). *Learning to listen, learning to teach: The power of dialogue in educating adults* (Rev. ed.). San Francisco, CA: Jossey-Bass.

Vockell, E. L. (2001a). Attribution theory. In *Educational Psychology: A Practical Approach* (Online Ed.) Chapter 5: Motivating Students to Learn. Retrieved from http://education.calumet.purdue.edu/vockell/EdPsyBook/Edpsy5/Edpsy5_attribution.htm

Vockell, E. L. (2001b). Metacognitive skills. In *Educational Psychology: A Practical Approach* (Online Ed.) Chapter 7: Teaching Thinking Skills. Retrieved from http://education.calumet.purdue.edu/vockell/EdPsyBook/Edpsy7/edpsy7_meta.htm

Vroom, V. (2009). Expectancy theory: Victor Vroom. Retrieved from http://www.valuebasedmanagement.net/methods_vroom_expectancy_theory.html

Vygotsky, L. S. (1978). *Mind in society: The development of higher psychological processes.* Cambridge, MA: Harvard University Press.

Wagaman, J. (2009, August 6). Steps for creating rules with students. *Allowing the Students to Create the Class Rules.* Retrieved from www.suite101.com/content/allowing-the-students-to-create-the-class-rules-a137146

Walther-Thomas, C., Korinek, L., McLaughlin, V. L., & Williams, B. (2000). *Collaboration for inclusive education: Developing successful programs.* Needham Heights, MA: Allyn and Bacon.

Wassermann, S. (1989, Summer). Children working in groups? It doesn't work! *Childhood Education*, p. 204.

Watson, J. (2005, May 21). Motivation by a challenge. Retrieved from http://ezinearticles.com/?Motivation-By-A-Challenge&id=37804

Wayman, A. (2010, June.). Reward yourself—You'll achieve more goals. Retrieved from http://www.aboutfreelancewriting.com/2010/06/reward-yourself-youll-achieve-more-goals/

Wayne, B. (2005). The power of talking out loud to yourself. Retrieved from http://www.possibilitypress.com/books/PDFs/The%20Power%20of%20Talking%20Out%20Loud%20to%20Yourself.pdf

Wayson, W. W. (1985). Rules for making rules that work for you. *Department of Educational Policy and Leadership.* Retrieved from www.hup.sjsu.edu/faculty/susanwilkinson/Content/178/6Rules%20for%20Making%20Rules.doc

Weikle, J. E. (1993, July). Self-talk & self-health. *ERIC Digest.* Retrieved from http://www.indiana.edu/~reading/ieo/digests/d84.html

Weiner, B. (1980). *Human motivation.* New York, NY: Holt, Rinehart & Winston.

Weiner, B. (2009, August). *The development of an attribution-based theory of motivation: A history of ideas.* Address given at meeting for the E. L. Thorndike Lifetime Research Achievement Award, Los Angeles, CA.

Weinstein, C. S., & Mignano, A. J., Jr. (2003). *Elementary classroom management: Lessons from research and practice,* (3rd ed.). Boston, MA: McGraw Hill.

Werner, E., & Smith, R. (1989). *Overcoming the odds: High-risk children from birth to adulthood.* New York, NY: Cornell University Press.

What IS Professional Dress? (2011, April 7). Retrieved from *Mystery Teacher*: http://lsturr.teacherlingo. com/archive/2011/04/07/what-is-professional-dress.aspx

White, J. (2009). The power of writing things down. Retrieved from http://www.divinecaroline.com/221 92/64852-power-writing-things

Whitlock, C. (2007, December 24). A green light for common sense. *The Washington Post.* Retrieved http://www.washingtonpost.com/wpdyn/content/article/2007/12/23/AR2007122302487.html

Whittier, J. G. (1866). *Maud Muller.* Boston, MA: Riverside Press.

Wiggins, G. (2010). Chapter 1: What's my job? Defining the role of the classroom teacher. In R. Marzano (Ed.), *On Excellence in Teaching* (pp. 7–29). Bloomington, IN: Solution Tree Press.

Wike, R., & Horowitz, J. M. (2006). Parental pressure on students: Not enough in America; Too much in Asia. *PewResearchCenter Publications.* Retrieved from http://pewresearch.org/pubs/55/parental-pressure-on-students-not-enough-in-america-too-much-in-asia

Williams, R. B. (1996). *More than 50 ways to build team consensus.* Arlington Heights, IL: IRI/Skylight Training and Publishing.

Wilson, L. O. (1997). Defining creativity. Retrieved from http://www.uwsp.edu/Education/lwilson/creativ/ define.htm

Wilson, R. (2010, July 23). Ethical code of conduct in teachers. Retrieved from http://www.ehow.com/ facts_6767350_ethical-code-conduct-teachers.html

Windle, R., & Warren, S. (2006). Section 4: Communication skills collaborative problem solving and dispute resolution in special education. *CADRE.* Retrieved from http://www.directionservice .org/cadre/section4.cfm

Winebrenner, S. (2001). *Teaching gifted kids in the regular classroom.* Minneapolis: MN: Free Spirit.

Winger, T. (2005, November). Grading to Communicate. *Educational Leadership—Assessment to Promote Learning, 63*(3), 61–65. Retrieved from http://www.ascd.org/publications/educational _leadership/nov05/vol63/num03/Grading_to_Communicate.aspx

Winston, J. S., Strange, B. A., O'Doherty, J., & Dolan, R. J. (2002, March). Automatic and intentional brain responses during evaluation of trustworthiness of faces. *Nature Neuroscience, 5*(3), 277–283.

Wisniewska, I. (1998, June). Designing materials for teacher autonomy. Forum, *36,* 24. Retrieved from http://exchanges.state.gov/forum/vols/vol36/no2/p24.htm

Wlodkowksi, R. J. (1984). Motivation and teaching: A practical guide. Washington, DC: National Education Association.

Wolfe, P., & Brandt, R. (1998, November). What do we know from brain research? *Educational Leadership—How the Brain Works.* Retrieved from http://members.shaw.ca/priscillatheroux/ brain.html

Wolk, R. (2010, April). Education: The case for making it personal. *Educational Leadership—Reimaging Schools, 67*(7), 16–21.

Wong, H. K., & Wong, R. T. (1998). *The first days of school: How to be an effective teacher.* Mountain View, CA: Harry K. Wong.

Wood, T., & McCarthy, C. (2002, December). Understanding and preventing teacher burnout. *ERIC Clearninghouse on Teaching and Teacher Education* ED477726. Retrieved from http://www.ericdigests.org/2004-1/burnout.htm

Worksheet. (n.d.). Worksheet: Writing and balancing chemical reactions. Retrieved from http://wolgemuthe.psd401.net/chemistry/06%20-%20balancing/documents/Worksheet%20-%20Balancing%20Chemical%20Equations.pdf

Wubbels, T., Brekelmans, M., van Tartwijk, J., & Admiral, W. (1999). Interpersonal relationships between teachers and students in the classroom. In H. C. Waxman & H. J. Walberg (Eds.). *New directions for teaching practice and research* (pp. 151–170). Berkeley, CA: McCutchen.

Wuest, D. (1999, April). Are you with it? PEC: Classroom Behavior/Learning Environment Article. *PE Central: The web site for health and physical education teachers*. Retrieved from http://www.pecentral.org/climate/april99article.html

Wright, J. (2005). Jackpot!: Ideas for classroom rewards. *Rewards and Incentives*. Retrieved from http://www.eatsmartmovemorenc.com/EatSmartSchoolStds/Texts/rewards_incentives.pdf

Wright, J. C., & Huston, A. C. (1981). Children's understanding of the forms of television. In H. Kelly & H. Gardner (Eds.). *Viewing children through television* (pp. 73–87). San Francisco, CA: Jossey-Bass.

Write-to-Learn Activities in the classroom. (n.d.) Retrieved from: http://www.ece.utah.edu/~cfurse/CLEAR/writing/Writing%20Handouts/Mini%20Lessons/Write1.doc

Young, L. P. (2009, November). Creativity in the classroom: Teaching and assessing creative thinking. Conference session conducted at the Southeastern Regional Association of Teacher Educators, Louisville, KY.

Zhao, Y. (2009). *Catching up or leading the way: American education in the age of globalization.* Alexandria, VA: Association for Supervision and Curriculum Development.

Zhao, Y. (2009, October 9). The mismeasure of education: Worthy knowledge in the age of globalization. *Yong Zhao*. Retrieved from http://zhaolearning.com/2009/10/22/the-mismeasure-of-education-worthy-knowledge-in-the-age-of-globalization/

Definitions, Idioms, and Synonyms

American Heritage Dictionary of the English Language, The (4th ed.). (2010). Retrieved from http://www.yourdictionary.com/

American Heritage Dictionary of Idioms, The (2nd ed.). (2003). Retrieved from YourDictionary.com website: http://idioms.yourdictionary.com/

American Heritage Stedman's Medical Dictionary, The (2nd ed.). (2002). Retrieved from Dictionary.com website: http://dictionary.reference.com

Cambridge Idioms Dictionary (2nd ed.). (2006). Retrieved from TheFreeDictionary website: http://idioms.thefreedictionary.com/

Collins English Dictionary—Complete & Unabridged, The (10th ed.). (n.d.). Retrieved from http://dictionary.reference.com/

Merriam-Webster. (2012). Retrieved from *Merriam-Webster Online:* http://www.merriam-webster.com/dictionary

Random House Dictionary. (2012). Retrieved from *Dictionary.com Unabridged*: http://dictionary.reference.com/

Online Etymology Dictionary. (2010). Retrieved from Dictionary.com website: http://dictionary.reference.com/

Roget's 21st Century Thesaurus (3rd ed.). (n.d.). Retrieved from http:// thesaurus.com/

Einstein's Life and Quotes

American Museum of Natural History (2002). Early years. Retrieved from http://www.amnh.org/exhibitions/einstein/life/index.php

Brainyquote. (2007). Quotes. Retrieved from *BrainyMedia.com*: http://www.brainyquote.com/quotes/authors/a/albert_einstein.html

Photo: Bettmann/Corbis. (2003). Person of the century. Retrieved from http://www.time.com/time/time100/poc/einstein_photo/einstein1.html

Photo Essay. (2003). Person of the century. Retrieved from http://www.time.com/time/time100/poc/einstein_photo/einstein1.html

Problem-Solving References

Bellanca, J., & Fogarty, R. (1986). *Catch them thinking: A handbook of classroom strategies.* Palintine, IL: Skylight.

Covey, S. R. (1991). *Principle-Centered Leadership.* New York, NY: Simon & Schuster.

Dewey, J. (1933). *How we think.* Boston, MA: D.C. Heath.

Elias, M. J., & Tobias, S. E. (1990). *Problem solving/decision making for social and academic success.* Washington, DC: National Education Association of the United States.

Gagné, R. M. (1985). *The conditions of learning.* (4th ed.). New York, NY: Holt, Rinehart, & Winston.

Polya, G. (2004). *How to solve: A new aspect of mathematical method.* Princeton, NJ: Princeton University.

Priestley, P., McGuire, J., Flegg, D., Hemsley, V., & Welham, D. (1978). *Social skills and personal problem solving: A handbook of methods.* Cambridge, England: Tavistock.

Russo, J. E., & Schoemaker, P. J. H. (1989). *Decision traps: Ten barriers to brilliant decision-making and how to overcome them.* New York, NY: Simon & Schuster.

Silva, M. C. (1990). *Ethical decision making in nursing administration.* Norwalk, CT: Appleton & Lange.

The steps of making the best decisions. (1987). *Here's Looking At You, 2000.* Roberts, Fitzmahan & Assoc., Inc.

Whetton, D. A., & Cameron, K. S. (Eds.). (1991). *Developing management skills.* New York, NY: Harper Collins.

Teacher and Coach Quotations

Brainyquote: http://www.brainyquote.com/

CreativeProcess.net: http://www.creativeprocess.net/moreposters/educators/

Encarta Encyclopedia: http://encarta.msn.com/encyclopedia

Pitino, Rick. Quote in Covey, S. R. (2004). *The 8th Habit: From Effectiveness to Greatness.* New York, NY: Free Press.

The Real Heroes Club: http://www.theheroesclub.org/mary_mcleod_bethune.php

Thinkexist: http://en.thinkexist.com/quotes/

Wikipedia: http://en.wikipedia.org/

Index

Supplements from A to Z

Supplements for each prescription contain the blackline masters and detailed explanations for putting the classroom management concepts and strategies into practice in the classroom. Follow the instructions on the next page to access the **Supplements from A to Z** online.

Prescription R$_X$ 1—Apply Active Engagement

A Quality Grouping
B Jigsaw Tasks
C LTC (Learner Teacher Checker)
D HOT Question Starters (Higher-Order Thinking)
E Surveys for Preferred Learning Styles, Conditions, and Activities
F Motivation and Activity Planning Forms

Prescription R$_X$ 2—Repeat High Expectations

G About Me Survey
H Homework Contract
I Inspirational Frames
J High Expectations Strategy Game

Prescription R$_X$ 3—Use Appropriate Assessments

K Unit and Lesson Design
L "Win-Win" Classroom Competitions
M Practice Book
N Practice Record Sheet
O Grade Book Magic (Secrets Revealed)
P Learning Journal

Prescription R$_X$ 4—Encourage Trustworthy Behavior

Q Mission, Vision, Principles, and Values
R Consequence Hierarchy and Behavior Support System
S Time Outs and Think Sheets
T Behavior Record Sheets
U Self-Management Record Sheets
V Clipboard Management

Prescription R$_X$ 5—Maintain Effective Communication

W Nonverbal Interactions—Self-Assessment
X Discussion and Dialogue Prompts
Y Conference Guidelines and Protocols
Z Classroom Management Plans and Checklists

Book Website and Discounts

Order *How to Cure the Classroom Management Blues: A Self-Help Survival Guide for Teachers* online at *www.classroommanagementblues.com*

Website

For more information, visit www.classroommanagementblues.com **or** www.classroomblues.com

Supplements and Resources

To access resources and download the ***Supplements from A to Z*** for the *Classroom Management Blues*, you will need to register online. The process takes a couple of minutes.

1. Go to **www.classroommanagementblues.com**

2. Select **Login**, and then **click here** to request a Login and Password.

3. Submit the form. Be sure to enter a valid e-mail address.

You will receive your Login and Password by e-mail within 24 hours M–F (excluding holidays).

Discounts

Quantity discounts are available for educational and training purposes. Discounts are also available to schools and other organizations. Contact Fostrom Press at inquiries@fostrompress.com

Fostrom Press

P.O. Box 437
New Albany, IN 47151-0437
inquiries@fostrompress.com

The **FOSTROM PRESS** logo—hands holding a sprouting plant across an open book—has its origin in the Proto-Germanic word **fostrom*, meaning "to encourage or help grow" in early 13th century of things and in the 1560s of feelings and ideas (Online Etymology Dictionary, 2010). **FOSTROM PRESS** publishes books that encourage and help teachers and learners grow.

Made in the USA
Charleston, SC
25 October 2012